Metrical Claims and Poetic Experience

Metrical Claims and Poetic Experience

Klopstock, Nietzsche, Grünbein

HANNAH VANDEGRIFT ELDRIDGE

OXFORD
UNIVERSITY PRESS

OXFORD

UNIVERSITY PRESS

Great Clarendon Street, Oxford, OX2 6DP,
United Kingdom

Oxford University Press is a department of the University of Oxford.
It furthers the University's objective of excellence in research, scholarship,
and education by publishing worldwide. Oxford is a registered trade mark of
Oxford University Press in the UK and in certain other countries

Published in the United States of America by Oxford University Press
198 Madison Avenue, New York, NY 10016, United States of America

British Library Cataloguing in Publication Data
Data available

Library of Congress Control Number: 2022908065

ISBN 978-0-19-285921-1

DOI: 10.1093/oso/9780192859211.001.0001

Printed and bound by
CPI Group (UK) Ltd, Croydon, CR0 4YY

Acknowledgments

I could not have written this book without the support of institutions and individuals willing to take an interest in a topic that is often perceived as fussy, arcane, and outdated. Institutional and financial support for this research was provided by the Office of the Vice Chancellor for Research and Graduate Education at the University of Wisconsin-Madison with funding from the Wisconsin Alumni Research Foundation. The Institute for Research in the Humanities at the University of Wisconsin-Madison enabled me to combine a Residential Fellowship with a semester of funding from the Faculty Sabbatical Leave Program (Office of the Provost, University of Wisconsin-Madison) so that I could spend a full year at the Institute, engaged in intellectually vibrant conversation with other fellows and consuming an embarrassing number of cookies at Monday seminars. The IRH provided additional support in the form of a Summer Humanities Research Fellowship, which provided funding for me to ask Natalie Gerber to read my work. Her generosity and acumen in commenting on all levels of chapters five and six improved them immeasurably. I have noted in those chapters the moments where her suggestions led me to a specific point, resource, or other intervention, but I want to acknowledge here the degree to which both her work and her comments on mine helped me work through contemporary metrical theories. Any errors are of course mine. Ann W. Harris, Assistant to the Director at the IRH, was not only incredibly helpful but extremely kind, making all of the logistics involved in combining funding sources, coordinating offices, and communicating with scholars at and beyond UW Madison downright pleasant. Robert von Hallberg wrote numerous letters of recommendation as I applied for funding and continues to be an interlocutor on humane academic writing and the ongoing cultural value of poetry. John Lysaker improved my first book immeasurably and helped launch this one by writing recommendation letters, and Lynn Keller offered generous feedback on an early proposal draft.

Ximing Lu's painstaking translation and contextualization of the Ancient Greek quotations or paraphrases opened the way into Nietzsche's rhythm notebooks for me; any errors in translation or transliteration are mine, not his. Sarah Ferchau meticulously checked references and footnotes, saving me dozens of hours as well as taking a generous interest in work outside her research expertise. Kevin Kurdylo worked magic on a humanities library acquisition budget and tracked down everything from feuilleton articles on meter that inexplicably referenced potatoes to elegies for German media theorists. Many other UW Madison librarians, library staff, and student workers went above and beyond during the Covid-19 pandemic, extending loan periods, tracking down electronic and physical sources, and helping me and countless other researchers access collections safely. I am grateful to Oxford University Press, particularly Jacqueline Norton, Karen Raith, and Aimee Wright for skillful guidance of this project through the waters of publishing, and to three anonymous reviewers for highly constructive feedback.

The College of Letters & Science and the Department of German, Nordic, and Slavic+ at UW Madison has been a collegial and intellectually stimulating place to write and teach. Thanks to the many students and colleagues willing to share my excitement and set me off on tangents about meter, often contributing their own examples of metrical delight. Sabine Gross not only wrote several rounds of recommendation letters but offered invaluable feedback on several chapters. Her energy and enthusiasm buoyed this project at a time when I wasn't sure there was anything there, and our collaboration on the 2019 Wisconsin Workshop on "Rhythms" and its published volume enriched my thinking immeasurably. Thanks to B. Venkat Mani—colleague, friend, fellow troublemaker, and grant proposal wordsmith—whose myriad intellectual accomplishments include the edited volumes whose essays have inspired my next research project. And thanks to Nâlân Erbîl and Nurettin Erkan for both shared and differing interests and fearless conversation.

I have had the privilege of exchanging work with Tatyana Gershkovich, Matt Handelman, Joela Jacobs, and especially my Madison colleague Sunny Yudkoff for some six or seven years. Their questions, corrections, and suggestions, as well as reading their work, have sharpened my thinking and writing; I look forward to every one of our meetings, and we have shared the challenges of building academic identities and careers. Joela, along with Peter Erickson, has been a dear friend and interlocutor over more than a decade as we build on what our shared graduate education included and lament (and remediate) what it left out. Thank you to Katie Somers—our writing (and life) accountability check-ins made the struggles of writing less lonely and the triumphs more fun. My thanks also extend to family members and friends in Madison and beyond: Deanna Cheung, Julian Sharifi, Rasoul Sharifi, Adam Stern (and Theo!), Sonja Klocke, Dean Krouk, Kit Tilmann, Megan Kenney, Peter Doksus, Janice Poehlman, Aygul Batyrshina, Jeff Durbin, and other compatriots.

My parents, Joan Vandegrift and Richard Eldridge, read and commented on numerous drafts, enriching my arguments and improving my prose—the remaining faults are no doubt where I foolishly disregarded their advice. More importantly, they inducted me into the metrical delights of language from *Now We Are Six* to *The Prelude*. My sister, Sarah Eldridge, is not only a brilliant colleague in German Studies but a fellow seeker of labor justice in the academy and collaborator in elaborate baking projects; I have learned an enormous amount from her work as well as her input on mine. Jonathan Eldridge's rendition of "Punch brothers, punch with care!" remains the gold standard for me, and his eye-rolling dismissal of pretentiousness and joy in being ridiculous on occasion are an inspiration. My brother-in-law and nieces are further connoisseurs of rhythms and silliness—thank you especially to Elena for loving *The Pout Pout Fish*. Finally, Marina Sharifi, my wife, is a constant source of love and support in ways innumerable and inarticulate. Thank you.

Thanks to the following rights-holders for permission to reprint works under copyright:

"Aporia Augustine (On Time)" translated by Michael Eskin. Copyright © 2013 by Upper West Side Philosophers, Inc., New York. Used by permission.

Excerpt from: Durs Grünbein, Gedichte. Bücher I–III. © Suhrkamp Verlag Frankfurt am Main 2006. Alle Rechte bei und vorbehalten durch Suhrkamp Verlag Berlin.

Excerpt from: Durs Grünbein, Nach den Satiren. Gedichte. © Suhrkamp Verlag Frankfurt am Main 1999. Alle Rechte bei und vorbehalten durch Suhrkamp Verlag Berlin.

"Biological Waltz" translated by Andrew Shields. Poetry Magazine, November 1998 (p.105).

Contents

List of Figures

Introduction

0.1 Metrical Claims

Human experience with patterned language cuts across geographical, cultural, and class boundaries. From the Epic of Gilgamesh and ancient Greek, Latin, and Sanskrit verse all the way to nursery rhymes and popular songs in contemporary cultures, language and rhythm form and inform being human. But the study of how metrical patterns are formed, how they develop, how they affect readers, and how they are combined with semantic content seems today to play almost no role in either general or scholarly investigations of poetry.[1] Inquiries into poetry's function for subjects and communities have driven a strong renewal of interest in lyric poetry in the last twenty years. Building on and moving beyond work this work, I argue that attention to metrical theory and practice bears on precisely these concerns.[2] What can patterns of syllables tell us about the experience of being human? How does using language in metrically specific ways in linguistic communities shape the communities and ourselves? Why should we care about poetic meter?

Metrical Claims and Poetic Experience takes up these questions. The "metrical claims" of my title are twofold. First, I argue that examining current and historical metrical theory and practice expands readers' and listeners' experiences of poetry and that such experiences are valuable acts of self-understanding, cultural

---

[1] Since roughly 2015 this state of affairs has shown signs of changing through work in the field of historical poetics: https://www.historicalpoetics.com/, accessed July 20, 2022. The group remains focused solely on the Anglo-American tradition, however. I discuss historical poetics and what I draw on from the field below.

[2] The boom in studies of the lyric in multiple American and European traditions is documented, to name just a few sources, in the 2017 issue of the *Journal of Literary Theory* dedicated to the topic of "theories of the lyric" and outlining in its introduction the need for international collaboration. Claudia Hillebrandt et al., "Theories of Lyric," *Journal of Literary Theory* 11, no. 1 (2017): 1–11; in S. Burt, "What Is This Thing Called Lyric?," *Modern Philology* 113, no. 3 (February 2016): 422–40, https://doi.org/10.1086/684097; Jonathan Culler, *Theory of the Lyric* (Cambridge: Harvard University Press, 2015); Klaus Hempfer, "Some Aspects of a Theory of Genre," in *Linguistics and Literary Studies / Linguistik und Literaturwissenschaft Interfaces, Encounters, Transfers / Begegnungen, Interferenzen und Kooperationen*, eds. Monika Fludernik and Daniel Jacob, linguae & litterae 31 (Berlin: de Gruyter, 2014), 405–22; Virginia Jackson, "Lyric," in *Princeton Encyclopedia of Poetry and Poetics*, 4th ed. (Princeton: Princeton University Press, 2012), 826–34; Dieter Lamping, "Eine Theorie des lyrischen Gedichts," *Recherches germaniques* 14 (2019): 31–7; Ingrid Nelson, "Poetics of the Rule: Form, Biopolitics, Lyric," *New Literary History* 50, no. 1 (2019): 65–89, https://doi.org/10.1353/nlh.2019.0004; Jahan Ramazani, *A Transnational Poetics* (University of Chicago Press, 2015) and *Poetry in a Global Age* (University of Chicago Press, 2020).

Metrical Claims and Poetic Experience. Hannah Vandegrift Eldridge, Oxford University Press.
© Hannah Vandegrift Eldridge (2022). DOI: 10.1093/oso/9780192859211.003.0001

examination, and care for language.[3] Second, I show that analyzing meter as it is discussed and deployed in different historical moments yields crucial insights about language and how human beings use it: meter illuminates the interplay of culture, cognition, emotion, and embodiment. Metrics is thus an ideal place to investigate the relations of language, culture, and the body as they shape human subjects.

I undertake this investigation in the German-language tradition of metrical theory and poetic practice. One reason for doing so is, of course, the contingent fact of my training as a Germanist. But the German tradition of metrical study is particularly fruitful in tracing the relation between cultural and aesthetic values because it is marked by deep disagreement about which poetic traditions should be models for German literature—and thus by disagreement about which phonological components of the language can or should be organized into metrical patterns. In consequence, a greater openness to different ways of making metrical patterns persists for longer and more different metrical systems find adherents than in other linguistic-cultural traditions. These uncertainties apply not only to the adaptation of Classical Greek and Latin meters into German but also to the rules governing Early Germanic verse practices.[4] Moreover, recent scholarship that interrogates the cultural values adhering to metrical theory and practice (rather than rhythm; see below) has primarily been focused on the Anglo-American tradition; looking to a different language expands, deepens, and complicates narratives of the claims made in and about meter and the poetic experiences it affords.

Ideas about the experiences meter can create are, I contend, best understood by bringing detailed examinations of particular linguistic traditions into contact with one another. Thus, this book should be understood as one starting point among many possible ones for reading together global metrical traditions (working out which traditions have had particular influences on one another and thus which international comparisons are especially illuminating would be another task for such comparison). Meter itself crosses cultures within a given poetic tradition, as metrical patterns are repeatedly "grafted from one language onto another."[5] That

---

[3] On the concept of "care for language" as challenging rather than reinforcing nationalist and racialized norms, see Yuliya Komska, Michelle Moyd, and David Gramling, *Linguistic Disobedience: Restoring Power to Civic Language* (Springer, 2018).

[4] For a comparison of European versification systems, see Mikhail L. Gasparov, *A History of European Versification*, trans. G.S. Smith and Marina Tarlinskaja (Oxford: Clarendon Press, 1996).

[5] Jahan Ramazani, "Lyric Poetry: Intergeneric, Transnational, Translingual?," *Journal of Literary Theory* 11, no. 1 (January 1, 2017), https://doi.org/10.1515/jlt-2017-0011. Ramazani instances both the adaptation of ancient Greek and Latin meters I have noted and the incorporation and alteration of Arabic meters in Persian poetry "in the aftermath of the Muslim conquest in the seventh century" (103). He elsewhere argues that meter and prosody shape the inherent transnationalism of poetry as a genre: "meter, rhythm, stanza, and other prosodic elements have always traveled across cultural and territorial boundaries; consider, for example, the Japanese haiku, famously anglicized by the imagists, or the Arabic ghazal, adapted for over a thousand years into Persian taking its canonical form in that language, Turkish, Urdu, German, and English" (Ramazani, *A Transnational Poetics* [University of Chicago Press, 2015], 56).

comparative work must begin with detailed attention to the particularities of one language tradition as the necessary basis for cross-language comparison. Although I focus on the German-language tradition, one could of course write several versions of this book's historical narrative for various European and international verse traditions. Each version would open further possibilities for learning from and about meter and for experiences of poetry. In giving one overview of the history of the German metrical and poetic tradition, I show both its particularities and its openness to cross-cultural influences.

To do so, I identify three transformative moments in metrical thinking in the German-language context and analyze these moments in the works of thinkers and poets who have engaged extensively with metrics both in their theoretical writings on poetry and in their poetic practice. Friedrich Gottlieb Klopstock (1724–1803) revolutionizes German metrics by the introduction of free verse and the imitation of Greek meters, Friedrich Nietzsche (1844–1900) articulates the radical historicity of meter as an embodied practice, and Durs Grünbein (b.1962) revitalizes traditional forms as he uses meter to challenge the assumptions of both metaphysics and natural science. Just as it would be possible to write versions of the history I trace here in different language traditions, it would be possible to choose different historical inflection points in the German poetic tradition. Klopstock, Nietzsche, and Grünbein, however, share several features that make them helpful for thinking about meter, language, and embodiment. First, they share interests in the ways German meters can adapt those of ancient Greek and Latin and in the connections between German and Greek and Roman culture more generally. They are, in consequence, particularly attentive to questions of cultural transmission and transformation on scales ranging from single syllables to entire value systems. Second, each poet draws on the newest natural-scientific work of his day to think and write about meter and the body, reaching beyond the discipline of poetic theory to make claims in exceptional detail about the bodily efficacy of meter. Moreover, all three are poet-thinkers who both theorize extensively about meter, language, poetry, and embodiment and also write poetry in a variety of meters and forms. Finally, each engages with and differs from the metrical and poetological theories and practices of his era in crucial ways, as I show by contextualizing and counterposing each poet (in Chapters 2, 4, and 6) in and against his era (Chapters 1, 3, and 5).

Using these three authors and the contexts in which they write, I show that metrical theory and practice illuminate the interaction between language, culture, and the body because meter is based on audible features of language used in everyday speech (such as pitch and accent). But unlike everyday language, meter deliberately organizes those features into particular patterns established in cultural and historical contexts. Thus, looking carefully at who counts what as which meter at what historical moment and why can reveal the individual and cultural commitments mapped onto the material features of the language. And because

those features are created by the human voice and experienced in human hearing, meter comes from and resonates in the human body. Klopstock, Nietzsche,
and Grünbein probe the relations between embodiment, subjectivity, and poetic
language in ways that both emerge from and challenge their particular historical
moments.

Because languages, cultures, and bodies change across history, poets and theorists of meter reflect on this interaction in historically specific ways; to understand
what meter does in our own moment, it is important to understand earlier metrical
theory and practice. Historical contextualization likewise forms a crucial basis for
trans-historical and trans-linguistic comparison: in order to see what Klopstock
does or doesn't share with (for instance) Milton or Hölderlin or Wordsworth, we
first need to understand how each poet responds to the pressing poetic questions
of his immediate cultural circumstances. (There may well be times when an international context is more influential for a given figure than the national one; in that
case, full understanding of both poetic-historical backgrounds will be even more
important.) Analyzing the backgrounds against which Klopstock, Nietzsche, and
Grünbein work is what lets their distinctive contributions emerge. I contend that
these contributions are worth reclaiming for poetry today.

Before turning to terminological clarifications and theoretical debates, I want
to give a brief example of what patterned language can (be imagined to) do: Mark
Twain's 1876 fable of metrical contagion, "A Literary Nightmare." The story begins
with a request:

> "Will the reader please to cast his eye over the following lines, and
> see if he can discover anything harmful in them?
>
> *Conductor, when you receive a fare,*
> *Punch in the presence of the passenjare!*
> *A blue trip slip for an eight-cent fare,*
> *A buff trip slip for a six-cent fare,*
> *A pink trip slip for a three-cent fare,*
> *Punch in the presence of the passenjare!*
> *CHORUS*
> *Punch, brothers! punch with care!*
> *Punch in the presence of the passenjare!*
>
> I came across these jingling rhymes in a newspaper, a little while
> ago, and read them a couple of times. They took instant and entire
> possession of me."[6]

At first charmed by the "jingling rhymes," the narrator grows increasingly dis-
tressed as he becomes unable to write or even to sleep; when, striving for relief,
he goes for a walk, he finds himself moving in step to "Punch, brothers, punch

---

[6] Mark Twain, "A Literary Nightmare," *The Atlantic Monthly* (February 1876): 167–9.

with care/ Punch in the presence of the passenjare!"[7] The narrator eventually cures himself by passing the verses on to his friend, a pastor, who inadvertently mixes them into a funeral oration—only to find his hearers equally affected:

> And the most distressing thing was that my delivery dropped into the undulating rhythm of those pulsing rhymes, and I could actually catch absent-minded people nodding time to the swing of it with their stupid heads. And, Mark, you may believe it or not, but before I got through the entire assemblage were placidly bobbing their heads in solemn unison, mourners, undertaker, and all.[8]

The friend's situation grows even more extreme than the narrator's: he becomes frenzied and ultimately falls into a trance through repeating the words. The story ends when the narrator announces that he has written for "a worthy, even a noble, purpose. It was to warn you, reader, if you should come across those merciless rhymes, to avoid them—avoid them as you would a pestilence."[9]

This admittedly humorous and extreme example underscores several central features of meter and rhythm. First, the characters' responses demonstrate meter's bodily efficacy: the narrator describes himself as "possessed" by the jingle; he walks in time to the lines; and the pastor's auditors bob their heads along to the "undulating rhythm." Second, the story foregrounds the ambiguous relation of sound patterning to content: at times the contagion seems to be in the beat alone (as when the pastor falls into its cadence), while at other times the mundane content of the lines adds to the indignity of their persistence (as when they appear in the narrator's writing). It's unclear if words, specifically, or just the beats, sounds, and/or movements lodge themselves in the hearers. Finally, the story hints at tensions between universal transmissibility and cultural or medial specificity: the narrator reads the lines in print while the pastor and the funeral attendees hear them out loud, suggesting that the lines cross media boundaries for universal effect. Nonetheless, in order to produce and to some extent perceive the lines, one must be fluent in English, especially to spit out the rapid-fire monosyllables of "blue trip slip," "buff trip slip" and "pink trip slip" and to pick up on the phonological spelling of "passenJARE," which not only enforces the rhyme but marks a social location in suggesting the class position of a train conductor. To understand the effects of Twain's metrical virus fully, we would have to consider the social locations (including class, geography, and race) of train conductors in 1876, the regional readership of *The Atlantic* and their dialects, pronunciations, or accents

---

[7] Twain, "A Literary Nightmare," 167.

[8] Twain, "A Literary Nightmare," 169.

[9] Twain, "A Literary Nightmare," 169. The notion of contagion and pestilence also appears in the title of an essay by Haun Saussy on rhythm's bodily efficacy, "Contagious Rhythm: Verse as a Technique of the Body," in *Critical Rhythm: The Poetics of a Literary Life Form*, eds. Ben Glaser, Jonathan Culler, Lazar Fleishman, and Haun Saussy (New York: Fordham University Press, 2019), 106–27.

as well as Twain's, and contemporaneous conventions for representing oral and informal speech in published writing, to name just a few of the relevant areas. But at the same time, the lines are entertaining, memorable, and effective even prior to those investigations, suggesting that its effects are not only the result of learned appreciation.

The questions Twain's story raises—How does meter affect the mind and the body? How does it relate to meaning? How is it transmitted? For whom and in what forms is it effective?—are precisely those addressed by the authors I treat in this book. Using Klopstock, Nietzsche, and Grünbein, I draw insights both into our lives with poetry and into how patterned language links language, culture, and the body. To understand their contributions, I first clarify—to the extent possible—what I mean by "meter" and how it relates to and interacts with a number of other terms, particularly "rhythm."

0.2 Meter versus Rhythm

Meter stands in a series of sometimes contrasting and sometimes overlapping terms or concepts, including rhythm, prosody, verse, lyric, poetry, and poetics. For much contemporary scholarship, meter appears as the least interesting of these concepts; late-twentieth- and early-twenty-first-century scholars seem in almost universal agreement with Gilles Deleuze and Félix Guattari's assertion that "meter is dogmatic, but rhythm is critical."[10] But although the distinction between meter and rhythm is both long-standing and canonical for European-American poetry and poetics (dating back at least to the fourth century BCE and Aristoxenus of Tarentum[11]), the definitions of each term overlap considerably. Moreover, the definitions of meter and rhythm undergo numerous shifts in their respective conceptual histories. Many contemporary theorists describe one or the other as an abstract pattern or schema and its realization—but they disagree on which of the two is the schema and which the realization.[12] Given these terminological confusions, I attend carefully in each chapter to the way the eras and thinkers I consider

---

[10] Gilles Deleuze and Félix Guattari, *A Thousand Plateaus*, trans. Brian Massumi (Minneapolis: University of Minnesota Press, 1987), 313.

[11] Aristoxenus contended that meter was a sub-phenomenon of rhythm and held that rhythm could best be examined in music, as the art form whose material organized by rhythm was the least affected by other factors or functions of the material. This distinction becomes central in nineteenth-century philology and is crucial for the work of Friedrich Nietzsche, whom I discuss in Chapter 4. Contemporary theorists and manuals simplify the debate by aligning so-called rhythmicians with music and metricians with philology; rhythm thus becomes broader, while meter remains a specifically linguistic phenomenon. See Aristoxenus, *Aristoxenus Elementa Rhythmica: The Fragment of Book II and the Additional Evidence for Aristoxenean Rhythmic Theory*, trans. Lionel Ignacius Cusack Pearson (Clarendon Press, 1990).

[12] Two relatively recent overviews in German illustrate this point: Christine Lubkoll explains that "while meter is the time signature, as it were, the abstract order of a verse text, rhythm is the concrete realization fitted to the prosodic factors of the language ("[w]ährend das Metrum die Taktart,

use "meter" and "rhythm." To give a rough preliminary definition, which subsequent chapters will complicate, I understand *meter* in poetry as syllable patterning. These patterns may be created in a number of ways (organized differences of length, pitch, and/or volume), and they interact with other elements of poetic language such as rhyme, line ending, and sound repetition (alliteration, assonance). Consequently, rhyme, line ending, and sound repetition may be metrical *features*, even if they are not themselves meters. *Rhythm*, conversely, is a much broader category of organization not limited to language, usually involving a combination of variation and repetition, either spatial or temporal; these may, but need not, include meter in language.

On the basis of this distinction, I briefly sketch the moves by which contemporary work divides meter and rhythm and the consequences of that division. Much of this theory strips questions of meaning, political stakes, embodiment, and effects on subjectivity away from meter and attributes them to rhythm.[13] Doing so gives rhythm a robust philosophical and theoretical pedigree while reducing meter to pedantic counting. Thus, for example, the introduction to a 2019 volume on rhythm notes the "slippery relation between the two terms" but quickly privileges rhythm, asserting that "meter now appears to require the supplement of rhythm to preserve the salience of sound-form within theories of the aesthetic or literary."[14] The use of "now" highlights that on this account, whatever the case was before, poets and readers/listeners *today* seem to need rhythm as a supplement to meter. In contrast to meter, rhythm "rarely gets described without some claim that it can be heard, felt, and shared because it has physical effects on bodies or tympanums."[15] These characteristics link rhythm to perception and embodiment, versus the merely formal, abstract, and inaudible nature of meter. As meter's palpable and perceptible counterpart, rhythm, in this reading, seems relevant to numerous physiological, media-theoretical, and philosophical questions, while meter does not.

Rhythm, then, is expansive, multimedial, and connected to meaning; it "expands beyond the domains of prosody and versification, and even of music and

---

gewissermaßen die abstrakte Ordnung eines Verstextes darstellt, ist der Rhythmus die den prosodischen Gegebenheiten der Sprache angepasste konkrete Realisierung," Christine Lubkoll, "Rhythmus und Metrum," in *Literaturwissenschaft. Einführung in ein Sprachspiel,* eds. Heinrich Bosse and Ursula Renner (Freiburg : Rombach, 1999), 103–122, 117), while Wilhelm Seidel argues that in opposition to the term rhythm, the term meter never designates a principle, but always a manifestation of the principle of rhythm ("[i]m Gegensatz zum Terminus Rhythmus bezeichnet der Terminus Metrum nie ein Prinzip, sondern immer nur eine Manifestation des Prinzips Rhythmus," Wilhelm Seidel, "Rhythmus," in *Ästhetische Grundbegriffe,* eds. Karl Barck et al., Vol. 5, [Stuttgart 2003], 291–314, 293). Translations mine when no citation is given.

[13] I analyze in detail the consequences of this marginalization of meter for contemporary metrics and poetic practice in Chapter 5.

[14] Ben Glaser, "Introduction," in Glaser, Culler, Fleishman, and Saussy, *Critical Rhythm,* 1–17, 7. Glaser questions further the implications for poetry of this turn away from meter and toward rhythm (2–3).

[15] Glaser, "Introduction," 6.

dance, to encompass the broader dynamics of sense-making."[16] Through the inter-rogation of its relation to meaning ("sense-making"), rhythm aligns with poetry in the canonical question of the relation between philosophy and poetry (while "meaning" corresponds to "philosophy"). David Nowell Smith—who asks per-haps the most clearly of any contemporary verse theorist what philosophy wants with rhythm—suggests that, for many philosophers, rhythm "names the dynamic unfolding/enfolding of sense."[17] This broad definition brings both promise and dif-ficulties. On the one hand, this meaning-based rhythm "seems far removed from questions of prosody or versification."[18] But on the other hand, defining rhythm as the unfolding of meaning or sense can (or could) direct us back to the specific workings of language on more and different levels than stressed and unstressed syl-lables, for example by calling attention to rhythm(s) of paragraphs, line lengths, intonational contours, or strophe-level organization.[19] Nowell Smith reflects care-fully on how philosophical considerations of rhythm neglect or appropriate its specific appearances in verse practice.[20] Analyzing thinkers such as Heidegger, Agamben, Derrida, and Kristeva, Nowell Smith reflects that when philosophers ask "how features of 'verse' can open on to a 'poetic' truth," the question of rhythm becomes a philosophical question.[21] At the same time, this philosophical valoriza-tion of rhythm (and thus poetry, as the type of language most defined by rhythm) threatens to elide poetic specificity: "there is a fine line between recognizing that poetry is 'other' to thinking, and transforming poetry into thinking's 'other.'"[22] As he points out, theory, not poetry itself, draws those distinctions; analyzing poetry as theory's or philosophy's other almost inevitably subordinates poetry to thinking.

Conversely, I demonstrate that attending to meter and considering the philo-sophical, political, and anthropological work undertaken by and in patterns of syllables helps fix our attention on the poetic and historical content and context, making clear that poetic questions about subjectivity, language, and embodiment

---

[16] David Nowell Smith, "What Is Called Rhythm," in Glaser, Culler, Fleishman, and Saussy, *Critical Rhythm*, 40–59), 40.

[17] Nowell Smith, "What Is Called Rhythm," 51.

[18] Nowell Smith, "What Is Called Rhythm," 51.

[19] Nowell Smith, "What Is Called Rhythm," 51. Of course, much of the history of metrical theory has taken precisely these questions as central to *meter*, not rhythm; that Nowell Smith thinks metrics does not ask these questions is a symptom of the reassignment of metrical questions to rhythm in the late twentieth century.

[20] He also notes the differences between Anglo-American/analytic and Continental philosophy apropos rhythm: "in continental Europe the transformation of the concept of rhythm becomes, if not a concept *for* philosophy, then a concept through which poetics sets itself in relation to philosophy, a concept through which philosophy tries to adopt a poetics" (Nowell Smith, "What Is called Rhythm," 41) and traces this tradition beginning with Hegel to Schopenhauer, Wagner, and Mallarmé (42).

[21] David Nowell Smith, "The Poetry-Verse Distinction Reconsidered," *Thinking Verse* 1 (2011): 137–60, 140.

[22] Nowell Smith, "The Poetry-Verse Distinction Reconsidered," 144. Nowell Smith makes this point here primarily apropos Heidegger but notes a similar move in Derrida: "Poetry's withdrawal from and resistance to philosophical questioning and vocabulary has become its characteristic trait; it too is now simply one more instance of 'deconstruction'" (147).

unfold in particular poems from particular authors in particular cultures at particular moments. Such meaning-making effects in the arenas of the linguistic, poetic, bodily, and political appear in yet another theorist who rejects or challenges meter in favor of an analysis—or, in his terms, critique—of rhythm: the French linguist, poet, and translator Henri Meschonnic, who remains relatively little-known in the Anglo-American academy.[23] Although Meschonnic articulates many of the effects of patterned language that I argue for, he attributes them to rhythm rather than meter; nonetheless (and despite several anti-meter polemics), Meschonnic hints at the kind of metrical practice I examine in Klopstock, Nietzsche, and Grünbein as historically variable, culturally shaped, and politically charged.

Meschonnic defines rhythm as "the organization of meaning in discourse,"[24] that is, as the singular event of making sense from this subject in this place in history and culture. Consequently, his theory of rhythm has effects for subjectivity, historicity, society, and politics—just the effects I find in *meter*.[25] Work on and in language becomes a political activity, because, following Wilhelm von Humboldt, Meschonnic sees discourse as shaped by and shaping a form of life. What Meschonnic calls "poetics" is therefore an ethical and political project in which a subject transforms and is transformed by language and life.[26] Meschonnic's rejection of meter and his absorption of formal features into philosophical questions rest on his view of language: his ethical-political "poetics of society" entails a challenge to the conception of language as a system of signs. He contends that taking language as a structure of arbitrary signs creates a binary mode of thinking that suppresses or forgets that the continuous use of language as creating meaning comes before the focus on language as a sign system. Meter sits comfortably within the discontinuous/binary sign paradigm because it chops language up into discrete syllables and feet, allowing for "scientific" study that distances the material properties of the sign from meaning.

It is therefore perhaps not surprising that Meschonnic outlines his theory of rhythm in *opposition* to meter and metrics, which are strongly associated with

---

[23] This is beginning to change: the last five years have seen the publication of *The Henri Meschonnic Reader*, the first large-scale collection of Meschonnic's work in English (*The Henri Meschonnic Reader: A Poetics of Society*, ed. Marko Pajević [Edinburgh, 2019]), and a 2018 special issue of *Comparative Critical Studies* dedicated to his work (*Comparative Critical Studies* 15.3 [2018], eds. Marko Pajević and David Nowell Smith). Both contain brief biographies and overviews of Meschonnic's works; see John E. Joseph, "Introduction," (in Pajević, *The Henri Meschonnic Reader*, 1–14) and Marko Pajević and David Nowell Smith, "Introduction: Thinking Language with Henri Meschonnic," *Comparative Critical Studies* 15, no. 3 (2018): 279–87, https://doi.org/10.3366/ccs.2018.0296).

[24] Pajević and Nowell Smith, "Introduction," 281.

[25] As Pajević and Nowell Smith explain, "Meschonnic's theory of rhythm entails a theory not just of discourse, but of the constitution of subjects in discourse, as they inhabit and transform their historical moment. What starts as a conceptual problem of linguistic rhythm extends outward to comprise an alternative approach to grasping language, the subject, and society" (Pajević and Nowell Smith, "Introduction," 282).

[26] Henri Meschonnic, "Realism, Nominalism: The Theory of Language Is a Theory of Society," in Pajević, *The Henri Meschonnic Reader*, 312–20, 312.

poetry and poetic *form*. He reads meter as an impoverished way of forcing poetry into an abstract formal pattern that enables readers to continue thinking of language as a system of signs. Metrics then becomes a "metaphysics of poetry" because it divides form and content, sloughing off the latter to create pure "form, inner, outer, proportion, symmetry, unit," which are, in his view, more like music than poetry.[27] Indeed, the most important problem with meter and metrics for Meschonnic is that, in his view, they separate syllable patterning from meaning, working on individual units of verse as single examples isolated from the rest of the poem or text.[28] Rhythm, in contrast, organizes discourse, and so it participates in or even enables the meaning-making of that discourse and is a semantic and not a formal-metrical principle.[29] Moreover, rhythm constitutes the subject: "rhythm is necessarily an organization or configuration of the subject in their discourse ... There cannot be a theory of rhythm without a theory of the subject, nor theory of the subject without a theory of rhythm."[30] This rapid ramification of rhythm, language, and subject both underscores the importance of rhythm, in Meschonnic's account, for culture and society, and reveals the way the particularities of poets' practices and syllable patterning expand (or disappear) into the literary, philosophical, political, etc. In this respect, Meschonnic is a paradigmatic case for the way contemporary investigations of meter and rhythm remove cultural, historical, political, aesthetic, and subjective significance from meter and attribute them to rhythm.

In contrast, I keep the specifics of metrical thinking firmly in view; somewhat surprisingly, there are moments where Meschonnic's work points the way toward doing so, especially in his remarks about particular verse practices in their historical appearances. He acknowledges that meters, too, participate in the project of sense-making: "since nothing of what is in language can be without an effect on sense, then not only rhymes have sense, and meters, but each consonant, each vowel, all the seen and heard materiality of words."[31] Moreover, he

---

[27] Meschonnic, "Metrics," 122. As Nowell Smith points out, Meschonnic's rejection of meter as artificially imported into language from music theory ignores musical practice and its phrase structures as well as music theory's interest in how music functions like a language (David Nowell Smith, "Rhythm-Sense-Subject, or: The Dynamic Un/Enfolding of Sense," *Comparative Critical Studies* 15, no. 3 (October 1, 2018): 357, https://doi.org/10.3366/ccs.2018.0300).

[28] As Nowell Smith explains, the syllables meter analyses are "discontinuous both in that they are isolated from each other, and as they are isolated from sense. They are subsequently measured into feet, or verse lines, formalized according to patterns of alternating stress and unstress, and then reconstructed into higher level units'" Nowell Smith, "Rhythm-Sense-Subject," 356.

[29] Marko Pajević, "Meschonnic's Theory of Rhythm, His Key Concepts and Their Relation," in Pajević, *The Henri Meschonnic Reader*, 15–31, 22; Hans Lösener, *Der Rhythmus in der Rede: Linguistische und literaturwissenschaftliche Aspekte des Sprachrhythmus* (Tübingen: Niemeyer, 1999), 5.

[30] Meschonnic, "Rhythm: What Is at Stake in a Theory of Rhythm" 69. Hence, as Lösener remarks, Meschonnic returns the subject to the study of language (Lösener, *Der Rhythmus in der Rede*, 6); whether this is as much of a return for disciplines other than linguistics could be debated.

[31] Meschonnic "Rhyme and Life," 182, trans. Andrew Eastman, in Pajević, *The Henri Meschonnic Reader*, 179–97.

succinctly frames the non-objectivity of metrics: "many examples show that a metrical scheme is not a linguistic emanation, but rather a relation between culture and language."[32] That is, metrical rules do not come solely from the phonological attributes of the language but are shaped by the culture(s) in which that language is used. I (unlike Meschonnic) show in detail how these multiple mutual shapings take place and why authors and cultures become attached to or invested in them. Meschonnic also acknowledges that "the histories of metrics and of language are often heterogeneous," with poets importing patterns from one language into another and then the second language's features influencing the metrical pattern, and that metrical "counting" changes over time.[33] Although Meschonnic reflects on the cultural lifetimes of particular meters (for example, he notes "the alexandrine was a way of relating to the world"[34]), he combines the idea that "a metrics is a collective attitude" with a reading of metrical forms as bodily and individually coercive: "Metrics is a hold of the social and cultural life on the individual subject ... The alexandrine is a bringing to heel. A singing parade."[35] I argue, over and against Meschonnic, that these forms are not always or necessarily unconscious or coercive. Rather, poets might—I contend, do—deliberately activate, challenge, and combine such forms in complex and nuanced ways, thus incorporating traditions of meaning-making and past poems, subjects, and discourses into their poetry.

Skepticism about poets' and theorists' contemporaneous accounts of their poetic projects forms a rather unexpected point of connection between Meschonnic and a completely separate approach to poetic meter that informs my modes of reading: so-called "historical prosody" or "historical poetics."[36] Historical poetics analyzes with exemplary care how different epochs and sometimes individual poets deploy particular forms and what cultural or ideological commitments underlie the use of those forms. Yopie Prins, one of the originators of the approach,

[32] Gabriella Bedetti and Henri Meschonnic, "Interview: Henri Meschonnic," *Diacritics* 18, no. 3 (1988), 93–111, 93.

[33] Henri Meschonnic, "Metrics: Pure Metrics or Discourse Metrics," trans. John E. Joseph, in Pajević, *The Henri Meschonnic Reader*, 127–8. His assertion that "linguistic frequency governs the types of verse" (Meschonnic, "Metrics," 128) falls short of the nuance in work by Marina Tarlinskaja, who demonstrates using statistical analysis of English iambic pentameter that cultural historical convention has a greater influence on metrical "irregularities" than phonological pressure. (See Marina Tarlinskaja, "What Is 'Metricality'? English Iambic Pentameter," in *Formal Approaches to Poetry: Recent Developments in Metrics*, eds. B. Elan Dresher and Nila Friedberg (Berlin: De Gruyter, Inc., 2006), 53–74, 64).

[34] Meschonnic, "Rhyme and Life," 186. Meschonnic acknowledges that we can and do continue to enjoy and play upon past forms, but that we cannot return to unreflective use of them: "Just as we listen to early music, as we continue to look at paintings which remain paintings. But we can no longer compose such music." Meschonnic, "Rhyme and Life," 187.

[35] Meschonnic, "Metrics," 119.

[36] Yopie Prins, one of the main exponents of this line of research, refers to it as historical prosody; others conducting similar projects use "historical poetics." Both have impressive collaborative projects: the Princeton Prosody Archive (https://prosody.princeton.edu/, accessed July 20, 2021) and the Historical Poetics website (https://www.historicalpoetics.com/, accessed July 20, 2021). Both, however, are relentlessly English-language focused.

shows that even apparently fixed and settled forms like the Sapphic stanza in English are realized differently by different authors at different times (and, I would add, in different languages). This analysis leads her to recast yet again the question of the relation between meter and rhythm: "[w]hat if literary concepts such as meter and rhythm are historically contingent and fundamentally unstable?"[37]As Prins argues, and as I demonstrate in detail in this book, "the phenomenology of poetic rhythm experienced in the present moment depends on how meter is theorized at different moments in history."[38] I diverge, however, from historical poetics in that I move beyond the exclusively English-language scope of historical prosody and historical poetics to show that attention to different traditions—here the German-language tradition—illuminates the variation in the cultural-political work undertaken by metrical theory and practice in different cultures at different times.[39]

Moreover, I argue for more deliberate activation of different forms, meters, and traditions on the part of poets, versus the unconscious commitments that historical poetics works to uncover. Metrical theorists, too, often interrogate the very definitions and attributes that both Meschonnic and readers in historical poetics accuse them of taking as given.[40] Rather than unconsciously adopting an ideology, a poet might choose to write one poem in (say) accentual folk verse and another in a modern hexameter or a modified Sapphic ode form, and I show that if readers miss the deliberate activation of a given verse tradition, we miss part of the meaning-making of the poet's discourse. My analyses of meter in its specificity as patterns of syllables that are then organized and worked on by other structures such as

---

[37] Yopie Prins, "Sapphic Stanzas: How Can We Read the Rhythm?" in Glaser, Culler, Fleishman, and Saussy, *Critical Rhythm*, 247–73, 251.

[38] Prins, "Sapphic Stanzas," 251. Prins herself succumbs to the contemporary rhythm/heard/felt versus meter/written/read dichotomy, even as she pleads for attention to be paid to the complex mutual definitions of meter and rhythm shaped by how metrical forms are defined, asking of the Sapphic stanza, "can we really hear this rhythm, even with a well-tutored ear, or is it a metrical effect that appeals to the eye?" (Prins, "Sapphic Stanzas," 255). Among other things, this highlights how difficult it is to abandon the metrical paradigms of our own cultures.

[39] Reading beyond English has the further benefit of avoiding embarrassment. Prins, in her article on hexameters, cites a distich from "Coleridge": "In the hexameter rises: the fountain's silvery column, / In the pentameter, aye: falling in melody back" (cited in Yopie Prins, "Metrical Translation: Nineteenth-Century Homers and the Hexameter Mania," in *Nation, Language, and the Ethics of Translation*, eds. Sandra Bermann and Michael Wood [Princeton: Princeton University Press, 2005], 229–56). The lines are, of course, a translation of Schiller's famous description of the elegiac distich—as Coleridge knew and Prins apparently does not: "Im Hexameter steigt des Springquells silberne Säule,/ Im Pentameter drauf fällt sie melodisch herab" (Friedrich Schiller, "Das Distichon," in *Sämtliche Werke*, Vol. 1, Munich³ (1962), 251–2.

[40] To give one example, in discussing the introduction of metrical "upbeats" or "downbeats" as musical terms inaccurately mapped onto language, Meschonnic claims that the idea "first appears, it seems, in an 1816 treatise on German metrics" (Meschonnic, "Metrics," 130). He seems unaware that, at precisely this moment, German-speaking authors were involved in a virulent debate over whether modern music could be a model for ancient Greek or modern German meters, how to take account of the relation between metrical foot and word boundaries, and effects of line endings—that is, many of the questions Meschonnic himself asks. I analyze that debate in detail in Chapter 3.

rhyme, line, strophe, or repetition show what happens when aesthetic, philosophical, and political claims remain tied to patterns of syllables in their particular
cultural, linguistic, and historical locations. Analyzing those patterns of syllables,
moreover, reveals that arguments about hexameter, folk verse, free verse, Sapphics, and so forth are also arguments about subjectivity, language, culture, and
embodiment.

One task of this book is to show in detail that what counts as which meter when
and for whom is anything but a matter of objective or neutral syllable counting;
that seeing who counts what as what meter and how reveals significant cultural,
aesthetic, and political stakes. This, of course, raises the question of how we recognize meter or metricality at all and, more practically, of how I ground the
metrical scansions of the poems I consider. Identifying a poem's metrical structures involves the combination of recognizing a known metrical pattern (if one is
present), consciously or unconsciously observing phonological norms (which are
especially definitive for multi-syllable words), and incorporating semantic interpretation (given that for German, as for English, stress both expresses and is to
some extent determined by lexical meaning).[41] Metrical description is thus never
entirely separate from performance, as David Nowell Smith argues: "scansion
becomes not a completed description of stress, but rather a series of performative
and interpretive choices; to scan a poem is not to construct a finished product,
it is a process of reading and re-reading, of listening, voicing, in order to activate
ever anew the sensorium that meter opens up."[42] These choices are not, however,
merely a matter of personal preference. In deciding whether a syllable is long,
short, or ambiguous, I refer to metrical patterns ("iambic pentameter"), the historical period ("this how the 1780s treated hexameter in German; by the 1810s
theorists were less strict"), the particular author ("oh yes, this is how Anna Luise
Karsch usually adapts Sapphic form"), or the author's or another person's audio
recording ("Barbara Köhler's readings of her Homeric poems make the hexameter
structure stand out—now I hear this is supposed to be long"). All of this information makes up what Reuven Tsur calls a reader's (in this case, my) "metrical set,"
a combination of background knowledge and cognitive structures that shape the
performance of a meter (and, I would argue, its identification).[43]

---

[41] Take, for instance, the phrase "He said he didn't take it," where emphasis on each word significantly
changes the meaning of the phrase ("*He* said he didn't take it" [but somebody else said he did]; "He *said*
he didn't take it" [but he did]; "he said *he* didn't take it" [but somebody else did] and so on). In certain
contexts, it might make sense to scan the phrase as iambic trimeter with an extra weak syllable: he
said he *did*n't take it, in which case some of the semantic emphases would work within the metrical
pattern ("he *said* he didn't take it") and some would not ("he said *he* didn't take it").

[42] David Nowell Smith, "Editor's Introduction: Scansion," *Thinking Verse* 3 (2013): 1–14, here 8.

[43] Reuven Tsur, *Poetic Rhythm: Structure and Performance: An Empirical Study in Cognitive Poetics*
(Apollo Books, 2012), 9. Tsur overemphasizes readerly cognition and competency, at the cost of ignoring the metrical traditions activated by the author. Nowell Smith describes learning to hear French
alexandrines as an adult, reflecting that as we learn and are exposed to a culture we get a "vague sense"
of what metrical rules "might be"; "this initial sense of what might be continues to govern how our ears

The interweaving of information, response, and performance underscores yet again that phonological-linguistic and metrical-historical-aesthetic judgments cannot be fully separated. As Nowell Smith points out, "each phonological claim contains a tacit aesthetic value judgment. And these value judgments then contribute to the lived history of the language, out of which arises—yes, linguistic-phonological structure."[44] Similarly, efforts to create a notation system or "score" that would more fully convey the realization of a metrical pattern or rhythm cannot evade the difficulties of interpretation—though the history of metrical theory has made numerous attempts at all-encompassing formal description, including the use of musical notation, phonological trees, and multi-level length or stress numbering systems. In the face of these limitations, I use a binary scansion notation with variations depending on whether the author presents German meter as using long and short (– ∨) or stressed and unstressed (/ x) syllables. This difference marks not an objective property of German phonology but the metrical tradition the author takes up. Moreover, because scansion and interpretation, schema and performance are intertwined, I cannot prove that my judgment that a syllable is long or short is correct, although I argue that attention to the particularities of meter in its historical details and theoretical presentations can and should guide those judgments. This explanatory power is one thing that the rejection of meter to focus exclusively on rhythm will miss.

To sum up: like philosophers interested in rhythm, I argue for the significance of patterned language, particularly meter, for arguments about aesthetics, subjectivity, politics, ethics, and language use. Henri Meschonnic does likewise, but adds a historical attention that I share. Like the exponents of historical poetics, and sometimes Meschonnic, I hold that poetic forms emerge from forms of life and that the way poets use meters expresses their cultural and political commitments and aesthetic values. Like historical poetics but *unlike* Meschonnic, I unsettle the firm distinction between meter and rhythm, which is itself an artifact of particular historical and cultural circumstances and has implications for the questions philosophers consider (about aesthetics, subjectivity, politics, ethics, and language use). Finally, however, I argue that poets themselves engage with different traditions and their implications for cultural politics more consciously and deliberately than either Meschonnic or practitioners of historical poetics allow. Rather than seeing poets as "prisoners of" the "linguistic-cultural habits" they inherit,[45] I show that poets and thinkers might be virtuosos of those very habits and the forms they

---

are trained by the poems they attend to, how they train themselves, how they are trained through discussion, through argument, reading, recitation" David Nowell Smith, "Training the Ear, or: On Learning to Hear the *Alexandrin*," *Thinking Verse* 3 (2014): 137–38.

[44] David Nowell Smith, "Verse Scored Free: Scansion, Recording, Notation," *Revue Française d'études Américaines* 153, no. 4 (2017): 45.

[45] Meschonnic, "Metrics," 144.

inform. Poets prove adept at negotiating the various stakes of different forms in different ways in their works, helping us as listeners and readers to experience poetry and language in new, rich, and surprising ways.

0.3 What Language, Which Culture, Whose Bodies?

At the same time, any reading together of culture, language, and the body faces the problem that this interrelation can lead and has led to various types of essentialism, where speaking a certain language, existing in a certain body, or living in a certain culture means that a subject exists in a certain, predetermined way. Scholars with culturally dominant identities, especially white scholars, have repeatedly used different kinds of essentialism to mark subjects that are other, especially subjects of other races, as lesser, underdeveloped, or non-autonomous. Rhythm, in particular, has a long history of activating white supremacist tropes of primitivism and savagery. In the face of this history and its continuation, I contend that analyzing meter in its particular historical context and remaining alert to the cultural and political work that metrical claims perform *disrupts* essentializing argumentative moves in several crucial ways.

First, meter negotiates between the species universal and the cultural particular: training and practice are as influential in experiencing meter in poetry as biology, or even more influential. Second, keeping in mind the politically charged nature of various metrical claims can help dismantle claims to universalism or neutrality, as analysis of the arguments made by subjects who want to position themselves as universal reveals their particular social, cultural, political, and historical locations. Finally, listening to different meters and striving to hear them opens listeners or readers to new and different poetic experiences, undercutting their tendencies to essentialism or appropriation.

In order to disrupt rather than unconsciously continue the tradition of essentialism that can emerge from thinking language, culture, and the body together, it is important to identify at least some of that tradition's exponents and inflection points. The tradition that Meschonnic extends from Humboldt, who in turn was influenced by Johann Gottfried Herder, aligns meter and rhythm with topoi of "primitive" language as particularly poetic and vivid, attributes that have fallen away in the "civilization" of the culture and its language.[46] We can trace a direct line from Herder's assertion that "every nation ... speaks according to how it thinks, and thinks according to how it speaks,"[47] to Humboldt's "belief in

---

[46] I discuss this narrative in Chapter 1; see e.g. Johann Gottfried Herder, "Versuch einer Geschichte der Lyrik," in *Werke*, ed. Wolfgang Pross, Vol. I. (Munich: Carl Hanser Verlag, 1984), 7–61.
[47] Johann Gottfried Herder, "Über die neuere deutsche Literatur. Fragmente. Zweite, völlig umgearbeitete Ausgabe," in Pross, *Werke*, 63–210, here 81.

a national mind whose character is shaped by language structure,"[48] and finally to Meschonnic's occasional succumbing to the "pull of the *idée fixe* that links facts about language to the culture of its speakers, indeed to their whole mode of thinking."[49] The risks of linking language to a specific, fixed form of life are enormous.

This danger affects not only direct links of culture, language, and body but contemporary attempts to connect rhythm and meter to any species-universal or scientific-biological body through associations with (for example) gait, heartbeat, or respiration. Virginia Jackson warns against the temptation to read rhythm as "a defining principle of verse" that "is traced back to a social, ideally communal rather than natural origin of poetry we have lost in modernity."[50] Jackson points to work by Jonathan Culler and Derek Attridge, both of whom claim that some kind of pre-cultural link between rhythm and the body is central to the existence and experience of poetry. Culler, for instance, asserts, "in its rhythmical character ... lyric is in touch with fundamental bodily rhythms: the timing of heartbeats, of breathing, of walking, of marching, of dancing."[51] Jackson is correct that such claims to naturalness shore up essentialism; she therefore calls readers to "trace the overdetermined origins of such versions of lyric rhythm" and develop a history of poetics (in her case particularly American poetics) that does not rely on naturalized-essentialized visions of culture.[52] Linguistics, like poetics, can slip into essentialism when making arguments for various language characteristics as products of mental architecture or cognitive structures, and the essentializing of language lies at a founding moment of the discipline.[53]

---

[48] John E. Joseph, *Language, Mind and Body: A Conceptual History* (Cambridge University Press, 2018), 150.

[49] John E. Joseph, "Language-Body Continuity in the Linguistics-Semiology-Poetics-Traductology of Henri Meschonnic," *Comparative Critical Studies* 15, no. 3 (October 1, 2018): 311–29, https://doi.org/10.3366/ccs.2018.0298, 317. Joseph notes this tendency particularly in Meschonnic's oppositions of "the Greeks" and "the Hebrews" in their languages and/as modes of thinking and culture (320). He asserts that we "need to ask whether and how we can avoid reading Meschonnic in an ethnic-essentialist way" (320) but seems to think that we can either "avoid" potentially essentialist thinking or "*choose* to be drawn to it with our eyes open to the risks of slipping from language to ethnic to racial essentialism, and ready with our arguments to forestall the slippage" (321).

[50] Virginia Jackson, "The Cadence of Consent: Francis Barton Gummere, Lyric Rhythm, and White Poetics," in Glaser, Culler, Fleishman, and Saussy, Critical Rhythm, 87–105, here 90. Jackson, as her title suggests, analyzes this account of rhythm in the work of American philologist and folklorist Francis Barton Gummere (1855–1919).

[51] Jonathan Culler, "Why Rhythm?," 21–39, 36.

[52] Jackson, "The Cadence of Consent," 90.

[53] On this point see John Joseph's critique that linking language with mental structure suggests "speakers of different languages do indeed have different innate mental properties" (John E. Joseph, *Language, Mind and Body: A Conceptual History* (Cambridge University Press, 2018), 1), a viewpoint that "would constitute a strange form of quasi-racism that is flatly negated by our experience of bilinguals, and of children taken from their birthplace for adoption at an early age who become monolingual speakers of the language of their adoptive family" (1–2). He analyzes the essentializing of language in linguistics in the nineteenth century: "At the start of linguistics as a 'scientific' historical inquiry with the work of Franz Bopp and Jacob Grimm, its cultural attraction and power lay in the promise it offered of rediscovering the original and true foundations of languages, cultures, and races" (222).

This important critique, however, begs the question of whether *any* recourse to bodily efficacy of meter or rhythm necessarily entails an essentialist-naturalist stance. One of the things meters—and the thinkers of meter I consider here—help us to see is that there is no pre-cultural (essential or natural) bodily experience. Haun Saussy rejects the commonsense belief that the body is pre-cultural or purely biological and describes how the body affected by patterned language is always already a body envisioned by culture and language: "What will count as a body is an effect of the representational or discursive means available to incarnate it. The body operative in our discourse is whatever we have the ability to speak, chart, compute, or perform—walk, dance, shimmy—into being."[54] Saussy references Marcel Mauss to reflect on the culturally-shaped body, and although he refers to "rhythm" his examples are meters:

> The body attentive to rhythm is, we can say without too much metaphorical exaggeration, a transformer. It takes a flow of energy (sonic pulses) and packages it into a specific form of current that is best able to travel in its particular cultural milieu. Among infantrymen, it will be a four-four measure; among hearers of ancient Greek epic, it will be dactylic hexameter; among hearers on the Scottish-English border, it will be the ballad stanza, and so forth.[55]

As Saussy points out, culture also shapes perception: the experience of hearing six pulses in two sets of three or three sets of two, in music in 6/8 or 3/4 time, is something that only someone with previous exposure to music in those time signatures can do.[56] Contra the idea that the effects of metrical patterning are purely biological or "natural," then, perception and experience occur in complex interactions with culture and physiology.

Moreover, even within a given cultural or linguistic sphere, physiology and cognitive architecture are not as universal as claims for the bodily efficacy of meter, rhythm, or poetry seem to assume. Neither heartbeats nor gait nor breath are homogenous or even regular: what meters might come from the push and slide of a wheeled mobility aid, and what prosody would speak to or with someone struggling to draw breath or with an arrhythmic heartbeat?[57] Non-neurotypicality of various kinds underscores that the neural processes that underlie claims about how poetry works in the brain are far more diverse than those claims typically

---

[54] Saussy, "Contagious Rhythm," 114.

[55] Saussy, "Contagious Rhythm," 116–7.

[56] Saussy, "Contagious Rhythm," 117.

[57] G. Gabrielle Starr links prosody and the motor centers in the brain on the basis that "metrical writing can evoke not only auditory imagery but the imagery of motion; as we time the words we 'hear,' motor centers of the brain ... are also active" Starr, *Feeling Beauty. The Neuroscience of Aesthetic Experience* (Cambridge, MA: MIT Press, 2013), 89. Rather than assume this means individuals with motor processing difficulties cannot appreciate metrical language, I invite consideration of the new poetics that different motor and other processing (dis)abilities might create.

admit. One way of addressing universalized cognitive claims about poetic language in general and meter in particular is to combine the perspectives of cognitive literary theory (which links human experience of literature to mental structures) and disability studies (which analyzes the construction, theorization, and experiences of the categories of ability and disability). In studies on autism and cognitive literary studies, Ralph Savarese collaborates with autistic authors to work toward a "dethronement of privileged neurotypicality."[58] They argue that autistics have a particular and valuable relationship to poetry—including its meters—and that poetry can serve as a bridge between neurotypical and autistic semantic and sensory processing. This challenge to cognitive universalism, crucially, does not use a deficit model, which would lament that not everyone can appreciate meter, but rather finds in non-neurotypical poetic experience a new understanding of how poetry works in the brain.

Moreover, individuals and cultures are not invariably or even normally monolingual: thinking in and about multiple languages can also disrupt essentialist notions about "natural" connections between language and culture, as all of Saussy, Pajević, and Joseph point out. Joseph argues that Émile Benveniste's conception of the "language-body nexus" is based on thinking through social positioning in relation to "other bodies and to society and its institutions,"[59] while Pajević points to Humboldt's notion of language as a *Weltansicht* to suggest that "thinking in another language relativizes any essentialist language notion."[60] Taking multilingualism alone as avoiding essentialism and the discrimination it creates strikes me as a bit too convenient—Humboldt, in particular, at best benefited from and contributed to the structures of colonialism as otherizing study of non-Europeans and at worst helped create categories that genocidal colonialism used to justify itself. But apropos *meter* in particular, attention to inter-language contact helps disrupt the idea that any particular meter is natural, given, or inherent to the language; as Saussy argues, "Contact between languages in verse form is a contact not between objects in themselves, but between the forms they take through comparison and reflexivity. The forms taken over from other languages will necessarily make the receiving language stumble, will break the inertia of its forward movement."[61] Because of its decentralized literary culture, the German-speaking tradition has been, as I show, not only particularly heterogeneous in its metrical practices but self-reflexively so, at least since the seventeenth century.

---

[58] See e.g. Ralph James Savarese, "What Some Autistics Can Teach Us about Poetry," in *The Oxford Handbook of Cognitive Literary Studies*, January 1 (2015), https://doi.org/10.1093/oxfordhb/9780199978069.013.0020. I am grateful to Natalie Gerber for calling the work of Savarese and his collaborators—especially Tito Mukhopadhyay—to my attention.

[59] Joseph, *Language, Mind and Body*, 319.

[60] Marko Pajević, "A Poetics of Society: Thinking Language with Henri Meschonnic," Comparative Critical Studies 15, no. 3 (October 1, 2018): 291–310. https://doi.org/10.3366/ccs.2018.0297, 303.

[61] Saussy, "Contagious Rhythm," 123.

Although meter has the advantage that it is harder to coopt to essentialisms precisely because its status as culturally and historically shaped is frequently more apparent than in rhythm, arguments about the universality of meter, about the particularity of meter, about its bodily efficacy, and about its disruption of categories of meaning and logic can be and have been coopted by essentialist and exclusionary positions. Claims that meter is universal can be hegemonic, as in Johan Jacob Breitinger's assertion in 1740 that metrical patterns express universal affects and consequently "the same passion would express and explain itself in an Iroquois in his rustic speech as by a Saxon"—a claim Breitinger felt entitled to make without knowledge of indigenous American languages and while European colonizers, some of them no doubt from Saxony, were murdering members of the Haudenosaunee nation.[62] Conversely, claims about linguistic particularity—that is, the features particular to German and their importance for metrical practice and the responses it invokes—can be exclusionary, as Richard Wagner's theories about Germanic alliterative verse and its implications for the soulful naturalness of the "German people" support his virulent antisemitism.[63] (The example of Wagner also demonstrates that religion, too, can be essentialized.[64]) And arguments that meter and materiality challenge not only meaning-making but subjectivity can land very differently for those whose subjectivity and modes of speech have been shut out from the discourses of high culture's poetry and academic metrical theory—for example, Friedrich Kittler's "discoveries" of the porousness and contingency of universalized (read: white male) subjectivity were hardly news to women of any race and people of color, whose subjectivity male and/or white academics frequently denied and deny.[65]

The three authors I consider most extensively in this book, not accidentally, are white men: especially because metrical theory took place (and takes place) in universities, its purviews have been as exclusionary as the institutions themselves;

---

[62] Johann Jakob Breitinger, *Fortsetzung der Critischen Dichtkunst: Worinnen die Poetische Mahlerey in Absicht auf den Ausdruck und die Farben abgehandelt wird, mit einer Vorrede von Johann Jacob Bodemer.* Faksimiledruck nach der Ausgabe von 1740 (Stuttgart: JB Metzler, 1966). (Continuation of the Critical Poetics: Wherein Poetic Painting is Treated with a View towards Expression and Color), 355.

[63] See e.g. Richard Wagner, "Oper und Drama" ("Opera and Drama"), in *Richard Wagner: Dichtungen und Schriften,* ed. Dieter Borchmeyer, Vol. 7, 10 vols (Frankfurt A.M.: Insel Verlag, 1983), 9–370. On philology and race in the 19th century in general see Tuska Benes, *In Babel's Shadow: Language, Philology, and the Nation in Nineteenth-Century Germany* (Detroit, Mich: Wayne State University Press, 2008).

[64] On religion as functioning in the essentialized-biologized ways that race does in its modern conception, see Geraldine Heng, "The Invention of Race in the European Middle Ages II: Locations of Medieval Race," *Literature Compass* 8, no. 5 (2011): 275–93, 10.1111/j.1741-4113.2011.00795.x. As Heng's title indicates, she also shows how "racial thinking, racial law, racial formation, and racialized behaviors and phenomena" were at work "in medieval Europe before the emergence of a recognizable vocabulary of race" (275).

[65] On this point, see John Durham Peters, "Introduction: Friedrich Kittler's Light Shows," in *Optical Media: Berlin Lectures 1999,* ed. Friedrich Kittler, trans. Anthony Enns (Cambridge: Polity Press, 2010), especially 7–9.

sometimes Klopstock, Nietzsche, and Grünbein are, too. I myself, as a white woman socialized in American society and trained in the American school and university systems, am equally influenced by the hierarchies and injustices of those structures. Klopstock, Nietzsche, and Grünbein show in numerous moments that one may be a virtuoso of linguistic cultural habits and at the same time shaped by white supremacy, sexism, and ableism. I analyze these moments but argue that nonetheless these three thinkers help de-essentialize the connection between language, culture, and the body through their consciously historical and particular metrical thinking and their poetry. Klopstock helps us understand that authors and readers have the power to shape a feedback loop between semantic meaning, metrical patterning, and bodily response. Nietzsche helps us understand that there can be no pre-cultural bodily experience nor any meter or rhythm "before" culture or history. Grünbein helps us understand the ways in which poetic forms and cultural positions live in the tensions of various systems of meaning making, whether philosophical or natural-scientific, and that our poetry and our bodies are shaped by that tension. Read together, they show how meter disrupts its own claims to universality and demonstrate that metrical powers and pleasures may begin unconsciously and feel natural, but may be consciously transformed, rejected, or reappropriated. All three help us refuse the idea that certain meters are natural or given, opening up different meters to new uses. In using Klopstock, Nietzsche, and Grünbein to attend to history, culture, and political work done by metrical patterns, we can block both manipulative affective responses to and appropriation of culturally situated meters.[66] Taking metrical claims seriously can call attention to and dismantle the gate-keeping of certain kinds of metrical practice as exclusively erudite or elite, placing hexameter, Sapphics, or sestinas on a continuum of practice and pleasure that includes pop songs, folk poetry, and children's literature. Doing this calls for a certain kind of openness, a willingness to take pleasure and move or be moved in a sometimes unexpected poetic experience.[67]

[66] To name an example from my own field, understanding how meters come about ought to give German 101 teachers pause before having their predominately white students write "Hip Hop Lieder" without understanding the genre's history. For a discussion of the harms of such tokenizing pedagogical approaches, see Adrienne Merritt, "A Question of Inclusion: Intercultural Competence, Systemic Racism, and the North American German Classroom," in *Diversity and Decolonization in German Studies*, eds. Regine Criser and Ervin Malakaj (Palgrave MacMillan, 2020), 177–96.

[67] Amongst the unexpected metrical delights I encountered while writing are the children's book *The Pout-Pout Fish* by Deborah Diesen (Farrar, Strauss and Girroux, 2008) and the occasional poem by the Tumblr site "Facts I Just Made Up" answering the question "Can you explain how crackers are made?," which begins: "First the cracker batter baker bakes a cracker batter batch/ then the cracker batter mixer door will open and unlatch/ so the batter mixer nozzle can descend onto the patch/ where the cracker batter spreads out for the nozzle to attach" (https://facts-i-just-made-up.tumblr.com/post/86186032503/i-spent-like-15-hours-on-this, accessed July 5, 2022).

0.4 Volume Overview

The book's six chapters are structured into three pairs. Each uses one chapter to introduce the guiding questions and challenges for metrical theory of the epoch (around 1750, around 1870, and around 1990) and shows how those debates emerge from and feed into broader questions of language, history, and subjectivity. In the second chapter of each pair, I show in detailed readings how Klopstock, Nietzsche, and Grünbein (respectively) take up and modify their epochs' metrical thought in their poetry and theory, inviting readers to experience patterns of syllables—and thus poetry and language—in new ways. Chapter 1, "Meter, Language, and the 'Whole Human,'" analyzes eighteenth-century debates on metrics in the context of Late Enlightenment aesthetics. Metrical theorists sought to understand how language plays a vital role in a subjectivity determined not only by reason but also by the emotions and the body as part of the quest for an aesthetics and anthropology of the "whole human." In Chapter 2, "Klopstock's Meters as Embodied Meaning," I show how Klopstock's unique contributions to metrical theory and practice emerge from and against this context.

In Chapter 3, "Disciplining Meter," I show how the development of new scholarly disciplines—historical and comparative linguistics, Germanic philology, and musicology—gave rise to conflicts over how meter should be measured and by whom. Chapter 4, "Nietzsche's Meters as Cultural Critique," takes up Nietzsche's poetry and his analyses of meter and rhythm in poetry and music. Nietzsche uses meter to show that embodied experience is always historically and culturally conditioned, that meter thus conditioned undermines claims to objective or "scientific" knowledge, and that historical difference cannot be overcome in artistic or cultural practice. Chapter 5, "From Meter to Media and Materiality," traces the development of attention to meter in the twentieth and twenty-first centuries as the field shifts from discussions of verse practice to accounts based on the natural sciences on one hand, and on the other to a more general thematization of meter within arguments about media and the so-called "materiality" of language and text. Finally, Chapter 6, "Grünbein's Metrical Paradoxes," takes Grünbein's own engagement with natural-scientific, metaphysical, and media-theoretical paradigms as a mode of thinking that highlights the resistance of both bodily and linguistic material to scientistic reductionism. Grünbein's varying treatments of meter in his poetry show how this resistance becomes poetically productive, articulating the location of modern subjectivity caught between metaphysics and materialism. The afterword will draw together commonalities between the three thinkers' approaches to metrics across historical differences and emphasize the ongoing importance of thinking about and experiencing metrical language.

1

Meter, Language, History, and the "Whole Human"

Between roughly 1730 and 1800, gallons of ink and reams of paper were dedicated to a long-running and occasionally vicious conflict over dactyls, trochees, and spondees—that is, over whether it is possible or desirable to produce hexameter in modern German. This chapter undertakes to show how the claims made about patterns of syllables both implicitly and explicitly draw on and support claims made about human language, culture, and subjectivity, using the hexameter debate as a central example. The hexameter debate reveals with particular clarity the extent to which metrical theory and practice rest on culturally-specific norms and ambitions; precisely for this reason, analyzing metrics and verse practice yields insights into those norms and the theories and philosophies behind them. I further contend that these insights are not merely of historical-philological value. Instead, attention to patterned syllables can reveal how human, embodied subjects take up specific types of language use in specific cultural traditions and simultaneously invite others outside their own cultural-historical embeddedness to read and be affected by that language use. Metrical theories thus perpetually probe the boundary between individual-historical particularity and anthropological-biological universals, revealing just how tenuous, porous, and contested those boundaries are.

The second half of the chapter follows the connection between metrical theory and the broader norms and theories of human language use and subjectivity that undergird it by analyzing narratives of the origin of poetry and meter. These narratives emerge from the various faculties of human subjects, in particular reason/cognition and emotion/sensation. In the eighteenth century, the so-called "Anthropologie des ganzen Menschen" (*anthropology of the whole human*) worked against the one-sided understanding of human subjectivity advanced by rationalist philosophy, which subordinated both the body and emotion to reason and created a dualist picture of subjectivity as divided between body and mind.[1] Human sensory (and eventually emotional) capacities in combination with rational capacities became the basis for what artworks do and how they do it;

---

[1] As I note below and discuss in detail in Chapter 6, recent philosophy and poetry have challenged this view of rationalist philosophy as the one-sided valorization of reason above all else; still, this was the view that the later eighteenth century strove to correct.

Metrical Claims and Poetic Experience. Hannah Vandegrift Eldridge, Oxford University Press.
© Hannah Vandegrift Eldridge (2022). DOI: 10.1093/oso/9780192859211.003.0002

conversely, the efficacy of artworks became a source of insight into human faculties and their interaction.

The eighteenth century saw the development of the disciplines of anthropology—in this broad sense meaning the investigation of the human, not in the modern sense of the study of culture or ethnology—and aesthetics— understood not as the subdiscipline of philosophy studying the fine arts but as a "science of things perceived."[2] Taken together, these disciplines help create an understanding nebst of language as a mediator between the intellectual and sensory components of human subjectivity. In turn, this theory of language leads to theories of the relation between the semantic and formal-material elements of language in poetic and philosophical or conceptual language. Metrical form, as perhaps the most striking sensory quality of an art form that uses (rational) language, becomes a central place for investigating the interplay of sensory and cognitive human capacities, and thus of human wholeness.

Seeing the connection between metrical practices and the theories of artistic achievement and human subjectivity that shaped and supported those practices lets Klopstock's unique contributions to theory and practice emerge in the next chapter as an exceptionally rigorous thinking through of the relations between meaning, meter, author, hearer, language, mind, and body. Moreover, Klopstock offers a counterweight to an ambivalence behind the ramification of metrics into these areas: as meter attains general anthropological or aesthetic importance, attention to particular poetic practice becomes increasingly unnecessary. That is, if meter is not dictated by a poetics of rules that assigns meters to genres but is, rather, the expression of universal human capacities as they develop in the history of language and/or culture, the metrical unfolding of any particular poem becomes secondary to the unfolding of those histories or capacities. In Klopstock, conversely, metrical theory emerges from and remains in constant dialogue with his poetic innovations; his poetic practice drives his metrical theory, which in turn never loses poetic or material particularity from view, even as it advances cultural, physiological, and anthropological claims.

1.1 Context: Metrical Theory and Practice in the Long Eighteenth Century

In the years between 1730 and 1805, German verse theory and practice were undergoing their greatest upheavals since the work of Martin Opitz more than

---

[2] Alexander Baumgarten, *Meditationes philosophicae de nonnullis ad poema pertinentibus*, trans. Karl Aschenbrenner and William B. Holther (Berkeley: University of California Press, 1954), 7. I have also consulted the German translation by Albert Riemann in *Die Aesthetik Alexander Gottlieb Baumgartens unter besonderer Berücksichtigung der* Meditationes Philosophicae de nonnullis ad poema pertinentibus *nebst einer Uebersetzung dieser Schrift* (Halle: Max Niemeyer Verlag, 1928). The German is "eine Wissenschaft vom sensitiven Erkennen" (Baumgarten/Riemann, 145).

a century earlier. Influenced by metrical forms from France and the Netherlands, Opitz's *Buch von der deutschen Poeterey* (1624) prescribed several metrical rules whose effectiveness derived no less from their simplicity than their accommodation of the phonological features of German.[3] Among other rules, Opitz insists on what came to be known as "alternating verse," defined by accent or stress (not length or duration).[4] This means, first, that only two-syllable patterns are permitted; Opitz rejects three-syllable feet, even when they are the only meters in the poem (a poem of entirely dactyls, for example, would transgress his norms). Moreover, alternating verse excludes so-called polymetrism: forms that use different types of feet (such as the Sapphic ode, which combines trochees and dactyls and varies them with free syllables). For Opitz, poetry must use only one foot type. Finally, he demands complete agreement between verse accent and word accent, whereas earlier Medieval and Baroque poets had considered the occasional placement of an unstressed syllable in a stressed position an aesthetic strength, emphasizing the poetic (that is, divergent from normal speech) character of a work.

Taken together, these rules governed German-language verse through the Baroque period and into the early modern, until the eighteenth century brought the beginnings of a reorientation.[5] While the majority of poetry in German between 1600 and 1750 is written in alexandrines or vers commun (a ten-syllable verse line ending on a stressed syllable and a caesura after the fourth or sixth syllables), in the middle third of the eighteenth century poets began to investigate antique meters, folk styles, and romance forms such as the sonnet or terza rima.[6] Klopstock's break from this tradition is prepared by the loosening of Opitz' rules in the theorists I analyze here, as well as by poets and poet-theorists such as Barthold Heinrich Brockes (1680–1747), Luise Adelgunde Victorie Gottsched (1713–62) Christian Fürchtegott Gellert (1715–69), Anna Luise Karsch (1722–91), and Christoph Martin Wieland (1733–1813).

Metrical theorizing, as the hexameter debate shows in detail, was both driven by and contributed to the expansion of verse forms used in German. Thus Klopstock's experimentation with free verse forms and adaptions or inventions based on Greek and Latin forms comes into being in the context of debates over the appropriate models for German poetry and what forms are natural to the German language. His free verse experimentation, in turn, influences both the early Goethe and Friedrich Hölderlin, who draws on Klopstock as well as the study of

---

[3] See e.g. Erwin Arndt, *Deutsche Verslehre* (Berlin: Volk und Wissen Verlag, 1996), 161–2 and Dieter Breuer, *Deutsche Metrik und Versgeschichte* (Munich: Wilhelm Fink Verlag, 2008), 168–72.

[4] Remigius Bunia argues that Opitz's most important contribution was noting the ambiguous stress of single-syllable words in German, which enabled him to prescribe strict alternation via the flexibility of reading monosyllabic words as either stressed or unstressed depending on context and position. Remigius Bunia, *Metrik und Kulturpolitik. Opitz, Klopstock, Bürger* (Berlin: Rippenger und Kremers Verlag, 2014), 87.

[5] "Beginnende Neuorientierung." Breuer, *Deutsche Metrik und Versgeschichte*, 185.

[6] Arndt, *Deutsche Verslehre*, 162, 207, 210.

Pindar (another strand in late-eighteenth-century poetry).[7] Hölderlin (who does not theorize about verse in any detail) also writes in elegiac distiches and multiple ode forms, a trait he shares with both Goethe and Schiller at the height of Weimar classicism. Partly as a reaction against Weimar Classicism's insistence on ancient forms, romantics such as Novalis (Friedrich von Hardenberg), Ludwig Tieck, Friedrich Schlegel, and Clemens Brentano turn to romance forms, folk forms, and German Medieval verse. And finally, in the last phase of his life, Goethe combines virtually all of these verse practices in the *summa metrica* of *Faust II*, in which his use of different meters fills in characterization, hints at connections across the work, and even ironizes speakers.[8] Goethe's metrical multiplicity becomes widespread in the nineteenth century (as I discuss in Chapter 3), with poets such as August von Platen (1796–1835), Friedrich Rückert (1788–1866), Annette von Droste-Hülshoff (1797–1848), Eduard Mörike (1804–75), and Conrad Ferdinand Meyer (1825–98) writing in any of sonnets, ghazals, distiches, odes, and other forms without much (or any) discussion of metrical theory.

This shift from a small range of acceptable meters and forms to a pluralistic metrical landscape occurs in tandem with two other transitions in metrical and poetic theory. First, theories of poetry developed from *Regelpoetik* (poetics of rules), in which content regulated form to create numerous micro-genres, to a poetics based on the division of literary works into the lyric, epic, and dramatic as three overarching genres, with wide formal variation within each.[9] Whereas the poetics of rules appealed to predetermined and ostensibly ancient norms for the deployment of a given metrical form, the poetics of genre often appealed to particular accounts of human cognitive and sensory faculties or development (as I discuss in the second half of this chapter). Meter, therefore, likewise shifts from being assigned by the content (an ode form for an ode; distiches for an elegy; iambs for satirical drama …) to being based on accounts of poetic features as activating emotion, bodily responses, images, and associations, as well as conceptual content.

The second transition in metrical theorizing emerges in response to the first: as metrical form and content cease to condition one another, the relation between

---

[7] On Hölderlin's interest in Pindar see (most recently) Elisa Ronzheimer, "'Wie wenn am Feiertage …'. Hölderlins Projekt eines individuellen Metrums," in *Poetologien des Rhythmus um 1800. Metrum und Versform bei Klopstock, Hölderlin, Novalis, Tieck und Goethe* (Berlin/Boston: de Gruyter, 2020), 53–77, especially 71–6. On Pindar's influence in the German poetic tradition, see John T. Hamilton, *Soliciting Darkness: Pindar, Obscurity, and the Classical Tradition*, Harvard Studies in Comparative Literature 47 (Cambridge, MA: Harvard University Press, 2004).

[8] Breuer uses the term *summa metrica* to describe *Faust II* and to describe the nineteenth century's pluralistic approach to meter and metrics (Breuer, *Deutsche Metrik und Versgeschichte*, 220–1). For a detailed account of the way Goethe's metrical practice is integral to the poetics of *Faust*, see Elisa Ronzheimer, "'Sceptische Beweglichkeit'. Metren in Goethes *Faust II*," in *Poetologien des Rhythmus um 1800*, 146–70.

[9] These rules of *Regelpoetik* derived from French adaptations of Greek and especially Latin norms. See Breuer, *Deutsche Metrik und Versgeschichte*, 185–6.

meter and meaning becomes a question. Faced with this question (and the struggle to decide what phonological elements of German were best suited to make meters with), eighteenth-century poets and poetic theorists developed the idea that semantic as well as so-called "mechanical" factors determine the way syllables can be organized and perceived in metrical patterns.[10] Whereas most thinkers (including Klopstock) aim for some combination of "mechanical" factors such as duration, volume, and/or pitch, Karl Philipp Moritz insisted that meter was defined solely in relation to the context in which the syllables appeared.[11] Significantly, he also notes the ways emphasis may vary depending on the speaker and context for performance, opening the question of potential conflict between speech accent and word accent, systematic versus realized language, and written versus performed poetry. Meter thus shifted from determining content to being determined by meaning in the course of the eighteenth century.

1.2 The Hexameter Debate, 1730–1800

This explosion of metrical practice and theory forms the context in which the hexameter debate emerged. That debate engages with all of the questions outlined above: genre norms, the relation of poetry to embodied human thinking and feeling, the way meters are made (and what they are made of), and their relation to meaning as conceived by the poet and performed or perceived by the speaker or hearer. I outline these debates in detail because they illuminate the broader questions in which technical features of prosody, phonology, scansion, and metrical counting become entangled: poetic quality, linguistic and cultural difference, national prestige, and authorial individuality.

Translation History and Examples

Within the metrical and poetic upheavals of the eighteenth century, the hexameter debate in particular emerged from disagreements over both theoretical premises and practical approaches to the translation of texts from Greek and Latin antiquity into German. It is difficult to overstate the extent to which translation, especially

---

[10] For a detailed account, see Joh. Nikolaus Schneider, *Ins Ohr geschrieben: Lyrik als akustische Kunst zwischen 1750 und 1800* (Göttingen: Wallstein Verlag, 2004), in particular section 2.2.2, "Metriktheorien zwischen 1750 und 1800 im Widerspruch."

[11] See Schneider, *Ins Ohr geschrieben*, 65. As Schneider points out, this is considerably easier for multisyllabic words than for monosyllabic ones; Moritz attempts to create a system for monosyllables depending on grammar (that is, what type of word the monosyllable is). Nouns and verbs receive the most emphasis, then pronouns, then prefixes if any, and finally grammatical endings denoting case and gender. See also Christian Wagenknecht, *Deutsche Metrik. Eine historische Einführung*, 5th edition, (Munich: C.H. Beck, 2007), 37.

metrical translation, was bound up in national and linguistic self-understanding.[12] Translation activity reached a peak in the last decades of the eighteenth century;[13] in the years leading up to this high point, the understanding of the task of the translator changed in accordance with altered conceptions of history, linguistic specificity, and metrical possibilities (a shift eventually theorized in Schleiermacher's distinction between foreignizing and domesticating translations).[14] During the early part of the century, translation practice was shaped by a loosely rationalist theory of language, according to which *all* language is the translation of thought into signs; translation from language to language was simply the substitution of one set of signs for an equivalent but different set.[15] The focus is thus on ease of comprehensibility in the target language.[16] Subsequently, translators adopted the idea of "compell[ing] German readers to experience the same impact which the poem had on its original readers."[17] This principle implicitly allows some deviation from the standard form of the target language and places original and target languages on a more equal footing. Some forty years later, that emphasis shifted almost fully to the original language, with translators demanding strict fidelity in matters of form, meter, and rhythm; since language was by now understood as the expression of a particular historical moment in the development of a people, nation, or culture, a translation should also express the difference of that culture from modern German.[18]

Hand in hand with the shift from natural-sounding reproduction of semantic meaning in the target language to fidelity to semantic and formal elements of the original language, there occurred a move toward ever more rigorous imitation and theorization of meter, in particular the meters of Greek and Latin, and especially hexameter. Hexameter was the meter of epic, particularly Homer and

---

[12] Manfred Fuhrmann, "Von Wieland bis Voss: Wie verdeutscht man antike Autoren?" *Jahrbuch des deutschen Hochstifts* 1987, 1–22, here 1.

[13] Fuhrmann, "Von Wieland bis Voss," 2.

[14] See Josefine Kitzbichler, Katja Lubitz, and Nina Mindt, *Theorie der Übersetzung antiker Literatur in Deutschland seit 1800* (Transformationen der Antike 9. Berlin: de Gruyter, 2009), 60–1.

[15] Manfred Fuhrmann makes this point apropos Wieland but draws on the general axioms of equivalence between languages in the early German Enlightenment. Fuhrmann, "Von Wieland bis Voss," 4.

[16] See for example Johann Christoph Gottsched's notes to his Horace translation that introduces his *Versuch einer Critischen Dichtkunst* (first edition 1730). Johann Christoph Gottsched, *Versuch einer Critischen Dichtkunst. Vierte, sehr vermehrte Auflage* (Darmstadt: Wissenschaftliche Buchgesellschaft, 1977; facsimile of fourth edition, Leipzig 1751), 6. Each edition includes the paratexts of the previous editions, and so I quote from the fourth edition even when discussing prefaces to the first, second, or third. All translations are mine.

[17] Jane Veronica Curran, *Horace's Epistles, Wieland, and the Reader: A Three-Way Relationship* (London: W.S. Maney and Son Ltd., 1999), 16.

[18] See Fuhrmann, "Von Wieland bis Voss," 9. The idea that nations or cultures progress along stages of development which are then necessarily expressed in their language implies at least a step toward the kind of essentialism I analyzed in my introduction. The incredible variation of metrical practices undermines the essential inevitability of the connection between language and nation or culture even as metricians appealed to essentialism to validate their theories. The most striking example of the shift in translation practice is the theory of Wilhelm von Humboldt.

Virgil, and the German attempt to write in hexameter was thus central to the question of whether modern literature could approach the greatness of its ancient predecessors and of what modern German literature should become.[19] It would be simplistic to assert a one-way relation of influence from translation practice to metrical innovation; indeed, it seems likely that an expanded sense of what was metrically possible in German (spurred on in no small part by Klopstock) supported calls for metrical rigor in translation, even as translation inspired the search for German equivalents of ancient meters.

The calculation of hexameters was a vexed issue because of the differing prosodic-phonological features of German, Greek, and Latin. The hexameter debate itself makes clear that there can be no objective, universal determination or definition along the lines of "hexameter is ..." What counts as hexameter for whom and for what reasons is culturally and historically determined. Nonetheless, it is possible to describe what both eighteenth-century German and modern metrical theory recognize as the characteristics of what counted as hexameter in Ancient Greek and Classical Latin. Both languages involve exact measurement of syllable *length*, and the organization of long and short syllables in given patterns creates metrical units referred to as feet, which are then combined to form lines.[20] Classical hexameter was defined, at the simplest level, as consisting of six feet, mostly dactyls (one long syllable followed by two short, – ∨ ∨), in which most but not all positions may have a spondee (two long syllables, – –) substituted for the dactyl:

$$| - \vee \vee | - \vee \vee | - \vee \vee | - \vee \vee | - \vee \vee | - \vee \vee |$$
$$\ \ \ 1 \qquad\ 2 \qquad\ 3 \qquad\ 4 \qquad\ 5 \qquad\ 6$$

There is thus no fixed number of syllables per line; rather, the length of time required to speak each line is equivalent, according to the principle that one long syllable is equal to two short syllables. German (like English) does not regulate syllable length as precisely; instead, most metrical patterning works by arranging equal numbers of more and less emphasized or accented syllables, with accent defined predominantly by volume and pitch (although length, mostly determined by vowel type, can also be a component in indicating emphasis).[21] Any attempt

---

[19] Fuhrmann, "Von Wieland bis Voss," 1.

[20] There are additional complex rules for the placement of a caesura or break in the line that must neither divide it into two equal halves nor let itself be confused with the line ending.

[21] Since German and Greek meters organize different phonological units, I use different notations for scansion in each. When discussing Greek meters, or efforts in German to create length-based scansion, I use – for a long syllable and ∨ for a short syllable. When discussing German meters, including hexameter that adapts Greek long syllables to German stressed syllables, I use / for a stressed syllable and x for an unstressed syllable. For a discussion of English use of hexameters, which began earlier than the German debate but was less widespread, only to be reintroduced by way of the German tradition and specifically Coleridge's reading of Klopstock, see Jeff Strabone, *Poetry and British Nationalisms in the Bardic Eighteenth Century: Imagined Antiquities* (Basingstoke, UK: Palgrave MacMillan, 2018), especially 19–23 and 272–4.

to create hexameter in German had to determine a functional equivalent to the differentiation between short and long syllables.[22]

Responses to the problem of differences in prosodic-phonological features between Greek, Latin, and German fell broadly into three groups: those which used German accented syllables as long syllables, unaccented as short; those which attempted to systematize syllable duration or quantity in German; and those who rejected hexameter entirely.[23] I refer to these groups as "latitudinarians," "rigorists," and anti-hexametrists, respectively.[24] In effect, then, the hexameter debate was a debate over which prosodic-phonological units were relevant to formal-metrical patterning in German, and in particular whether elements other than stress can be described systematically enough to serve as the basis of metrical patterns.[25] Parallel to the calls for increasingly rigorous adherence to original meters in translation, the general trend in the mid-to-late eighteenth century was toward considering ever greater numbers of factors in German prosody with ever increasing detail. Whereas translations of ancient texts from the 1750s and before were typically in alexandrines (a verse type adapted from Romance languages) or even prose, those from the 1770s and 1780s moved from iambs to increasingly carefully calculated hexameters, culminating in the six-level length-based scansion system advanced by Johann Heinrich Voß in his *Zeitmessung der deutschen Sprache* (Time-Measurement of the German Language, 1802). Following (and partially in response to) Voß, there occurred a backlash against metrical exactness (or pedantry) and the adoption of more intuitive but less precise practices of versification.[26]

---

[22] While some authors carefully distinguish between Latin, Greek, and German prosody, they continue to use "long" and "short" to differentiate between what are in fact accented and unaccented syllables, while others claim that German has length-based meters and no pitch accents, etc. The conceptual blurring between "long" and "accented" had already begun in post-classical Latin: because originally an "accented" syllable was a "long," "long" was, conversely, used to mean "accented" in medieval Latin, which moved toward accentual scansion. Leif Ludwig Albertsen, *Neuere deutsche Metrik* (Bern: Peter Lang, 1984), 98.

[23] See Clémence Couturier-Heinrich, "Autorität und Konkurrenz. Zur Reaktion von Goethe und Schiller auf Vossens Hexameterlehre und –praxis," (in *Voß' Übersetzungssprache. Voraussetzungen, Kontexte, Folgen*, eds. Anne Baillot, Erica Fantino, and Josefine Kitzbichler [Berlin: De Gruyter, 2015)] 7–92) for a description of those groups, including their main practitioners.

[24] I borrow the terminology of "Latudinarier" and "Rigoristen" from Couturier-Heinrich (Couturier-Heinrich, "Autorität und Konkurrenz," 72).

[25] For a discussion of this problem as guiding the main theories of German meter, see Bunia, *Metrik und Kulturpolitik*, 12.

[26] Fuhrmann, "Von Wieland bis Voss," 15. Fuhrmann's chronology makes clear the extent to which Klopstock was ahead of contemporaneous metrical theorization: the first volume of Klopstock's *Messias* appeared in 1748, while the metrically demanding final cantos appeared in 1773. Fuhrmann explains that many of the developments occurred in the friendly competition between members of the Göttinger Hainbund: Gottfried August Bürger, Friedrich Leopold Stolberg, and Johann Heinrich Voß, all of whom were influenced by Klopstock (16). See also Erika Fantino's account of Voß's role in the paradigm shift from prose and alexandrines to appropriations of ancient metrics. (Erica Fantino, "Johann Heinrich Voß als junger Dichter und Übersetzer antiker Lyrik. Zur Entfaltung seiner rigoristischen Methode," in Baillot, Fantino, and Kitzbichler, *Voß' Übersetzungssprache*, 1–32, 12.) The ambivalence with which the Weimar Classicists responded to Voß is symptomatic of ambivalence

The hexameter debate was thus more or less unofficially decided in favor of hexameters, but only as defined by the latitudinarians, who viewed German meter as constructed using accentuation alone.[27] But the period leading up to this practical consensus is an ideal place to examine the poetic and philosophical principles that underlie metrical theorizing, particularly because the debate was not a sequential development from one position to the next. Instead, conflicting practices and theories exist side by side in a discourse that continued across several decades and in which all of rigorist hexameter, latitudinarian hexameter, and non-polymetrical verse were live options that created an exceptional plurality and polyphony of German verse forms.

To modern readers/hearers (and possibly to our eighteenth-century counterparts), the differences can be quite fine, sometimes even indistinguishable, as the following examples of translations of the first few lines of the *Iliad* illustrate. For comparison, here are two eighteenth-century English translations. First, James MacPherson's prose version:

> The wrath of the son of Peleus,—O goddess of song, unfold! The deadly wrath of Achilles: To Greece the source of many woes! Which peopled the regions of death,—with shades of heroes untimely slain ...[28]

Next, an iambic translation by William Cowper:

> Achilles sing, O Goddess! Peleus' son;
> [x / |x / | x / |x /| x /]
> His wrath pernicious, who ten thousand woes
> Caused to Achaia's host, sent many a soul
> Illustrious into Ades premature ...[29]

In German, Johann Heinrich Voß's rigorist translation from 1793 uses atypical translations of Greek names in an effort to make certain syllables long, in particular Πηληϊάδεω (Pēlēïádēs, the son of Peleus):[30]

---

toward metrical rigor more generally: Goethe and Schiller admired but were also critical of Voß's systematicity. Both asked him to correct hexameter works early in their careers—avoiding mistakes in meter was a matter of authorial dignity—while later condemning him for a pedantry that stifled poetic creativity. See Couturier-Heinrich, "Autorität und Konkurrenz," 73. She adds that the relation between Goethe, Schiller, and Voss indicates that, for a brief time, metrical correctness was a marketing tool (91).

[27] For example, Friedrich Hölderlin (1770–1843), one of the great German poets in antique meters, simply adopts without theorization the principle that a Greek long syllable is a German accented syllable.

[28] James MacPherson, *The Iliad of Homer. Translated by James Macpherson, Esq; in two volumes* (London, 1773), 1.

[29] *The Iliad and Odyssey of Homer, translated into English blank verse, by W. Cowper, of the Inner Temple, Esq.* (Dublin, 1791), 3.

[30] Voß published fragments of a hexameter translation of the *Odyssey* in 1777 and 1778 and a full translation in 1781. See Josefine Kitzbichler, "Übersetzungstheoretischer Paradigmenwechsel um

Singe den|Zorn, o |Göttin, des | Peleia|den A|chilleus,
[– ∨ ∨ | –   – | –   ∨ ∨ | – ∨∨ | – – | – ∨∨]
Ihn, der entbrannt den Achaiern unnennbaren Jammer erregte
Und viel tapfere Seelen der Heldensöhne zum Aïs
Sendete ...[31]

Johann Jacob Bodmer's latitudinarian translation (begun in the 1750s and published in 1778) uses the more traditional "Peliden," adheres closely to standard
German word order, and drops some of the adjectives to condense Voß's and
Homer's three lines spilling onto a fourth into two. He also uses the widespread
German adaptation that allows the occasional use of a trochee (/ x) instead of a
spondee (/ /), here in the final foot of the line, an adaptation necessary because
it is very difficult for a multi-syllable word in German to have two equally strong
stresses:

Sing, o | Göttinn den | Zorn des Pe|liden, der | Unheil und | Jammer
/   /| /   x   x| /   x   x|/ x   x| / x   x | /   x
Ueber die Griechen gebracht, die Helden zu Pluto gesendet ...[32]

Gottfried August Bürger (who published fragments of his translation in 1771 and
more in 1776) rejects hexameters entirely, choosing instead the iambic meter
endorsed by the German language's first great poetic theorist, Martin Opitz, and
used in Milton's enormously influential *Paradise Lost*:

Sing, Göttin, den unsel'gen Groll Achills,
/   /| x / |x/ | x   / | x /
Des Sohnes Peleus, welcher tausend Weh
Auf die Achäher lud, in's Todtenreich,
So viele Starken tapfre Seelen trieb ...[33]

The irregularity of the first line helps avoid the monotony complained of by anti-
iamb polemicists;[34] the frequent dropped syllables ("unsel'gen" for "unseligen,"

1800," in Kitzbichler, Lubitz, and Mindt, *Theorie der Übersetzung antiker Literatur in Deutschland seit 1800*, 15–28, 21.

[31] Johann Heinrich Voß (trans.), *Homers Werke (Ilias und Odyssee). Übersetzt von Johann Heinrich Voss; mit 25 Radirungen nach Zeichnungen von Bonaventura Genelli* (Stuttgart: J.G. Cotta, 1876).

[32] *Homers Werke. Aus dem Griechischen. Übersetzt von dem Dichter der Noachide* (Johann Jakob Bodmer). Zürich: Orell, Gessner, Füesslin und Compagnie, 1778.

[33] *Sämmtliche Werke*, Vol. II. Göttingen: Verlag der Dieterichschen Buchhandlung, 1844.

[34] It also echoes the stressed first syllable in the immediate command to the muse in *Paradise Lost*, although Milton establishes the iambic meter in the preceding five lines: "Of Mans First Disobedience, and the fruit/ Of that forbidden tree, whose mortal taste/ Brought death into the world, and all our

"in's" for "in das," "tapfre" for "tapfere") both maintain the meter and perhaps suggest oral presentation in written notation. These three translations were in progress concurrently, albeit with varying starting and finishing points; the arguments made to justify each belie their apparent similarities and indicate the degree to which metrical practice and theory were irrevocably tied up in cultural, aesthetic, and anthropological commitments.

Rigorists

In keeping with the complicated chronology I have described, both the earliest and the latest theorists in the debate outlined here were rigorists: Johann Christian Gottsched in his *Versuch einer critischen Dichtkunst* (Attempt at a Critical Poetics, 1730) and Johann Heinrich Voß in his *Zeitmessung der deutschen Sprache* (Time-Measurement of the German Language, 1802). Gottsched insists that German hexameters, based on length not accent, are possible and can expand the resources of German verse.[35] In particular, he argues that German possesses genuine spondees, enabling a hexameter that follows classical models in mixing dactyls and spondees.[36] Although in 1730 Gottsched laments that connoisseurs of unrhymed verse in Virgil or Horace fail to appreciate in German the euphony that they admire in ancient authors, in the 1751 edition he qualifies that the intervening years of hexameter attempts have been so disappointing that he almost regrets having hoped for them.[37] He accuses German authors of failing to read Latin with the correct length-based scansion: "and so it happens, that one reads the most beautiful hexameter of *Virgil* or *Claudius* like a lame and limping prose, and never gets the enchanting euphony in the ear that a properly pronounced verse ought actually to have."[38] Gottsched thus coopts the traditional literalization of the metaphor of poetic "feet" to characterize bad reading as "lame" and sees a deprivation of the ears as a result. (In doing so, he establishes an able-bodied gait as normative and uses mobility differences as a metaphor for poetic deficits.) Moreover,

---

woe,/ With loss of Eden, till one greater Man/ Restore us, and regain the blissful seat, / *Sing Heav'nly Muse*" (my emphasis)." (John Milton, *Paradise Lost* [London, 1795], 4).
[35] Gottsched, *Critische Dichtkunst*, 385.
[36] Gottsched, *Critische Dichtkunst*, 396.
[37] Gottsched, *Critische Dichtkunst*, 397–98.
[38] Gottsched, *Critische Dichtkunst*, 398. He describes his own learning to scan Latin hexameter by singing in a subsequent essay. Because music intuitively incorporates note duration, holding the "long" syllables for double the length of the "short," rather than landing on them loudly or at a higher pitch (as in accent-based scansion) was easier. Gottsched, "Gutachten, von der heroischen Versart unsrer neuen biblischen Epopeen" (Assessment of the Heroic Meter of our New Biblical Epics), in Hans-Heinrich Hellmuth and Joachim Schröder, eds. *Die Lehre von der Nachahmung der antiken Versmaße im Deutschen. In Quellenschriften des 18. und 19. Jahrhunderts. Mit kommentierter Bibliographie* (Munich: Wilhelm Fink Verlag, 1976, 15–24, 16).

he complains that the mania for ancient meters has led to the use of hexameter in inappropriate genres or contexts, such as love poems, or in elegies without intervening lines of pentameter.[39] In sum, then, Gottsched wants imitation of ancient meters to expand the horizons of German poetry, but when the poetry written in those meters transgresses the norms he establishes elsewhere in the *Critical Poetics*, he uses accusations of inadequate metrical rigor to discredit it.[40]

Johann Heinrich Voß likewise argues in favor of hexameter from a rigorist standpoint that denies any significant differences between the possibilities of the meter for Greek, Latin, and German. In the introduction to his translation of Virgil's *Georgics* (published in 1789), Voß defines German hexameter as a series of four-beat *Takte* (measures or bars) consisting of dactyls and spondees.[41] As the term "Takt" indicates, he sees metrical feet as analogous to musical measures and uses musical notes to represent syllables.[42] Voß is not the first theorist to use musical notation,[43] but his doing so indicates the detail with which he attempted to systematize temporal duration for use in German prosody. Voß' agenda has cultural-pedagogical undertones: by the 1780s, Homer was established as the ideal of literary production, and emulating him in German opened the possibility of broadening his efficacy and example even to those who did not speak or read Ancient Greek.[44] Voß also attempts to direct pronunciation using orthography (for example in his spelling of "Peleiaden" in the *Iliad* translation cited above). This innovation was much mocked by more latitudinarian theorists, especially Georg Christoph Lichtenberg in his 1781 essay "On the Pronunciation of the Sheep of Ancient Greece, Compared with the Pronunciation of their

[39] Gottsched "Gutachten von der heroischen Versart ..." 17

[40] Erica Fantino points out the divergence from Gottschedian norms apropos Voß in particular, but the work of Bodmer, Breitinger, and Klopstock already transgressed these norms, which included the rejection of inspiration over technique, and an insistence on the proximity of logical/rational thought to syntax, including poetic syntax, and consequently a polemic against inversions in word order. (Fantino, "Johann Heinrich Voß als junger Dichter und Übersetzer antiker Lyrik," 1–2).

[41] Johann Heinrich Voß, "Aus der Vorrede zur *Georgica* Übersetzung" (From the Preface to the *Georgics* Translation, in Hellmuth and Schröder, *Die Lehre von der Nachahmung der antiken Versmaße im Deutschen*, 242–49), 242.

[42] Specifically, Voß argued for an understanding of each hexameter foot as a measure of 2/4 time, in which a spondee is two quarter notes, a dactyl is a quarter note followed by two eighth notes, and a trochee is a dotted quarter note followed by an eighth note (Voß, "Aus der Vorrede zur *Georgica* Übersetzung," 242–3).

[43] Ten years earlier, Joshua Steele's *Prosodia rationalis* had offered a depiction of the verse structure of *Paradise Lost* using musical notation. The emergence of this strategy had to do with changing notations for and theories of musical measure and rhythm in the eighteenth century, the beginning trend of studying musical and speech or poetic rhythm together, and the emergence of *Taktmetrik* (bar metrics) toward the end of the century. See Joh. Niklaus Schneider's illuminating overview of acoustics in the eighteenth century for a treatment of the interaction between musical measure and poetic meter (Schneider, *Ins Ohr geschrieben: Lyrik als akustische Kunst zwischen 1750 und 1800* [Wallstein Verlag, 2004], section 2.2.2.3, "Theorien des musikalischen Taktes und ihr Einfluß auf die Verslehre" [Theories of Musical Measure and their Influence on Metrics]).

[44] Fantino, "Johann Heinrich Voß ...," 2.

Modern Brothers on the Elbe; or on Beh, Beh, or Bäh ..."[45] Here, again, metrical debates become intertwined with cultural politics, as the debate over spelling that could help with proper scansion overlaps with more general discussions of orthography, pronunciation, and the standardization of language.[46] Voß mobilizes orthography to support meter in a cultural agenda that sought to prove the fitness of German for the highest literary achievement by making it closer to Ancient Greek.

Latitudinarians

Latitudinarian theorists tend to emphasize the differences between Greek and German, arguing that German hexameter can never achieve the standards of its predecessors, but that it remains nonetheless a valuable poetic resource. Friedrich Nicolai, for example, remarks in a 1781 review of Friedrich Wilhelm Zachariae's hexameter translation of *Paradise Lost* that it would be foolish to deny the possibility of German hexameter given Klopstock's success in the meter, but claims that even the best hexameters in German are only an approximation of Ancient verse.[47] Comparing Greek, Latin, and German, Nicolai adds that while the first two calculated their metrical feet based on precise measurements of clearly defined syllable lengths, Germans must rely on their variable pronunciation.[48] In consequence, imitation cannot be grounded by metrical rules but only by approximate auditory cues. In a different review, Nicolai makes clear that more careful prosodies of German and additional rules cannot compensate for the lack of the harmony that classical languages possess: "Our hexameter will never attain the euphony of those in Greek and Latin. The inflexible nature of our language and the lack of spondees will not permit it."[49] His assertion illuminates the extent to which criticism of meter and judgment of poetic quality become intertwined: whereas rigorists criticize poets for failing to create length-based hexameters, Nicolai suggests that poetic genius can compensate for the differences in ancient and modern metrical possibilities—up to a point.

[45] "Über die Pronunciation der Schöpse des alten Griechenlands, verglichen mit der Pronunciation ihrer neuern Brüder an der Elbe; oder über Beh, Beh, oder Bäh ..." For more detail on this conflict, see Armin Schäfer, "Wieland liest die Briefe des Horaz," in *Wieland Übersetzen: Sprachen, Gattungen, Räume,* eds. Bettine Menke and Wolfgang Struck (Berlin: De Gruyter, 2010), 83–103.
[46] Klopstock produced his own efforts at spelling reform in "Über die deutsche Rechtschreibung. Eine Beilage zum zweiten Theile der Campischen Erziehungsschriften" ("On German Spelling. An Appendix to the Second Part of Campe's Pedagogical Writings") (1778).
[47] Friedrich Nicolai, "Rezension zu F.W. Zachariae, Das Verlohrne Paradies" (1761, "Review of F.W. Zachariae's *Paradise Lost*"), in Hellmuth and Schröder, *Die Lehre von der Nachahmung der antiken Versmaße im Deutschen,* 61–9, 62.
[48] Nicolai, "Rezension zu F.W. Zachariae ...," 62
[49] Friedrich Nicolai, "Zu einer Young-Übersetzung eines Ungenannten" ("On an Anonymous Translation of [Edward] Young"), in Hellmuth and Schröder, *Die Lehre von der Nachahmung der antiken Versmaße im Deutschen,* 70–9, 70.

The conditions, limits, and possibilities of attaining classical euphony appear in almost comical detail in Carl Wilhelm Ramler's 1756 introduction to his translation of Batteux's *Les Beaux-Arts réduits à un même principe* (1746, The Fine Arts Reduced to a Single Principle). Ramler describes the differences between German and Greek phonology, taking the latitudinarian view that emphasis must replace duration in German meters, before proceeding to describe his system with such precision as to out-rigor the rigorists. He argued that *if* German authors 1) observe the difference between high and low pitch accents, 2) make their scansion entirely unambiguous, 3) avoid too great a similarity between the ending of each verse or between the end of a verse and its internal caesura, 4) place the words so that the interaction of their sounds creates a pleasing variety, 5) refrain from linking vocalized and silent letters to create the "little howl" (*kleines Geheul*) of a *hiatus* (long vowels at the end of one word and the start of another) and the crashing together of four or more consonants to displease the ear and strain the tongue, 6) place a single-syllable caesura in the middle of the line unless a higher euphony can be achieved through not doing so, and 7) achieve said euphony through variation and onomatopoeia, German poets will have done the best they can: "Then we can make German hexameter as euphonious as the difference between languages allows."[50] Given the difficulty of attaining these conditions, it is not surprising that many theorists concluded that German could only produce only a kind of inexact hexameter or abandoned the prospect entirely based on prosodic differences. Nonetheless, latitudinarian theorists maintained that the variability and innovation polymetrism in general and hexameter in particular bring to German verse are worth the struggle of reconciling German and ancient prosody to avoid what they frequently criticized as an unbearable tick-tock of iambic verse.

Other latitudinarians take a more critical view of metrical *theorizing*, either reserving it for scholars or rejecting it entirely as irrelevant. Johann Jacob Bodmer, for example, remarks in 1749 that "professional scholars," hung up on pedantic debates, "will be the last to recognize the perfection of German hexameter."[51] Most readers, per Bodmer, ought simply to read hexameter like rhetorical prose.[52] This mode of reading works, he claims, precisely because of the success of latitudinarian adaptations: he asserts that Klopstock so successfully adapts the rules of hexameter to the German language (for example permitting trochees instead of spondees in some feet) that no one need analyze its use.[53] And like Nicolai, Bodmer attributes the necessity of the adaptation to the difference in languages, not to any defect

---

[50] Carl Wilhelm Ramler, "Ist der römische Hexameter der deutschen Sprache möglich?" (1756, Is Latin Hexameter Possible for the German Language?), in Hellmuth and Schröder, *Die Lehre von der Nachahmung der antiken Versmaße im Deutschen* 35–45, 36.

[51] Johann Jacob Bodmer (presumed), "Aufgefangener Brief, 1749" (found/intercepted letter) in Hellmuth and Schröder, *Die Lehre von der Nachahmung der antiken Versmaße im Deutschen*, 9–13, 13.

[52] Bodmer, "Aufgefangener Brief," 13.

[53] Bodmer, "Aufgefangener Brief," 12

on the part of the poets, informing his addressee that "if you and others, to whom Homer's verse is known, find this German verse improper, then you must not hold it against the German language that it is not Greek."[54] The fitting of verse practice to language and the historical differences between languages thus appear as arguments on both sides of the debate; they also, as I show below, became crucial to the linking of metrical considerations to narratives of history and culture more broadly.

In the entry on "Hexameter" in his *Allgemeine Theorie der Schönen Künste* (General Theory of the Fine Arts), published in 1771 (vol. 1) and 1774 (vol. 2), Johann Georg Sulzer shares the view that Klopstock's work justifies German hexameter but considers the state of metrical theorizing in Germany to be itself a point of analytical interest.[55] The article describes hexameter simply as a verse with six feet of two or three syllables without discussing which phonological elements the meter uses. In the entry for "Prosody," however, Sulzer reflects on the difficulties that hexameter in particular and polymetrism in general have brought to a previously straightforward topic: "Forty years ago the prosody of the German language seemed to be a topic that had very little difficulty. The poets limited themselves to a small number of verse types, which mostly consisted of only one kind of foot."[56] He reports that everyone knows that ancient prosody was based on the binary difference between long and short syllables, whereas in German length is only one (secondary) consideration amongst several that determine emphasis, including semantic importance and comparison to surrounding syllables.[57] German prosody therefore seems to be "a far more artificial matter ... than Greek prosody," and a full German prosody, including a theory of euphony, remains, in his view, to be written (Sulzer 929). Latitudinarian stances thus did not reject metrical theorizing entirely; with variations among individual authors, they reflected on the place and usefulness of such theorizing for different readers and authors in different contexts.

Anti-Hexametrists

The anti-hexametrist camp, which includes such illustrious Enlightenment figures as Gotthold Ephraim Lessing and Christoph Martin Wieland, receives perhaps its most detailed (and personal) defense in August Gottfried Bürger's justification of his own iambic translation of the *Iliad* in the form of a dialogue between a proponent of German hexameters and a defender of iambic verse, published in Wieland's

---

[54] Bodmer, "Aufgefangener Brief," 12

[55] Johann Georg Sulzer, "Hexameter," in *Allgemeine Theorie der Schönen Künste*, vol. 1, 4 vols (Leipzig, 1771), 536–7, 536.

[56] Sulzer, "Prosodie," (in *Allgemeine Theorie der Schönen Künste*, 928–9), 928.

[57] Sulzer, "Prosodie," (in *Allgemeine Theorie der Schönen Künste*, 928–9), 928.

Teutsche Merkur in 1776.[58] Bürger's representative, "A," bases his arguments on the differences between languages, acknowledging that, indeed, Homer wrote in hexameter, but he also wrote in Greek.[59] He argues that precisely the kind of exact calculation of syllable duration Voß attempts is impossible in German:

> Our language, whose measures are filled mostly with *whole* and *half* and only very few *quarter-notes*, should imitate Greek easily and well? Greek, with its multiply divisible measures, with all its *half-*, *quarter*, *eighth-* and *sixteenth-notes*? And German should fill out the measure of every hexameter in such a way that it is neither too long nor too short?[60]

This level of detail allows Greek verse to dance; German poetry must walk instead, and if allowed to do so can proceed with dignity, whereas if forced to imitate its forebear it becomes burlesque.[61] Hexameter, "A" allows, may work in shorter, original poems in German where there is no Greek or Latin for comparison and where themes for which the words are unmelodious can be avoided, but he seeks to prove by way of looking for metrical feet in prose texts that series of iambs (which appear much more often by coincidence) are more natural to German than hexameter.

In Bürger's view, then, the quest for German hexameter was nothing more than a symptom of "Obsession with imitation, damned imitation!," ignoring the cultural politics behind hexametrists' imitations of Greek and Latin meters in particular.[62] Given the absence of true dactyls and spondees in German, "A" argues that any attempt to produce the quantity of German hexameters necessary for an *Iliad* make the work "the most unpleasant ear-torture."[63] Ears should be enough, in Bürger's view, to determine that hexameter is ideal for Greek, but disastrous for German, and "A" adds mouths as a figure for the origin of and differences between languages: "Whether or not hexameter is the most perfect verse that ever fell from the lips of the muses, it would still be as unnatural to a German *Iliad* as for example maintaining the word order of the original language against the spirit of our own

---

[58] Lessing critiques German hexameters in a review of Johan Jacob Bodmer's *Noah* (Lessing, "Rezension zu Johann Jacob Bodmers Noah," in Hellmuth and Schröder, *Die Lehre von der Nachahmung der antiken Versmaße im Deutschen*, 14); Wieland did attempt hexameter in a few translation projects, but ultimately rejected it for translation. See Christoph Martin Wieland, "Eine neue hexametrische Übersetzung der Illiade" ("A New Hexameter Translation of the Iliad") and "Ein Wort von Herrn Voßens Einwendungen gegen die teutschen Monatsnamen" ("A Word on Mr. Voss's Objections to the German Month Names") in *Der Teutsche Merkur*, both cited and discussed in Schäfer, "Wieland liest die Briefe des Horaz," 90–9.

[59] Gottfried August Bürger, "An einen Freund über seine teutsche Illias" ("To a Friend, On His German Iliad," in Hellmuth and Schröder, *Die Lehre von der Nachahmung der antiken Versmaße im Deutschen*, 158–71), 159.

[60] Bürger, "An einen Freund," 59

[61] Bürger, "An einen Freund," 160.

[62] Bürger, "An einen Freund," 163

[63] Bürger, "An einen Freund," 169.

would be. Let everyone speak and sing as his beak is shaped!"[64] The perfection and beauty of Greek hexameter are, for Bürger, irrelevant, since they belong to Greek, not German; he has "A" go so far as to assert that if Homer had been German, he, too, would have written in iambs.[65] Here, then, historical and prosodic differences are not grounds for producing non-standard German, as they will be for Humboldt (nor are different varieties of and approaches to translation theorized, as they will be in Schleiermacher). Instead, they ground a call for natural-sounding German in meters that make extensive use of German's most striking prosodic-phonological feature: the binary difference between accented and non-accented syllables.

Johann Gottfried Herder intensifies the relation between prosodic-phonological and cultural-historical differences as the grounds for differing metrical practices. Writing in his fragments "Über die neuere deutsche Literatur" (On Recent German Literature), he investigates "what meters are—not possible but *natural* to our language."[66] He explains that German is too complex for polymetrical verse because of the differences between its accentual structure and that of Greek.[67] Moreover, because he considers monosyllables in German long, he argues that it is difficult to compose fluid, natural-sounding verses or periods: "Our entire period obtains ... something stiff and prosaic."[68] Herder derives a final piece of evidence against German polymetrism from the history of German lyric, pointing out that the Germans' poetic predecessors, "the Skalds," "never sang polymetrically in the Greek manner."[69] In order to see which, if any, Greek feet emerge by coincidence in German poetry, Herder examines German free-verse poetry.[70] In a free-verse ode by Klopstock, Herder locates spondees, trochees, and iambs; "dactyls—can only be found in participles and few other words; and our one-syllable words are really too undetermined and prosaic for the remaining multisyllable steps."[71] Herder's recommendations for German verse practice are

---

[64] Bürger, "An einen Freund," 163. Interestingly, this may be a fixed but non-normative link between language and body: mouths are shaped to produce certain kinds of language, but Bürger does not suggest here that some mouth shapes are better than others or that languages represent more or less developed cultures.

[65] Bürger, "An einen Freund," 163.

[66] Johann Gottfried Herder, "Über die neuere deutsche Literatur. Fragmente. Zweite, völlig umgearbeitete Ausgabe," in *Werke*, ed. Wolfgang Pross, vol. I (Munich: Carl Hanser Verlag, 1984), 63–210, 97.

[67] He describes German as "too full-toned," compared to Greek, which was "high-toned" and had "high and low [i.e. pitch] accents" in addition to long and short syllables. Perplexingly, Herder asserts that German has syllable length but not pitch; this is correct insofar as pitch/intonation is not precisely measured or controlled in German. Herder, "Über die neuere deutsche Literatur," 97.

[68] Herder, "Über die neuere deutsche Literatur," 98.

[69] Herder, "Über die neuere deutsche Literatur," 98. Klopstock, as we shall see in the next chapter, argues the opposite, even purporting to find hexameter in Old Saxon texts.

[70] Somewhat counterintuitively, he asserts that if German cannot not produce Greek metrical feet in free rhythms, it is even less likely to do so in bound speech. Herder, "Über die neuere deutsche Literatur," 98.

[71] Herder, "Über die neuere deutsche Literatur," 99.

therefore shaped by adherence to both historical and national particularity, making a decisive link between culture, language, and thought: "Every nation thus speaks according to how it thinks, and thinks according to how it speaks."[72] He attends to the characteristics of (modern) German in order to uncover its aesthetic possibilities and to give recommendations for literary production.[73]

Herder extends his theories of historical and cultural difference past recommendations for meter to the possibility of poetry as such, thus tying his connection between culture, language, and thought to a teleological development.[74] In a further section of the letters on literature he explains that the Greeks lived in a still-poetic cultural age, which had by his era disappeared: whereas for the Greeks poetry was "singing nature," for moderns it has become "an art that beautifies language in order to please."[75] Any imitation must therefore run up against the differences in culture and epoch. He reminds the reader that close attention to the material properties of language offers insight into the "spirit" of the culture that created and uses it: "Let one observe German's bodily structure, from the mechanics of individual members to the construction and form of the whole; let one learn to see the spirit in it, that shaped it, that enlivens and moves it."[76] And meter, in particular, renders cultural identity audible, as "A listening ear will recognize and hear in our language, too, and in the rustling of our feet and the unhurried measure of our steps: who we are."[77] Even as Herder firmly asserts the difference between cultures and between epochs—and critiques unthinking or rigid imitation of even the most prestigious cultures—his theorization of the *Volksgeist* and his links between spirit, language, and body aids in the establishment of modern race theory (despite Herder's own criticism of the concept of race[78]). In keeping with his attention to meter and the material features of language more generally as related to their cultural particularity, Herder argues that what moderns should take or learn from ancient or older languages is neither their meters nor their verse construction, but their characteristic individuality.[79]

---

[72] Herder, "Über die neuere deutsche Literatur," 81.

[73] Herder, "Über die neuere deutsche Literatur," 123.

[74] Although Herder, as this paragraph demonstrates, is deeply ambivalent about the "progress" of culture, the categories of "developed" and "primitive" his narrative helps to entrench and the characteristics of language he links to that narrative form a key moment in the establishment of non-European cultures as "primitive" and the link between meter and especially rhythm and tropes of "savagery." See my discussion of Herder's role in cementing a racialized essentialism in language and poetry in the introduction, Section 0.3.

[75] Herder, "Über die neuere deutsche Literatur," 164.

[76] Herder, "Über die neuere deutsche Literatur," 91. The grammatical gender of "language" as feminine (*die Sprache*) in German makes Herder's personification of the language much stronger, e.g. "the spirit that has shaped, that moves and enlivens *her*."

[77] Herder, "Über die neuere deutsche Literatur," 92.

[78] Michael Forster, "Johann Gottfried von Herder," in *The Stanford Encyclopedia of Philosophy*, ed. Edward N. Zalta, Summer 2019 (Metaphysics Research Lab, Stanford University, 2019), https://plato.stanford.edu/archives/sum2019/entries/herder/ (accessed July 5, 2022).

[79] Herder, "Über die neuere deutsche Literatur," 199.

In Herder, as in Gottsched, questions of metrics and especially hexameter move past problems of translation to questions of original verse composition in German, but with diametrically opposed results. Whereas Gottsched hoped for renewal of German verse via ancient meters (even if the efforts in that direction did not satisfy him), Herder holds that the differences between languages are too great for any such productive imitation to occur. Not in its outcomes, but rather in its details and its supporting arguments, the hexameter debate shows how technical questions of prosody, phonology, and scansion become implicated in genre poetics, poetic quality, and linguistic and/or cultural difference. In what follows, I look past the passionately argued hexameter debates to more general claims about prosody, including stories of its origins and development, its interaction with semantic meaning, and its emotional/affective and sensory/physiological impact to draw out the anthropological and aesthetic claims made for prosody.

1.3 Ramifications

I uncover the ramifications of claims about meter that emerge through the hexameter debate in the narratives eighteenth-century theorists offer about the origin and history of meter and language, including the recommendations they derive from these origins for verse practice more generally, and the accounts of how human perception, sensation, and cognition worked in the mind and the body that were radically revised in the course of the eighteenth century. Perhaps surprisingly (at least in a contemporary context), meter is vital to both of those accounts. Indeed, meter becomes a central topic in narratives of the history of language and culture that shape theoretical accounts of the origin of poetry and its development (a subset of debates over the origin of language) in the mid-to-late eighteenth century. All of these narratives attribute important anthropological functions to poetry: it developed in response to human capacities, needs, or desires. And each theorist I consider weaves together anthropological, aesthetic, and poetic considerations in making recommendations for German verse practice with the goal of moral, emotional, and physiological efficacy—ideally, all three in interaction with one another.

To twenty-first-century ears, the linking of anthropology, poetics, and aesthetics requires some explanation. In the years leading up to the hexameter debate and the broader explosion in metrical experimentation, the German Enlightenment was engaged in a re-evaluation or reclaiming of sense perception as a source of knowledge from its banishment in Cartesian rationalism.[80] Aesthetics,

<hr>

[80] See Stefanie Buchenau, *The Founding of Aesthetics in the German Enlightenment* (Cambridge: Cambridge University Press, 2013), 11–2, for a discussion of this narrative of the German Enlightenment as plausible but in need of further investigation as to *why* philosophers such as Christian Wolff

in its eighteenth-century definition, was a crucial component in understanding all human faculties and thus in anthropology as the science of the "whole human." Prior to its career as the term for the subgenre of philosophy treating the fine arts, "aesthetics" was derived from the Greek *aisthesis*, "sensation" or "perception" (as opposed to *noesis*, "intellect" or "reason").[81] The phrase "whole human" (in German "der ganze Mensch") grounded the claim that not only reason but sensibility (*Empfinden* or *Empfindung*) is inherent to human subjectivity[82]. Thus the German term *Empfinden* can refer to a combination of perceptual data, bodily-sensory input, and emotional affectation; understanding the whole human thus necessarily entailed overcoming dualisms such as mind/body, reason/emotion, and ratiocination/perception. Human sensory (and eventually emotional) capacities in combination with rational capacities became the basis for what artworks do and how they do it; conversely, the efficacy of artworks became a source of insight into human faculties and their interaction. Meter, as perhaps the most striking sensory quality of an art form that uses (rational) language, becomes a central place for investigating the interplay of sensory and cognitive human capacities, thus of human wholeness.

In shifting from an organization based on positions in a debate to one treating single authors in chronological order, I am attempting to trace the inflection points in a major shift in eighteenth-century theorizing about meter and poetry. Gottsched, the first figure I discuss, is perhaps the last great German theorist of *Regelpoetik* (poetics of rules), in which poetic accomplishment involves the adherence to inherited rules that unify form and content. He also, however, links different elements of poetry (such as sound or image versus truthful imitation of life) to an account of human sensory and cognitive faculties.[83] Gottsched thus

---

and Gottfried Wilhelm Leibniz undertook this rehabilitation. The view of Descartes as a one-sided rationalist has, of course, been called into question in more recent philosophy, but for the purposes of the generation of German philosophers following Descartes, the Cartesian view is the one of the *Meditations* that insists on the unreliability of sense perception for knowledge. Grünbein pleads the case of a non-rationalist Descartes in the poem and essays I discuss in Chapter 6.

[81] Ernst Stöckmann, "Von der sinnlichen Erkenntnis zur Psychologie der Emotionen. Anthropologische und ästhetische Progression der Aisthesis in der vorkantischen Ästhetiktheorie," in *Physis und Norm. Neue Perspektiven der Anthropologie im 18. Jahrhundert*, eds. Manfred Beetz, Jörn Garber, and Heinz Thoma (Göttingen: Wallstein Verlag, 2007), 69–106, 69. As I discuss below, the term was first used by Alexander Baumgarten, who defined aesthetics as the "science of things perceived [scientia sensitive quid cognoscendi]" Baumgarten, *Meditationes philosophicae de nonnullis ad poema pertinentibus*, 7.

[82] Buchenau, *The Founding of Aesthetics in the German Enlightenment*, 167. At the same time, this shift modified but continued a normative view of subjectivity as defined primarily (but now not exclusively) by reason and language use—a sort of eighteenth-century version of contemporary assumptions of neurotypicality. Moreover, even as the theory of the "whole human" broadened the range of faculties associated with subjectivity, it established normative valuations of kinds of knowledge, behavior, and sensation that could be ascribed to different groups (women, non-white and/or non-Christian, non-European) in different degrees and thus used to privilege some subject identities (white, male, European, Christian) over others.

[83] Gottsched's division of the faculties, like many eighteenth-century thinkers', is based on the philosophy of Christian Wolff. As Stefanie Buchenau notes, "The Wolffian philosophy was thus the ground

initiates the transition from *Regelpoetik* to a philosophical poetics, in which analysis and presentation of rules is gradually replaced by attention to the way poetry appeals to and develops specific human faculties. Herder, the last figure in this chapter, represents the culmination of this shift: he seeks to develop a philosophy of beauty based entirely on human sense perception and unites the history of human culture so tightly to the development of reason that he views the creation of true poetry, appealing to all of reason, emotion, and sense perception, as impossible in the prosaic modern era. The intervening figures—Breitinger, Baumgarten, and Sulzer—mark moments in this transition which place varying emphases on the different faculties that make up the whole human and accord meter variable roles in the appeal to those faculties.[84]

Johann Christoph Gottsched

Gottsched holds that the task of works of art is to present "the general truths of morality" in a particular and concrete form that makes them more present and effective than does abstract knowledge of those truths.[85] Poetry thus seeks to affect the reader in order to move "the innermost parts of the soul" in a more moral direction.[86] As his narratives of their origins show, both poetry and meter arise in response to anthropological and physiological givens. In his *Critische Dichtkunst*, Gottsched offers two origin stories for poetry. In the first, a "lively mind, of good temperament" finds its (or rather, his) blood heated and vital spirits awakened by food or drink; "so he perhaps began to sing for joy, and to show his enjoyment also through speaking certain words in the process."[87] Alternatively, "a shepherd in

on which, in the two decades between 1721 and 1740, a common aesthetic project was progressively formulated." Buchenau, *The Founding of Aesthetics in the German Enlightenment*, 86.

[84] Since giving a full history of eighteenth-century aesthetics, or even of the idea of sensate cognition in eighteenth-century German aesthetics, is beyond the scope of this project, I limit my discussion to theorists who treat meter centrally in their discussions of poetry. Lessing, as discussed above, was a vehement opponent of German imitations of Greek meters, and otherwise discusses versification (mostly iambs and alexandrines) largely apropos his theories of tragedy. Mendelssohn considers rhyme and meter largely in reviews, such his discussion as Ramler's translation and introduction of Batteux, in one of his contributions to the *Briefe, die neueste Literatur betreffend*. On Lessing, and the influence of Baumgarten, Mendelssohn, and Meier, see David E. Wellbery, *Lessing's Laocoon. Semiotics and Aesthetics in the Age of Reason* (Cambridge: Cambridge University Press, 1984). Georg Friedrich Meier, although he was enthusiastic about Klopstock's *Messias*, discusses its content rather than its versification in his *Beurtheilung Des Heldengedichts, Der Meßias* (Halle: Carl Herrmann Hemmerde, 1749); he polemicizes in favor of rhyme-free poetry in a preface to Samuel Gotthold Langes *Horatzische Oden* titled "Vom Werthe der Reime" ("On the Value of Rhymes," Georg Friedrich Meier, "Vom Werthe der Reime," in *Horatzische Oden*, by Samuel Gotthold Lange, ed. Georg Friedrich Meier [Halle: Carl Herrmann Hemmerde, 1747], 2–21). For more general discussion of pre-Kantian German aesthetics, see (in addition to the *Stanford Encyclopedia of Philosophy* cited above) Paul Guyer, *A History of Modern Aesthetics: The Eighteenth Century* (Cambridge University Press, 2014).

[85] Guyer, "18th Century German Aesthetics."

[86] Gottsched, *Critische Dichtkunst*, 23.

[87] Gottsched, *Critische Dichtkunst*, 82.

love, in whose heart was moved and his blood stirred by the presence of a graceful shepherdess during the long while he attended his grazing herds" may have imitated the birds in an attempt to attract the attention and awaken the desire of his beloved.[88] As the use of the term "sing" in the first example and the idea of imitating the birds in the second attest, for Gottsched, song as wordless vocalization precedes poetry and is related to a physiological excitation, which then stimulates the organism sufficiently that words are added to the song. Poetry thus occurs as the natural extension from bodily excitation to vocalization that both expresses emotion and calls it forth in others.[89]

Meter, in turn, arose through efforts to make words easier to sing. Gottsched hypothesizes that the earliest poetry was "raw and coarse" without regular patterns of syllables.[90] Eventually, however, the difficulty of fitting melody and words together prompted more careful syllable counting.[91] He suggests that the Greeks, gifted with "very sensitive hearing," were the first to discover that maintaining an equal number of syllables per melodic unit made song easier, and then to refine this discovery by paying greater attention to the patterning of long and short syllables.[92] From this theory of the introduction of meter, the step to a poetics of genre is relatively short: as soon as the Greeks discovered the patterning of syllables, they noticed that certain patterns worked well with certain types of song, and thus codified the multiplicity of verse genres found in Greek and Latin.[93] According to Gottsched, Northern cultures, including Germanic peoples, were less gifted hearers and so developed rhyme instead of polymetrism; these cultures continued to count the numbers of syllables in each line only loosely,[94] at least until the influence of Greek and Latin introduced them to more exact meters.[95]

The argument that specific meters emerged with and for specific types of poetry is fully in keeping with Gottsched's poetics of rules, which is implicit in his criticisms of those who use hexameter in inappropriate genres. Much of the *Critische Dichtkunst* works to establish rules for the use of particular feet as appropriate to particular genres and to correct their misuse. Gottsched emphasizes the (Horatian) idea that poetic technique is a matter of using each meter correctly, lamenting that in modern Germany "People are making epics in elegiac, and love laments in heroic verses. People are making panegyrics in the common satirical mode:

---

[88] Gottsched, *Critische Dichtkunst*, 82.
[89] Gottsched, *Critische Dichtkunst*, 68–9.
[90] Gottsched, *Critische Dichtkunst*, 69–70.
[91] Gottsched, *Critische Dichtkunst*, 73.
[92] Gottsched, *Critische Dichtkunst*, 73. Note the way Gottsched attributes bodily characteristics—sensitive ears—to a culture as a whole. He likewise groups "Germanic peoples" and "northern cultures" (as opposed to Greek "southern" culture) together as harder of hearing.
[93] Gottsched, *Critische Dichtkunst*, 73.
[94] Gottsched, *Critische Dichtkunst*, 73–4.
[95] Gottsched, *Critische Dichtkunst*, 79.

and satire first rises to the heights of an epic and plunges into the language of the mob."[96] This genre mixing ignores the relations, established in the Classical tradition (though not as unambiguously as Gottsched implies), between verse and content.[97] Because verse is inseparable from genre (and thus content), Gottsched dedicates only one chapter of the work to a general discussion of the euphony created by meter and rhyme, and ends it with the suggestion that readers seek more particular information for themselves.[98] His readers had ample opportunity to do so, as Gottsched turns in the second and third parts of the *Critische Dichtkunst* to a catalogue of poetic genres and their practitioners.

Johann Jakob Breitinger

The question of how much individual genius rather than adherence to traditional rules determines aesthetic quality and aesthetic truth forms the primary disagreement between Gottsched, on the one hand, and Breitinger (with his poet-colleague Johann Jakob Bodmer), on the other. In keeping with his greater emphasis on individuality, Breitinger focuses in his own *Critische Dichtkunst* on both the poet's and the audience's emotions.[99] He attends less to deployment of particular meters in "correct" genres, and instead analyzes the power of meter in activating human emotions in the pathetic or "heart-stirring mode of writing" (which he ties to human physiology in a catalogue of linguistic symptoms of emotional arousal). Like Gottsched, he describes poetry as beginning from expressive vocalization; he argues that this original poetry is then accidentally refined by human auditory perception.[100] Thereafter, early poets analyzed the source of "euphony in speech to derive metrical rules and systems directed toward a pleasing harmony and evaluated by human hearing.[101] These rules, in Breitinger's view, progress in culturally specific ways to fulfill a universal desire for harmony. Thus, nations with more sensitive ears show a faster and more significant development of meter.[102] Breitinger draws an analogy between different meters and the different gaits of individuals

---

[96] Gottsched, *Critische Dichtkunst*, 19, n. 29.

[97] Gottsched, *Critische Dichtkunst*, 21, n. 32.

[98] Gottsched, *Critische Dichtkunst*, 416.

[99] Johann Jakob Breitinger, *Fortsetzung der Critischen Dichtkunst: Worinnen die Poetische Mahlerey in Absicht auf den Ausdruck und die Farben abgehandelt wird, mit einer Vorrede von Johann Jacob Bodmer*. Faksimiledruck nach der Ausgabe von 1740. (Continuation of the Critical Poetics: Wherein Poetic Painting is Treated with a View towards Expression and Color, Stuttgart: JB Metzler, 1966). The title taken from Gottsched underscores the great degree of commonality between the two thinkers; once the relations between them had soured from disagreement into polemic, Gottsched remarked in his preface to the third edition of his *Critische Dichtkunst* (1742) that Breitinger's work so clearly lacked everything essential to a poetic handbook that no one could possibly confuse the two, despite the shared titles (Gottsched, *Versuch einer Critischen Dichtkunst*, XIX–XX).

[100] Breitinger, *Fortsetzung der Critischen Dichtkunst*, 16.

[101] Breitinger, *Fortsetzung der Critischen Dichtkunst*, 16.

[102] Breitinger, *Fortsetzung der Critischen Dichtkunst*, 18–9.

with varying temperaments and of different nations.[103] The connection between metrical feet and the body's gait is, of course, a long-established topos, but in keeping with his emphasis on arousal and expression of affect Breitinger links the trope to affective as well as national temperaments, foreshadowing Herder's merging of body, language, and spirit.

Since appealing to the emotions remains Breitinger's highest poetic priority, it follows that his comments on verse practice are guided by the goal of having meter support content, and in particular content of the highest and most pathetic tone. Unlike Gottsched, he contends that these relations of support cannot be matters of universal, objective rules, although he notes Homer as the greatest creator of a "beauty of meter" that unites meter and meaning.[104] Instead, Breitinger draws an analogy with the dualism between soul and body to describe the relation between euphony (the goal of meter) and meaning, arguing that "no matter how great the beauty of a verse with respect to euphony may be, it is only ever the beauty of a soulless corpse."[105] That is, even given the drive to harmony or formal balance, symmetry cannot by itself be poetically effective. As Breitinger's attention to the relation between form and meaning as such, rather than in given genres, suggests, correctness remains secondary to emotional efficacy, and Breitinger relies on emotion and hearing to determine successful verse practice. Verse practice is thus not a sign of erudition or a mark of poetic skill, but a tool for the activation of human emotion that is, for Breitinger, the highest mark of poetic quality.

He then describes how this activation works: poetry uses words, "signs for thoughts," to transmit images in the poet's mind directly to the imagination of the reader or hearer.[106] These images are derived from the workings of the imagination as it is led by understanding and judgment; understanding or cognition thus continue to play a role even in the most poetic speech.[107] Poetic speech also, however, follows the patterns of affectively excited speech: "the moving and pathetic mode of writing is nothing other than an unforced imitation of the way of speaking that nature places in the mouth of anyone who is aroused by a passion."[108] As such, it does not follow grammatical or logical rules observed by rational discourse and instead exhibits "haste" (via leaving out logical-grammatical connector words), repetition, and hyperbole.[109] Using quasi-medical vocabulary, Breitinger

---

[103] Breitinger, *Fortsetzung der Critischen Dichtkunst*, 442.

[104] He gives the *Odyssey*'s description of Sisyphus and his boulder as an example: "This twofold movement is admirably expressed in the flow of the verses; how the stone is rolled upwards in the four first lines with different spondees, mixed with the necessary moments of pause, then finally falls back down in a single line of pure dactyls." Breitinger, *Fortsetzung der Critischen Dichtkunst*, 31.

[105] Breitinger, *Fortsetzung der Critischen Dichtkunst*, 35.

[106] Breitinger, *Fortsetzung der Critischen Dichtkunst*, 6.

[107] Breitinger, *Fortsetzung der Critischen Dichtkunst*, 9.

[108] Breitinger, *Fortsetzung der Critischen Dichtkunst*, 353–4.

[109] Breitinger, *Fortsetzung der Critischen Dichtkunst*, 373, 376–8.

describes further "Symptomata" of affective arousal and affective speech, such as conflating present and absent objects and persons, speaking for and as others, narrating the past as present, and evoking presence via direct address.[110] This combination of characteristics, taken together, makes the unusual word order and occasional dropping of words demanded by strict meters (like hexameter) a virtue rather than a defect: deviations from standard German testify to emotional arousal.

Breitinger insists that these affects and their expression in speech are universal because human nature is universal: "The same passion would express and explain itself in an Iroquois in his rustic speech as by a Saxon."[111] (As I noted in the introduction, it is telling that Breitinger feels entitled to generalize about "Iroquois" and "Saxons" while only having familiarity with the latter. Virtually all of the theorists I consider in this section assume rather than invite universality.) Drawing on the classical argument that the poet must experience an emotion to create it, Breitinger gives an extended analogy between human souls and instruments tuned to each other: "The souls of all people are like an identical instrument that is strung with as many strings as there are passions."[112] Only an instrument with a string of the same note as the one that is struck will resonate in response; therefore, a poet seeking to touch an emotion in a hearer must sound the same tone in himself.[113] While the idea that the poet must feel an emotion in order to excite it is at least as old as Horace, the metaphor of emotional affectation as musical sound, in particular the comparison between a specific faculty of the soul and the strings of an instrument, depended upon changing conceptions of human physiology emerging along with the disciplines of aesthetics and anthropology. Earlier paradigms that described the nerves with images of "pipes" and "fluid" were replaced with a model that explained nerve excitation as fibers set into vibration.[114] In this metaphorical system, nerves could be characterized, at least provisionally, as the "seat of sensitivity" and described as tensed or released, like strings stretched to resonate at a specific pitch.[115] Since the poet can only achieve emotional "resonance" with the reader by activating his own affects, Breitinger argues that the poet should learn to understand human affects and passions, rather than studying repertoires of poetic or rhetorical figures.[116]

[110] Breitinger, *Fortsetzung der Critischen Dichtkunst* 389–96.
[111] Breitinger, *Fortsetzung der Critischen Dichtkunst*, 355.
[112] Breitinger, *Fortsetzung der Critischen Dichtkunst*, 359.
[113] Breitinger, *Fortsetzung der Critischen Dichtkunst*, 359.
[114] Carsten Zelle, "Klopstocks Diät—das Erhabene und die Anthropologie um 1750," in *Wort und Schrift: Das Werk Friedrich Gottlieb Klopstocks*, eds. Kevin Hilliard and Katrin Kohl, Hallesche Forschungen 27 (Tübingen: Niemeyer, 2008), 101–27, 113.
[115] Zelle, "Klopstocks Diät," 113.
[116] Breitinger, *Fortsetzung der Critischen Dichtkunst*, 371–2.

Alexander Baumgarten

The interweaving of questions of aesthetics and questions of psychology is like-wise central for Alexander Baumgarten. Once Baumgarten establishes the idea of poetic speech as a kind of discourse that produces perfection pleasing to the sense perception as well as reason, aesthetics becomes a point of insight into those faculties, a kind of *Seelenkunde* (study of the soul).[117] Baumgarten develops the idea of aesthetics from a consideration of poetry; in his view, poetry is governed by rules that are different from but complementary to the rules of formal logic, even as poetry is not devoid of logical or cognitive content. Furthermore, meter is instrumental in his derivation of the term *aesthetics* because it is a central component of speech that is both sensory *and* rule-bound, effective for sensory perception *and* reason.[118] In Baumgarten's model, poetry's task is to use "imagery drawn from the senses" to convey truth more vividly and with more practical relevance than can abstract cognition.[119] (Here he is in agreement with both Gottsched and Breitinger.) And because poetry's discourse is a matter of concrete images in a particular medium, its perfection may be a matter of the sensory images depicted, the words themselves as the medium in which those images are conveyed, or in the relation between image and medium;[120] Baumgarten thus holds that the sensory components of a work of art are not mere vehicles for the conveyance of truth but have their own type of perfection, which is itself a source of pleasure.[121] This is a significant departure from Gottsched's insistence that medium is a by-product of certain types of content and from Breitinger's assertion that formal symmetry on its own produces no pleasure.

Baumgarten works out the relation between representations and their medium in the *Meditationes philosophicae de nonnullis ad poema pertinentibus*, where he explains that "the several parts of a poem" are "(1) sensate representations, (2) their interrelationships, (3) words [, or the articulate sounds which are represented by the letters and which signify the words]."[122] After analyzing the ways the

---

[117] Kevin Hilliard describes this as a convergence of observation of art and psychology in Baumgarten, Mendelssohn, and others. Kevin Hilliard, "Die»Baumgartensche Schule«und der Strukturwandel der Lyrik in der Gefühlskultur der Aufklärung," in *Gefühlskultur in der bürgerlichen Aufklärung*, eds. Achim Aurnhammer, Dieter Martin, and Robert Seidel, Frühe Neuzeit 98 (Tübingen: Niemeyer, 2004), 11–22, 14.

[118] Guyer, "18th Century German Aesthetics." There is some ambivalence as to whether Baumgarten's theory represents the valorization of sensation against reason or the cooptation of the former by the latter. Buchenau argues for the valorization of sensation (Buchenau, *The Founding of Aesthetics in the German Enlightenment*, 146), Stöckmann for its continuing domination by reason (Stöckmann, "Von der sinnlichen Erkenntnis zur Psychologie der Emotionen," 88).

[119] Guyer, "18th Century German Aesthetics."

[120] Guyer, "18th Century German Aesthetics."

[121] Guyer, "18th Century German Aesthetics."

[122] Aschenbrenner and Holter leave out the linking of words to articulated letters and sounds. The original is "voces sive soni articulati litteris constantes earum signa" (Baumgarten, *Meditationes philosophicae de nonnullis ad poema pertinentibus*, reprinted in Aschenbrenner/Holter [eds.], 7).

representations in a poem may be combined, Baumgarten discusses the medium of poetry: "words," considered as "articulate sounds."[123] He emphasizes that poetry exhibits perfection specifically in its verbal-acoustic medium, as judged by the ears: "Since the poem, taken as a series of articulate sounds, excites pleasure in the ear ... there must also be a perfection in it ... and indeed the highest perfection."[124] He then turns to a discussion of metrics, defining the "quantity of a syllable" as "that property which cannot be known apart from association with another syllable."[125] Baumgarten, drawing on Cicero, defines "measure" as occurring when "long and short syllables are so mingled that pleasure of the ear ensues"; and because pleasing the ears is poetic, so too is measure.[126] "Measure" refers both to the loose organization of syllables in prose and to the full organization of syllables in poetry: "The kind of measure that, through the ordering of all syllables of the discourse, promotes pleasure in the ear is called *meter*. If measure determines pleasure through many syllables following one another without any definite order, it is called *rhythm*."[127] Meter entails more order than rhythm, and so metrical speech is more poetic than mere rhythmical speech: "Since meter produces sense impressions ... and since these have the greatest extensive clarity, they are to that degree the most poetic ... Thus it is highly poetic to observe most carefully the laws of meter."[128]

Baumgarten immediately qualifies that meter or verse do not by themselves make something a poem.[129] He remarks that the traditional definitions of poetry—as "bounded discourse" or as "imitation of actions or of nature"—are neither contradictory of nor dependent on one another. Both, however, are insufficient.[130] And this inadequacy prompts him to derive the field of aesthetics. Baumgarten argues that there must be a logic of sense perception and emotion, which can be developed in a "science of sensitive cognition."[131] This new science is that of *aisthesis*, "the science of perception, or *aesthetic*."[132] In Baumgarten's model, poetry's perfection is perfection for sensibility, while the perfection of what he calls

---

[123] Baumgarten, *Meditationes philosophicae*, 69.

[124] Baumgarten, *Meditationes philosophicae*, 70. The ellipses indicate my omission of Baumgarten's references to the previous sections in the *Meditationes* where he takes himself to have defined or demonstrated the claim advanced.

[125] That is, a syllable's quantity is not apparent from letters alone (either the vowel sound or the number of letters). Baumgarten, *Meditationes philosophicae*, 71.

[126] Baumgarten, *Meditationes philosophicae*, 73.

[127] Baumgarten, *Meditationes philosophicae*, 74.

[128] Baumgarten, *Meditationes philosophicae*, 75.

[129] Baumgarten, *Meditationes philosophicae*, 74.

[130] Baumgarten, *Meditationes philosophicae*, 76.

[131] Baumgarten, *Meditationes philosophicae*, 39. The Latin is "scientia sensitive quid cognoscendi"; Aschenbrenner and Holter leave out the final clause in which the most condensed definition appears; Riemann has "eine Wissenschaft vom sensitiven Erkennen" (Baumgarten, *Philosophische Betrachtungen*, 145).

[132] Baumgarten, *Meditationes philosophicae*, 78.

"distinct cognition" is perfection for reason, and neither is inferior to the other.[133] This enables Baumgarten's claim that aesthetics is *both* a science of sensibility and one of poetry";[134] studying the types of perfection that appeal to sensation and emotion offers insight both into those faculties and into the creation of poetry that is itself the source of such perfection.

Johann Georg Sulzer

Both the importance of emotion or affect and the attention to medium-specific pleasures of formal organization increase in the work of Johann Georg Sulzer.[135] Moreover, he emphasizes the subjective response to beauty over the objective characteristics of a beautiful object.[136] Beauty becomes a source not of objective or external knowledge about the world but of subjective or internal *self*-knowledge; it is a source of insight into human sensations and perceptions, rather than a datum for cognition.[137] Consequently, the moral purpose of all the arts is the development in the individual of sensation and eventually moral sensations, as opposed to the cognitive purposes of philosophy.[138] Drawing, like Breitinger, on the metaphor of sympathetic strings, Sulzer differentiates two methods for the artist to arouse *Empfindung*: either he must experience the emotion in himself, or he must depict the object that arouses emotion so vividly that it calls forth the emotion in the recipient as if it were present.[139] For this reason, the artist must not write too generally or universally; abstract ideas are the province of philosophy; the particularity required for the arousal of sensation belongs to the fine arts.[140]

Sulzer derives poetry's origins and its features from its fundamental nature as expression and evocation of emotion.[141] The earliest poetry, Sulzer speculates, was brief "moral proverbs or also very short expressions of some surging passion ...

---

[133] Buchenau, *The Founding of Aesthetics in the German Enlightenment*, 171. Baumgarten thus differentiates poetic representations from non-poetic, fully logically determined ones: "Distinct representations, complete, adequate, profound through every degree, are not sensate, and therefore, not poetic" (Baumgarten, *Meditationes philosophicae*, 42). That is, poetry has certain capabilities and perfections that fully rational, cognitive representations do not.

[134] Buchenau, *The Founding of Aesthetics in the German Enlightenment*, 172.

[135] Stöckmann, "Von der sinnlichen Erkenntnis zur Psychologie der Emotionen," 97.

[136] Sulzer makes this point directly in the essay on "Empfindung (Schöne Künste)" ("Sensation [Fine Arts]"), in the *Encyclopedia of the Fine Arts*:" "In cognition we are occupied with the object as a thing that lies entirely outside of us; in sensation, however, we give more attention to ourselves, to the pleasant or unpleasant impression, that the object makes on us than to its qualities." Sulzer, "Empfindung (Schöne Künste)" (in *Allgemeine Theorie der Schönen Künste* 311–6), 311.

[137] Stöckmann, "Von der sinnlichen Erkenntnis zur Psychologie der Emotionen," 100.

[138] Sulzer, "Empfindung," 311.

[139] Sulzer, "Empfindung," 314. Like Breitinger, Sulzer takes for granted that the qualities that define "human nature" are those that white Europeans designate.

[140] Sulzer, "Empfindung," 315.

[141] Sulzer, "Dichtkunst. Poesie," (in *Allgemeine Theorie der Schönen Künste*, 250–8), 252.

that were sung while dancing."[142] He adds, "in this era it was not yet art";[143] rather, poetry was heightened but fully natural expression without rules or techniques. Later, poets noticed the efficacy of certain forms and began to study and deploy them more systematically.[144] Meter, as one such efficacious form, is not a defining feature of poetry for Sulzer, but it is linked to poetry's goal of arousing sensation and emotion. Because the tone of a given poem must fit with its *Empfindung*, the poem must have a certain rhythmical quality due of the nature of *Empfindung* itself, "because the sensation is always the same, and always turns around itself."[145] And this natural rhythmic quality explains the origins of metrical verse: "From this we can understand to some extent the origin of verse"; because both meter and sensation are dynamically self-referring, "One can thus say that verse is natural to poetry."[146] Different poetic genres and their different verse forms come not from poetic tradition but from the differences in individual poets and sensations.[147] Furthermore, because meters themselves have characteristic emotions or sensations associated with them (Sulzer's example is the cheerful tone of triple meters versus more serious duple meters), verse enables the poem to maintain a consistent affective or sensory tone, versus the flux of representations or concepts in the individual words.[148] Hexameter works particularly well for epic poems, which do not present only a single affective tone due to their length, because hexameter lines combine duple and triple feet and vary from line to line. Shorter poems, which strive to maintain a single sensation or emotion across their entire length, must use more uniform verse forms.

The nature of sensations also makes rhythmic repetition necessary to maintain a single sensation across the course of a poem: sensations are most intense at their onset and then decrease in strength.[149] Without metrical repetition, they would quickly die away. In verse, however, with each measure or beat, "before the prior impression is entirely exhausted the next one arrives, and thereby there occurs to some extent an adding up, a piling up of sensation and effectiveness through which the mind/soul is ever more inspired."[150] In this model, rhythm not only maintains sensation and effectiveness but heightens them throughout the poem, with effects that Sulzer describes using the physiological vocabulary of nerve excitation: "This can go so far that finally the entire system of nerves begins to move" and, heightened by new impulses before the previous ones die away, becomes faster and faster

---

[142] Sulzer, "Dichtkunst. Poesie," 253.
[143] Sulzer, "Dichtkunst. Poesie," 253.
[144] Sulzer, "Dichtkunst. Poesie," 253.
[145] Sulzer, "Gedicht," 434.
[146] Sulzer, "Gedicht," 434.
[147] Sulzer, "Dichtkunst. Poesie," 251.
[148] Sulzer, "Rhythmus; Rhythmisch (Redende Kunst, Musik, Tanz)," 975–85, in *Allgemeine Theorie der Schönen Künste*, 982.
[149] Sulzer, "Rhythmus; Rhythmisch," 981.
[150] Sulzer, "Rhythmus; Rhythmisch," 982.

"so that a sensitive mind/soul can be driven to distraction."[151] The physiological effectiveness of rhythm testifies to its relation to innate human faculties and behaviors; Sulzer remarks that rhythm is "nothing artificial" but has "a natural sensation at its foundation."[152] Sulzer's discussion of meter and rhythm thus illuminates his complex combination of formalist and moral concerns for artwork; although he begins the article by defining rhythm merely as *"order in tone and movement"* and announces he will analyze it as entirely separate from content, he nonetheless uses the basis of rhythmical and metrical efficacy in and for human physiology to tie meter to *Empfindung*, which overcomes cognition as the central project of the arts.

Johann Gottfried Herder

In a final step, Johann Gottfried Herder joins poetic practice so tightly to the historical development of human reason and human culture that the emotional efficacy and directness of true poetry become impossible in the face of modern culture's rationalism: throughout his career, he narrates the progression of language from its natural origins to a poetic age into prose and ultimately philosophy.[153] Poetry's original (now lost) emotional and physiological directness are, for him, an indication of its human rather than divine origins.[154] Instead, the first poetry was religious (that is, addressed by humans *to* the gods, not coming *from* the gods), and priests were the first poets. Their purposes led to poetry's characteristic features of brevity, sensuousness, and unusual diction: poetry is "a short, sensual prayer full of carefully chosen strong words."[155] To this initial description Herder adds the qualities of accentuation and song: "And when this prayer is in a language that lets its accents be heard very strongly? Then this poetry already walks on polymetric feet: people speak it in high tones and—*sing it therefore*: a *natural raw song of poetry*."[156] Early meters thus result naturally from the heightened accentuation of early language. In "Über die neuere deutsche Literatur" (On Recent German Literature), Herder describes the effects of such language, explaining that early language drew on tone and gesture to convey passion and emotion.[157] This language was therefore a "language of affect" shaped by the senses (rather than logic).[158]

---

[151] Sulzer, "Rhythmus; Rhythmisch," 982.
[152] Sulzer, "Rhythmus; Rhythmisch," 980.
[153] This narrative appears in the "Versuch einer Geschichte der Lyrik" (Attempt at a History of the Lyric), in "Über die neuere deutsche Literatur" (On Recent German Literature), and of course (albeit more indirectly) in the "Abhandlung über den Ursprung der Sprache" (Treatise on the Origin of Language); it is implicit in the ambivalence toward language and its effects on sensory experience in the "Viertes Wäldchen" (Fourth Forest) of the *Kritische Wälder* (Critical Forests).
[154] Johann Gottfried Herder, "Versuch einer Geschichte der Lyrik," in Pross, *Werke*, 7–61, 19.
[155] Herder, "Versuch einer Geschichte der Lyrik," 29–30.
[156] Herder, "Versuch einer Geschichte der Lyrik," 30.
[157] Herder, "Über die neuere deutsche Literatur," 145.
[158] Herder, "Über die neuere deutsche Literatur," 145.

The qualities he ascribes to poetry, including meter, are thus derived from anthropological dispositions and needs and adapted to human sensory capacities and development.

The development of human culture and the development of language move in parallel: after its poetic youth, language reaches a period of "beautiful prose" and finally the "philosophical era of language" in which modern Germans live.[159] Meter, in later epochs, is no longer a natural feature of poetic speech but an artificial technique or set of rules retroactively applied to prosaic language. (Here we can see a criticism of Gottsched's poetics of rules.) This progression correlates with the rise of rational thought; because modern peoples reason about so much, they lose the vividness that motivated and appeared in early poetry.[160] Herder is adamant that the epochs of language (poetic, prose, and philosophical) cannot coexist; initially all language was poetic language, which was then suppressed by prose, and in the philosophical age of language "we have merely versified philosophy, or mediocre poetry."[161] No set of metrical rules or theories can overcome this fundamental historical and cultural difference (hence Herder's rejection of hexameter, as I discussed above). Indeed, Herder sees metrical constraint as restricting emotion and imagination, which must either be damaged by or damage any strict meter: "The painting of the imagination can bear no bound meter, unless either it or the meter suffers."[162] Modern culture's best chance at anything like the efficacy of true poetry from the childhood of the species is to be as unbound by rules (and thus meters) as possible. Whereas meter was natural to and thus effective in early poetry, in modern German culture it becomes a hindrance to affective and physiological efficacy.

Herder asserts a (historically variable) relation between human language and human cognitive and emotional capacities.[163] He thus accords language a robust role in the development of human logical reasoning: "In our upbringing we learn thoughts through words, and the nannies who shape our tongues are thus our first teachers of logic."[164] Thought, and with it cognition, is impossible without language, and thus language defines the boundaries of human thought.[165] Poetry, in particular, combines the sensory-intuitive and cognitive-rational elements of language.[166] (It should be noted that Herder is arguing systematically rather than historically here: he is making a point about the interrelation of

---

[159] Herder, "Über die neuere deutsche Literatur," 148
[160] Herder, "Versuch einer Geschichte der Lyrik," 35.
[161] Herder, "Über die neuere deutsche Literatur," 163. Herder analyzes fully philosophical language in some detail in an entire "Fragment" on Alexander Baumgarten (183–7).
[162] Herder, "Über die neuere deutsche Literatur," 101
[163] This variability does hinder outright essentialism despite the alignment of language, culture, body, and thought Herder establishes.
[164] Herder, "Über die neuere deutsche Literatur," 79.
[165] Herder, "Über die neuere deutsche Literatur," 79.
[166] Herder, "Über die neuere deutsche Literatur," 79.

language and thought.) By virtue of its dual constitution, poetry is capable of arousing poetic affects, moving the lower faculties of the soul, and inflaming the imagination.[167] Studying language, in particular poetic language, can offer insight into the unity of human sensory and rational faculties, even as modern humans are so dominated by the latter that they can no longer produce poetry that unites the two.

Unifying not only reason and sensation but thought and physiology, Herder makes clear that the sensory elements of language work directly on the body, as evidenced in his description of the auditory satisfactions of (specifically German) poetry: "The ear feels bliss and voluptuousness when it can drink in this euphony of its language with long draughts, when it hears strength and gentle weakness, sweetness and dignity, slowness and speed, noise and silence, movement and decorum blended in tones, when it finds all of these tone colors in the inner construction of the words."[168] Poetry, then, is language created to suit to the capacity for sensory pleasure of the human ear—the most effective poetry will be the poetry in a speaker's or culture's own language. Herder works out the connections between different artistic media and the human senses in the fourth *Kritisches Wäldchen*, his unfinished effort to elaborate a systematic account of the effectiveness of different art media by way of their relation to the senses of sight, sound, and touch.[169] For Herder, any attempt to explain aesthetic experience based on properties of the artwork alone or even on a special sense for formal properties cuts that experience off from the fundamentally human capacities, in particular our senses, that enable it.[170]

The task of aesthetics, then, is to understand how each art form developed from the physiology of the specific sense out of which it arose. Herder argues that three senses are of primary importance to aesthetic perception and experience: hearing, touch, and sight. For purposes of meter and poetry, of course, hearing is the crucial sense, and Herder contends that because European aesthetics has, like its philosophy, been dominated by the sense of sight, it is ill-equipped to give an account of "the pleasurable" for the ears.[171] Herder speculates that a more musical culture with a better understanding of the connection between music and the soul might have developed a "philosophy of tones" with "euphony" rather than "beauty" as its leading term.[172] Although Herder carefully separates the senses in his analysis, he explains that in experience they always interact, and that therefore the concepts

[167] Herder, "Versuch einer Geschichte der Lyrik," 19.
[168] Herder, "Über die neuere deutsche Literatur," 105
[169] Robert Norton, *Herder's Aesthetics and the European Enlightenment* (Ithaca, NY: Cornell University Press, 1991), 139.
[170] Guyer, "18th Century German Aesthetics."
[171] Johann Gottfried Herder, "Kritische Wälder oder Betrachtungen über die Wissenschaft und Kunst des Schönen. Viertes Wäldchen: Über Riedels Theorie der Schönen Künste (1769)," in Pross, *Werke*, 57–240, 96 and 99.
[172] Herder, "Viertes Wäldchen," 99–100.

of both truth and beauty are the result of this interaction.[173] Hence the plurality of aesthetic media, experiences, judgments, and tastes; any science of aesthetics must concern itself with understanding the human sensory capacities from which such judgments and experiences emerge.

This science no longer needs metrical theorizing; understanding poetry is not, as it was in Gottsched, a matter of accounting for relations between verse, genre, and content that align with expert judgments; a *Critische Dichtkunst* no longer requires a catalogue of examples. The very attention to the whole human—including sensation, emotion, reason, and physiology—that made metrical speech such a characteristic example of the interaction between these elements can now proceed straight to theories of those faculties, mirroring Herder's own narrative of the progression to modern culture as one in which poetry becomes philosophy.

* * *

The narrative I have traced from Gottsched to Herder, by way of Breitinger, Baumgarten, and Sulzer, interweaves aesthetics and anthropology, understood as the exploration of all human faculties, ever more tightly. It moves from emphasizing rational cognition alone, with sense perception and aesthetics understood as making an inevitably deficient contribution to knowledge, to a view of sense perception and reason as complementary forms of knowledge, to a valorization of sensation and affect as the key to the moral efficacy of art works. Likewise, it progresses from normative definitions of poetry and beauty based on poetic tradition to "critical" or "philosophical" derivations of each term from human faculties. At the same time, the discipline of aesthetics becomes increasingly independent of detailed description of genres, features, and characteristics of individual artworks in order to delineate its object. Gottsched's critical poetics still demands a catalogue of poetic genres in order to explain what poetry is and how it works; Baumgarten uses the characteristic of metrical language and the feature of imitation to outline a conceptual and terminological gap into which he places the concept of an "aesthetics"; Breitinger subordinates metrical achievement to emotional efficacy; Sulzer argues that verse is natural to poetry, but its presence also requires explanation; Herder turns from artworks to the senses, albeit not without the promise that artworks themselves could be better understood through a more thorough knowledge of the faculties that underlie them.

There are, of course, nuances to this narrative—on the balance of Herder's career, one could hardly accuse him of ignoring particular artists or artworks—but globally speaking, the more poetry in particular and art in general are understood as expressions of the development of human culture or society, the capacities of the human senses, or even the physiology of the species, the less the particularities of

---

[173] Herder, "Viertes Wäldchen," 106.

individual artworks can be taken to define the investigations of aesthetic. It is, then, not a coincidence that metrics become less central to definitions of art and poetry from Gottsched to Herder. The more aesthetic and anthropological dignity meter attains—a dignity underscored by the enormously high stakes of the hexameter debate—the less important particular metrical practice becomes in understanding poetry. Meter becomes merely one feature among others on the sensory side of language used to please or activate the senses. In my next chapter, I turn to Klopstock as offering a counterpoint to this narrative. His theories of poetry are as ambitious, as physiologically rooted, and as culturally specific as any of the theorists' I have analyzed here. But by making metrical efficacy the center of his poetic theorizing, Klopstock maintains an attention to poetic practice and the particularities of bound language that defies the disappearance of metrics into anthropological faculties or aesthetic theories, highlighting the complexity of interplay among language, culture, and the human in its rational and sensory components—that is, the "whole human."

2

Klopstock's Meters as Embodied Meaning

In the previous chapter, I presented the eighteenth-century debate over the possibilities and pitfalls of hexameter in German to demonstrate two crucial arguments of this book. First, the hexameter debate shows that registering or producing a meter is never solely a matter of tallying objectively present syllables according to the phonological givens of a language but is always culturally and historically determined. Second, these cultural and historical determinations reveal the broader cultural politics, aesthetic goals, and anthropological arguments (with their implications for subjectivity) that underly metrical theorizing. I now turn to Klopstock's metrical theory and practice as showing how a historically grounded, non-scientist metrics can illuminate and enrich our own experiences of meter and thus of reading poetry more broadly. Klopstock provides a vocabulary and categories of analysis to understand the complex interaction between poet, meter, content, and listener as a processual feedback loop that develops and builds on its prior moments across the course of a poem.

While I do not contend that every aspect of Klopstock's metrical theory is universally applicable either today or historically, his theory and practice can help us understand our own experiences of metrical language, which have been obscured by the various idea of metrics as arcane technique, as mere objective counting, or as entirely divorced from semantics. This chapter reads Klopstock's metrical theory and practice as an effort to speak to and call forth what the theorists of the previous chapter called the "whole human": a subjectivity that is defined by the interrelation and interaction of body, reason, and affect or sensation. Meter can help recover or create a whole humanity precisely because it is not constituted solely by the phonology of a given language but is instead—like the subjects it seeks—shaped by the interplay between language, culture, and the body. Moreover, the fact that the links between meter, meaning, affect, and body are more flexible and more open than generally acknowledged lets Klopstock's accounts of metrical efficacy avoid the universalizing claim that meters work the same way for every hearer. For most considerations of meter, both historical and contemporary, the fact that, say, dactyls do different things in different places has been taken as evidence that accounts of meter supporting content are illusory; for Klopstock, the fact that (e.g.) dactyls do different things in different places is evidence *for* the varying and complex ways meter supports or can support content. What I call Klopstock's metrical thinking reveals that insisting on some kind of universally applicable iconicity (in

Metrical Claims and Poetic Experience. Hannah Vandegrift Eldridge, Oxford University Press.
© Hannah Vandegrift Eldridge (2022). DOI: 10.1093/oso/9780192859211.003.0003

the Peircean/Saussurean sense) as the only relation between meter and meaning has foreclosed thick description of their interaction in our metrical experience.

2.1 Klopstock's Context and Major Works

Friedrich Gottlieb Klopstock, born in Quedlinburg in 1724, sits somewhat askew to scholarly narratives of eighteenth-century German (-language) literature.[1] Often taken as the initiator of modern German literary and especially poetic language, including the emphatic subjectivity that characterized the "Sturm und Drang" (Storm and Stress),[2] he nonetheless writes within the framework of Baroque humanistic models, particularly in the importance he places on rhetoric.[3] As a religious poet writing in the century of philosophy and the Enlightenment[4], he is often associated with sentimentalism and the overflowing of emotion.[5] Following his education at the famous Schulpforta (at which Fichte and Nietzsche would later be pupils), Klopstock was influenced by the work of Bodmer and Breitinger, in particular their emphasis on the sublime and their loosening of the rules of imitation espoused by Gottsched, with the effects on language discussed in the previous chapter. In part because Klopstock does not fit neatly into accounts of increasing secularization or developing autonomy of art in literary histories of the eighteenth century, he has not enjoyed much critical attention in the last hundred years or so of German Studies, especially in the United States; he is someone whose name everyone knows but whom nobody has read much of, with the exception of a few frequently anthologized poems.

Klopstock's literary projects are unusually heterogeneous. Possibly the most influential of his works are the poems in free rhythms he published during the 1750s, which opened up the possibility of free-verse poetry in German for the generations that followed him. (Goethe's early lyric, Hölderlin, Nietzsche, and Expressionists such as Gottfried Benn and Georg Trakl are all unthinkable without Klopstock's innovations.) The work that made his reputation is the Christian hexameter epic The Messiah (Der Messias), whose twenty cantos were published between 1748 and 1773, and which for many theorists established unequivocally that hexameter in German was not only possible but could be combined with a high degree of poetic achievement. In the early 1760s, Klopstock adapts antique

---

[1] See e.g. Kevin Hilliard and Katrin Kohl, "Einleitung," in Wort und Schrift: Das Werk Friedrich Gottlieb Klopstocks, eds. Kevin Hilliard and Katrin Kohl, Hallesche Forschungen 27 (Tübingen: Niemeyer, 2008), 1–5.

[2] See e.g. Eric A. Blackall, The Emergence of German as a Literary Language, 1700–1775 (Cambridge: Cambridge University Press, 1959).

[3] Kevin Hilliard, Philosophy, Letters, and the Fine Arts in Klopstock's Thought (London: Institute of Germanic Studies, 1987).

[4] Hilliard and Kohl, "Einleitung," 5.

[5] See e.g. Hilliard, Philosophy, Letters, and the Fine Arts, 25.

odes to German and invents some thirty new ode strophes, which emerge from several years of intensive metrical theorizing;[6] during this time, he combines his interest in antique meters with attention to old Germanic or so-called "Bardic" forms, even asserting that he has found hexameters occurring naturally in the Old-Saxon "Heliands-Lied" written in alliterative verse (*Stabreim*).[7] In addition to writing several types of religious text (dramas based on Biblical stories and hymn strophes intended to be sung to Luther's chorales), Klopstock also engages extensively with cultural politics and pedagogy, including a grammar in dialogue form and a set of spelling reforms designed to make written German closer to the language as it was spoken.[8] All of these projects bespeak his focus on hearing and sound, rather than writing and reading, and his rejection of theoretical systematicity.

Although Klopstock considers metrical questions over a span of more than fifty years in letters, essays, dialogues, odes, and epigrams, he never completed a systematic metrics, tending instead to publish pieces as "fragments" that incorporate sections of essays started far earlier and intended for publication in other contexts.[9] Questions of hexameter serve as his primary point of entry into theoretical debates, since they foreground problems of prosody and adaptation of ancient meters; he theorizes very little about his free-verse poems and not much about his adaptations of antique ode forms, in part because both found widespread critical acceptance.[10] In addition to their fragmentary and patchwork qualities, Klopstock's texts on metrical theory are made difficult by his somewhat laconic

---

[6] For the argument that this period represents the high point of Klopstock's metrical innovations, and was the source from which he drew much of his metrical practice and, later, metrical theory. See Hans-Heinrich Hellmuth, *Metrische Erfindung und metrische Theorie bei Klopstock* (Munich: Wilhelm Fink Verlag, 1973), 58ff.

[7] See Mark Emanuel Amtstätter, *Beseelte Töne. Die Sprache des Körpers und der Dichtung in Klopstocks Eislaufoden*, Studien und Texte zur Sozialgeschichte der Literatur 107 (Berlin: De Gruyter, 2005) for a discussion of the influence of the Heliand-Lied on Klopstock's ode strophes.

[8] The *Grammatische Gespräche* (Grammatical Conversations, Altoona: 1794) and "Über die deutsche Rechtschreibung" (On German Orthography, 1774). Other projects addressed to German cultural and political life included the *Deutsche Gelehrtenrepublik* (The German Republic of Letters), published in 1774, which envisioned an elaborate structure of government by guilds of artist elites. (Friedrich Gottlieb Klopstock, "Die Deutsche Gelehrtenrepublik. Ihre Einrichtung, Ihre Gesetze, Geschichte des letzten Landtags," in *Friedrich Gottlieb Klopstock. Ausgewählte Werke*, ed. Karl August Schleiden [Munich: Carl Hanser Verlag, 1962], 875–929). These projects can tip into bloodthirsty nationalism; although much of Klopstock's German chauvinism appears to be linguistic, not nationalist, as a spur to the German *Kulturnation* to produce literary works equal not only to their modern European counterparts but to the Ancient Greek world (see e.g. Katrin Kohl, *Friedrich Gottlieb Klopstock* [Stuttgart: Metzler Verlag, 2000], 17–9), his Germanophilia is clearly nationalist in the most violent possible vein in his *Hermann* dramas (see e.g. Mark-Georg Dehrmann, "Klopstocks totaler Krieg - Zur Neuedition von Klopstocks Hermann-Dramen": literaturkritik.de," accessed July 5, 2022, https://literaturkritik.de/id/14395).

[9] Hellmuth, *Metrische Erfindung*, 18–9; thus parts of an "Abhandlung vom Sylbenmaasse" ("Treatise on Metrics") started in 1764 to make their way into the *Gelehrtenrepublik*, the *Grammatische Gespräche*, and the second half of *"Vom deutschen Hexameter"* (On German Hexameter, 1779), Hellmuth, *Metrische Erfindung*, 35).

[10] Hellmuth, *Metrische Erfindung*, 45.

writing style and a reluctance to engage in theoretical debate at all, asserting that poetic achievement should speak for itself; when he finally does answer the charges of other authors, he is polemical.[11] Klopstock's frequent use of dialogue form enables him to present opposing positions, but since he repeatedly struggles to resolve tensions between traditional metrics and his own theoretical inventions and poetic practice, his texts remain conflicted, occasionally even contradictory, and open-ended.[12] I do not, therefore, attempt to present a systematic account of the development of Klopstock's metrical theory across his career, nor do I offer an overview of every treatment of metrics in his essays, dialogues, epigrams, odes, and treatises. Instead, I sift through Klopstock's writings on metrics to elaborate the key elements of his theory and practice, focusing especially on the idea of *Mitausdruck* or co-expression as a resource for conceptualizing and articulating metrical experience.

2.2 Klopstock's Metrical Thinking

Mitausdruck

Leiserer, lauterer Mitausdruck der Gedanken des Liedes
Sei die Bewegung des Verses. Sooft er diesem Gesetz nicht
Treu und hold ist, gehet er nur, um zu gehn; und verirrter
Tritt er einher, wenn er gar anwandert gegen den Inhalt.
Doch stets treuen Gehorsam verbieten nicht wenige Worte,
Und die Stellungen, welche der Sinn und die Leidenschaften
    ordnen,
Auch Gedanken, die dem Verein mit Bewegung sich weigern.
Deutsche, strebet, ihr könnts, nach dem Kranze der seltensten
    Untreu![13]

[Softer yet, louder still co-expression of the thoughts of the song
May the movement of verse be. Whenever to this law
It is not true and fair, it walks only to walk; and further
It strays, if it stumbles against the content.
But not paltry few words forbid full faithful obedience,
And the placings that order the sense and the feelings and
    passions,
And there are thoughts that refuse to combine with the movement.

---

[11] Hellmuth, *Metrische Erfindung*, 20–1.
[12] Hellmuth, *Metrische Erfindung*, 19.
[13] Klopstock, Friedrich Gottlieb. *Epigramme. Text und Apparat.* ed. Klaus von Hurlebusch (Berlin: de Gruyter, 1982), 54.

Germans, strive for, you'll reach it, the wreath of least frequent
betrayal!]

(My translation)

This epigram, written sometime between 1795 and 1803, introduces the central tenet of Klopstock's metrical theory and practice: verse is a kind of movement (*Bewegung*) that should be, to varying degrees, *Mitausdruck* (coexpression) of the thoughts or semantic content of a poem. Klopstock coalesces this definition into a single sentence in his dialogue grammar: "Meter is co-expression through movement" ("Silbenmaß ist Mitausdruck durch Bewegung").[14] *Mitausdruck* is Klopstock's neologism for the complex interrelation between specific expression in language (including word choice, word order, sound, and meter) and the ideas expressed; given the curious neologism, I use the German term throughout. Crucially, Klopstock holds that this is not a relationship of preordained correspondence (or non-correspondence) but an interaction created anew in each text. This chapter's primary goal is to understand how such coexpression works in the mutual influencing of content (understood as both affectual/emotional and conceptual, as the epigram's use of "senses" and "passions" reveals[15]) and verse practice. *Mitausdruck*, I argue, provides a framework for understanding our metrical experiences as meaning-bearing in complex ways that go beyond the unidirectional subordination of sound to sense.

Several other explications and qualifications of the conception of the movement of verse as *Mitausdruck* appear in the epigram and help underscore its complexity. First, the epigram uses metaphors of volume (louder, softer) to describe the degree of *Mitausdruck*, again implying the priority of spoken over written language and also indirectly insisting on the material presence of poetic expression. (Curiously, "lauterer" can also mean "purer," shifting the idea of degrees of *Mitausdruck* into a different register.) Second, Klopstock literalizes the canonical metaphor of meter as consisting of *feet* and poetry as gait (again, of course, making assumptions about bodies and their movement), which locates verse as *Bewegung* in the body and anticipates his use of the term *Bewegung* both for the movement of language in poetic production and for the affective response of hearer reception. Moreover, he distinguishes between verse as *Mitausdruck* and verse for technique's sake (that "gehet ... nur, um zu gehn"/ walks only to walk). Although the epigram enters an implicit critique of the latter, Klopstock develops an account of the pleasure and significance produced by the repetition of (initially) contentless verse forms, making them bearers of indirect meaning. But he also, in the epigram and elsewhere,

---

[14] Klopstock, *Grammatische Gespräche*, 146
[15] See also Torsten Hoffmann's discussion of G.E. Lessing's irate comment that Klopstock "calls *thinking* what other honest people call *feeling*" (cited in Torsten Hoffmann, *Körperpoetiken: Zur Funktion des Körpers in der Dichtungstheorie des 18. Jahrhunderts* [Munich: Wilhelm Fink Verlag, 2015], 154, my translation).

acknowledges the difficulty of attaining full convergence between verse movement and content, and relativizes the law ("Gesetz") of adherence to content by modifying the goal to the least frequent transgression ("der seltensten Untreu"). In calling for the following of this law, he makes a culturally or linguistically specific appeal to Germans to strive for metrical achievement. Finally, the poem erases any decisive distinction between metrical theory and practice by presenting metrical principles in poetic form. In what follows, I present the aspects of Klopstock's understanding of meter that show how such *Mitausdruck* works, in particular how it relies on and indeed celebrates subjective experience, associative or metaphorical thought, and embodied particularity.

Subjectivity of Metrical Experience

Klopstock's most extended theoretical rumination on meter is the 1779 text "Vom deutschen Hexameter" (On German Hexameter), which aggregates much of his metrical thought up to that point.[16] The text responds to and quotes extensively from Gottfried August Bürger's anti-hexameter polemic in defense of his own iambic translation of the *Iliad*.[17] But in fact only the first half of "On German Hexameter" deals directly with issues of hexameter adaptation; the second shifts to an elaboration of Klopstock's own metrical principles, originally developed as part of an essay called "Abhandlung vom Sylbenmaaße" (Treatise on Meter) begun in 1764. Like much of Klopstock's writing on poetry, "On German Hexameter" prioritizes specific examples over abstract rules and poetic practice over theoretical consistency.[18] He also emphasizes the impossibility of full congruence between meter and content, which he now calls "perfect or complete [*vollendete*] metrical beauty" ("Vom deutschen Hexameter" 152): even Homer, he contends, falls short of that goal, and "overall, 'more often' or 'less often' and 'more' or 'less' are so operative here, and the goal, that of complete metrical beauty of verse, is so

[16] Hellmuth, *Metrische Erfindung*, 55. Since the critical historical (Hamburg) edition has not yet published the text, I use the edition by Winfried Menninghaus (Klopstock, Friedrich Gottlieb, "'Vom deutschen Hexameter,'" in *Gedanken über die Natur der Poesie. Dichtungstheoretische Schriften*, ed. Winfried Menninghaus (Frankfurt a.M.: insel taschenbuch, 1989), 60–157)and subsequently cite in the text as "'Vom deutschen Hexameter.'" All translations are mine.

[17] Gottfried August Bürger, "An einen Freund über seine teutsche Illias," in *Die Lehre von der Nachahmung der antiken Versmaße im Deutschen. In Quellenschriften des 18. und 19. Jahrhunderts. Mit kommentierter Bibliographie*, eds. Hans-Heinrich Hellmuth and Joachim Schröder (Munich: Wilhelm Fink Verlag, 1976), 158–71; see my discussion in Chapter 1, Section 1.2.4 (Anti-Hexametrists).

[18] Curiously, Klopstock's own hexameter practice does not exhibit the fit between metrical units and semantic content that he elaborates here. Hellmuth argues that this is likely because Klopstock's metrical theories are derived from his ode strophe inventions, and not from hexameter, which was an inherited meter and thus constrained him more than did the metrical forms he invented and used starting in the early 1760s; Hellmuth contends that "Vom deutschen Hexameter" is to some extent a theoretical ossification of Klopstock's practice into a system ex post facto (Hellmuth, *Metrische Erfindung*, 263).

unreachable that one can be quite far from it and still be second [only to Homer]" ("Vom deutschen Hexameter" 152). As in the epigram, Klopstock acknowledges that the goal cannot be fully reached; he focuses on comparatives (more often or more seldom, more or less) as what count or are valid (*gelten*) in poetic achievement.

Moreover, Klopstock insists on and indeed celebrates the subjectivity of metrical experiences, as he focuses on the interaction of perception and effect with phonological givens. In fragments from the unpublished "Treatise on Meter" he explains that he is interested primarily in the expressive capacities of verse, its "influences on our soul."[19] In "On German Hexameter," he points out that the strict ratio of two short syllables to one long syllable in Greek meters does not apply to German, and gives two sentences that, according to durational rules, should be "gleichzeitig" (of equal time): "Wut, Wehklag', Angstausruf laut aufscholl von dem Schlachtfeld" and "Eile dahin, wo die Lanz und das Schwert im Gedräng dich erwarten" ("Fury, woeful lament, cry of fear ring forth from the battlefield" and "Hurry there, where the lance and the sword in the crowds await you," "Vom deutschen Hexameter" 133). But, he continues, we hear them as different: "Who does not hear very different durations in them, great slowness in the first, and much speed in the second?" ("Vom deutschen Hexameter" 133) He includes a semantic cue for speed in the second example, the command *Eile* (hurry), indicating the way semantic and metrical impressions influence one another. Using an analogy of the perception of time, he explains "It is a similar case, (I do not say an *identical* one, because in language long and long, short and short are not exactly the same), when one hour seems long to us, another passes by quickly. It depends not at all on what is an hour by the clock, but what it is according to our conception" ("Vom deutschen Hexameter" 133). Klopstock does not abandon duration entirely, but he insists on the importance of subjective-perceptual criteria in any analysis of the effects of meter.

Indeed, Klopstock criticizes those who attend only to theory and not to the effects of poetry: "One sees that I approach the matter from the side of its effects. I know very well that one does this quite seldom in theoretical questions of the arts; but I also know that precisely this tendency has led to no little confusion and error" ("Vom deutschen Hexameter" 135). Attention only to theory in abstraction from effect on hearers causes "confusion and error." Klopstock holds that metrical theories miss the most important aspects of their object when they focus only on rules (recalling his relativization of his own laws with "mehr oder weniger") and neglect experience.

---

[19] Archival MS # F_2, KN 41, 343^V, cited in Hellmuth, *Metrische Erfindung*, 224. In the afterword to his edition of Klopstock's poetological texts, Menninghaus describes Klopstock's awareness of meter as suspended between "mechanical" and "subjective-phenomenological" poles. (Winfried Menninghaus, "Klopstocks Poetik der schnellen 'Bewegung,'" in Menninghaus, *Gedanken über die Natur der Poesie. Dichtungstheoretische Schriften*, 259–361, here 302–3).

Klopstock's Terminology: *Wortfüße, Zeitausdruck, Tonverhalt*

Klopstock's attention to perception underpins perhaps his primary metrical innovation, a shift in the units of metrical counting from canonically defined feet (dactyls, spondees, iambs, etc.), which he calls "Versfüße" or "künstliche Füße" ("verse feet" or "artificial feet"), to what he calls "Wortfüße" or "word feet." This shift is crucial in understanding how *Mitausdruck* works in Klopstock's metrical thinking. Whereas a verse or artificial foot is, per Klopstock, a matter of "alternations and sequences" that "supposedly lie hidden in the words," word feet consist of as many words as are heard as one unit according to their content ("Vom deutschen Hexameter" 130).[20] He contrasts the verse feet and word feet in a line of hexameter, giving the verse feet first (Figure 2.1).

There are six artificial feet (five dactyls and a spondee), but only four word feet.[21] Klopstock justifies this innovation by arguing that the hearer will not perceive the artificial feet, only the word feet, and it is thus useless to theorize about the effects of the former: "The artificial feet hidden in the word-feet do not concern the hearer at all. He doesn't hear them; he only hears the word-feet; and makes his judgment about the verse based only on them" ("Vom deutschen Hexameter" 131). Three points are worth noting here in the vocabulary of contemporary metrical theory (rather than Klopstock's' terminology): first, the word-foot theory implies absolute convergence between a metrical schema and its prosodic-phonological

Fig. 2.1 Word feet and verse feet in hexameter (Adapted from Klopstock, *Vom deutschen Hexameter*, 130)

[20] He qualifies that some words (the examples he gives have four and five syllables) are too long to be linked with others, and holds that they are their own word foot ("Vom deutschen Hexameter" 130).

[21] "Terribly rang the winged thunder-song in the army's hordes." In the interest of space and clarity, I have modified Klopstock's formatting (he puts each foot on a separate indented line; I have consolidated them onto one line with the feet separated by |). Although Klopstock holds that there are durational components in German verse (as I discuss below), he also insists that German hexameter cannot and should not fully follow Greek rules; I consequently use the scansion markings for German accentual meters from my first chapter, rather than those I used for verse that purported to use exclusively durational components.

realization,[22] since it is, second, based on specific semantic units that fill in the syllables.[23] Third, although Klopstock does not seem to realize it, this adaptation reflects the phonological particularities of German, which has much more strongly marked word boundaries than Ancient Greek or Latin.[24] Thus, although Klopstock makes the argument for his new unit of analysis based solely on perception, it also hints at his consistent combination of semantics and meter and at his arguments for meters that fit the particularities of the language in which they are used.

The unit of the word foot forms the basis for Klopstock's analysis of verse and its impact as movement or "Bewegung," which should be the *Mitausdruck* of the poem's content. To explain the expressive work done by the word feet, Klopstock divides their movement into two components: what he calls "Zeitausdruck" (time expression) and "Tonverhalt" (tone/accent relation). While *Zeit* in *Zeitausdruck* refers fairly unambiguously to duration, *Ton* has multiple meanings: it can refer to sound (as in *tönen*, to sound/resound) or to accent (as in *Betonung*—emphasis, stress, or accentuation). Once again, given Klopstock's neologisms and their ambiguities, I use the German terms. Klopstock thus recognizes both durational and accentual components; he combines them, however, with semantic cues and asserts that the latter will outweigh both in determining which syllables most appropriately fill long/emphasized slots in his metrical structures.[25]

Zeitausdruck refers to the ratio of long and short syllables in a metrical unit: "The movement of the words is either fast or slow. It has, viewed from this perspective, *Zeitausdruck*. This designates primarily sensory-material qualities, and then also certain qualities of sensation or passion" ("Vom deutschen Hexameter" 126). A word foot with many long syllables is slower than one with more short syllables.[26] *Zeitausdruck's* expressive qualities work primarily by way of analogy or association: *Zeitausdruck* "expresses something of sensation or passion only in so far as slowness or speed are qualities thereof" ("Vom deutschen Hexameter" 136). Speed or slowness can be a quality of verse that matches qualities of the emotion,

---

[22] See Mark Emanuel Amtstätter, *Beseelte Töne. Die Sprache des Körpers und der Dichtung in Klopstocks Eislaufoden*, Studien und Texte zur Sozialgeschichte der Literatur 107 (Berlin: De Gruyter, 2005), 33.

[23] See Hellmuth, *Metrische Erfindung*, 77 for a discussion of how the combination of semantic and phonological criteria for designating metrical units makes it difficult to apply Klopstock's theory outside his own work.

[24] Remigius Bunia, *Metrik und Kulturpolitik. Opitz, Klopstock, Bürger* (Berlin: Rippenger und Kremers Verlag, 2014), 213–4.

[25] Hellmuth (*Metrische Erfindung*, 224) and Menninghaus ("Klopstocks Poetik," 296–7) corroborate the blending of length- and accent-based scansion; Menninghaus ("Klopstocks Poetik," 298) and Amtstätter (*Beseelte Töne* 34–5) emphasize the priority of semantic considerations in the ultimate determination of what Klopstock calls "Länge."

[26] Klopstock focuses not on the static ratio of long to short syllables but on the variation in that ratio across feet and lines, meaning that *Zeitausdruck* can be "steigend" (rising), "fallend" (falling), or "schwebend" (hovering), which he uses to mean wavering between slower and faster ("Vom deutschen Hexameter," 130ff.).

thought, or object depicted, and Klopstock later adds that these associations can also be somewhat looser: "That which is related in a certain proximity to the slow or the fast belongs to that which *Zeitausdruck* comprises" ("Vom deutschen Hexameter" 136). He gives the example of Homer using a slow spondaic hexameter to express heaviness of the food laden on a table ("Vom deutschen Hexameter" 136); the associative connection between slowness and weight makes the slow *Zeitausdruck* appropriate to the heavy-laden table.

As the focus on syllable duration indicates, the concept of *Zeitausdruck* fits quite smoothly with traditional durational metrics and emerges relatively early in Klopstock's metrical theorizing.[27] *Tonverhalt*, on the other hand, does not appear as a specific term until the publication of "On German Hexameter" in 1779 and seems to have accentual components, making it difficult to reconcile with the categories Klopstock inherited from classical metrical theory. Klopstock recognizes the possibility of different types of metrical efficacy at least by the 1764 draft of the "Treatise on Meter," where the characters in the dialogue debate whether the *order* in which syllables appear plays a role in the effect of verse on the hearer, or merely the *number* of long and short syllables.[28] As defined in "On German Hexameter," *Tonverhalt* describes the "agreeing, or contrasting, relations [of longs and shorts] among each other" ("Vom deutschen Hexameter" 126). Both the name (Ton*verhalt*) and the definition (relations, *Verhältnisse*) emphasize relation and proportion, but with connotations of conduct, behavior, or decorum; Adelung's dictionary notes that *Verhältnis* "expresses all of what in Latin is expressed by *respectus, relatio* and *proportio*."[29] Name and definition thus already hint at potential affective expressiveness of arrangement.

Klopstock's presentation of the ways in which *Tonverhalt* is or can be expressive of content is more difficult to follow than the connotations of *Zeitausdruck*. He explains that "The gentle, the strong, the lively/cheerful, the vehement, the solemn/majestic, and the uneasy/turbulent are, or can be, qualities of sensation or passion. This seems to me to be the embodiment of that which *Tonverhalt* can express" ("Vom deutschen Hexameter" 136). First, Klopstock describes the different kinds of *Tonverhalt* in affective/content-bearing terms (mild, strong, cheerful, vehement, solemn, majestic, and uneasy), as opposed to the more material fast and slow of *Zeitausdruck*. Moreover, he foregrounds their role as qualities (*Beschaffenheiten*) of sensation and passion (*Empfindung und Leidenschaft*), rather than as material-sensory qualities whose association with content beyond speed or slowness is metaphorical. He does, however, also see the possibility of metaphorical

---

[27] Hellmuth, *Metrische Erfindung*, 224–5.

[28] Hellmuth *Metrische Erfindung* 236–8. Hellmuth also reproduces the (as yet unpublished) fragments from the Klopstock archive.

[29] Johann Christoph Adelung, "Verhältniß," in *Grammatisch-kritisches Wörterbuch der Hochdeutschen Mundart mit beständiger Vergleichung der übrigen Mundarten, besonders aber der oberdeutschen* (Leipzig, 1793-1801), columns 1057–60.

"Sanftes" : "/ x / x x lieblichtönende."	"x / x x / x des Baches Gelispel."
["Mild" : "/ x / x x lovely ringing."	"x / x x / x the brook's whispers."]
"Starkes" : "x / / der Ausruf."	"x x x / / / da es vom Sturm aufbraust."
["Strong" : "x / / the outcry."	"x x x / / / as it flares up from the storm."]
"Muntres" : "x x / x x der geflügelte."	"/ x x / x Silbergewölke."
["Cheerful" : "x x / x x the winged."	"/ x x / x silver clouds."]

Fig. 2.2 Word feet by *Tonverhalt* (Adapted from Klopstock, *Vom deutschen Hexameter*, 138)

associations with the qualities listed as *Tonverhalte*: "That which stands in a certain proximity to the listed qualities also belongs to that which *Tonverhalt* encompasses" ("Vom deutschen Hexameter" 136). *Tonverhalt*, comprising seven attributes and their metaphorical associations, thus appears to have considerably greater expressive range than *Zeitausdruck*.[30]

But Klopstock never explains why these seven attributes are those that can be expressed by particular syllables in particular orders or relations to one another, and instead of defining (e.g.) a "munterer Tonverhalt" (cheerful tone relation) via abstract characteristics, he lists several word feet that, in his view, exhibit the *Tonverhalt* in question. Moreover, all of the examples given contain words whose content fits, either directly or metaphorically, with the "Tonverhalt" (Figure 2.2).[31]

Word feet with the same *Tonverhalt* tend to share several characteristics: those listed under "Sanftes" (mild or gentle), for example, have frequent [x /] or [/ x] alternation and all of the examples listed end on a short/unstressed syllable; word feet described as "Starkes" (strong) often have two more of one type of syllable in a row and almost all end on a long/stressed syllable. "Heftiges" (vehement) uses frequent alternation and usually ends on a long/stressed syllabe, [/]. "Ernstes" (solemn) exhibits a high ratio of [/] to [x] and ends on either; "Feierliches" (majestic) has a similar ratio to "Ernstes" but all of the examples end on [x]. In the restless *Tonverhalt* ("Unruhiges"), all of the example feet have sharply contrasting groups of [x] and [/] and in my subjective estimation seem more difficult to pronounce ("tödliches Geschoß" [deadly missile] "der abtrünnige" [the reprobate]) ("Vom deutschen Hexameter" 138-9). In keeping with Klopstock's emphasis on

---

[30] For corroboration on this point, and the development of the idea of *Tonverhalt* in Klopstock's work, see Hellmuth, *Metrische Erfindung*, 256ff.

[31] All examples are from "Vom deutschen Hexameter," 138. Since the scansion is clearly marked in German, I have not attempted to maintain it in my translations, because to do so would distort the semantic connections I am trying to point out. Moreover, all of Klopstock's terms are adjectives turned into nouns, e.g. "The Mild" rather than "Mild." This is much more unusual in English than in German, and so I have translated to the adjectival form.

practice, effect, and subjective perception, however, there is no abstract principle or definition that can be extended to all the examples in a group, much less from his identifications of specific *Tonverhalte* to other poets or theorists.

Movement: *Wortbewegung*

I have listed Klopstock's examples and my proposed commonalities between them at some length to illustrate the kind of search for patterns and connections that Klopstock's metrical thinking invites his readers to undertake. The thought that relations of syllables might be lulling or clashing or solemn exemplifies the kind of metaphorical associations with syllable patterns he strives to elicit, and his use of examples that include words whose connotations correspond to the affect of the *Tonverhalt* mentioned illustrates how for him semantic and material qualities interact. Both, as will become clear, direct the hearer's or reader's attention, and, in the ideal situation of production and reception, will support one another for rapid conceptual, emotional, and even corporeal efficacy.

The semantic elements working into the definition of Klopstock's various *Tonverhalte* already suggest the degree to which both *Zeitausdruck* and *Tonverhalt* complicate the relation between meter and content. Klopstock's discussion of the way *Tonverhalt* and *Zeitausdruck* interact makes clear that the expressiveness of *Mitausdruck* need not always mean a direct, iconographic relation between *Zeitausdruck*, *Tonverhalt*, and semantic meaning. Moreover, his discussion begins to show that and how our attention to metrical expressiveness is and should be semantically directed. He explains that *Zeitausdruck* and *Tonverhalt* always work simultaneously, but too much of one destroys the effect of the other: "*Zeitausdruck* and *Tonverhalt* are always together and work simultaneously; but this only under the condition that neither of the two is *noticeably stronger* than the other. For in this case the effect of the weaker one ceases" ("Vom deutschen Hexameter" 128, italics in original). If *Tonverhalt* and *Zeitausdruck* are in balance, they work together. But, conveniently, when only one of the two fits with the content of the verse, the hearer disregards the other: "As soon as only the *Zeitausdruck*, or only the *Tonverhalt* fits with the ideas; then the fitting one rings out, so that the other will not be noticed over it" ("Vom deutschen Hexameter" 149). He gives examples in which only one of *Tonverhalt* or *Zeitausdruck* fits the content of the line but prioritizes the ideal working together of *Zeitausdruck* and *Tonverhalt* to fit content. Klopstock's description of the way whichever of *Zeitausdruck* or *Tonverhalt* fits semantically obscures whichever of the two does not fit shows his understanding of the semantic steering of attention to meter, which, for him, should be used to poetic advantage.

The interaction between *Zeitausdruck* and *Tonverhalt* is what Klopstock calls *Wortbewegung* (word movement), and it is for him the most important part of metrics: "This is the extent of what I call word movement. It is the main task for verse practice" ("Vom deutschen Hexameter" 128). To sum up the components of Klopstock's metrical theory thus far, then, verse consists of word feet (*Wortfüße*), which are semantic-phonological groupings not of syllables but of words. Word feet possess the qualities of time expression (*Zeitausdruck*) and tone relation (*Tonverhalt*), which are both conditioned by and condition the expression of content as the hearer perceives it. They interact to create movement (*Bewegung*), a word that gestures both toward material-phonological unfolding of syllables across time and to the affective impact of those syllables in their material and semantic identities. And *Bewegung*, as the epigram that I cited at the outset of this chapter asserts, must strive to be coexpression of the thoughts (*Gedanken*, including sensation, "Sinn," and passion, "Leidenschaften") of the poem. That *Mitausdruck* is not a one-way relation between content and meters that universally fit that content's connotations begins to emerge in the emphasis on subjective perception, the possibility of metaphorical rather than iconic correlations between meter and content in both *Zeitausdruck* and *Tonverhalt*, and the semantic steering of their perception.

Functions and Effects of *Mitausdruck*

The question of expressive or affective qualities of organizations of syllables raised by Klopstock's theory of *Mitausdruck* also requires him to introduce several distinctions and qualifications to ensure that verse does not become separate from or even dominant over the content of the poem. A generation later, in romanticism, the autonomy of sound, largely in rhyme and assonance, will become a primary poetic goal; Klopstock, as the epigram I cited to open this chapter makes clear, rejects the idea of autonomous poetic materiality.[32] First, Klopstock distinguishes sharply between meter ("Silbenmaß" or his term, word movement, "Wortbewegung") and sound ("Klang" or sometimes, confusingly, "Ton"). And he recognizes that because true onomatopoeia is rare, sound can only occasionally support content directly, making it less important to expression:

> Euphony, or the sound of words as it fits overall or in particular to the content, through strength or gentleness, euphony is not unimportant to verse practice at

---

[32] Here I differ strongly from Menninghaus, who sees Klopstock as suggesting the autonomy of metrical efficacy. This is because Menninghaus operates with a strict dichotomy between formal autonomy and correlation with meaning, whereas I show that Klopstock works with a range of connections between semantic meaning and formal expressiveness. I do agree that the exploration of this range is a step on the way to romanticism's valorization of *Sprachmusik*. On the distinction between Klopstock and poetics of musicality, see also Joh. Nikolaus Schneider, *Ins Ohr geschrieben. Lyrik als akustische Kunst zwischen 1750 und 1800* (Wallstein Verlag, 2004), 138.

all; but it is of weaker expression [than movement]. Moreover it is rarely found in detail. For there are really not many words in languages whose sound agrees with their sense.

("Vom deutschen Hexameter" 128)

He acknowledges that euphony has some role to play in verse and uses the terms "Sanftes" (mildness) and "Stärke" (strength), both of which also refer to tone relations, to describe the potential correlation between sound and content, but prioritizes *Bewegung* (a phenomenon of meter not euphony) as a bearer of expression.

Later Klopstock will suggest that even when the sounds of the words directly conflict with the content (*Wortsinn*), they can be pleasing as "leerer Schall" that is "für das Ohr allein da" (empty sound, there for the ear alone, "Vom deutschen Hexameter" 100). But this pleasure remains subordinate to the *Mitausdruck* of metrical movement, at least officially: in an epigram that recalls the one with which I opened this chapter, Klopstock stages an argument between "Silbenmaß" and "Wohlklang."

> Silbenmaß, ich weiche dir nicht, behaupte mich, ziehe
> Dir mich vor! "Wohlklang, ich liebe das Streiten nicht. Besser
> Horchen wir jeder mit wachem Ohr dem Gesetz', und vereinen
> Fest uns. Wir sind alsdann die zweyte Seele der Sprache."[33]

> Verse measure, I won't give way to you, give you preference to me;
>   I assert
> myself here! "Euphony, I do not love fighting. Better
> We each obey the law with alert ears, and unite
> Ourselves firmly. Thereupon we are the second soul of language."

(My translation)

Euphony speaks first, but the vehemence with which it ("he," in the personifications supported by German noun genders) asserts itself suggests it challenges a general view or preconception of the primacy of meter. Moreover, in the context of Klopstock's other remarks on meter and sound, the admonition of *Silbenmaß* to follow the law (the phrase drops the usual prefix "ge" from "gehorchen," to obey, making it identical to "horchen," "to listen") and unite, rather than argue, reads as the *noblesse oblige* of the dominant party. The final sentence, asserting that unified meter and euphony are the "second soul of language," echoes the doubling in Mit*ausdruck*; the material elements of language serve a coexpressive purpose to the ideas and emotions of the poem.

[33] "Der doppelte Mitausdruck" (Double coexpression), Friedrich Gottlieb Klopstock. *Epigramme. Text und Apparat.* Ed. Klaus von Hurlebusch (Berlin: de Gruyter, 1982), 53.

Klopstock formulates the interrelation of euphony, meter, emotion, and images as a type of content in the earlier programmatic ode "Der Bach," which establishes an extended parallel between poetry and the flowing of water from a spring to a stream swelling into a river ("Quelle," "Bach," "Strom") in the first two strophes. In the first published edition, the third strophe names euphony and verse explicitly:

> Wohllaut gefällt, Bewegung noch mehr;
> Zur Gespielin gab dem Herzen ich sie.
> Diesem säumt, eilet sie nach; Bildern folgt,
> Leiseren Tritts, ferne sie nur. (12–15)[34]

The movement of verse has greater powers of pleasing than euphony; verse, too, has a closer relation to affect (the heart) than it does to images ("Bilder" can mean metaphorical associations, or any mental representations in the content of a poem). Meter's power comes from its association with affect.

In the later (1798) edition of the poem, Klopstock adds a discussion of the creation of content prior to the strophe I cited and follows it with a more detailed description of metrical movement:

> Inhalt, den volle Seel', im Erguß
> Der Erfindung, und der innersten Kraft,
> Sich entwirft, strömet; allein lebend muß,
> Will es ihm nahn, tönen das Wort.
> ...
> So säumet, und so eilt sie nicht nur:
> Auch empfindungsvolle Wendung beseelt
> Ihr den Tanz, Tragung, die spricht, ihr den Tanz
> All ihr Gelenk schwebt in Verhalt.[35]

No matter how abundantly content flows forth from the soul, the word must be alive if it is to correspond to (or coexpress) that content. The verse describing euphony, movement, heart, and image now elaborates on what it means for words to be alive. In the next strophe, Klopstock returns to the words "säumen" and

---

[34] "Euphony pleases, movement still more/ To the heart as a playmate I gave her/ She tarries and hurries after it; images/ she follows in soft steps, at a distance." Klopstock, Friedrich Gottlieb, "Der Bach," in *Oden*, ed. Horst Gronemeyer and Klaus Hurlebusch, vol. 1, 2 vols. (Berlin: de Gruyter, 2010), 270–5. The critical edition, which I cite here, gives the 1771 version and the 1798 version on facing paces; I discuss both and cite using the abbreviation HKA I.1 [page #]. For the entire poem and my translation, see the appendix ("Poems and Translations").

[35] "Content, which the full soul in its outpouring/ of invention, and of the innermost force/ creates for itself, streams; but being alive/ The word must resound, if it will approach." / "Not only does it tarry so, hurry so/ But also turn [expression] full of feeling ensouls/ its dance, speaking bearing, its dance/ All its joints sway in relation." HKA I.1, 271

"eilen" used to describe the relation between the tarrying heart and the hurry-ing meter and contrasts them to a more sensitive expressiveness. In a note to the later edition he explains "the former the *Zeitausdruck*, the latter the *Tonverhalt*"; "eilen" (tarrying) and "säumen" (hurrying) thus refer to increase and decrease of speed in time expression.

Here, as in "On German Hexameter," *Tonverhalt* is more complicated; Klop-stock describes it first as "turn [Wendung] full of feeling" that "ensouls" the dance of meter. Moreover, the word "Wendung" can refer either to the physical move-ment of turning or twisting or to (as in English) a turn of phrase or linguistic expression (*Redewendung*). The next clause calls what the note clarifies as *Ton-verhalt* "Tragung, die spricht"; a nominalization of the verb "tragen," whose more relevant definitions include to carry, hold, bear, or support, describing *Tonver-halt* as a vehicle of expression that is itself expressive. Finally, the poem depicts metrical movement, personified as female via the gender of *Bewegung*, as dance, emphasizing that movement by repeating the phrase (a word-foot) "Ihr den Tanz" [/x/, her dance, the dance for/of her] twice in a single line. This underscores the symmetrical structure of each of the last two lines in Klopstock's ode schema in the ode, which he gives at the beginning (as shown in figure 2.3):

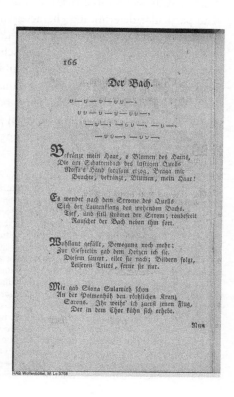

Fig. 2.3 "Der Bach." (Friedrich Gottlieb Klopstock, *Oden*. Hamburg, 1771, 166)

The symmetry of line three [/ x /, / x x /, / x /] and line four [/ x x /, / x x /], marked clearly at the word-foot boundaries with commas, contrasts with the asymmetry of the first two lines, [x / x / x / x x /] and [x x / x / x / x x /], where Klopstock does not mark the word-foot boundaries. The ode thus articulates the complex interrelations of euphony, meter, and content; *Wohlklang* can be pleasing, but only meter, especially through *Tonverhalt*, can become an expressive vehicle of expression.[36]

The problem of purely material pleasure raised by euphony also occupies Klopstock in his considerations of meter alone. In the essay "Vom gleichen Verse" (On Equal Verse) written during the period of intense metrical experimentation in the 1760s, he distinguishes "metrical expression" from the "beauty of rhythm," which comes from attractively symmetrical relations of syllables; here, too, he subordinates sound pleasurable merely to the ears to expressive metrical arrangement.[37] "On German Hexameter" separates "bedeutende ... Bewegung" (literally "meaningful/significant movement"), the kind of meter expressive of content he praises, from "wiederholte Bewegung" (literally "repeated movement"), merely symmetrically or pleasingly arranged syllables and links the latter to music rather than poetry. But Klopstock does not deny the value of such acoustic pleasure entirely; ideal poetry should use both kinds of metrical movement to its advantage: "The particular/determining characteristic of a good meter is therefore significant and repetitive movement, and the *double metrical force* [*doppelte metrische Kraft*] produced by them" ("Vom deutschen Hexameter" 112, emphasis in original). Klopstock goes further, however, and suggests that the repetition of patterns can itself be a source of pleasure, via the expectation and satisfaction they can create for the reader across the course of a specific poem. And indeed, his ode practice often places unusual word feet at particularly significant places, freighting them with significance internal to the poem to create a kind of localized metrical

---

[36] I return to the idea of expressive signs in my discussion of Klopstock's conception of language below. "Der Bach" also bears on questions of cultural particularity, as the speaker announces himself crowned by the Bardic deities Nossa and Braga, then the Christian muse "Siona Sulamith"; he encourages himself to "bolder momentum" ("kühnere[n] Schwung") of metrical invention rather than merely imitating the alcaic ode form; he appeals to Ossian and rejects "Nachahmer" (imitators) of Latin forms (HKA I.1, 272–5; see again the appendix with the full poem and my translation). It is characteristic of Klopstock's metrical thinking that these questions appear in interaction with one another.

[37] Klopstock, Friedrich Gottlieb, "Vom gleichen Verse. Aus einer Abhandlung vom Silbenmaße," in Menninghaus, *Gedanken über die Natur der Poesie. Dichtungstheoretische Schriften*, 35–54, here 36. Originally published as a preface to the fourth volume of the *Messiah*, the "treatise" begins in dialogue form and then lists thirty-six ode strophes by category. I return to those strophes, and "On Equal Verse" in my discussion of the twentieth canto of the *Messiah* below. The title refers to the repetition of the metrical pattern from strophe to strophe across the poem, as opposed to (for example) hexameter verse, which (in addition to not being broken into strophes), may be differently realized line by line provided the total time of syllables remains the same. An accurate but highly technical translation would be "On Homostrophic Verse. From a Treatise on Meter". On "Vom gleichen Verse" and its relation to Klopstock's other large-scale collection of strophe schemata, "Lyrical Meters" ("Lyrische Sylbenmaasse"), published privately in 1764, see Hellmuth, *Metrische Erfindung*, 65.

iconicity.[38] For Klopstock, then, the relation between meter and content (and also, though less centrally, sounds of letters and content) is a spectrum that ranges from support to metaphorical association to localized iconicity to independence to disagreement.

This spectrum shows that Klopstock's semanticization of meter involves degrees and complications: without ever formulating it directly or in abstraction of other points in his discussions, he develops a metrics that postulates a feedback loop between imagination, content, and meter, with each influencing the others and creating effects that interact across the space of a poem. And this vision of metrics is once again grounded in the particulars of German language. Klopstock explains, in the course of differentiating Greek from German meters, that whereas Greek worked solely by way of duration (determined by vowel type and consonant combination), German operates primarily by semantic criteria: "The syllable duration of the Ancients was produced only by the ear; it was mechanical. Ours bases itself on concepts (sensation and passion are not excluded here)" ("Vom deutschen Hexameter" 80). Once again, Klopstock insists on the importance of passion and sensation as well as conceptual content. Their role for meter becomes the basis of the difference between antique and modern meters: German meter always includes semantic components because the most emphasized words (or parts of words) are those that are the most conceptually significant. He clarifies: "The words and syllables are long for us when they express main concepts and short when they express secondary concepts" ("Vom deutschen Hexameter" 90). This differentiation relies on Klopstock's budding recognition of accentual components in metrics: within multi-syllabic German words, syllables with the word root rather than prefixes or endings receive the greater stress.[39] He reiterates that this does not mean mechanical considerations play no role in German, however; in situations of ambiguous stress, mechanical duration determines which syllables are long ("Vom deutschen Hexameter" 80).

As the discussions of *Zeitausdruck* and *Tonverhalt* above demonstrate, the interpenetration of meaning and meter (or metrical movement) goes beyond stress on semantically important syllables, however, to affinities between kinds of movement and the "sensations and passions" that are (for Klopstock) the prime subjects of poetry. All of these things together begin to illuminate Klopstock's most direct account of the *effects* of meter. He notes toward the end of "On German Hexameter" that "impressions of meter" are in fact greater than one would expect given the limitations on what can be expressed metrically (speed and slowness in *Zeitausdruck*, the seven attributes of *Tonverhalt*, the metaphorical associations with both).

---

[38] Amtstätter gives a detailed and convincing account of how Klopstock uses unusual word feet to structure his ice-skating odes of the 1760s (Amtstätter, *Beseelte Töne*, 86–7).

[39] See e.g. Jürgen Esser, *Rhythm in Speech, Prose and Verse. A Linguistic Description* (Berlin: Logos Verlag, 2011), 23–5.

And he proposes the following cause: "We receive the representations [Vorstellungen] produced in us by the words according to their meaning not quite as fast as those representations produced by the words through their movement. In the first case we transform the sign into the signified; in the second the movement seems to us directly to *be* what it expresses" ("Vom deutschen Hexameter" 148). Here, metrical movement short-circuits semantic content: movement seems not to represent but simply to *be* what it expresses.[40] The nuances of *Zeitausdruck* and *Tonverhalt* as well as the interaction between merely material sound and meter and their expressive/significant counterparts indicate that Klopstock is not making the implausible claim that there is a direct iconic relation between meter and the many varieties and shades of meaning expressed in poetry. Rather, the complexities of his metrical system allow for a much more capacious notion of how movement can arouse *Vorstellungen* independently from, in relation to, metaphorically associated with, and aligned with words.

Helped by his earlier discussions of the way *Zeitausdruck* and *Tonverhalt*, as kinds of movement (*Bewegung*), themselves express (especially) affective content, Klopstock can now shift the rhetorical ideal of the audience being moved by language inside language itself[41]: the movement of syllables moves the hearer, rendering the semantic medium fully transparent and letting the reader experience the objects of depiction as though they were present. He elaborates further that "the feeling and imagination of the hearer" ("Vom deutschen Hexameter" 148) contribute to this experience, insisting that the hearer has a role to play in the creation of *Mitausdruck* by way of her emotional and imaginative associations and connections. One of the most important aspects of Klopstock's metrical thinking is that he does not seek to banish such associations as too individual or insufficiently objective. Instead, he celebrates and invites them; individual association, subjective experience, embodiment, linguistic particularity are necessary components of his view of meter as *Mitausdruck* in which meter and content interact in ways that correspond to each of those components as they belong to and shape whole human subjects.

2.3 View of Language and Subjectivity

Understanding Klopstock's assertion that the representations of the meter reach the hearer faster than those of the meaning requires an examination of his picture of how language works. Throughout his career, he describes words as signs

[40] Schneider characterizes this as the coincidence of signifier and signified (Schneider, *Ins Ohr geschrieben*, 136).

[41] Menninghaus points this out, but without recognizing that the discussion of *Zeitausdruck* and *Tonverhalt* as themselves as affective "Bewegung" are what makes it possible (Menninghaus, "Klopstocks Poetik," 305).

("Zeichen") that represent thoughts or ideas ("Gedanken") and insists on the priority of those ideas over what he calls "Ausdruck," that is, the particular expression of ideas in linguistic signs (see for example "Vom deutschen Hexameter," 61). In this respect, he is consistent with the theories of language espoused by authors such as Gottsched, Breitinger, and Baumgarten that I discussed in the previous chapter. But Klopstock has an unusually detailed account of how specific components of "Ausdruck" as linguistic expression interact with content. Furthermore, he differs from Gottsched and Baumgarten, especially, in undermining distinctions between conceptual and affective content: Klopstock classifies both emotion and reason as "concepts" ("Begriffe"). His analysis of the effects of expressive subcomponents relies on a view of language as coming from and working on the body, meaning that meter and poetry are centrally corporeal phenomena for him. Some elements of these views are not unusual for the mid-to-late eighteenth century (in part because Klopstock both influenced and was influenced by the theorists I discuss in Chapter 1), but the implications Klopstock draws from them for his metrical theory and practice, and the elements of those views his poetic practice prompts him to emphasize, make his metrical thinking an especially consequential experiment with poetic practices of the whole human.

Expressive Signs

Klopstock gives his most detailed analysis of the interaction between the meaning of words and the signs that express meaning in "On Equal Verse": "Everything that language can say, it says through the meaning of words, in so far, that is, as words, as tones chosen as signs, have a certain content, without considering the sound or the movement of these tones; through the Zeitausdruck insofar as the movement, and the Tonausdruck [tone expression], insofar as the euphony helps to express" ("Vom gleichen Verse," 37–8). Klopstock's terminology is not fully developed at this point; he distinguishes "Tonausdruck" from "Zeitausdruck" and affiliates the former with euphony ("Wohlklang") and the latter with movement ("Bewegung"), his term for metrical expressivity. (Because Klopstock associates Tonausdruck here with euphony and not with meter, it is not equivalent to Tonverhalt, which appears only later.) The sentence lists the components of signification in order: language expresses what it expresses (or rather, says what it says) first through the meaning of the words as sounds chosen as signs that express content independent of the sound or the movement of those sounds; second, through the movement of Zeitausdruck, and, third and last, through the sounds of the "tones" of the signs.

Although he lists the meaning of the words ("Wortsinn") first, Klopstock says relatively little about it; in one of his earliest essays on poetry, he explains that the words must fit the thoughts or ideas the poet wishes to convey, that some words have lost all force or emphasis through usage and are not fitting for poetry, and that others do not fit with the affect of the poem.[42] And he immediately shifts to discussions of material features: in particular the interacting elements of euphony or dissonance ("Wohlklang" and "Übelklang," "Von der Sprache der Poesie," 25) and word order ("Wortstellung"). Not only should the order of the words reflect the order of the thoughts; euphony can justify slight divergences from standard word order ("Von der Sprache der Poesie," 28). Klopstock makes similar arguments in the essay "On Word Order" ("Von der Wortfolge"), and notes both there and in "On the Language of Poetry" that poetry, in particular, should use word order to highlight the most affectively moving elements of the thought by putting those first (see "Von der Sprache der Poesie," 28). As with the representations that are conveyed more quickly by meter than by the words themselves, Klopstock attends to the expressive capacities of the arrangement of the linguistic signs themselves.

These capacities enable the poetically advantageous illusion (*Täuschung*, a positive principle in Klopstock's poetics) of material presence of the object conveyed— the illusion confuses the word as sign for the object or emotion it expresses. Klopstock returns to this idea in his discussion of *Tonverhalt, Zeitausdruck,* and their expressive capacities. He notes that he has said, in the name of accuracy, that both express qualities (*Beschaffenheiten*) of sensations and passions (*Empfindungen, Leidenschaften*) rather than expressing those sensations or passions themselves ("Vom deutschen Hexameter," 137). The word expresses the sensation, passion, or object by its meaning, not, strictly speaking, its *Tonverhalt* or *Zeitausdruck* (or those of the word-foot in which it appears). But he remarks further that his readers might object "that the hearer, swept away by the liveliness of his participation, doesn't think of this difference, but believes he hears the passion itself, in the movements of the words, too" ("Vom deutschen Hexameter," 137); listeners moved by a poem hardly stop to ask whether their response comes from the meaning of the words or the arrangement of the words as material signs with durational and accentual qualities. The poet can and should use this to his advantage ("Vom deutschen Hexameter," 137). Klopstock invariably prefers emotionally engaged to learned readers; here, he shows that the affective responses to material signs, activated primarily by way of *Zeitausdruck* and *Tonverhalt*, enable a more direct communication than the encoding and decoding of semantic meaning into those signs.[43] This theory of language undergirds the notion of *Mitausdruck*, in which the signs of language themselves become expressive and, through a complex variety of metaphorical, affective, imagined, material, and conceptual connections, correspond to the meanings expressed by the words.

---

[42] Friedrich Gottlieb Klopstock, "Von der Sprache der Poesie," in Menninghaus, *Gedanken über die Natur der Poesie. Dichtungstheoretische Schriften*, 22–34, here 25. Hereafter cited in text.

[43] Schneider translates this argument into the vocabulary of eighteenth-century media aesthetics, in particular the discourse of natural and artificial signs (Schneider, *Ins Ohr geschrieben*, 133).

Embodied and Culturally Embedded Language

The confusion of signifier with signified and the greater rapidity of representations from movement of interacting *Zeitausdruck* and *Tonverhalt* relies on the rapidity of sensory, specifically bodily perception as opposed to rational cognition and processing.[44] In the epigram with which I began the discussion of Klopstock's metrical terminology, the metaphorics of volume emphasized spoken language and the shift to word feet rather than verse feet rests on auditory perception; he consistently prioritizes the judgments of the ear over those based on abstract principles or theoretical systems.[45] Per Klopstock's conception of poetry as emerging from and being received in the body, the ears mediate between the quasi-corporeal movement of verse *feet* and the conceptual or affective content of poetry.[46] Indeed, the syntax of his description of how *Tonverhalt* is perceived actually locates ears in the foot: "Concerning *Tonverhalt*, the ear compares in the feet ..." ("Vom deutschen Hexameter," 130).[47] The continuation of the sentence, "... in the feet: syllables with syllables," makes clear that Klopstock is not in fact positing a physiological impossibility, but instead beginning a list of what the ears compare in verse feet. Nonetheless, by his own arguments about the significance of word order, the falling together of feet and ears is striking. He consistently returns to and strives to literalize the metaphor of verse as the movement of feet, as in the epigram's stylization of verse as "gait" (*Gang*) or in his even more striking presentations of poetry as dance. Perhaps most famously in his poems on ice-skating, Klopstock uses dance as the unity of affective and bodily movement, correlating the two.[48] Klopstock layers the movement of the body, the movement of the soul, and the movement of verse, shifting from mental intellection to bodily engagement as the principal means of both speech and perception.[49]

The ode "Sponda" ("Spondee"), written in 1764, exemplifies the idea of poetry as dance by personifying metrical feet; here, the canonical feet of Greek meters (the "künstliche Füße" or artificial feet in "On German Hexameter"), which the speaker sends on a search for the missing spondee in German. (The difficulty of having two truly equal syllables in a row in German was a common reason for discarding or adapting hexameters in the debates analyzed by the previous chapter.) "Sponda," like all of the odes published in the "Lyrische Syllbenmaasse. als M.S. für

---

[44] See Schneider, *Ins Ohr geschrieben*, 139 and Hoffmann, *Körperpoetiken*, 155.
[45] Katrin Kohl also points out Klopstock's "radikale Orientierung seiner Sprachtheorie an der gesprochenen Sprache" (Kohl, *Friedrich Gottlieb Klopstock*, 54) as evident in both "On German Hexameter" and in his phonologically based suggestions for spelling reform (Kohl, *Friedrich Gottlieb Klopstock*, 54–5). Hoffmann points out the irony that Klopstock urges his readers to trust their ears and then writes poetologies (Hoffmann, *Körperpoetiken*, 145)
[46] Hoffmann, *Körperpoetiken*, 145.
[47] Hoffmann, *Körperpoetiken*, 162.
[48] Amtstätter, *Beseelte Töne*, 22–3.
[49] Amtstätter, *Beseelte Töne*, 23.

Freunde" (Lyric Meters. as MS for Friends), begins with a diagram of the metrical pattern, perhaps an effort on Klopstock's part to overcome the deficiencies of the print medium and to direct declamation:

$$x / x / x / x x /,$$
$$x x / x / x / x x /$$
$$/ x /, / x x /, / x /,$$
$$/ x x /, / x x /^{50}$$

The poem then admits the charms of Greek meters (lines 5–6) but explains that Germans ("Teutons Volk") prefer the dance once led by "Braga," the old Nordic God of poetry. These songs, however, are now lost; the Greek songs are escapees from ruins of Ancient cultures ("ruinentflohen"). But the spondee seems to have been lost like the Bardic songs; the speaker laments "Sponda! dich such' ich zu oft, ach! umsonst;/ Horche nach dir, finde dich nicht!" ("Spondee! I seek you too often, alas, in vain/ Listen for you, finding you not!" 15–6). Underscoring the centrality of listening and sound, the next strophe surrounds the question "in welche Grott' entführtest du sie,/ Sprache, mir?" (And in what grotto did you steal her away,/Language, from me? 18–9) with an appeal to Echo, who softly repeats the speaker's call; describing Spondee's "tönender Schritt" (resounding tread), it links the metaphorics of foot and sound.

Although Spondee does not answer, the other canonical verse feet gather, seemingly to lament their lost compatriot, but also to assert their own rights. To make sure his readers identify the personified feet accurately and appreciate their interactions, Klopstock clarifies in a note in the 1798 edition: "(der Daktylos) Dieser Fuß / x x. Hier folgen auch die übrigen, welche in der Ode vorkommen: Choreos /x. Kretikos /x/. Choriambos /xx/. Anapäst xx/. Jambos x/. Bacheos x//. Didymäos <xx /x>. (Die anderen Päone sind: x/xx, /xxx, xxx/.) Pyrrhichios <xx>."[51] Each appears and states its attributes, possible functions, or historical roles, e.g.

> Erhaben trat der Daktylos her:
> Bin ich Herrscher nicht im Liede Mäoons?
> Rufe denn Sponda nicht stets, bilde mich
> Oft zu Homers fliegendem Hall. (ll.25–8)[52]

---

[50] Friedrich Gottlieb Klopstock, "Sponda," in Gronemeyer and Hurlebusch, *Oden*, 243–5, hereafter cited by line number. See the appendix for the full poem and my translation.

[51] / (the dactyl) This foot /xx. Here follow the others that appear in the ode: Choreos /x. Kretikos /x/. Choriambos /xx/. Anapäst xx/. Jambos x/. Bacheos x// Didymäos <xx/x>. (The other paions are: x/xx, /xxx, xxx/.) Pyrrichios: <xx>. Note to line 30.

[52] Dactylus entered, sublime:/ Am I not ruler in Mäoons song?/ Call then Sponda not constantly, form me/ Often to make Homer's flying resound.

The feet compete with each other and compare themselves, using the vocabulary of dance, gait, and tread ("trat ... her," "schwebende[r] Gang," and "Kothurn," the sandal worn during tragedy performances):

> Jambos, Apolls alter Freund,
> Hielt sich nicht mehr, zürnt und begann:
>
> Und geh nicht ich den Gang des Kothurns?
> Wo ..., Baccheos schritt in lyrischem Tanz:
> Stolze schweigt! ha, Choriamb, töntest du,
> Daktylos, du, tönt' ich nicht mit?[53]

"Iamb" resents the claims of Choriamb, Baccheos, Anapest, and Dactyl, insisting that it, too, can be heard in all of those feet; because the strophe form ends with a choriamb surrounded by two cretics in the third line and two choriambs in the fourth, one can indeed find five iterations of a short syllable followed by a long syllable (/ x /,/x x / / x / and / x x /, / x x /), in addition to the distinctly iambic beginning of each strophe. Interestingly, however, the second two lines of each strophe are the ones in which Klopstock marks word feet, *not* canonical feet, and the fact that Iamb can claim hidden appearances inside other feet (which have non-iambic canonical functions) may be a subtle critique of verse foot metrics, which ignores word boundaries and can be applied to any syllables within the line that happen to fit the pattern. In this case, the poem's depiction of the failed search for the lost spondee (even the speediest foot, rapid "Pyrrhichios" [xx], cannot find it) may enter a metrical argument for the shift to linguistically and culturally particular word feet.

In his odes on ice skating, Klopstock proposes an origin for the metrical movement of word feet: the movement of the poet's body on the ice, in a further layering of verse movement and bodily movement that likewise continues (and intensifies) the contrast between Greek and Old Germanic models touched upon in "Sponda." The four ice-skating odes, "Der Eislauf" ("Ice-Skating" 1764), "Der Kamin" ("The fireplace," which exists in an untitled version from 1779 and heavily revised as "Der Kamin" in the 1798 publication), "Braga" (a proper name for a Nordic god, 1766), and "Eisode" ("Ice ode," 1767?, revised as "Die Kunst Tialfs" [Tialf's Art] in the 1798 edition) all extend their thematizations of bodily movement past verse alone to discussions of health, energy, and even, in "Der Kamin," blood and nerves:[54]

---

[53] Ll. 41–4, "... Iamb, Apollo's old friend/ Held back no more, grew cross, and began./ And do I not walk the tread of the Kothurn?/ Where ... Baccheus stepped in lyrical dance: / Proud one, be silent! Ha, Choriamb, when you sound/ Dactyl, you, do I not sound too?" My underlining in the German marks crypto-iambs.

[54] Since I only quote small sections from each poem, I do not give full translations.

Mit Gefühle der Gesundheit durchströmt
Die frohe Bewegung sie,
Da die Kühlungen der reineren Luft
Ihr eilendes Blut durchwehn,
Und die zarteste des Nervengewebs
Gleichgewicht halten hilft.[55]

The speech situation of "Der Kamin" complicates its praise of vigorous movement through skating, as we learn in its final section that the speaker remains
huddled by the fireplace breathing the steam of his punch (ll.78–87). Perhaps for
this reason, the poem differs the most formally from the other ice-skating poems
and Klopstock's odes in general: the earlier version uses a hexameter-like mixture of dactyls and trochees in long lines (in fact they are longer than hexameter),
while the 1798 edition breaks up the lines, emphasizing the regular appearance of
[/ x x / x /] almost every other line. The other ice-skating odes, written using Klopstock's ode strophes developed in the years surrounding their composition, make
similar arguments without the contradiction between speaker and speech; the
metrical difference suggests that perhaps only those who are themselves moving
can shape language into the word-feet of the ode forms.

Moreover, the ringing of skates on the ice as the skater steps forward models the
interaction between movement/meter and euphony/sound: the movement produces the sound, making them inseparable, but *Bewegung* is the source. Thus, in
"Eisode," "Wie des Telynors Lenzgesang aus der Kluft zurücke,/ Tönt unter ihrem
Tanze der Krystall" (HKA I.1 310)[56], while "Der Eislauf" contrasts the silence
of the fields with the ringing of steel skates on the ice and now uses the word
"Kothurn," which referred to the iamb's gait in tragedy in "Sponda," to refer to ice
skates:

Wie schweigt um uns das weiße Gefild!
Wie ertönt vom jungen Froste die Bahn!
Fern verrath deines Kothurns Schall dich mir,
Wenn du dem Blick, Flüchtling, enteilst.[57]

---

[55] Friedrich Gottlieb Klopstock, "Der Kamin," in Gronemeyer and Hurlebusch, *Oden*, 252–7, ll. 56–
61. "With feeling of health the happy/ Movement streams through them,/ As the cooling of purer air/
Pervades their hurrying blood/ And the finest tissue of the nerves helps/ Keep equilibrium." Hereafter
cited by line number.
[56] Friedrich Gottlieb Klopstock, "Eisode. / Die Kunst Tialfs," in Gronemeyer and Hurlebusch, *Oden*,
310–9, ll. 21–2.
"As Telynor's springtime song from the chasm back/ tones the crystal under their dance."
[57] Friedrich Gottlieb Klopstock, "Der Eislauf," in Gronemeyer and Hurlebusch, *Oden*, 249–51, ll.
29–32. "How the white fields are silent around us!/ How the track rings from the young frost!/ Far
away the sound of your kothurn reveals you to me,/ When from my glance, fleeting one, you fly."

"Der Kamin" and "Braga" use very similar vocabulary, and the latter in particular links feet and verse in its description of the (fantasized) Bardic god of poetry skating away:

> Er entschwebt, sein Kranz
>
> Rauscht wie von Westen, und es wehet ihm sein goldenes Haar!
> Seiner Ferse Klang fernte sich hinab am Gebirg,
> Bis er endlich in der Düfte Gewölk
> Unter dem Hange des Gebirgs verschwand.[58]

"Ferse," meaning the heel of the foot, is a homophone of "Verse" (verses, as in line of a poem); in Klopstock's orthography reform, "F" replaces "V" in most instances, making metrics ("Verskunst") *Fers*kunst, thus importing the literalization of the metaphor of verse *feet* into German orthography. And the primary objective of Klopstock's reforms was to make written language conform more closely to spoken language, once again underscoring the necessary interaction of feet and ears.[59]

Klopstock joins *Verse* and *Ferse* himself in a note on the vision of Braga. In the sixth strophe, Braga appears, and in the fourteenth, speaks:

> Ich, der **B**egeisterer des **B**arden und des **S**kalden, ich,
> **T**ön' es, **T**elyn, laut! **h**ör' es du am **H**ebrus! erfand,
> Vor der Lanze, und dem **St**urme vorbey
> **S**iegend zu **sch**weben! und den **sch**önen **S**ohn
>
> **S**iphias lehrt' ich es![60]

The description of Braga teaching the art of ice skating to subsequent generations activates tropes of Old Germanic culture in Klopstock's repertoire (using martial imagery; Klopstock consistently compares the steel of skates with the steel of spears and lances). Moreover, it maps techniques of Old Germanic alliterative verse (*Stabreim*) on to the ode meter, as I have marked using bold type in the quoted example (T, h, St/Sch, and S). During the years of ode experimentation, Klopstock also studied Old Saxon and Old Norse poetry intensively;[61] the imitation in "Braga" was so successful that his friend Carl Friedrich Cramer mistook it for a reproduction of the Old Norse *Edda* (Klopstock's source for much

---

[58] Friedrich Gottlieb Klopstock, "Braga," in Gronemeyer and Hurlebusch, *Oden*, 280–2, ll. 70–4. "He glides away, his wreath// Rustles as if in the west wind, and his golden hair waves!/ His heel's sound moves away along the rocks/ Until finally in the perfumed clouds/ He disappears under the slope of the mountain." Hereafter cited by line number.

[59] See Klopstock, "Über die deutsche Rechtschreibung" and Kohl, *Friedrich Gottlieb Klopstock*, 54.

[60] "Braga," ll. 59–63. My bold type to mark alliteration. "I, inspirer of the bards and the skalds, I/ Let the Tyln sound it, it be heard on the Hebrus, discovered/ How to fly in front of the lance, and sweep / victorious past the storm and to the beautiful son// Siphias I taught it!"

[61] See Amtstätter, *Beseelte Töne*, section 4.

of the "Bardic" or "Skaldric" mythology in the odes, including the names "Tialf" and "Braga"[62]), explaining as much in the edition of the odes published in his five-volume *Klopstock. Er; und über ihn*. In response, Klopstock added his own note in the 1798 edition: "I took neither this, nor anything else that appears in the ode, from the Edda. I had not yet read the passage from it that Cramer includes in his notes at the time when I wrote the ode. I formed its meter on the ice according to [following the shape of] my movements" (note to l. 61). Despite his enthusiasm for old Germanic forms as a culturally specific predecessor to set against Ancient Greek, Klopstock denies imitating the Edda and instead asserts the meter's origins in the movements it describes. But Cramer's error emphasizes the degree to which embedding verse practice in the body is culturally particular. Unlike twenty-first-century theories of metrics that insist on the body as a universal anthropological constant, Klopstock's metrics remind us that not only verse but the body is shaped by culture and language.[63]

Klopstock's discussion of *Tonverhalt* likewise illuminates the extent to which his appeals to physiological characteristics also insist on linguistic and cultural particularity. In the first half of "On German Hexameter," answering Bürger's charges that it is impossible to write German hexameters (see Chapter 1 Section 1.2, "Anti-Hexametrists"), Klopstock elaborates both similarities and differences between "Greek and German long [syllables]"("Vom deutschen Hexameter," 83). He recognizes that both Ancient Greek and modern German as languages have longer and shorter syllables and also accented and unaccented syllables but distinguishes between how each language used duration and accent in metrical organization. He explains that whereas in Greek duration was the primary characteristic of a "long" syllable, in German the length is determined by "Erhebung" (raising) or "Anstrengung" (exertion) of the voice: "The Greek and the German long are therefore not a little different, that in the former *normally* only the duration or the time of the enunciation, in the latter the raising or exertion of the voice, and specifically a stronger one, *continually*, and more than the duration, comes into effect" ("Vom deutschen Hexameter," 83). He defines length by the characteristics of the voice, and ties its perception to the conditioning of the ear: "In hearing long syllables, our ears attend not so much to the time the speaker spends on the syllable, but how he spends his time. We like to hear the accent/tone, with which he pronounces the long syllable" ("Vom deutschen Hexameter," 82). As in the epigram, Klopstock locates verse in the body and insists on the cultural and linguistic particularity of metrical patterning.

---

[62] See Friedrich Gottlieb Klopstock, "An M. Denis, 6. und 9. September 1767," in Gronemeyer and Hurlebusch, *Oden*, 430. This study is part of his nationalist cultural project of seeking to develop a Germanic culture comparable to Greek or Roman culture.

[63] See Hoffmann for more on this point, although he ties cultural particularity solely to the ears (Hoffmann, *Körperpoetiken*, 152).

2.4 The Metrical Sublime: The "Triumphgesänge" of the *Messiah*

In turning to the twentieth canto of the *Messiah*, I analyze one of the most striking instances of Klopstock's metrical thinking. Even here, the distance between metrical theory and poetic practice is minimal, since Klopstock's verse practice rests on and shapes his theorizing: the final canto of the *Messiah* is both partial impetus for and one outcome of Klopstock's strophe invention. Moreover, in "On Equal Verse," the preface to the first publication of the last five cantos, he prints metrical schemata of those forms organized according to their "lyrical time-expression" (*lyrischer Zeitausdruck*), inviting readers into the culminating volume of his life's work by way of a metrical treatise. As I explained, *Zeitausdruck* emerged relatively early in Klopstock's metrical thought; it is thus not surprising that he uses it as an analytical category here. He has not yet theorized tone relation (*Tonverhalt*), although he was manifestly aware that not only the total quantity of syllables but also their positional arrangement affected metrical experience.[64] I therefore do not attempt a detailed application of Klopstock's conceptions of *Tonverhalt* and *Zeitausdruck* that would account for every syllable of every line in the text. To do so would ossify Klopstock's notion of *Mitausdruck* into a systematicity that his metrical thinking forbids and that obscures the interaction between culture, language, and the body. Instead, I use the strophe schemata and their designations of *Zeitausdruck* only as a starting point to consider the possible associative connections between tempo and content. I take Klopstock's later discussion of the interaction between *Zeitausdruck* and *Tonverhalt*, in which semantic content directs the reader/hearer's attention to metrical features, as a cue to look for elements of metrical movement that interact with content in metaphorical, innovative, and sometimes ambiguous ways.

The Context of the *Messiah* and the Task of the Twentieth Canto

The *Messiah* has a complex publication history, including multiple editions, both authorized and unauthorized, of each volume (which contained groups of between three to five cantos plus forewords and other paratexts including an index of names and summaries of each canto). The first cantos, I–III, were

---

[64] In a letter from October of 1764, for example, he first responds to his interlocutor's criticisms of his meters, poses a series of questions about Greek metrics, and then adds "I don't want to ask you: whether the rhythm of these feet is different ... but what is the effect of their difference?"; between the two parts of the sentence he lists every possible combination of two short and two long syllables (//xx, xx//, x/x/, /x/x, /xx/, x//x) (Friedrich Gottlieb Klopstock, "An Ebert, Oktober 1764," in *Briefe*, ed. Helmut Riege, vol. Briefe IV.1 (Berlin: de Gruyter, 2003), 239).

published in 1748, the final cantos, XVI–XX, in 1773, and Klopstock continued to revise the work thereafter, bringing out a new edition in 1799. He was highly aware of and responsive to critical reception, particularly of his hexameter; the work on the *Messiah* itself likewise influenced his conceptions of metrics as he sustained German hexameter over thousands of lines of verse.[65] Moreover, he wrote non-linearly, devising a general plan for the entire work from the outset and working episodically, adding and rearranging episodes as his poetic practice and theory developed (HKA IV.3, 181). The work rests on an exceptionally ambitious cultural and religious program: its form insists that modern German language and culture are capable of hexameter epic that competes with Homer; its subject asserts the possibility of specifically Christian epic rivaling Milton; taken together, they represent an extended performance of the idea that poetry, in all its formal-material features, can undertake the affective-subjective work of revelation.[66]

The first sentence announces the *Messias'* purpose, replacing the canonical appeal to the muse with a command from the poet to his soul: "Sing, unsterbliche Seele, der sündigen Menschen Erlösung" ("Sing, immortal soul, of sinful mankind's redemption," I.1).[67] Mixing Biblical episodes, Miltonian echoes, and Klopstock's invention, the next (ca.) 19,000 lines narrate the days immediately prior to Jesus' crucifixion, his death, the resurrection, and the Last Judgment, depicting scenes on earth, in heaven, and in hell.

The twentieth canto presents particular problems for poetic composition: its task is not to introduce new content but to make the redemption of humankind present to readers "under the aspects of eternity and infinity" (HKA IV.3, 340). Klopstock portrays the ascension by way of the triumphal choirs of angels and resurrected human souls as Jesus ascends, and to represent the multiplicity of

---

[65] The text of the *Messiah* and the critical apparatus associated with it occupy six full volumes of the critical edition, edited by Elisabeth Höpker-Herberg. I cite them using the abbreviation HKA (for Hamburger Klopstock Ausgabe) followed by the section number (Werke IV) and then the volume number (1–6). On the organization of the HKA, see https://www.sub.uni-hamburg.de/sammlungen/nachlass-und-autographensammlung/klopstock-arbeitsstelle/hamburger-klopstock-ausgabe.html (accessed May 24, 2022). See HKA Werke IV.3, 184–5 and 199; for a description of Klopstock's practice of reading unpublished sections to friends or in public presentations and revising based on hearer reactions, see HKA Werke IV.3, 206–8.

[66] Nor does the importance of the bodily disappear in explicitly religious poetry: Klopstock attempts to reconcile the apparently competing claims of earthly and spiritual love in his various versions of the autobiographically inflected episode of Semida and Cidli (Canto IV, 651–599 and 740–889, canto XV, 1376–1549), both of whom Jesus raised from the dead and who struggle with the implications of their spiritual renewal for their mortal love, ultimately finding immortal love in their transfiguration. After the death of his wife, Meta Klopstock (née Moller) in childbirth, Klopstock adds a second Cidli, wife of Gedor, who is the "Gefährtin/ Dieses Lebens" (companion/ of this life) as well as "jenes ewigen Lebens" (that eternal life) (XV. 422–3), and whose death mirrors Meta's (see HKA IV.3, 301 and Bernd Aurochs, *Die Entstehung der Kunstreligion*, [Göttingen: Vandenhoeck & Ruprecht, 2006], 231–2).

[67] For the twentieth canto, the critical edition prints the 1799 (Göschen) edition of the text, as it "represents the work at the stage of its most extensive editing by Klopstock" (HKA Werke IV.3, 253), in volumes IV.1 and IV.2 of the section "Werke" (works). I cite by canto number and line number in the text.

voices he uses thirty-six different strophe forms developed during his period of intense metrical experimentation in the mid-1760s (HKA IV.3, 341). His overview of those thirty-six strophes in the preface to the first publication of Cantos XVI–XX, "Vom gleichen Verse," serves not only as an experiment in theorizing verse but as a reader's aid (HKA IV.3, 355): as Klopstock had ample opportunity to judge from the largely negative reactions to the private publications of sections from the *Triumphchöre*,[68] the sheer plurality and volume of strophe forms (and the syntax they elicit and support) puts enormous demands on its recipients.[69]

And indeed, the twentieth canto frustrates efforts to describe its metrical practice in straightforward categories; although the strophe schemata in "Vom gleichen Verse" make it possible to identify the lyric time expression of every chorus, it is difficult to determine the appropriate level of detail for analysis, as virtually every pattern that appears has an exception somewhere within the 1187 lines of the canto. (For example, Klopstock does not use different strophe forms to distinguish human and angelic speakers; different strophe types are separated by epic contextualization in hexameter—that is, every chorus stays in a single strophe form—except for a long passage that alternates between Klopstock's so-called "fast, alternating" strophes and "transitioning [*übergehende*]" strophes from lines XX.510–76.) This complexity, moreover, emphasizes important aspects of the represented content. First, Klopstock uses metrical heterogeneity that frustrates any systematic overview to suggest the sheer number of singers; the choirs include not merely all the orders of angels and the entire harvest of earth's redeemed souls from all of history but also souls from other planets or worlds who observe and praise the resurrection and ascension. Klopstock underscores the enormous numbers of singers in his vocabulary as well, for example in "Haufen schauten; allein bald wurden die Haufen zu Schaaren,/ Bald die Schaaren zu Heeren" (Masses watched; but soon the masses became multitudes, the multitudes hosts, XX.585–6). Second, both meter in its attribute as the organization of time on line-by-line or strophe-to-strophe levels and the macrostructural relations created by repetition of strophe forms separated by wide expansions of text mimic the complex relation to temporality and history in the canto: not only are the events narrated "under the aspect of eternity" (as it was in the beginning, is now, and will be forever, amen),

---

[68] He published twenty "Triumphchöre und –lieder" (Triumphal Choruses and Songs) in March 1764 and twelve "Fragmente" (Fragments) from the twentieth canto in May 1766 as "M.S. für Freunde" (MS for Friends, HKA IV.3, 343ff.); in part responding to confusion in response to the former, Klopstock included the metrical patterns of the strophe type for each choir in the second pre-printing (HKA IV.3, 343).

[69] For example, Klopstock's sister-in-law, Elisabeth Schmidt, complains to him in a letter from April 1764, "The triumphal choirs strike me peculiarly, I cannot understand this new German and the strange constructions at all, I'll soon be studying myself stupid ... I said in the first read-through, Klopstock has forgotten that he and we have not yet been amongst the angels" (Friedrich Gottlieb Klopstock, "Von Elisabeth Schmidt, April 1764," in Riege, *Briefe*, 232.

but Klopstock depicts the fulfillment of numerous Biblical prophecies, layering a dizzying number of Old Testament and New Testament references in single lines, strophes, or choruses.

To meet the challenge of depicting overwhelming volume and infinite temporality, and, more importantly, the significance of redemption through Jesus for all of creation, Klopstock creates what I am calling the metrical sublime, where the way the complexity and multiplicity of metrical forms exceeds the capacity for analysis mirrors the overwhelming joy of resurrection and the incommensurability of the divine with human understanding, much less representational abilities. And just as the understanding runs up against its own limits and is thrown back within itself, so too the twentieth canto as song (Gesang) repeatedly reflects on its own limits and thematizes sound and song. Thus both the narrative instance in hexameter and the choirs themselves note their own hesitancy and daring in singing Jesus' praise. After a hexameter introduction that situates the events "Weit schon über den Wolken" (Already far above the clouds, XX.1), the angel Gabriel speaks first, commanding the choirs to sing: "Fanget bebend an, athmet kaum/ Leisen Laut, denn es ist Christus Lob,/ Was zu singen ihr wagt!" (Begin trembling, barely breathe/ Soft sound, for it is Christ's praise/ That you dare to sing! XX.5–7); once started, he suggests the singers will gain confidence "die Ewigkeit/ Durchströmt's! tönt von Äoon fort zu Äoon!" (Eternity/ Flow through it! Ring from eon forth to eon! XX. 7–8).[70] Both the alliteration in "Leisen Laut ... Lob" (soft song ... praise) and the consonance in "tönt ... Äoon" (ring ... eon), as well as the metaphorical connection of song and fluidity in "Durchströmt's," are characteristic for the entire canto.

The choirs repeatedly take the act of song—specifically praise—as their theme or topic, as in lines XX.471–94, in which a choir of Seraphim commands all of nature to sing God's praise: "Ertönet sein Lob, Erden, tönt's, Sonne, Gestirn!/ Ihr Gestirn' hier in der Straße des Lichts, hallt's feyernd,/ Des Erlösenden Lob! siehe, des Herrlichen,/ Unerreichten von dem Danklied der Natur!// Lobsing', o Natur ..." (XX.471–5).[71] Klopstock relies on sound to evoke not only positive emotions and songs of praise, but also torment, damnation, and fear: he uses neologistic composites such as "Wehklagen" (woe-laments) as well as alternations between crying out and falling silent to convey the pain of the damned, as in a passage drawing on Numbers 16:27–37, in which the earth swallows Abiram, Kora, and Dathan, because they "provoked the Lord:" "O der Angst Stimme, die herrufend vom Abgrunde/ Dumpf tönte, aus Staubwolken zum Licht auf umsonst klagte!/ Und

---

[70] I do not translate all 1187 lines of the canto; instead, I give my own translations of what I cite either in notes or, in the case of brief phrases, in the text. For the several strophes I analyze in their entirety, I give both original and translation in the text.

[71] "Let sound his praise, let it ring, Sun, Stars!/ You stars here in the streets of light, resound it celebrating/ The praise of the redeemer! See, of the mighty, unreached by the thanksgiving song of nature!// Sing praise, o Nature!"

nunmehr sterbend noch graunvoller schwieg, furchtbarer,/ Verstummt, schreckte, als hinsinkend sie Wehklag' ausrief!" (XX.225–8).[72] All of these strategies repeatedly direct the hearer's attention to sonic patterning in the text, even as those patterns far exceed the capacity for complete systematization, the more so in the live performance that was Klopstock's ideal.

The New Strophes in "On Equal Verse"

Klopstock's preface, "On Equal Verse," offers a framework for describing the tempo of each strophe, with some limited connections to affective dispositions. The main types of verse are rising (*steigend*), falling (*sinkend*), alternating (*abwechselnd*), transitioning/merging (*übergehend*), and hovering/suspended (*schwebend*), which describe types of relationships between speed and slowness. The identity of a strophe is thus not a question of the total number of long or short syllables but (anticipating *Tonverhalt*) of their relation and proportion across a line; Klopstock explains that "slowness and speed have degrees. If the slowness or the speed increases, then the strophe *rises*; and *falls*, when one of the two decreases" ("Vom gleichen Verse," 35). When either speed or slowness "now decreases, and now increases; then the strophe *alternates*," and "if the one or the other remain approximately the same, then it [the strophe] *hovers*"; finally, strophes can "*pass* from slowness *over* to speed, or from the latter to the former" ("Vom gleichen Verse," 35). Thus Klopstock arrives at the categories of "fast, rising strophes" (*Schnelle, steigende Strophen*), "fast, alternating strophes" (*Schnelle, abwechselnde Strophen*), "slow, rising strophe" (*Langsame, steigende Strophe*), "slow, sinking strophe" (*Langsame, sinkende Strophe*), "slow, alternating strophes" (*Langsame, abwechselnde Strophen*), "fast, hovering strophe" (*Schnelle, schwebende Strophe*), and "transitioning strophes" (*Übergehende Strophen*). There are some obvious asymmetries: the fast strophe examples include rising, alternating, and hovering, while the slow strophe examples given are rising, falling, and alternating; moreover, Klopstock gives different numbers of examples for each type, from the single "fast, hovering strophe," "slow, rising strophe," and "slow, falling strophe," to eight "fast, alternating strophes" and fifteen "transitioning strophes" (this last reflecting the fact that they are of course not broken into subcategories of "slow" and "fast"). These examples all use different meters, leading to the total of thirty-six strophe forms, which appear unequally throughout the twentieth canto, as my mapping them out across the 1187 lines showed: some appear only once as a single strophe, others only once but as multi-strophe

---

[72] "Oh the voice of fear, that calls from the abyss/ Sounds dully, from clouds of dust up to the light in vain!/ And now dying fell still more horribly silent, more terribly/ Fall silent, daunted, as it calls out woe-lament!"

sequence, others still once in the first half and once in the second, and finally some as many as seven times (the first type of fast, hovering strophe).

Once again, then, Klopstock's metrical practice refuses full systematization, in keeping both with his emphasis on effect and the ways in which the sublime content of the twentieth canto exceeds representational and rational capacities; indeed in "On Equal Verse" he acknowledges the difficulty of fully distinguishing each strophe type even when they are organized by tempo, much less in the flood of variety of the twentieth canto: "I don't demand that you think of all this while I read aloud; it is enough for me if you pay attention to the impression that the movement of the strophes makes on you" ("Vom gleichen Verse," 45). These impressions, then, are the most important aspect of Klopstock's meter, and thus a suggestion for considering the strophe forms of the twentieth canto. For example, the various types of "slow" strophe appear in depictions of pain, damnation, death, and ruin, whether in Old Testament stories, prophecies of downfall, or the condemnation of those not saved. Klopstock uses "slow" strophes for, e.g., lines XX.225–8, whose "slow, rising strophes" describe the Earth swallowing Abiram, Kora, and Dathan in Numbers 16; ll. XX.210–3, a "slow, sinking strophe" depicting the death of the Pharaoh's army from Exodus 14; ll. XX.231–4, a "slow, alternating strophe" on the fall of Jericho in Joshua 6; and ll. XX.914–7, the last appearance of a slow (alternating) strophe depicting the throwing of the damned into a lake of fire from Revelation 20. Other content-tempo links are less straightforward; Klopstock uses "fast, alternating" strophe types frequently and for longer sections (the choirs vary in length from single four-line strophes to the sixty-eight line choir that alternates between a "fast, hovering" and a "transitioning" strophe type from lines XX.509–76) and tends to create series or clusters of strophe types with intervening hexameter sections (as for example the series of "transitioning strophes" between lines XX.800 and 899). In each case, the unsystematic and flexible connections create metrical networks of association across sections of the canto.

The Seven Cities in Revelation

One way of approaching this type of non-systematic patterning is to examine sections with a single Biblical source, and thus fairly consistent themes, and analyze the different strophe types used. In a sequence that from lines 725-818 that begins with a hexameter section introducing the reference to Revelation and describing Patmos, and continues uses five strophe types interleaved with hexameter, Klopstock takes up the fates of the seven churches listed in Revelation 1:11: "What thou seest, write in a book, and send it unto the seven churches which are in Asia; unto Ephesus, and unto Smyrna, and unto Pergamos, and unto Thyatira, and unto Sardis, and unto Philadelphia, and unto Laodicea." Klopstock treats the cities in that order, which obscures the mapping of the cities' fates onto metrical patterning: for the city of Smyrna, described in unambiguously positive terms in Revelation 2:8–10 (and in lines XX.758–61), he uses a "fast, rising strophe." For a city with an unambiguously negative fate, Sardis (lines XX.783–94), Klopstock uses a slow (alternating) strophe, in keeping with the association of slow strophes with pain and damnation. The cities of Ephesus (Revelation 2:1–7 and lines XX.748–55), Pergamos (Revelation 2:12–17 and lines XX.763–70), and Thyatira (Revelation 2:19–28 and lines XX.772–9) are more ambiguous, mixing good and bad deeds; the text of Revelation in all three sections emphasizes repentance ("Buße" in the Luther version) and Klopstock uses the first fast, alternating strophe from "On Equal Verse," where long and short syllables remain more or less in balance and in roughly consistent ratios across the strophe.

Finally, the characterization of Laodicea and its fate (Revelation 3:17–21 and lines XX.811–8) are ambivalent, tending to the negative: "I know thy works, that thou art neither cold nor hot: I would thou wert cold or hot" (Revelation 3:15) and "As many as I love, I rebuke and chasten: be zealous therefore, and repent. Behold, I stand at the door, and knock: if any man hear my voice, and open the door, I will come in to him, and will sup with him, and he with me" (Revelation 3:19–20). If the city repents, some will be saved; Klopstock appears pessimistic, however, both in his use of the subjunctive ("vernähme den Ruf Laodicea noch"— *if* Laodicea *were* to hear the call, or if only it heard, XX.811) and his deployment of a "transitioning" verse. And this particular transition (the third of the transitioning schemata in "On Equal Verse") moves from faster (associated with the saving of the cities) to slower (associated with damnation): the first line has eight short and four long syllables, the second has four short and six long, the third five and six, and the third an equal proportion of long to short syllables, six of each. The ratios thus shift from 2:1 to 1:1 across the course of the strophe, suggesting that Laodicea will share the fate of Sardis with its slow strophe.

The repetition of strophe forms—that is, their use at multiple points in the twentieth canto—strengthens the associations of strophe types with content, here with damnation or salvation. Thus the suggestion that Laodicea is ultimately condemned becomes stronger through its metrical association with the destruction of Babel in lines XX.703–10, the only other appearance of the third "transitioning strophe" type. The depiction of Sardis' negative fate shares its slow, alternating form (the third such form in "On Equal Verse") with lines XX.445–60, which merge numerous prophecies of the destruction of Jerusalem and the temple and are some of the most violent in the canto: "Geh unter! geh unter, Stadt Gotts!/ In Kriegsschreyn! in Rauchdampf! und Glutstrom!" (Perish! Perish, city of God!/ In cries of war! in pillars of smoke! and streams of fire!, lines XX.445–6). Conversely, Smyrna and Philadelphia share their strophe forms with sections explicitly marked as song, in Smyrna's case lines XX.96–701, in which seraphim sing the creation of the world, and in Philadelphia's lines XX.471–94, where the entire section is a jubilant command to the whole of nature to sing. And the mixed cases of Ephesus,

Pergamos, and Thyatira take part in a metrical narrative of destruction, repentance, and redemption that stretches across more than 1000 lines: the first "fast, alternating" verse in "Vom gleichen Verse" first occurs in lines XX.74–93, narrating Zechariah's vision of the crowning of Joshua (Zechariah 3:1–10). In the next occurrence, lines XX.320–79 follow Ezekiel 31:1–17, describing God as avenger ("Rächer") and destroyer of all those who "Blutgier/ Lechzten"("pant with bloodlust," XX.322–3), but the book of Ezekiel ends with prophecies of salvation. The three cities called to repent make the fourth, fifth, and sixth uses, and finally, in the seventh section (lines XX.1112–31) "Sieben Erstandne, die ersten unter den Menschen" (Seven of the resurrected, the first among humans) praise God and Jesus for their redemption, noting the incommensurability between their mortality and finitude ("Endlichkeit," XX.1112) and the greatness of God's mercy.

Such networks of metrical associations, created by the repetition of strophes, by the clustering of strophe types around certain themes, and the interaction of both, run through the entire canto, though as I indicated above they hardly explain every syllable of it. They are, moreover, an example of the way Klopstock's conception of *Mitausdruck* creates links between meter and content that move past direct iconicity: here, a broad or weak iconistic connection between the metrical feature of slowness or heaviness, and correspondingly to weight, extends to the physical sinking of damnation and the metaphorical weight of sin, as well as to the difficulty or struggle associated with the pain of depicting such themes, to a general association of slow strophes with themes of fear, pain, and death which is then reinforced by the use of slow strophes to portray such topics, creating a feedback loop between material feature, semantic association, and aural perception. It should, in theory, be possible to trace such networks for fast and transitional strophes as well, but I do not do so both for reasons of space and because of a certain tension in Klopstock between the command simply to listen and the inclusion of highly technical strophe schemata in "On Equal Verse." Indeed, it seems highly implausible that listeners could map out associations in such detail, although Klopstock's own letters, attempts at musical notation, metrical diagrams, and marked-up copies of the manuscript suggest he was working at this level of precision. But the presence of the twentieth canto and the metrical diagrams in the same volume suggests that Klopstock calls for some kind of interaction between emotional response (including being overwhelmed by volume and multiplicity), analysis of metrical patterning through text, the frustration of complete systematicity, and a more finely honed attention.

Lines XX.612–26

Taken together, the strophe diagrams and triumphal choirs invite readers to attend to our metrical experiences, meaning both the ways in which we do things with meter (make connections, compare, contrast) and the things meter does to us (triggers associations, frustrates expectations, gets into our ears and under our skin). In turning by way of conclusion to a single choir, I hope to show how this kind of honed attentiveness to metrical experience deepens the pleasure we might take in reading even—especially?—difficult, syntactically demanding, and metrically complex poetry. Lines XX.612–26, just after the midpoint of the canto, are spoken by a single human figure, one of a married couple introduced as mortals ("Sterblichen," XX.698) in a hexameter section from lines XX.595–603. Klopstock has both the man and the woman speak, and introduces them using almost identical diction that underscores their love for each other and for God: "Indem der Schatten des Baumes, /Ihnen Hütte jetzt, und Kühlung sanfterer Lüfte/Weht', und der Bach mitscholl, erhob sie die Stimme der Andacht, /Sie, die liebte den Herrn, und ihres Lebens Gefährten" (XX.600–3) and "Als der Schatten des Baums, und Kühlung sanfterer Lüfte/ Weht', und der Bach mitscholl, erhob er die Stimme der Andacht,/ Er, der liebte den Herrn, und seines Lebens Gefährtin" (XX.608–10).[73] The woman speaks first, commanding her soul to elevate itself to the heavenly choirs and join their song; then her "life's companion" begins:

> Selbständiger! Hochheiliger! Allseliger, tief wirft, Gott!
> Von dem Thron fern, wo erhöht du der Gestirn' Heer schufst,
> Sich ein Staub dankend hin, und erstaunt über sein Heil,
> Daß ihn Gott hört in des Gebeinthals Nacht!
>
> Durch feyrende, lautpreisende Psalmchöre des Sternheers bebt
> Mein Gebet auf zu dem Thron deß, der im Lichtreich herrscht!
> Vom Beginn selig macht! Labyrinthweg' uns empor
> Zu dem Thron führt, wo unerforscht Er herrscht!
>
> Hochheiliger! Allseliger! Unendlicher! Herr, Herr, Gott!
> O erhör du mein entzückt Flehn von dem Grabthal her!
> Von der Nacht stammelts auf zu des Chors Halleluja;
> O erhör's, Gott! und mein verstummt Flehn auch!
>
> Gott! mache den toderbenden glückseliger. Gott! trockn' ihm
> Die Betrübniß von der Wang' ab! doch ist Elendslast
> In der Nacht hier sein Theil, so begnad' ihn mit Geduld!
> Und o leit' ihn, daß er am Thron anschau!
>
> [Self-sufficing! High-holiest! All-blessed, before you, God!
> From the throne far, where on high you made the stars' throngs,
> A dust speck throws itself in thanks, amazed at its salvation,
> That God hears him in the night of the valley of bones!

---

[73] "As the shadow of the tree, and the cooling breezes/ Blew, and the brook echoed too, she [he] raised a voice of devotion/ She [he] who loved the Lord and her [his] life's companion."

Through solemn, loud-praising psalm choirs of the stars' legion
    trembles
My prayer up to the throne of him who reigns in light's kingdom!
From the beginning makes blessed! Labyrinth path leads us
Up to the throne, where unexplored He reigns!

High-holiest! All-blessed! Unending! Lord, Lord, God!
O hear you my rapturous plea from the grave's abyss,
From the night it stammers up through the choir's Hallelujah;
O hear it, God! and my mute prayer too!

God! make the one born to death more blissful. God, dry
The sorrow from his cheek! but if misery's weight
In the night here is his part, then bless him with patience!
And o lead him, that he may gaze at the throne!]

Lines XX.611–26, like virtually every choir in the twentieth canto, are both exceptional and typical. Klopstock's use of dramatic addresses to God, marked by exclamation points and repeated apostrophic appellations, as well as the highly inverted syntax and the use of neologistic compound words as both nouns ("Gebeinthals" [valley of bones/skeletons, XX.614], "Psalmchöre" [psalm choirs, XX.610], "Lichtreich," "Elendslast" [light kingdom, misery's weight, XX.624]) and adjectives ("lautpreisend" [loud-praising, XX.615], "toderbenden" [death-inheriting, XX.623]), are characteristic for much of the canto. The passage's Biblical referents are Psalm 28 ("Unto thee will I cry, O LORD my rock; be not silent to me: lest, if thou be silent to me, I become like them that go down into the pit. Hear the voice of my supplications, when I cry unto thee, when I lift up my hands toward thy holy oracle" 1–2) and several references to God wiping the tears from the faces of the pious, e.g. Isaiah 25:8 ("the Lord GOD will wipe away tears from off all faces"), Revelation 7:17 ("God shall wipe away all tears from their eyes") and Revelation 21:4 ("And God shall wipe away all tears from their eyes"). Psalm 23 ("the valley of the shadow of death," 4) echoes in the words "Gebeinthals Nacht" (night of the valley of the bones, XX.614) and "Grabthal" (grave valley, XX.620), and the word "tief" (deep, XX.611), the topography of valleys, and the act of crying out to God suggest Psalm 130 ("Out of the depths have I cried unto thee, O LORD. Lord, hear my voice," 1–2). As a whole, then, the strophes are split between praise and supplication, joy and fear, (eternal) life and death.

This doubleness likewise appears in the metrical form of the lines: they are the only occurrence of the second type of slow, alternating strophe from "On Equal Verse," and the only instance of a slow strophe that does not portray damnation or destruction. But the speaker does dwell on his distance from God, his mortality, and the contrast between his prayer or plea and the angelic choirs; he characterizes earthly life as taking place in "des Gebeinthals Nacht" (the night of the valley of bones) and in the "Grabthal" (literally "grave valley"). The strophe's meter is particularly noticeable in its difference from the normal prosodic patterns of German, which, like English, rarely has multiple strong/long syllables in a row and tends to alternate between stressed and unstressed syllables; the strophe, however, has frequent patterns of two or three strong syllables per Klopstock's annotations of its schema:

> //xx, //xx, //xx, ///,
> xx//, xx//, xx///,
> xx//x/, xx/, /xx/
> xx//, xxx///.

(HKA IV.6, 23).

The series of three long/emphasized syllables, which end three of the four lines of the strophe, are especially striking, and Klopstock uses a variety of strategies (monosyllables, compound words, directional prefixes, etc.) to achieve them. Like many of the strophes designated as "fast," the section explicitly discusses song and sound in several places ("feyrende, lautpreisende Psalmchöre" [celebrating, loud praising psalm choirs, XX.615], "Mein Gebet" [my prayer, XX.616], "erhör ... Flehn" [hear ... plea, XX.620], "des Chors Halleluja" [the choir's halleluja, XX.621], "O erhör's Gott" [oh hear it, God, XX.622]), but here prayer and pleading, radically different from the praise and hallelujas of the angels, are tentative ("bebt" [trembled, XX.615], "stammelt" [stammers, XX.621]) and threaten to fall silent ("verstummt" [falls mute, XX.622]).

Klopstock's efforts at outlining the strophe in musical notation (in a letter to Johann Wilhelm Ludwig Gleim from July 1764) emphasize its slowness: he gives the tempo marking "lento e grave" and renders the strophe in 3/2 time, using almost exclusively half- and quarter-notes. This stands in particular contrast to what comes before and after. In the strophe sung by the woman of the couple, human song still appears as tentative ("bebenden Gesang" [XX.607]), but here the choirs of the redeemed are like the human figure: they once (per the past-tense verb "stammelten") stammered their praise as she now does (XX.606–7). Perhaps more striking are the direct syntax, compared to the strophes sung by her "Lebens Gefährten" (life's companion), and the fast, alternating verse type (#6) used only here; both fit the movement of the soul, which line XX.604 describes as swinging or swooping ("Schwinge dich empor, Seele"), as opposed to the labyrinthine path and syntax of her male counterpart.

Following line XX.626, the singer (said male counterpart) does fall silent ("Also sang er, und schwieg" [XX.627]), before beginning again in a different meter (the only one not explicitly included in "On Equal Verse," a version of the ionic strophe Klopstock discusses at the end of his preface (see "Vom gleichen Verse," 50–3) with every line broken into two shorter lines and printed without strophe breaks).

This much-faster meter begins jubilantly, commanding the harp to sound and his song (now "Psalm" [XX.634]) to rise to God's throne (XX.633–4); it turns to the inadequacy of human praise and conceptions of God (like a painting of sunrise that turns to twilight compared with an actual sunrise [XX.647–9]) and then once again to the "Elend" (misery, XX.665) of mankind and the "Labyrinthweg" (labyrinth path, XX.668) that leads to God. The speaker laments that the voice of fear ("Der Angst Stimme" [fear's voice, XX.681]) mixes itself with the "Loblied der Himmel" (praise song of the heavens, XX.680), and ends by merging the tears shed at graves with thankful tears of bliss (XX.686).

Neither Klopstock's diction nor his meters, then, disregard human mortality, loss, and suffering even in the joy of resurrection. Moreover, the specific speech situation of a loving couple and the gendered marking of their speech (the woman speaks more directly and confidently, in a meter associated with redemption, the man more with more convoluted syntax and more uncertainty, in a meter associated with pain) hints both at the poem's earlier considerations of the connection and conflict of earthly and mortal love and the autobiographical elements of Klopstock's sorrow for Meta's loss: it seems the woman reaches heaven first, leaving her companion to struggle and mourn, recalling an episode (likewise autobiographically inflected) in the fifteenth canto in which a woman blesses her husband on her deathbed and reminds him of the immortal life and love that awaits them. This reference within the text and to Klopstock's biography contradicts a different association of the loving couple in a hut beneath the trees, namely Ovid's Baucis and Philemon, who are rewarded by the gods for the hospitality of their hut by (at their request) dying at the same moment and being transformed into an intertwined linden and oak tree (Ovid, *Metamorphoses*, 8.616–724). The allegorical-referential level of the passages, then, points to a kind of wish-fulfillment fantasy, in which Klopstock wrote the lifetime of love he and Meta were unable to share into his narration of redemption; the meter belies this wish-fulfillment, halting the soul's flight into heaven with heavy-syllabled line-endings and labyrinthine syntax.

* * *

The tension generated by the multi-layered affiliations and contradictions between meter, allusion, and content, I want to say, deepens readers' or listeners' appreciation for and affective engagement with the *Messiah*, perhaps especially for twenty-first century listeners more attuned to human pathos than to ecstatic depictions of divine redemption. In seeking to move his readers through the movement of language, Klopstock relies on metrical efficacy to support content even as he seeks to activate his readers' attentiveness to that efficacy. In addition to the cerebral satisfaction (not to be discounted) of following metrical patterns across large volumes of text and at the same time the pleasure of finding poetic language to offer more than can be assimilated into such patterns, Klopstock offers us a way of indexing our experience of metrically complex language, attending neither solely to a rush or swell of sound nor discarding any relation between meter and thematic content that is not universally valid as a shaping of sound by sense. *Mitausdruck*, then, becomes a resource for excavating and articulating the expressiveness of poetry more fully, showing the ways in which the complicated, variable, and subjectively perceived relations between language in its inseparable material and signifying components make poetry the place where the whole human—cognitive, affective, embodied, and culturally conditioned—speaks itself.

3

Disciplining Meter

In 1799, the renowned Leipzig philologist Gottfried Hermann begins his monumental *Handbook of Metrics* by castigating his colleagues for "worship of everything old in modern times," a love for "everything obscure and mysterious," "faintheartedness ... in the face of apparently insurmountable difficulties," and "neglect of philosophy."[1] Clearly, the stakes of metrical theory and practice remain high, and tongues remain sharp. In this chapter, I show what those stakes are by situating metrical thinking within the context of nineteenth-century German culture, the years after Klopstock's death and leading up to Nietzsche's career. Doing so will uncover what cultural, aesthetic, and philosophical problems were investigated through questions of patterns of syllables roughly 120 years after the figures in my first and second chapters, reminding us again that the supposed objectivity of metrical counting is always illusory. Tracking the metrical developments of the nineteenth century will also help to show the ways in which Nietzsche, the focus of the fourth chapter, both engages with and departs from thinking about meter and rhythm in his era. Doing so, in turn, will foreground what elements of his theories we might want to reclaim for our own understanding of meter as a central component of poetic experience, one that illuminates the complex interplay between language, culture, and the body. Whereas the eighteenth-century metrical debates had focused on cultural prestige and the effort to move bodies as well as minds, the nineteenth century's thinking about meter foregrounds questions of disciplinary identity and cultural difference.

Thinking about meter in the nineteenth century is dominated, at the most general level, by two very broad (and sometimes overlapping) questions: 1) How foreign or distant are the meters of past or other cultures? That is, can members of one culture imagine or understand, much less experience, the metrical achievements of another? 2) How do we study meter? Specifically, is metrics a science (*Wissenschaft*), and what does it mean to be "scientific" (*wissenschaftlich*)? Who measures what and how? These questions get posed in specific ways in the different disciplines that began to define themselves as the forerunners to modern university disciplines: classical philology, Germanic philology (which split into modern and Old Germanic branches, plus literary studies and linguistics), historical and comparative linguistics (which developed in tandem with

---

[1] Gottfried Hermann, *Handbuch der Metrik* (Leipzig: Gerhard Fleischer dem Jüngern, 1799), IV. Translations mine.

Metrical Claims and Poetic Experience. Hannah Vandegrift Eldridge, Oxford University Press.
© Hannah Vandegrift Eldridge (2022). DOI: 10.1093/oso/9780192859211.003.0004

philologies of non-classical languages but also adopted the methodologies of natural sciences such as physiology), as well as musicology (which was gradually beginning to articulate distinctions between music criticism, history, theory, and acoustics).

In this chapter, I first give a brief overview of the historical, political, and cultural shifts that these changes reflect. I then follow the two questions—how distant are the meters of past or foreign cultures? and how should they be studied?—into the two areas of metrical theorizing most important for Nietzsche: classical philology and musicology. Not coincidentally, they are also the two disciplines in which thinking about meter and rhythm were central to disciplinary identity.

3.1 Translation and Literary Contexts

In the eighteenth century, as I outlined using the hexameter debate, the interplay between problems of translation and poetic innovation drove metrical theory to a previously unheard of level of precision and contentiousness. Shifts in translation practice mirrored shifts in literary and academic culture as a whole starting in the 1820s and especially following the death of Johann Wolfgang von Goethe in 1832: a sense of belatedness, a turn away from classical (both Latin and Greek) to modern European languages, and persistent questions about audience and efficacy—pedagogical, political, or aesthetic.[2] The literary history of the nineteenth century uses several overlapping designations for time periods or tendencies, for example the so-called "Biedermeier" (from ca. 1820–50, characterized by resignation and quietism[3]), the more political *Junges Deutschland* and *Vormärz* movements or groups (from ca. 1830–50[4]), and a heterogenous and developing

---

[2] On literary trends see, for example, Clayton Koelb and Eric Downing: "After the death of Goethe the pace of innovative literary production slackened for a time in Germany. The middle years of the nineteenth century—the four decades from roughly 1830 to 1870—produced a number of significant writers of drama, poetry, and fiction, but the period was by no means so intense as the turn of the century had been." Clayton Koelb and Eric Downing, "Introduction," in *German Literature of the Nineteenth Century, 1832–1899*, vol. 9, Camden House History of German Literature (Rochester, NY: Camden House, 2005), 1–19 (2). Josefine Kitzbichler titles her section on the years after Goethe's death "Ende der Übersetzungstheorie?" (End of translation theory?), noting that translation shares the sense of belatedness with the arts generally. Josefine Kitzbichler, Katja Lubitz, and Nina Mindt, *Theorie der Übersetzung antiker Literatur in Deutschland seit 1800*, Transformationen der Antike 9 (Berlin: de Gruyter, 2009), 73–5.

[3] Thomas Pfau, "Between Sentimentality and Phantasmagoria: German Lyric Poetry, 1830–1890," in Koelb and Downing, *German Literature of the Nineteenth Century, 1832–1899*, 207–50. See also Annemarie van Rinsum and Wolfgang van Rinsum, "IV.4.1 Biedermeier als kulturhistorischer Begriff," in *Deutsche Literaturgeschichte*, vol. Band 6: Frührealismus 1815–1848 (Munich: dtv, 1992), 181–4 and on lyric in particular Annemarie van Rinsum and Wolfgang van Rinsum, "IV.4.2 Die Lyriker," in *Deutsche Literaturgeschichte*, 185–213.

[4] Annemarie van Rinsum and Wolfgang van Rinsum, "III.3.5 Politische Lyrik des Vormärz," in *Deutsche Literaturgeschichte*, 168–78.

realism (from ca. 1850–90[5]). Anticipating my discussions in this chapter and the turn to Nietzsche in the next, Clayton Koelb and Eric Downing introduce their literary history of the nineteenth century by noting that "The transition from the quiet mid-century to the intensity of the 1870s, 1880s, and 1890s is also marked by a shift in the kinds of cultural activity that dominated the literary scene. Two of the most significant literary figures of the 70s and 80s were not poets, dramatists, or novelists but rather a composer, Richard Wagner (1813–83), and a classical scholar turned philosopher, Friedrich Nietzsche (1844–1900)."[6] The years prior to this transition, unsurprisingly, exhibited a number of conflicting trends with regard to metrical practice.

To begin with, metrical theory moved outside the realm of both literary production and translation practice; choosing to write in a specific meter no longer necessarily entailed a particular cultural and/or political commitment, and translators rarely theorized their methodologies—certainly not in the detail that Klopstock and others had done. The Biedermeier period, in particular, produced a "vast array of lyric writing," driven in part by "encyclopedic collecting and microscopic studying of lyric forms"[7] that "reflect[ed] the Biedermeier era's preoccupation with the collecting and inventory-taking of cultural artifacts";[8] thus "a number of poets (Platen, Lenau, Geibel, Rückert) explore a broad array of classical, modern, and experimental forms by scrupulously apprenticing themselves in a vast array of forms (Ghasel, terza rima, sestina, epigrammatic poetry, sonnet, alexandrine, ottava rima, canzone, ballad, ode, hymn) and then refining their prosodic possibilities."[9] Here, then, the previous century's valorization of the Ancient world yielded to a formal pluralism that adopted and adapted forms from Ancient and modern literatures. (We might also see this in the expansion and collection of forms as a parallel to the expansion and accumulation of material resources in European colonialism.) The aesthetic of collecting (*sammeln*) extended to poetic practice: authors as well known as Eduard Mörike assembled and edited anthologies, frequently stylized as a "Blumenlese" (florilegum), that included their own poetry and translations (sometimes previously published, sometimes lightly modified) of antique and other modern European authors.[10] For the *Junges Deutschland* and *Vormärz* authors, translation could democratize "Bildung," making it accessible to those without a classical education; both groups criticize metrical translations as

---

[5] Dietmar Goltschnigg, "Vorindustrieller Realismus und Literatur der Gründerzeit," in *Geschichte der deutschen Literatur*, ed. Viktor Žmegač, vol. Band II/1 1848–1918, 1980, 1–108, particularly the subsection on "Lyrik und Versepik" (42–59).

[6] Koelb and Downing, "Introduction," 4.

[7] Pfau, "Between Sentimentality and Phantasmagoria," 217.

[8] Pfau, "Between Sentimentality and Phantasmagoria," 223.

[9] Pfau, "Between Sentimentality and Phantasmagoria," 223.

[10] Kitzbichler, Lubitz, and Mindt, *Theorie der Übersetzung*, 133.

producing "dead rhythms" (*todte Rhythmen*), preferring versions that emphasize the contemporary and especially political relevance of Ancient texts.[11]

Some poets of the *Vormärz*, which produced more verse writing than *Junges Deutschland*, write political poems (often stylized as songs) and depict contemporary social and especially industrial reality, creating a "Poetik der Eisenbahnen und Dampfmaschinen" (poetics of railroads and steam engines).[12] But lyric is not at the forefront of German literature's shift into realism; Pfau remarks that "Were one pressed to name a single overarching and dominant feature of German lyric poetry after 1830, it would probably have to be the genre's enduring uncertainty as to its own social legitimacy and efficacy."[13] And while the number of translations increases throughout the nineteenth century, it does so in parallel with growth in the book market as a whole.[14] Finally, efforts to return to metrical principles in translation around the middle of the century are far less strict than their eighteenth-century predecessors and remain the province of epigonal formalists and traditionalists. Against this background, Wagner's *Gesamtkunstwerk* theories and libretti inspired by old Germanic verse and Nietzsche's radical critiques of language and highly ironized poetry appear emphatically new.

3.2 New Disciplines

Until the middle of the century, the shift in literary and cultural hierarchies away from antique literature leaves existing academic disciplines relatively untouched even as revolutions in university structures and priorities create new disciplines.[15] As my discussion below outlines, much of classical philology continues to appeal to authorities established between 1790 and 1810. Unlike the eighteenth century, the nineteenth century treats philology, poetics, and hermeneutics as separate fields, in what Kitzbichler, Mindt, and Lubitz characterize as a "drifting apart of different discourses," each of which has widely varying functions and contexts for translation.[16] Both sides of a raging debate over the proper object and methods of philology (here exclusively: classical philology) ban translation from the tasks of the philologist, treating it as *unwissenschaftlich* (unscientific).[17] (To say nothing of writing their own poetry or adapting the maxims of classical authors for their modern German counterparts, as Gottsched, Bodmer, Breitinger, and Klopstock had done.) Only near the end of the century does translation cease to be a "taboo

[11] Kitzbichler, Lubitz, and Mindt, *Theorie der Übersetzung*, 81–3.
[12] van Rinsum and van Rinsum, "III.3.5 Politische Lyrik des Vormärz," 168–78.
[13] Pfau, "Between Sentimentality and Phantasmagoria," 207.
[14] Kitzbichler, Lubitz, and Mindt, *Theorie der Übersetzung*, 78.
[15] Kitzbichler, Lubitz, and Mindt, *Theorie der Übersetzung*, 78.
[16] Kitzbichler, Lubitz, and Mindt, *Theorie der Übersetzung*, 78, my translation.
[17] Kitzbichler, Lubitz, and Mindt, *Theorie der Übersetzung*, 195.

topic" for classical philology and gain recognition as a method of exegesis or a useful step in interpretation.[18]

Instead, translations of both classical and modern languages into German are taken up by the newer departments of literary studies (*Literaturwissenschaft*) or modern German literature, which emerge concurrently with (and sometimes as part of) departments of *Germanistik*—a term whose scope was (and still is) itself a matter of disagreement. Many of the same developments that drive changes in the book market and translation practice likewise influence the establishment of new departments and disciplines: the increased self-assurance of a bourgeoise that expected educational politics to correspond to its interests (including commercial/industrial purposes), the extension of the demand for subject-specific university education for *Gymnasium* teachers to modern language educators (not just teachers of Greek or Latin), and the growing number of social-professional societies that function as a "link between school and university and an expression of increased bourgeois national consciousness."[19] The university system was undergoing equally significant (and not independent) revolutions in its organization, based on the "shift from general learnedness (*Gelehrsamkeit*) to disciplinary expertise, the dissolving of the hierarchy of the faculties, reform of the university to emphasize research, and the increasing independence of individual disciplines."[20] Within the study of languages, the rise of historical and comparative paradigms for inquiry in what would come to be called *Sprachwissenschaft* (language sciences; sometimes translated as linguistics) eventually assists Germanic philology in establishing itself as a scientific discipline distinct from the literary interpretation of texts.[21]

In the early- to mid-century, classical philology serves as a paradigm for the emerging disciplines and their corresponding departments: most professorships for the modern languages start as *Doppelprofessur* positions, with dual appointments in a classical and a modern language, or later in two modern languages.[22] Unlike classical philology, however, the new philologies split relatively quickly into literary studies and linguistics, the former concerned with modern texts (and areas such as aesthetics and poetics)[23] while Germanic philology turns to the project of

---

[18] Kitzbichler, Lubitz, and Mindt, *Theorie der Übersetzung*, 195.

[19] Jürgen Storost, "158. Die 'neuen Philologien', ihre Institutionen und Periodica: Eine Übersicht. XXV. The Establishment of New Philologies in the 19th Century Die Herausbildung neuer Philologien im 19. Jahrhundert Le développement des nouvelley philologies au XIXe siècle," in *History of the Language Sciences—Geschichte der Sprachwissenschaften—Histoire des Sciences du Langage.*, ed. Sylvain Auroux et al., vol. 2 (Berlin/Boston: De Gruyter, 2008), 1241. My translation.

[20] Uwe Meves, "160. Die Entstehung und frühe Entwicklung der Germanischen Philologie. XXV. The Establishment of New Philologies in the 19th Century Die Herausbildung neuer Philologien im 19. Jahrhundert Le développement des nouvelley philologies au XIXe siècle," in Auroux et al., *History of the Language Sciences*, 1286. My translation.

[21] Meves, "Die Entstehung und frühe Entwicklung," 1286.

[22] Storost, "Die 'neuen Philologien,'" 1243.

[23] Storost, "Die 'neuen Philologien,'" 1243.

producing editions of historical Germanic texts.[24] These scholars use historical-comparative methods to define themselves as scholars or professionals and to distinguish themselves from their literary-studies counterparts: "Aspirations to being scientific, professionalization and specialization formed the key words for the recognition of German philology ... as a scientific/academic discipline that included (historical) linguistics as a sub-field and let the fields of textual interpretation and modern literature lie fallow to a great extent."[25] The divisions within the field were not unequivocally celebrated: by the 1840s, there were calls to bridge the "divide between old and new philologies, between philologists and linguists,"[26] and at the close of the century the linguist Hermann Paul warned that the necessary division of labor between linguistics and literary history (*Sprachwissenschaft* and *Literaturgeschichte*) had become too great a separation.[27]

Scholars in each of these emerging disciplines—comparative and/or historical linguistics,) Germanic philology, and (modern) German literary studies—take up questions of metrics. Given the influence of classical philology on the new areas, it is not surprising that several versions of the questions with which I opened the chapter appear here, too: how foreign are the meters of other cultures, and how (and by whom) should meter and metrical theory be studied? While of course investigators of modern German literature do not take on the question of accessibility of historically distant metrical practice directly, their texts include accounts of adaptations of other meters to German and often raise questions of which phonological components of German were organized into metrical patterns in what kind of units (lines, strophes, half-lines, etc.) in ways that echo the inquiries of classical philology, Old Germanic philology, and comparative linguistics. All of these disciplines pose the question of their proper objects and methods across the century: is metrics a science, and what does being scientific mean? In the remainder of this section I give a brief example of the questions raised by investigations of meter before turning to the higher-profile and more contentious status of metrics in classical philology.

Historical Linguistics and Germanic Philology: Jacob Grimm

Jacob Grimm, best known in non-academic contexts for his collection of fairy-tales with his brother Wilhelm, is at the forefront of the newly developing discipline of historical linguistics; although thinkers such as Johann Gottfried Herder had developed a robust sense of historical change and development across human

---

[24] Meves, "Die Entstehung und frühe Entwicklung," 1286.
[25] Meve, "Die Entstehung und frühe Entwicklung," 1286, my translation.
[26] Storost, "Die 'neuen Philologien,'" 1242, my translation.
[27] Meves, "Die Entstehung und frühe Entwicklung," 1287.

culture, Grimm's approach is decidedly more empirical.[28] Whereas Herder, for example, narrates a story of the (ambivalent) progress of languages in general from poetic to rational (see Chapter 1), Grimm's four volume *Deutsche Grammatik* (German Grammar), published between 1819 and 1837, analyzes "the facts of the German language, in its varied forms and with its cousins, over some fifteen stages."[29] Here, then, the historical method underscores that a properly scientific approach is historical and empirical, not (necessarily) systematic in the sense of being derived from a set of first principles.[30]

In the first volume of his *Deutsche Grammatik*, Grimm offers a "Remark on prosody," in which he finds it puzzling that modern German poetry seems to attend exclusively to "tone/sound or accent" (*ton oder accent*) rather than "laws of quantity," particularly given that German does distinguish between long and short vowels.[31] He notes that Romance languages and modern Greek lost the quantitative categorizations that appeared in Ancient Greek and Latin, and proposes that historical investigations of German should ask whether German, too, previously had length-based principles and what elements might remain in the modern version of the language.[32] Although Grimm does not say so explicitly, his suggestion hints at an underlying principle of similarity, or at least similar developments, between German(ic) and Greek as well as Latin and Romance languages; rather than asking which if any are accessible to modern poets or hearers, he appears to hope that scholars might use analogies between language families to illuminate the less-studied groups. He also reflects (here, negatively) on the relation between metrical rules and phonological elements of a language, pointing out that the absence of rules governing quantity in Germanic metrics is not unequivocal

---

[28] N.E. Collinge, "156. The Introduction of the Historical Principle into the Study of Languages: Grimm. XXV. The Establishment of New Philologies in the 19th Century Die Herausbildung Neuer Philologien im 19. Jahrhundert Le Développement des Nouvelley Philologies Au XIXe Siècle," in Auroux et al., *History of the Language Sciences*, 1210–23. Collinge sees some of this as specific to Germany: "In Germany more than elsewhere, there developed an ethnic, empirical, and non-aprioristic stance, even within disciplines that had seemed theory-driven." ("Introduction of the Historical Principle," 1212) He also notes that Grimm "rejected the equation of language with a decaying natural organism possessed of a life cycle" and "accepted that language change is unstoppable ('unaufhaltbar') and that it guarantees a tongue's individuality" (Collinge, "Introduction of the Historical Principle," 1221).

[29] Collinge, "Introduction of the Historical Principle," 1213.

[30] "Historical" and "empirical" do not mean non-essentialist; both the linguistics and the fairy-tale projects are the Grimms' efforts to find the voice and spirit of a people in its language. On race, nationalism, and philology, see Tuska Benes, *In Babel's Shadow: Language, Philology, and the Nation in Nineteenth-Century Germany* (Detroit, Mich: Wayne State University Press, 2008) and Sarah M. Pourciau, *The Writing of Spirit. Soul, System, and the Roots of Language Science* (New York: Fordham University Press, 2017). John E. Joseph remarks that "At the start of linguistics as a 'scientific' historical inquiry with the work of Franz Bopp and Jacob Grimm, its cultural attraction and power lay in the promise it offered of rediscovering the original and true foundations of languages, cultures, and races" (Joseph, *Language, Mind and Body*, 222).

[31] Jacob Grimm, *Deutsche Grammatik*, 2nd ed., vol. 1 (Gütersloh: Druck und Verlag von C. Bertelsmann, 1893), 10–1. All translations are mine; I give the original German where connotations are ambiguous or different from English.

[32] Grimm, *Deutsche Grammatik*, 11.

evidence against quantity in the language: "The law of quantity can be present in a language and even still effective, without being used in poetry."[33] He then argues in the opposite direction, suggesting that there are perhaps traces of quantitative criteria operative in the (at the time not fully understood) rules governing rhyme practice in the Old High German poet Otfrid as well as in Middle High German.[34]

Grimm also exercises considerable care to explain what makes up the phonological features he postulates as the basis for metrical rules, a version of the question of what, precisely, metrics measures. He follows the section on prosody with a "Remark on accent" and differentiates between a) sound (*"laut (sonus)"*), as the "pronunciation of the voice," b) tone or accent as "the raising or sinking of the voice that accompanies the sound," and c) quantity, which measures "continuous sound."[35] The relation between quantity and accent in Germanic languages forms the basis of extensive discussion between Grimm and Karl Lachmann, the author of an unpublished but widely circulated manuscript, "On Old High German Prosody and Versification."[36] Grimm defers to Lachmann on the question of quantity versus accent, and regrets that "We can only set up a few propositions, but we are missing the living connection"[37] (a question of the in/accessibility of past meters). He acknowledges that the only clear rules in Old and Middle High German verse dictate accentuation and alliteration but reflects "Still there is something so natural in the measuring of time that for this reason I don't want to deny it to Old High German poetry ... You are more experienced in our metrics than I and can verify what is true or false in my views."[38] Lachmann initially rejects quantity entirely as a principle for Germanic verse and compares Old High German with Italian for sharing a "consistent conflict between observation of *Hebungen* and *Senkungen*, or number of syllables.[39] Eventually, however, he appears convinced by Grimm's evidence regarding rhyme and prosody in *Deutsche Grammatik*: which authors consider which words to rhyme indicate that there was some quantitative component at work as well.[40]

[33] Grimm, *Deutsche Grammatik,* 13.
[34] Grimm, *Deutsche Grammatik,* 13–5.
[35] Grimm, *Deutsche Grammatik,* 17.
[36] Karl Lachmann, *Über althochdeutsche Prosodie und Verskunst. Mit Beiträgen von Jacob Grimm.*, ed. Ursula Hennig, vol. 59, Hermaea Germanistische Forschungen (Tübingen: Max Niemeyer Verlag, 1990). See Hennig's introduction for an account of the circulation of the manuscript in the nineteenth century, leading to its discovery in Grimm's estate (Ursula Hennig, "Einleitung," in Hennig, *Über althochdeutsche Prosodie und Verskunst. Mit Beiträgen von Jacob Grimm,* 1–56.)
[37] Cited in Henning, "Einleitung," 14.
[38] Cited Henning, "Einleitung," 14.
[39] "Hebung" and "Senkung" literally mean "lift" and "fall" or "increase" and "decrease"; in German discussion of metrics (both Germanic and Greek or Latin) the terms refer to positions or functions in metrical patterning that could be realized in various ways, as Lachmann's discussion of what kind of accents could go in each of a *Hebung* or *Senkung* indicates. (See Hennig, "Einleitung," 15).
[40] See Henning, "Einleitung," 15–6. Sarah Pourciau gives an overview of the discoveries in nineteenth-century Germanic philology regarding *Stabreim* (alliterative verse) as what she calls "an indigenous alternative to the classical tradition of Greek metrics" (Pourciau, *The Writing of Spirit,* 120) whose quantitative measures dominated the discussion until the mid-to-late 1870s (Pourciau, *The*

Grimm's use of the possessive pronoun—"*our* metrics"—apropos the very metrics he laments not having sufficient information to understand hints at the way
in which historical and especially comparative arguments could be used to shore
up claims of linguistic uniqueness, which not infrequently shifted to claims of ethnic or racial belonging or difference.[41] (Wagner will use the insights of Germanic
philology to insist that only German can restore the unity of sound and meaning, language and music, to create the *Gesamtkunstwerk* of the future, as I discuss
below.) But comparative arguments could also assert fundamental relationships
and similarities between different languages and cultures.

Comparative Metrics: Rudolf Westphal

Rudolf Westphal, the only figure to publish in all of the disciplines I consider in this
chapter, uses other authors' documentation of shared plot elements between the
oldest literatures of Indo-Germanic languages as the starting point for investigations of whether they might also have shared forms, particularly metrical forms.[42]
He admits that any "comparative Indo-Germanic metrics" would be limited in
scope to very earliest forms potentially shared between the cultures of India, Per-
sia, Greece, and Germany, but hopes that understanding them could illuminate
the later metrics of each language.[43] He argues that rhythm as such (independent
of language, music, etc.) has two defining characteristics: equality of time units
and the organization of said time units into groups by an overarching marker,
the so-called ictus.[44] And then he lists the prosodic-phonological elements of each

Writing of Spirit, 299). Because Pourciau's argumentative trajectory aims at a rereading of Saussure, she
largely ignores the degree to which accent and quantity were disputed categories in nineteenth-century
(to say nothing of eighteenth-century) classical philology as well.

[41] See Pourciau for an argument about the role of philology in uncovering qualities used to make
claims for German particularity or superiority; though it is not always clear that the phrases she
cites have the normative valence she attributes to them, the linking of language, culture, and race is
unmistakable (Pourciau, *The Writing of Spirit*, Ch. 3 "Verse Origins").

[42] Rudolph Westphal, "Zur vergleichenden Metrik der indogermanischen Völker," *Zeitschrift für
vergleichende Sprachforschung auf dem Gebiete des Deutschen, Griechischen und Lateinischen* 9, no.
6 (1860), 437; all translations mine. Westphal is a polymathic figure whose relevance to almost all of
the nineteenth century disciplines in this chapter is surprising given his obscurity today: born in 1826,
he initially studied theology at Marburg before beginning to learn Sanskrit and Arabic in order to study
comparative and Indo-Germanic grammar. In 1846 he added classical philology to his already broad
interests. He published widely and rather hastily in comparative metrics, historical philology, modern German meter, history of Greek music, modern German music, and other fields. His works on
German music—based on his knowledge of Ancient Greek rhythmical theory—were largely rejected
by performers and composers, including Franz Liszt, but received enthusiastically by the music theorists Carl Fuchs and Hugo Riemann. (August Roßbach, "Westphal, Rudolf," in *Allgemeine Deutsche
Biographie, Band 42*, 1897, https://www.deutsche-biographie.de/pnd117327026.html#adbcontent.)

[43] Westphal, "Zur vergleichenden Metrik der indogermanischen Völker," 438. (All translations
mine.)

[44] Westphal, "Zur vergleichenden Metrik der indogermanischen Völker," 438. The notion of the
ictus, present in philology from Richard Bentley on, will be Nietzsche's primary enemy in his metrical
texts.

language that can be used to demarcate time units and their groupings: syllable length, accent placement, total numbers of syllables, some combination, or none of the above.[45] He believes he finds identical structures in the earliest transmitted forms of each culture, associated with attention to number of syllables and accent, which then developed into prosodies based on length or a combination of length and accent.[46]

Westphal's attention to the elements of rhythm independent of language comes from his commitment to the rhythmical theory of the 4th century BCE philosopher and music theorist Aristoxenus, to which he adheres throughout his career and in the many disciplines in which he writes. The proper method for metrical investigation, by Westphal's Aristoxenian lights, must combine an abstract definition of rhythm in general (of which meter is a species) with historical and comparative investigation of the ways meters developed from first principles over time. Westphal also shows a commitment to empiricism in his insistence that Aristoxenus derived his system from existing poetic practice, not as an abstract theory. Westphal uses similar argumentative strategies—general definition, comparison, historical development—in his study on German meter: in the preface, he complains that "What has thus far been said about this [metrical form] in appendices to German grammar or writings about poetics is far from a truly scientific penetration of this object, and even the most important fundamental concepts ... have hardly been articulated."[47] For Westphal, being scientific entails incorporating the (empirically derived and confirmed) theories of Aristoxenus; his work on modern German meters is less technical than his works on comparative or classical metrical theory and practice, but in organization, terminology, and designation of metrical units it is essentially the same.

Physiological Metrics: Ernst Brücke

One year later, Ernst Brücke, a professor of physiology, took the question of scienticity to its logical extreme in *Die physiologischen Grundlagen der neuhochdeutschen Verskunst* (The Physiological Foundations of New High German Metrics), in which he asserts his right to look at "bound speech" based on his previous work in the physiology of language and criticizes metrical theory for getting mired in debates over first principles and falling behind verse practice.[48] Brücke rejects not only classical metrics, which he sees as distorting scholars'

---

[45] Westphal, "Zur vergleichenden Metrik der indogermanischen Völker," 439.
[46] Westphal, "Zur vergleichenden Metrik der indogermanischen Völker," 454
[47] Rudolf Westphal, *Theorie der Neuhochdeutschen Metrik* (Jena: Carl Doebereiner, 1870), IX, my translation.
[48] Ernst Brücke, *Die physiologischen Grundlagen der neuhochdeutschen Verskunst* (Vienna: Carl Gerold's Sohn, 1871),III. All translations from Brücke are mine.

understanding of German meter, but also any poet's own statements, focusing instead on mouths and ears: "The verses that the living mouth speaks and the living ear hears are an object of natural-scientific investigation, entirely independent of the principles that led the poet in their composition, entirely independent of the patterns that were before him, and entirely independent of the views held about metrics when those patterns developed."[49] Emphasizing the importance of exact measurement, Brücke defines accent as the result of physiological processes: "The greater the pressure under which air moves through the glottis, the louder the tone of the voice becomes, and the louder the consonant sounds that the flow of air in the oral cavity creates. Accent is this intensification of tone and sound."[50]

Brücke attempts to measure both the strength of these intensifications and, in an appeal to the quantitative elements of metrics, the intervals between them by purely physiological means: using an instrument developed to measure blood pressure that turns at a consistent speed, he attaches one end of a dowel to a pen, the other to his lip, and speaks various verse forms, such that the consonants are marked by bumps in the line on the drum that increase in size according to the emphasis on the syllable (see Figure 3.1).[51]

The question of accessibility of past or foreign cultures disappears: Brücke demands investigations of the *living* mouth as it speaks (Greek verse forms!) and defines accent in physiological terms as created by "muscles that are able to change

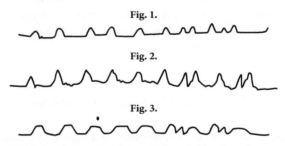

Fig. 1.

Fig. 2.

Fig. 3.

Fig. 3.1 Alcaic verse forms with syllables "pap," "bam," and "ba" (Ernst Brücke, *Die physiologischen Grundlagen der neuhochdeutschen Verskunst*, 33)

---

[49] Brücke, *Die physiologischen Grundlagen*, IV.

[50] Brücke, *Die physiologischen Grundlagen*, 2.

[51] Brücke, *Die physiologischen Grundlagen*, 32–4. Haun Saussy describes the creation of instruments to measure sound, language, accent, and dialect in the nineteenth century: using developments in "physics, medicine, physiology, and linguistics," Thomas Young, Carl Ludwig, Etienne-Jules Marey, and others invented a "family of kymographs," machines in which "a writing point was propelled by the energy of some external process and made to represent the stages of that process by moving across a space defined by minutely subdivided time and some other variable of interest" (Haun Saussy, *The Ethnography of Rhythm: Orality and Its Technologies* [Fordham Univ Press, 2016], 93. Saussy notes further, "Graphic methods were the Big Data of their time" (93).

the volume of the chest cavity" subdivided into syllables by the larynx.[52] What counts as meter, then, is only what can be counted or measured by empirical observation of physiological phenomena.

3.3 Classical Philology

Brücke's physiologically defined empiricism contrasts sharply with understandings of what it meant to be scientific or methodological in classical philology at the beginning of the nineteenth century, a contrast of both discipline and decade. Early in the century (that is, some seventy years before Brücke), classical philology is riven by a debate over its proper object and method between, not coincidentally, two metrical theorists: Gottfried Hermann and August Böckh.[53] The participants characterize the conflict as one between "word-philology" and "object-philology" (*Wortphilologie* and *Sachphilologie*), meaning the study and establishing of correct editions of texts versus attention to broader objects such as the history of law as well as material objects including coins and grave inscriptions. In fact, the two sides share significant common ground: "For Hermann, mastery of language included wider expertise and for Böckh language was one object of philology among others."[54] The disagreement arose initially from Böckh's rejection of Hermann's principles for distinguishing metrical units in the former's 1811 edition of Pindar;[55] because meter is taken to be, per Wilhelm von Humboldt, the "royal road to the innermost national character of the Greeks," granting privileged access to otherwise unreachable past culture, metrical theory becomes a struggle over who could claim such access.[56] Hermann accuses Böckh and the *Sachphilologen* in general of pursuing non-linguistic realia to conceal their lack of diligence in the study of language, while Böckh complains of "hardly even word- but rather syllable- and letter criticism";[57] what the debate reveals, however, are different conceptions of philology as a discipline or science. Whereas for Hermann philology is a rational practice applied to a finite task,[58] Böckh conceives of the discipline as

---

[52] Brücke, *Die physiologischen Grundlagen*, 84.

[53] The spelling of Böckh's last name varies between Boeckh and Böckh. I use the latter as what is given on the title page of the work I discuss below, *Über die Versmasse des Pindaros*.

[54] Christian Benne, *Nietzsche und die historisch-kritische Philologie*, Monographien und Texte zur Nietzsche-Forschung 49 (Berlin: De Gruyter, 2005), 52. See also Thomas Poiss, "Zur Idee der Philologie. Der Streit zwischen Gottfried Hermann und August Boeckh," in *Gottfried Hermann (1772–1848)*, eds. Kurt Sier and Eva Wöckener-Gade (Tübingen: Narr Francke Attempo Verlag, 2010), 143–63, here 143.

[55] Poiss, "Zur Idee der Philologie," 144–5.

[56] Poiss, "Zur Idee der Philologie," 148: "Metrik ... als Königsweg zum innersten Nationalcharakter der Griechen." Once again, Humboldt's essentialist linkage of language and culture is clear: there is *one* innermost national character expressed in meter as a feature of language.

[57] "kaum mehr Wort- sondern Silben- und Buchstabenkritik," Cited in Poiss, "Zur Idee der Philologie," 150.

[58] Poiss, "Zur Idee der Philologie," 154.

a "meta-science" (*Metawissenschaft*) whose identity consists in the infinite nature of its work: "Precisely in its infinity do we find the essence of the science."[59] As my more detailed discussion of both Hermann and Böckh below draws out, neither the degree of access to ancient cultures nor the objects through which that access was achieved—even within language—was uncontentious; for the moment, I want to emphasize the centrality of metrical theory to the question of disciplinary identity at the outset of the period I treat in this chapter.

Metrics as (Kantian) Science: Gottfried Hermann

For Gottfried Hermann, whose works are still considered the "first modern systematic treatment of metrics,"[60] to be scientific means to be Kantian: he adopts wholesale Kant's conception of "Wissenschaft" as a system based on first principles in all of the areas in which he published: aesthetics, poetics, metrics, grammar and hermeneutics.[61] In metrics, this means replacing the purely empirical existing metrics—based on observation of verse types—with a rational metrics that would develop universal laws of rhythm from a general definition.[62] In his *Handbuch der Metrik*, Hermann explains the ways in which metrics is or is not a science: "If by metrics one understands the enumeration and explanation of all types of verse, then it is a science that by its nature can never be completed. For rhythms are infinitely numerous, and there can be no rule that would restrict their number."[63] If, however, metrics means "the science of the universal rules of rhythm and the knowledge of the most common types of verse that are the basis of all others, along with the rules of applying rhythm in every possible genre of verse," then metrics can be a completable science.[64]

Having defined metrics in terms of (better: as the science of) rhythm, Hermann then defines rhythm as "the sequence of units of time [*Zeitabtheilungen*] according to a law."[65] This lawfulness is what distinguishes rhythm from any old sequence of time units; it is, moreover, the basis of rhythm's identity as a science (only what is law-driven can be a *Wissenschaft* in Hermann's sense). He then sets out to establish

[59] "Gerade in der Unendlichkeit liegt das Wesen der Wissenschaft," in Böckh's posthumously published *Enzyklopädie and Methologie der philologischen Wissenschaft*, from which he lectured, cited in Poiss, "Zur Idee der Philologie," 155. Poiss notes the proximity of this concept of philology to that of Friedrich Schlegel, and suggests Schleiermacher as Böckh's point of access to Schlegel's thought.

[60] Michael Schramm, "Hermann und Kant. Philologie als (Kantische) Wissenschaft," in Sier and Wöckener-Gade, *Gottfried Hermann (1772–1848)*, 98.

[61] Schramm, "Hermann und Kant," 84–5.

[62] Clemence Couturier-Heinrich, "Gottfried Hermann, un philologue kantien," *Revue germanique international* 14 (2011): 77.

[63] Gottfried Hermann, *Handbuch der Metrik*, IX.

[64] Hermann, *Handbuch der Metrik*, X.

[65] Hermann, *Handbuch der Metrik*, 1.

that the law of rhythm must be formal, objective, and a priori.[66] Specifically, the law of rhythm must be objective because different individuals perceive it the same way (i.e. is not dependent on subjective perception), formal because it does not have to do with the specific filling in of time units (with, e.g., particular words in a particular language), and a priori because it is not contingent or arbitrary.[67] Because rhythm is lawful sequence of units of *time*, in particular, Hermann appeals to Kant's analogies of experience from the *Critique of Pure Reason* (preservation of substance, causality, and reciprocal effects [*Wechselwirkung*]) to develop his a priori law of rhythm, but, unlike Kant, Hermann establishes a necessary relation between causality and *Wechselwirkung*, whereby causality is determined by reciprocal action.[68] Because rhythm is objective and temporal, and causality is the objective ground of all sequential things, "Thus the law of rhythm is causality" (Hermann, 4). But causality is not sufficient to define rhythm because it doesn't specify anything about the relation of *magnitudes* of cause and effect between units of time, which is what (for Hermann) the law of rhythm ought, by definition, to determine. Consequently, Hermann adds the idea of reciprocal effects or action (*Wechselwirkung*) and states that "the law of rhythm is the time-form of causality determined through reciprocal effects."[69]

This definition confronts Hermann with the problem of defining a first cause: how does the sequence of moments of time governed by laws of proportion of cause and effect get started to begin with? Simply proposing a previous cause within the sequences of time would lead to an infinite regress (what caused *that* cause, etc., etc.), and so Hermann suggests the existence of an external cause or "Kraft" (force).[70] This first cause manifests itself as a "beginning from its own force" (Anheben aus eigener Kraft), which Hermann links to a contentious term in metrical theory, the ictus: "This beginning from its own force is called *ictus*." (Hermann, 12). The concept of the ictus comes from the English philologist Richard Bentley (the only modern metrical theorist Hermann mentions approvingly), who used it in the commentary to his 1726 edition of Terence's comedies to designate the markings of the beginning of each unit within a verse structure (through stress, percussion, or dance movement). In Bentley's view it coincided with pitch accent, though this is a matter of continuing disagreement in the twenty-first century.[71]

---

[66] Hermann, *Handbuch der Metrik*, 3.

[67] See Hermann, *Handbuch der Metrik*, 2–3 and Schramm, "Hermann und Kant," 101.

[68] See Couturier-Heinrich, "Gottfried Hermann," 77 and Schramm, "Hermann und Kant," 101–2. Hermann does not refer to Kant or disagree with him explicitly; he outlines the insufficiency of the notion of causality alone for the law of rhythm in section 12 (4–5).

[69] Hermann, *Handbuch der Metrik*, 4: "Also ist das Gesetz des Rhythmus die durch Wechselwirkung bestimmte Zeitform der Caussalitat."

[70] I am omitting Hermann's arguments about the necessary equality of time units within the system of reciprocal effects.

[71] For an account of this debate, and a discussion of why it is so difficult to determine whether any such thing as an ictus existed in Latin, see Benjamin Fortson, *Language and Rhythm in Plautus: Synchronic and Diachronic Studies* (Walter de Gruyter, 2008).

Hermann aligns the ictus with what he calls the "arsis," which is the free cause of which the ictus is a manifestation.[72] Since he explains that the term arsis comes from the "Erhebung der Stimme" (raising of the voice),[73] he certainly seems to map ictus onto accent; what follows the free causes of the arsis Hermann calls the thesis, which is fully determined by the impetus of the arsis. As such, the theory of the ictus, which Hermann arrives at due to his need to be fully scientific in a Kantian sense, raises two versions of the question of the accessibility of Ancient meters and their proximity to modern German and its speakers: first, the question of the interplay between quantity and accent and, second, the question of whether the ictus formed a regular beat analogous to or identical with modern notions of *Takt*, understood as beat, bar, or measure (for example, ¾ time in modern music is referred to as ¾ "Takt").

Hermann addresses the question of accent and duration in a chapter called "Von den Accenten," in which he distinguishes what he calls "prosodic rhythm" (meaning quantity) from "accentual rhythm."[74] He contends that no rhythm at all is possible without determinate relations of long and short syllables in sequence, and that accent is entirely separate from quantity but can create its own rhythm by way of the contrast between accented and unaccented syllables.[75] Ideally, however, these rhythms should work in concert:

> Because the quantity of the words is already determined, and therefore also already has its own determinate rhythm, therefore the rhythm of the accent, whenever it is different from the prosodic [quantitative] rhythm, cannot cancel out this rhythm and its quantity; rather, it must be unified with the prosodic rhythm in such a way that both rhythms remain, and only those syllables in which the measurement of each rhythm is different, attain an intermediate length.[76]

Hermann holds that Greek and German are the same in this respect—both languages need to negotiate both types of rhythm—and, unusually, gives a German example of length and accent interactions, with _ designating a prosodically long syllable, U a prosodically short one, and 'marking the ictus:

Prosodic:	_ '_U unschúldig	' _ _ U lángsamer
Accent:	'_ U U únschuldig	_ '_ U langsámer[77]

---

[72] Hermann, *Handbuch der Metrik*, 13.
[73] This terminology reverses the usage in the Ancient rhythmicists and most metricists, where *arsis* (rise) and its opposite, *thesis* (fall), refer to the rise and fall of the foot, and thus thesis designates strong/accented/long and arsis designates weak/unaccented/short. I clarify which usage each theorist is following in the subsequent sections.
[74] Hermann, *Handbuch der Metrik*, 44.
[75] Hermann, *Handbuch der Metrik*, 44.
[76] Hermann, *Handbuch der Metrik*, 45.
[77] Hermann, *Handbuch der Metrik*, 45–6.

He explains that proper pronunciation combines the two, such that "unschuldig" and "langsamer" scan the same way when spoken, with a long and stressed first syllable, a medium length stressed second syllable, and a short and unstressed third syllable:

'_ Ú U únschúldig

'_ Ú U lángsámer

Hermann seldom addresses questions of performance or pronunciation, but he extends the question of accentual versus prosodic rhythm to a comparison of Greek, Latin, and German, noting that Greek meters demand divergent pronunciation from everyday speech, while Latin and German do not.[78]

Accent also seems to play a role for Hermann in fitting the prosodic-phonological components of language, which exist independently of the laws of rhythm, to a rhythmical or metrical pattern. He remarks that each language has its own rhythm as a source for euphony and expression, and adds that the rhythm of the verse and the rhythm of the words must agree: "Now if the rhythm of the verse is to be expressed in the rhythm of the words, then the rhythm of the words must be united with the rhythm of the verse in such a way that neither cancels out the other."[79] Hermann's vocabulary is remarkably similar to his description of the necessary agreement between quantitative and accentual rhythms, and his discussion of how verse rhythm and prosodic-phonological features can, in fact, influence quantity and thus metrical patterning seems nearly to identify the "rhythm of the words" with accent itself: "This unification of the rhythm of the words with the rhythm of the verses shows itself first in the caesura, second in the determination of the syllable quantity/meter [Sylbenmaaß] by the rhythm, third in the determination of the syllable quantity/meter [Sylbenmaaß] by the rhythm of the words, or the accent."[80] Accent, the phonological feature most familiar to speakers of modern German and the one used in German metrical patterning, has a much more robust function in Antique metrics than Hermann's initial focus solely on units of time (Zeitabtheilungen) in defining the laws of rhythm would suggest, hinting that perhaps those rhythms could be more similar to those of their modern counterparts than he admits.

The role of accent, if indeed it does fall together with the ictus, in defining metrical groups or units, thus poses the two questions I argue are central to thinking about meter in the nineteenth century: first, the ictus raises a version of the

---

[78] He gives the specific example of Terence, referring to Bentley's work in helping readers understand the pronunciation, and remarks that if one does not understand the role of accent, Terence's verses will sound harsh, but if one incorporates it, they gain the advantage over Greek verse that they don't injure the ordinary accent placement in the words (Hermann, Handbuch der Metrik, 49).

[79] Hermann, Handbuch der Metrik, 38.

[80] Hermann, Handbuch der Metrik, 38–9.

question of meter's scienticity, since it forces theorists to determine what, precisely, they are counting and how. And the question of metrical units likewise raises the question of *Takt*, given that determining whether Greek metrics had recurring units of equal size like modern musical measures depends to a great extent on which units are under discussion. The issue of *Takt* shows how the questions of whether metrics is a science and whether foreign or past meters are accessible overlap: if whatever units a given philologist counts produce something like the beats of modern music, then Ancient meters are fundamentally similar to their German counterparts. Hermann decisively rejects the idea of *Takt* in Ancient meters in his preface, where he discusses the differences between Greek and modern music. He contends that Ancient music was organized solely by the rhythm of the melody, with the consequence that Greek music was extremely fluid and variable with regard to the organization of time.[81] But Hermann introduces some ambiguity in his explanation that the divisions rhythmical rows (*Reihen*) of language superimposed a rhythmical structure (that of the words and the metrical schema) on the melody, therefore functioning in some ways like modern musical measures or time-signatures.[82] The most important difference, however, and the reason Hermann rejects efforts to reconstruct Greek music that import modern time signatures, is that the units of the rhythmical row are not all the same size; although twentieth-century music introduced changes of time signature (e.g., Stravinsky's use of 2/4, 2/16, 3/16, and 2/8 in the first five measures of the "Danse Sacarale" in *The Rite of Spring*), in 1799 the rule that all measures in a single section of a piece of (European art) music must be the same size was absolute.

Much depends, for Hermann, on the correct identification of rows as metrical units—not only the correct scansion and pronunciation but also any impression moderns might form of what Greek poetry actually sounded like, since poetry was invariably performed with music and dance. Unfortunately, precisely where to draw dividing lines between small-scale units of rows, to say nothing of lines or strophes, is not so easy to determine. In the final section of the *Handbuch der Metrik*, Hermann presents seven strategies for correctly dividing a text into strophes and lines: first, the philologist must identify known rhythmical patterns;[83] second, he must attend to the punctuation of the transmitted text;[84] third, most line endings align with word endings, though not all of them;[85] fourth (and most reliably), line endings always have an indeterminate (or anceps) syllable, though this must not be confused with an indeterminate syllable mid-line;[86]

[81] Hermann, *Handbuch der Metrik*, XIX–XX.
[82] Hermann, *Handbuch der Metrik*, XXIII.
[83] Hermann, *Handbuch der Metrik*, 232.
[84] Hermann, *Handbuch der Metrik*, 233–5.
[85] Hermann, *Handbuch der Metrik*, 236–7.
[86] Hermann, *Handbuch der Metrik*, 237–8.

fifth, the philologist should check hiatus placement;[87] sixth, consider whether the word-rhythm of words broken at potential line endings allow a division at that point.[88] The seventh approach, however, departs from the realm of rules: after considering all of the rules listed, the philologist must apply his "innate feeling for the beauty of rhythm and his educated taste. For whenever the above rules do not apply, then nothing but feeling can decide. This cannot be learned by rules, however; rather, like poetry itself, it is a gift of nature that can be refined by education/cultivation [*Bildung*] but not created."[89] At this point, then, science comes to an end: feeling replaces universal laws precisely at the point that would determine what the metrician is supposed to count and when the counting of those units (defined by quantity, accent, or both) would address the question of how much Ancient poetry is like or unlike modern meter and music, thus of how well modern listeners might be able to envision or hear the meters of past and foreign cultures.

Philology as Unending Task: August Böckh

To recapitulate: at the outset of the nineteenth century, to be scientific in metrical matters means to be systematic, a priori, ahistorical, formal, and objective. Perhaps unsurprisingly, the moments where Hermann falls short of these qualities—in the final sections on strophe and line division—begin the controversy with August Böckh that sets up opposing camps for disciplinary identity for the next several decades.[90] In his text on Pindar's meters (*Über die Versmasse des Pindaros*, 1809), Böckh credits Hermann for moving past the misleading theories of second and third century BCE Grammarians, but writes that he follows "erroneous side paths," in particular in emphasizing theory over observation.[91] Böckh identifies "criteria of division of verse" ("*Kriterien der Versabtheilung*") as the most important element of understanding rhythm: "if one wants to become familiar with a rhythm, it is necessary above all else to be able to determine its beginning and end"[92] Hermann's argument, Böckh points out, is circular: the philologist must know the rhythmical rules to establish the rhythmical units (of foot, line, etc.), but the units determine the metrical rules.[93] Moreover, Hermann permits word breaks across rhythmical units, which conflicts with his own principle of agreement between

---

[87] Hermann, *Handbuch der Metrik*, 244.
[88] Hermann, *Handbuch der Metrik*, 249.
[89] Hermann, *Handbuch der Metrik*, 265–6.
[90] For an account of the elements of this debate that remain unresolved in the twenty-first century, see Gauthier Liberman, "Hermann et la colométrie pindarique de Boeckh. Révolution et contre-révolution en métrique," in Sier and Wöckener-Gade, *Gottfried Hermann (1772–1848)*, 197–219.
[91] August Böckh, *Über die Versmasse des Pindaros*. Berlin: Realschulbuchhandlung, 1809.
[92] Böckh, *Über die Versmasse des Pindaros*, 24–5.
[93] Böckh, *Über die Versmasse des Pindaros*, 26.

verse and language rhythm: "The rhythm of the language and the rhythm of the verse should agree everywhere, and this harmony is disturbed if the rhythm of the words continues further than the rhythm of the verses extends."[94] Böckh also objects to Hermann's method: in his view, proof of the presence or absence of word breaks should be "a posteriori analytic," "not through reasoning from general grounds, but through historical-critical demonstration of laws that lie in the poems themselves and are discoverable in the poems through a precise analysis of them."[95] In contrast to Hermann, then, for Böckh proper scientific methodology proceeds from exact observation that can only subsequently be developed into general laws, not from a system from which all manifestations of meter or rhythm are derived.

Böckh also disagrees with Hermann on the relation between meter and music, both Ancient and modern. He criticizes Hermann for ignoring the mutual shaping of large-scale verse and musical structures, particularly in authors like Pindar, who writes in complex, variable, and large-scale structures that are nonetheless not lawless or chaotic.[96] Music and rhythm, per Böckh, can give much more information about each other than Hermann allows, and he adds that Hermann's refusal to take Ancient music theory into account obscures the "consistency and simplicity of our rhythmical systems, and at the same time its agreement with the views of the best musical theorists on the topic of measure [*Takt*]."[97] Böckh poses the question of *Takt* explicitly in a chapter called "Whether the rhythms of the Ancients, in particular those of Pindar, had *Takt*," and clarifies that this means the question "whether the rhythms also had a gait that moved along in equal intervals of time, or whether the times were unequal."[98] Böckh claims that equal time intervals are necessary: without them, "the manifold alterations of rhythm would have no unity; the multiplicitous could not be grouped together and would have no beauty."[99]. He resolves the apparent contradiction between (for example) the occasional allowed occurrences of a dactyl ($\_$ u u) in trochaic ($\_$ u,) rhythms by way of "dotted notes and pauses," including slight variabilities in the lengths of long and short syllables, which average out without distorting the rhythm.[100] Böckh closes his treatise with an afterword outlining his disagreements with Hermann along precisely the lines I explicated: Hermann ignores music, is theoretical/systematic rather than historical/empirical, and misinterprets his own law of the equality of time intervals to reject *Takt* as a commonality between Ancient and modern meters.

[94] Böckh, *Über die Versmasse des Pindaros*, 42.
[95] Böckh, *Über die Versmasse des Pindaros*, 45.
[96] Böckh, *Über die Versmasse des Pindaros*, 165-6.
[97] Böckh, *Über die Versmasse des Pindaros*, 191-2.
[98] Böckh, *Über die Versmasse des Pindaros*, 178-9.
[99] Böckh, *Über die Versmasse des Pindaros*, 179.
[100] Böckh, *Über die Versmasse des Pindaros*, 181.

Music's Challenge to Philology: August Apel

To reiterate, the apparently esoteric question of whether or not Ancient rhythms had *Takt* (measure, beat) emerges from a combination of the questions that determined metrical theory in the nineteenth century: what units, marked by the phonological features of which languages, are organized in ways that were similar or dissimilar to modern rhythms, and which of systematic, a priori or historical and empirical approaches are more scientific and thus better qualified to undertake investigation of Ancient meters? Writing in the years surrounding the debate between Hermann and Böckh, the jurist August Apel adds a further challenge: is philology in fact the right discipline to investigate meter and rhythm? In an extended series of articles published, fittingly, in the *Allgemeine musikalische Zeitung* (General Musical Journal) between 1807 and 1808, Apel complains that "The theory of rhythm would long since have been clear and comprehensible to everyone, if knowledge of music were not lacking on the side of the theoreticians, and on the side of composers the inclination to or capability of the necessary abstraction."[101] Modern German, in his view, poses little difficulty; nobody disagrees that accent determines verse, confirmed wherever there might be any doubt by the presence of rhyme at line endings and printing in clearly separated strophes.[102]

For Apel, modern and Ancient rhythms are fundamentally the same, and the reason modern hearers do not perceive their similarities is that philologists, following their pet theories rather than using their ears, distort Ancient rhythms and then demand that listeners praise what they have effectually invented.[103] If these distortions were cleared away, "the ancient verses reveal ... song that is quite comprehensible, at times very pleasing, and not at all strange to us."[104] Apel defines *Takt* as a necessary component of rhythm ("There is measure [*Takt*] in all rhythms, rhythm without measure cannot be conceived of by the very nature of rhythm"[105]) and remarks that since the laws of rhythm are based on laws of nature, "nobody need be surprised that they are the same in Ancient verse and modern music."[106] Like Böckh, he criticizes Hermann for not living up to his own Kantian standards, according to which "it befits every science to rest on firm principles," and contends that Hermann ends up making subjective, empirical, and a posteriori claims;[107]

---

[101] August Apel, "Über Rhythmus und Metrum," *Allgemeine musikalische Zeitung* 10, no. 1, 2, 4, 18, 19, 20, 21, 41, 42, 44 (1807-1808): 1–10, 17–26, 33–40, 49–62, 273–84, 289–98, 305–12, 321–31, 641–9, 657–68, 689–98.

[102] Apel, "Über Rhythmus und Metrum," 2.

[103] August Apel, *Metrik*, 2nd ed., vol. 1, 2 vols (Leipzig: Verlag der Weygand'schen Buchhandlung), 1834, IV.

[104] Apel, *Metrik*, V.

[105] Apel, *Metrik*, 13.

[106] Apel, *Metrik*, 14.

[107] Apel, *Metrik*, 40.

thus, "he has not achieved the derivation of the theory of rhythm from a single principle, indeed despite its appearance of systematic rigor his work lacks a scientific foundation entirely."[108] Apel extends his criticism from Hermann to metrical theorists and philology as a whole, arguing that they have covered the Ancient world in a "sheen of unreachable excellence" and thus for reasons of cultural prestige reject any equivalence between Ancient and modern rhythms.[109]

The discussion of the proximity between Ancient and modern music and rhythms, in the form of controversy over *Takt*, as well as the more technical disagreements over the role of accent and length, continued more or less unabated until Nietzsche's studies in the late 1860s and into the work of his teachers and scholarly sources. Friedrich Ritschl, Nietzsche's primary mentor, still felt compelled to address Apel's work in a piece in the periodical *Rheinisches Museum für Philologie* in 1842, called simply "On Metrics."[110] In the context of a discussion of specifically Latin verse that included attention to accent as an influence on syllable quantity, Ritschl glosses Apel's supposition that "probably we would find Greek accentual verse if we knew how to look for it" and notes that Apel gives no evidence for this statement, which "would contradict all of our understandings of Hellenic art."[111] Ritschl differentiates Greek and Latin verse practice and historical periods within each; he reflects on how text-critical decisions should be made and under what conditions rules are established. He proposes grammar as a first criterion in establishing whether a text has been corrupted in transmission, overriding rhythmical or metrical considerations, but also implies that metrical faults suggest faulty textual transmission.[112] Although he cites Hermann as an authority for certain editorial decisions, Ritschl is committed to historical-empirical principles: he proposes that to determine whether a given text is in a particular meter, a philologist should investigate whether the meter was attested at the time the text was produced, not whether the meter or text adheres to universal laws of rhythm.[113]

Reclaiming Aristoxenus: August Rossbach and Rudolf Westphal

The work of August Rossbach, in collaboration and eventual disagreement with Rudolf Westphal, introduces a further distinction into metrical theory: namely, the difference between rhythm as such and the material in which it appears. This distinction comes from a theorist who will become enormously important

---

[108] Apel, *Metrik*, 46.
[109] Apel, *Metrik*, 538.
[110] Friedrich Ritschl, "Zur Metrik," *Rheinisches Museum für Philologie* Neue Folge, 1 (1842): 277–302.
[111] Ritschl, "Zur Metrik," 301.
[112] Ritschl, "Zur Metrik," 278–9.
[113] Ritschl, "Zur Metrik," 284.

to Nietzsche's thinking about rhythm: Aristoxenus of Tarentum. According to Aristoxenus (in texts transmitted indirectly by subsequent treatises, of which Westphal released an edition) rhythm itself is a shaping or forming principle shared between art forms: "The forming, creating principle that brings law and regularity into the indifferent masses of tones, words, and movements."[114] He thus differentiates rhythm from what he calls the rhythmizomenon (ῥυθμιζόμενον), that is, the material that can be shaped by rhythm, but can equally well exist without rhythm.[115] Language, as a rhythmizomenon, poses particular problems because it already exists as an interrelated system of rules (grammar, syntax), unlike uncodified gestures or sounds that can be organized into dance or music. Rossbach follows Aristoxenus in defining metrics as the study of how language, specifically, can be rhythmicized.[116] The error of the Grammarians, per Rossbach, is to have attempted to establish a metrics that ignored the underlying rules of the rhythmicists (i.e. Aristoxenus): "A metrics without the foundations of Ancient rhythmics must more or less fall into the same error as the Ancient Grammarians, who cut through the vital nerve of the poetic forms and reduced meter to a schematism lacking the spiritual principle, the rhythm."[117]

In the history of metrical scholarship Rossbach gives in his introduction, he charges that Hermann, too, creates a dead metrics divorced from the principles of rhythm, while Apel and others who attempt to attribute modern rhythms to Greek meters end up in "unphilological dilettantism."[118] He sums up, "We do not need the principles of modern music in order to restore Ancient rhythms to meter; the remains of the Ancient rhythmicists, as slight as they are, when studied intensively together with scattered notes of other writers, give sufficient information."[119] The few remaining fragments, per Rossbach, illuminate much more than the small amounts of text would suggest because of their systematicity ("every sentence of the rhythmicists is a mathematical exercise that must be resolved and only finds resolution in comprehension of the other propositions/sentences [Sätze]."[120] Here, then, the criteria of systematicity and scienticity apply to the Ancient theorists themselves; in keeping with the trend toward valuing empirical-historical scholarship that developed across the nineteenth century, Rossbach praises Aristoxenus for combining history/tradition and science/system: "His

---

[114] August Rossbach, *Metrik der griechischen Dramatiker und Lyriker nebst den begleitenden musischen Künsten*, Bd. 1, 2 Bde. (Leipzig: Teubner, 1854) 7–8.

[115] Rossbach, *Metrik der griechischen Dramatiker und Lyriker*, 8. In his translation of Aristoxenus' fragmentary *Elementa Rhythmica*, Lionel Pearson renders *rhythmizomenon* as "rhythmicizable," conveying the potential or capacity for the material to be made rhythmic. Aristoxenus, *Aristoxenus Elementa Rhythmica: The Fragment of Book II and the Additional Evidence for Aristoxenean Rhythmic Theory*, trans. Lionel Ignacius Cusack Pearson (Clarendon Press, 1990).

[116] Rossbach, *Metrik der griechischen Dramatiker und Lyriker*, 19.

[117] Rossbach, *Metrik der griechischen Dramatiker und Lyriker*, 19.

[118] Rossbach, *Metrik der griechischen Dramatiker und Lyriker*, VIII.

[119] Rossbach, *Metrik der griechischen Dramatiker und Lyriker*, 20.

[120] Rossbach, *Metrik der griechischen Dramatiker und Lyriker*, VIII.

most positive propositions come from empiricism and historical tradition, they report first-hand experience and what is still present in the life of the nation and everywhere support themselves on established norms from the classical epoch, that he [Aristoxenus] could unify into a scientific connection [*wissenschaftlichen Zusammenhang*]."[121]

Because Rossbach follows Aristoxenus in understanding music and metrics as manifestations of rhythm in (different, but frequently combined) *rhythmizomena*, his approach to the question of whether not Ancient meters had *Takt* attends much more closely than earlier discussions did to specifically which units are being measured as equal or unequal. This links the question of scienticity—here, in the form of what, specifically, metrics counts and how those units are identified—to the question of the familiarity or foreignness of past rhythms. Rossbach notes that different groups of scholars have answered the question "Did antique *melos* have the measure [*Takt*] of modern music?" with "yes," others with "no," and suggests that instead an answer to the question requires careful clarification of what "Takt" refers to.[122] In modern music, *Takt* means "a group of tones that is unified to a coherent whole by a stronger emphasis on one, through lesser intension on the others," that is, "*the single measure*, insofar as it—as 3/8, 3/4, or 3/2 measure—constitutes the smallest unified element of music."[123] Per Rossbach, *Takt* in Ancient meters is a collection of elements joined into a coherent unit by an ictus defined by strength of intension ("The unity of the moments of time into a measure rests on the stronger intension, with which one of the moments is emphasized above the others"[124]), and indeed Rossbach notes that "in this sense the measure of modern and Ancient music is fully shared."[125]

But significant differences arise in the second sense of *Takt*, when the term is used specifically to mean "*Taktgleicheit*," that is, equal intervals of time from ictus to ictus.[126] Here, modern and ancient meters are quite different, and Rossbach quotes Aristoxenus' explanation that while the smallest units of time (which Aristoxenus calls *chronoi protoi*—first times) are equal in size, they are grouped in units of different numbers: "The signals of each foot remain constant in

---

[121] Rossbach, *Metrik der griechischen Dramatiker und Lyriker*, 3.
[122] Rossbach, *Metrik der griechischen Dramatiker und Lyriker*, 161.
[123] Rossbach, *Metrik der griechischen Dramatiker und Lyriker*, 161.
[124] Rossbach, *Metrik der griechischen Dramatiker und Lyriker*, 23.
[125] Rossbach, *Metrik der griechischen Dramatiker und Lyriker*, 161. It should be noted that Rossbach separates ictus from word accent, which he defines not as a question of emphasis but solely as one of pitch: "The ictus has frequently been confused with the word: 'accent', that is, pitch ... Ictus and word accent coincide in accentual poetry, such as older Latin or Germanic. In Greek the ictus is independent of pitch, as is the case everywhere when the poetry is sung rather than spoken, since in this case the ictus falls sometimes on a higher, sometimes on a lower pitch. Nobody would cast doubt on the identity of the word accent with higher pitch" (Rossbach, *Metrik der griechischen Dramatiker und Lyriker*, 24). In fact contemporary phonologists consider accent to be marked by a combination of pitch, volume, and possibly duration; see e.g. Kristin Denham and Anne Lobeck, *Linguistics for Everyone*, 2nd edn (Boston: Wadsworth, 2013).
[126] Rossbach, *Metrik der griechischen Dramatiker und Lyriker*, 163.

number and length, whereas the divisions that result from *rhythmopoiia* are subject to great variation."[127] (Again, similar to the combinations of multiple time signatures in, e.g., Stravinsky.) But the degree to which the combination of identically- and differently-sized components into groups and sub-groups creates structures of equal size or different size in each of Ancient or modern verse or music depends on the unit in question, which is again a matter of terminology and counting. Rossbach points out that one definition of *pous* refers to "what is called the single measure [*Takt*] in our music," but that in another sense it refers to "the combination of multiple single measures to a single row [*Reihe*], the periodic phrase in our music."[128] And as Rossbach quite rightly points out, modern music, too, does not invariably combine equal numbers of measures to build phrases or themes: "Typically groups of two and two or four and four measures do combine themselves, but almost every piece of music of the classical masters exhibits more elaborate rhythmical structures with intertwined phrase structures."[129] Rossbach's example is the beginning of Mozart's *Marriage of Figaro*.

Although Rudolf Westphal reports in the letter he writes to Rossbach, as a preface to his edition of Aristoxenus' fragments that he has come to disagree with Rossbach on the "fundamental propositions" of rhythm and meter, in fact his critical apparatus to the texts shares a great deal with Rossbach's metrics.[130] In particular, Westphal (like Rossbach) emphasizes Aristoxenus' combination of empiricism and systematicity;[131] he attends to rhythm as an underlying structure of all three of poetry, dance, and music;[132] like Rossbach, he distinguishes carefully between *pous* as individual measure and as larger group, making the analogy to modern music based on phrase structure rather than on than single measure size.[133] By the time Westphal published his *General Greek Metrics* in 1865, however, he was linking modern German music to Ancient Greek poetic and musical structures far more tightly than Rossbach permits.[134] On the question of how close German music and Ancient meters are—that is, the question of how foreign those meters are to modern German readers—Westphal makes somewhat contradictory claims: on one hand, he asserts that rhythm rests on an

---

[127] Aristoxenus, trans. Pearson, 13; Rossbach cites this passage in Greek, 164. "Signals" here refers to "*sēmeia*" (signs), i.e. the marking of *chronoi protoi* in the text. "Rhythmopoiia" refers to the creating of rhythmical structures in a specific *rhythmizomenon*.

[128] Rossbach, *Metrik der griechischen Dramatiker und Lyriker*, 22.

[129] Rossbach, *Metrik der griechischen Dramatiker und Lyriker*, XX.

[130] Rudolf Westphal, *Die Fragmente und die Lehrsätze der griechischen Rhythmiker* (Leipzig: Teubner, 1861).

[131] Westphal, *Fragmente und Lehrsätze*, VII.

[132] Westphal, *Fragmente und Lehrsätze*, 6.

[133] Westphal, *Fragmente und Lehrsätze*, 188–9.

[134] Rudolf Westphal, *Allgemeine griechische Metrik* (Leipzig: Teubner, 1865).

innate anthropological sense for order,[135] while four pages earlier he complains that Germans have lost their sense of the importance of rhythm: "Our modern feelings do not want to take rhythm as something consistently and essentially necessary either for poetry or for music. A great part of our poetic works, epic and dramatic, have fully cast rhythmical form aside and appears before us in the free robe of unbound speech, without our considering it less of a poetic artwork ... Our sacred and worldly opera music, as well, abandons strict rhythms for long sections."[136]

Westphal returns to the comparative approach he used in his essay on comparative Indo-Germanic metrics, linking the earliest forms of poetry to strophe-types present in Nordic and Iranian languages, therefore also likely Greek poetry.[137] And to consider how Ancient Greek poetry might have built itself up from smallest to largest structures, Westphal turns to modern German music and poetry: "It is a very striking coincidence, that the technics [Technik] of Ancient music designates the same melodic and rhythmic section, that is called 'period' by the new musicians, with the word [periodos], and that the first and second parts of the period [periodische Vorder- und Nachsatz] correspond to the word [kola], that is the limbs/members [Glieder] of the period for the Ancients."[138] Following up on the insight that similar names refer to similar structures and functions, Westphal demonstrates the organization of kola (members, limbs, Glieder) which he divides into periods using Goethe's ballad "Der König in Thule":

> "Es war ein König in Thule   Vordersatz
> Gar treu bis an den Grab,   Nachsatz [ll.1-2= "Periode"]
> Dem sterbend seiner Buhle   Vordersatz
> Einen goldenen Becher gab   Nachsatz [ll.3-4= "Periode"][139]

Here, then, Westphal proceeds on the basis of absolute identity on a medium-sized structural scale between Ancient Greek and modern German poetic forms. He notes, however, that because in antiquity composer and poet were the same person, there was complete agreement between melodic structure and verse structure, whereas for moderns such agreement is not required.[140]

Westphal then uses comparative methods to analyze the means of fitting together linguistic and rhythmical structures: the rhythm can fit both accent *and*

---

[135] Westphal, *Allgemeine griechische Metrik*, 187.
[136] Westphal, *Allgemeine griechische Metrik*, 183
[137] Westphal, *Allgemeine griechische Metrik*, 196.
[138] Westphal, *Allgemeine griechische Metrik*, 198–9.
[139] Westphal, *Allgemeine griechische Metrik*, 201.
[140] Westphal, *Allgemeine griechische Metrik*, 201.

quantity (although he admits that no such poetic tradition exists to his knowledge); rhythm can structure quantity *or* accent, or it may shape *neither*.[141] He gives extensive comparative and historical discussions of Sanskrit, Greek, Persian, and German, and notes that regardless of which phonological characteristic is organized metrically, all four languages develop larger (multi-foot or multi-line) structures and almost invariably align those structures with semantic units.[142] Westphal dedicates the most space to Greek in a discussion of ictus and word accent that complicates their relationship: in Greek, he compares the ictus with sforzando or marcato in music, while accent is exclusively a matter of higher and lower pitch for both Greek and German.[143] In German, pitch accent almost always coincides with the rhythmical ictus because the high pitch frequency (i.e. accent) typically falls on the root (semantically important, intensionally marked, highest-pitch) syllable.[144]

Westphal notes that the question of larger-scale units becomes even more complex in Old High German verse, in part because even forty-five years after Grimm and Lachmann, the precise rules that regulate lines and sub-units have not been determined, and so it remains difficult to delineate what *Takte* might or might not be equal and/or analogous to modern musical phrase structure.[145] In keeping with his combined philological and cultural-comparative approach, Westphal explains that in order to understand a particular appearance of a given meter, readers must take into account the entire historical context and development of verse forms within a given culture.[146] Consequently, he argues against calling German alternating verse "iambic" or "trochaic," since both are duple meters of equally long but unequally stressed syllables in German, but triple meters of unequally long (and ambiguously stressed) syllables in Greek.[147] Westphal gives his ultimate ruling on the relation between Ancient and modern music and verse in his history the of music of Antiquity and the Middle Ages (which Nietzsche cites in *The Birth of Tragedy*): Ancients and moderns have the same rhythmical basis but have developed and executed their rhythmical traditions differently across their histories.[148]

---

[141] Westphal, *Allgemeine griechische Metrik*, 221.

[142] Greek is something of an exception, in that classical Greek poetry allows word breaks within cola and ideas across line breaks (Westphal, *Allgemeine griechische Metrik*, 222).

[143] Westphal, *Allgemeine griechische Metrik*, 231.

[144] Westphal, *Allgemeine griechische Metrik*, 231.

[145] Westphal, *Allgemeine griechische Metrik*, 242.

[146] Westphal, *Allgemeine griechische Metrik*, 246. He also racializes this context and metrics in general, claiming for example that "the [east] Indian" has not adapted the "hard strength of unmediated strong bar elements [*Tacttheile*]" because "his whole nature is too soft and delicate for that" (Westphal *Allgemeine griechische Metrik*, 246). See Pourciau Ch. 3, "Verse Origins," for further discussion of the use of metrical characteristics to shore up claims of German superiority.

[147] Westphal, *Allgemeine griechische Metrik*, 256.

[148] Rudolf Westphal, *Geschichte der alten und mittelalterlichen Musik* (History of Ancient and Medieval Music, Breslau: Verlag von F.E.C. Leuckart, 1865), 125.

An Attempted Synthesis: Wilhelm Brambach

By 1870, Wilhelm Brambach, whom Nietzsche criticized for his continued adherence to the theory of the ictus, could both give an overview of the history of metrics and complain that "the majority of philologists have turned away from metrical studies since metrics has apparently become dominated by music."[149] In his *Rhythmical and Metrical Investigations*, Brambach is somewhat less critical, noting that attempts to consider Ancient rhythms from the perspective of contemporary music had existed since the fifteenth and sixteenth centuries.[150] He reports on Friedrich Ritschl's rejection of full agreement between ancient and modern rhythms, in particular of the "three fundamental assumptions" of "1) essential agreement in the arena of rhythm between Ancient and modern music; 2) inexorable demand for equality of measures ([*die Taktgleichheit oder Gleichtaktigkeit*]) for the concept of music; 3) complete falling together and coincidence of metrics and music in quantitative-rhythmical relation."[151] But Brambach follows Ritschl in recommending better knowledge of (modern) music to philologists studying meter. Both Brambach and Ritschl demand that proponents of the *Gleichtaktigkeit* of Ancient meters should be better acquainted with modern music, as Ritschl (as cited by Brambach), demonstrates with examples: "I will forgo quoting the examples of change of meter [*Taktwechsel*] that F. Ritschl has taken from our folk songs and generously shared with me; likewise the suggestive samples he includes of an Alsatian national dance or the curious fugue compositions of Anton Reicha, or even Wagnerian Operas. It is a fair demand that our philological guildsmen who argue for the axiom of *Gleichtaktigkeit* should make themselves rather more familiar with the history of music than tends to be the case."[152] Following this advice, I turn now to the questions in music theory that lie beneath its controversies over metrical and rhythmical structures.

3.4 Music Theory

As the conflicts between Hermann, Böckh, Apel, Ritschl, and Brambach have already shown, analysis of modern music is one strategy for attempting to gain insight into Ancient, especially Greek, poetry and music. Music has (or might have) this capability both because poetry was almost invariably sung and accompanied by music in the Ancient world and also, especially once theorists such as Rossbach and Westphal explicate Aristoxenus' work on rhythm, because music

---

[149] Wilhelm Brambach, "Kritische Streifzüge. II. Metrik und Musik," *Rheinisches Museum für Philologie*, Neue Folge, 25 (Critical Debates. II. Meter and Musik.1870), 237–8.

[150] Wilhelm Brambach, *Rhythmische und metrische Untersuchungen* (Leipzig: Teubner, 1871), V.

[151] Brambach, *Rhythmische und metrische Untersuchungen*, IX.

[152] Brambach, *Rhythmische und metrische Untersuchungen*, IX–X.

is the modern art form that most clearly makes use of rhythmical structures and their organization. One reason this debate recurs with such vehemence had little to do with metrical theory per se, but rather the developments of European—especially German—music in the nineteenth century: if modern music is a model for understanding Ancient verse, that model itself undergoes enormous changes, particularly in the increasing complexity of phrase structures of music both with and without words from Haydn to Mozart to Beethoven to Brahms to Wagner. The expansions of and irregularities in phrase structure and the discussions of the role of words for music especially but not only in opera, introduced over the years from 1800 to 1870, as well as the work in music theory that strove to take account of them, expand the repertoire of models provided by modern music. These "sweeping changes in temporality"[153] reflect their own set of aesthetic and cultural positions, whose protagonists influenced Nietzsche, Arthur Schopenhauer, Eduard Hanslick, and Richard Wagner. I cannot, of course, give a full presentation of the main issues in any of those theorists here; I use the questions raised in their work to outline the dilemmas and inquiries with which music theory found itself confronted—including, with Hanslick's appointment to the first chair of musicology in Vienna, the question of its own disciplinary identity—and the way in which thinking about musical rhythm responds to those questions. I then turn to the treatments of musical rhythm in Westphal as well as in Hugo Riemann and Carl Fuchs, both of whom are influenced by Westphal and the latter of whom prompts Nietzsche's final ruminations on meter in 1888.[154]

Philosophical and Cultural Foundations:
Schopenhauer, Wagner, and Hanslick

Schopenhauer remains relatively unknown for much of his lifetime, but, due to the exceptional status he accords to music in his philosophy, his work finds a prominent reception beginning with Wagner's enthusiastic attention in the 1850s and continuing into the 1870s and 1880s.[155] Specifically, Schopenhauer claims

[153] Lewis Rowell, "Time in the Romantic Philosophies of Music," *Indiana Theory Review* 25 (2004): 139–75.

[154] On Riemann's place in the "white frame" of music theory, see Philip A. Ewell, "Music Theory and the White Racial Frame," *Music Theory Online* 26, no. 2 (September 2020), https://doi.org/DOI:10.30535/mto.26.2.4. Ewell also enters a compelling argument that even the most formalist of analytical practices cannot be divorced from their originators' white supremacist views (in his article, the racism of music theorist Heinrich Schenker, which music theory as a discipline has claimed can be severed from his formal/structural analyses of music).

[155] Günter Zöller, "Schopenhauer," in *Music in German Philosophy: An Introduction.*, eds. Stefan Lorenz Sorgener and Oliver Fürbeth, trans. Susan H. Gillespie (Chicago: University of Chicago Press, 2010), 121–40. Zöller links this late-breaking enthusiasm to the resonance of Schopenhauer's philosophy with the cultural-historical moment following failed 1848/1849 revolutions: its resigned, apolitical

that music, unlike the other art forms, is a "representation of the will,"[156] understood in Schopenhauer's dualist system not merely as part of human psychology but the "arational foundational character of reality as an externally existing drive and compulsion."[157] Both this special status and the notion that music functions as a universal language that can express universal emotion—e.g. "pain itself" or "joy itself" rather than pain or joy about something in particular—proves appealing to composers and theorists of music,[158] even as Schopenhauer's argument that music represents the unrepresentable will is paradoxical[159] and the "analogies" he establishes between music and the phenomenal world as objectifications of the will are flimsy.[160] (For example, he claims that melody in a piece of music is to the ground bass as the human is to the natural world.[161]) But Schopenhauer does offer an intuitively appealing account of the way in which music seems to reveal something important about human emotion and to express human feeling and striving in a different, more innate and embodied, mode than discursive, conceptual speech.[162]

Two central ideas from Schopenhauer—music as lacking representational content and music as emotively expressive—formed opposite sides of perhaps the most famous music-critical polemic of the German nineteenth century: the writings of Eduard Hanslick and Richard Wagner. As Gunter Zöller points out, Schopenhauer's idea that music is "modifications of the will in the medium of tones" seems at least analogous to Hanslick's contention that music is "tönend bewegte Formen" (sounding moving forms).[163] But in the same text, "On the Musically Beautiful: A Contribution to the Revision of the Aesthetics of Music," Hanslick sets out to destroy what he calls "*Gefühlsästhetik*" (aesthetics of

---

pessimism and culture of art worship fit neatly into the self-understanding of the reading classes (Zöller, "Schopenhauer," 134).

[156] Zöller, "Schopenhauer," 127.

[157] Zöller, "Schopenhauer," 122.

[158] Zöller, "Schopenhauer," 128

[159] "Since the Will itself stood outside time, and time and space alike were forms of the *principium individuationis* by which phenomena and the Ideas are made known to us in their plurality, music to him was absolutely independent of the phenomenal world and therefore could scarcely be bound by time" (Rowell, "Time in the Romantic Philosophies of Music," 149).

[160] Alex Neill, "Schopenhauer," in *The Routledge Companion to Philosophy and Music*, eds. Theodore Gracyk and Andrew Kania (New York: Routledge, 2011), 347; Rowell calls the analogies "naïve" (Rowell, "Time in the Romantic Philosophies of Music," 149).

[161] Robert W Hall, "Schopenhauer's Philosophy of Music," in *A Companion to Schopenhauer*, ed. Bart Vandenabeele (Malden, MA: Wiley-Blackwell, 2012), 165–77.

[162] Hall glosses Schopenhauer's claim as asserting that music produces a kind of knowing as feeling that represents what can't be represented (Hall, "Schopenhauer's Philosophy of Music," 170); see also Rowell, "Time in the Romantic Philosophies of Music," 149 and Neill, "Schopenhauer," 347–8.

[163] Cited in Zöller, "Schopenhauer," 133. For an ongoing debate about Hanslick's Schopenhauerianism, see Tiago Sousa, "Was Hanslick a Closet Schopenhauerian?," *The British Journal of Aesthetics* 57, no. 2 (April 1, 2017): 211–29, https://doi.org/10.1093/aesthj/ayx008; Mark Evan Bonds, "Aesthetic Amputations: Absolute Music and the Deleted Endings of Hanslick's Vom Musikalisch-Schönen," *19th-Century Music* 36, no. 1 (2012): 3–23, https://doi.org/10.1525/ncm.2012.36.1.003; and Christoph Landerer and Nick Zangwill, "Hanslick's Deleted Ending," *The British Journal of Aesthetics* 57, no. 1 (January 1, 2017): 85–95, https://doi.org/10.1093/aesthj/ayw056.

feeling).[164] Hanslick links his call for a new aesthetics, one that will be attentive to
what is specifically musical in the "musically beautiful," to a shift from subjectivity
to objectivity, from feeling to science: "The drive towards an objective cognition of
things, as far as it can be attained by human research, had to overthrow a method
that began with subjective feeling, took a walk through the periphery of the phenomenon to be examined, only to return to feeling.[165] In order to be empirical
and objective, the new "research" that replaces subjective "systems" must derive
the "laws of beauty" of each art medium from the "characteristics of its materials,
its technique."[166] Here, then, systematicity has become unscientific, while medial
specificity combines with empiricism to create an aesthetics that analyzes what
is unique to musical beauty, in particular: "The primary element [*Urelement*] of
music is euphony [*Wohllaut*], its essence *rhythm*."[167] The "material" in which the
primal element of euphony and the essence of rhythm express themselves is "tone";
per Hanslick, the *only* thing these tones express are *"Musical Ideas,"* which are
interrelations of tonal forms that are beautiful in themselves, like the unfolding
of an arabesque or the movements of a kaleidoscope.[168]

Hanslick hypothesizes that composers insist on the importance of feeling
because they undervalue the sensory and want to compose for the heart rather
than for the ears, forgetting that all beauty is perceived by way of the senses.[169]
He rejects the idea that music is a language, universal or otherwise, because in
language sound or tone is merely a means to an end, whereas in music "Ton" is
a "Selbstzweck," an end in itself. Moreover, the notion of music as a language has
produced compositions that, as they strive to be expressive, disrupt the alignment
of large-scale rhythmical structures of symmetry ("Rhythmus im Großen, als die
Uebereinstimmung eines symmetrischen Baues") with micro-rhythmic moments
of individual elements ("Rhythmus im Kleinen, als die wechselnd-gesetzmäßige
Bewegung einzelner Glieder im Zeitmaß").[170] An aesthetics of music must take on
the task of establishing the boundary between music and language[171] ; Wagner
appears as a particularly frequent offender.[172] In fact, Hanslick's primary criticism of Wagner is that the latter prioritizes a-musical expressivity over what is
particularly and beautifully musical, to the point of becoming pathological: he
calls Wagner's "Lehre von der '*unendlichen Melodie*'" (theory of 'endless melody')

---

[164] Eduard Hanslick, *Vom Musikalisch-Schönen. Ein Beitrag zur Revision der Ästhetik der Tonkunst*,
ed. Dietmar Strauss (On the Musically Beautiful. A Contribution to the Revision of the Aesthetics of
Music, Mainz: Schott, 1990), 9. Strauss' edition prints the successive revisions in parallel; I therefore
cite it rather than the published English translations and give my own translations.
[165] Hanslick, *Vom Musikalisch-Schönen*, 21.
[166] Hanslick, *Vom Musikalisch-Schönen*, 23.
[167] Hanslick, *Vom Musikalisch-Schönen*, 74.
[168] Hanslick, *Vom Musikalisch-Schönen*, 75–6.
[169] Hanslick, *Vom Musikalisch-Schönen*, 76–7.
[170] Hanslick, *Vom Musikalisch-Schönen*, 74.
[171] Hanslick, *Vom Musikalisch-Schönen*, 102
[172] Hanslick, *Vom Musikalisch-Schönen*, 99.

"formlessness raised to a principle," "systematized non-music," and "a nerve fever written out on five music staves."[173] Polemics aside, the conflict between them, at least on Hanslick's terms, included debates over what it meant to be "scientific," questions about the tasks of music aesthetics as a discipline, and reflection on the interaction of small- and large-scale rhythmical units within a particular medium—that is, precisely the questions that motivated both the new disciplines and classical philology in same decades.

Richard Wagner's remarks on rhythm are embedded in the prose texts he produced throughout his career. His writings are less concerned with thinking through music-theoretical problems than with responding to musical, cultural, or political "stimuli."[174] Wagner has no reason to consider the problems of *Wissenschaftlichkeit* that the scholars writing in professional disciplines do; his works thus exhibit a rapid layering of cultural, aesthetic, philosophical, and political questions starting in the late 1840s: "Art and politics can stand in for each other, each seeking a revolutionary reorganization of its principles."[175] In addition to prompting a convoluted writing style with jumbled metaphors, this means that Wagner's aesthetic and philosophical judgments cannot be separated from his anti-semitism, German chauvinism, racial prejudice, and misogyny.[176] His works index the way in which analyses of culture and history in this period easily slide into nationalist and ethnic mythologizing, a tendency to which theorists of meter are not immune.[177] Wagner's texts grapple with problems of the expressiveness (and means thereof) of music, especially the relation between vocal and instrumental music,[178] and he calls for a new synthesis of art forms in the name of improving society in both *Opera and Drama* and *The Artwork of the Future*.[179] In the former, he blames the sorry state of opera on the fact that music, by rights a means to the ultimate end of drama, had become the main purpose of opera.[180] The encounter with Schopenhauer's work in 1854 provokes Wagner into rethinking this relation and offers him a further tool to refute Hanslick. Wagner eventually arrives

---

[173] Hanslick, *Vom Musikalisch-Schönen*, 11.

[174] James Treadwell, "The Urge to Communicate: The Prose Writings as Theory and Practice," in *Cambridge Companion to Wagner*, ed. Thomas S. Grey, Cambridge Companions to Music (Cambridge: Cambridge University Press, 2011), 181. He adds that for Wagner, "the stimulus is never far off; Wagner writes on a subject when that subject is directly in front of him" (181).

[175] Treadwell, "The Urge to Communicate," 184.

[176] Thus Wagner claims Felix Mendelssohn's music is superficial, heartless, and intellectually polished, mirroring his criticism of Jews as rootless, cosmopolitan, and able only to achieve learnedness rather than true cultivation or *Bildung*. See e.g. Richard Wagner, "Über das Dirigieren," in *Beethoven/Über das Dirigieren* (Darmstadt: Wissenschaftliche Buchgemeinschaft, 1953), 69–140, 118ff.

[177] See again Pourciau, *The Writing of Spirit* Ch. 3, "Verse Origins," and, specifically on Wagner, Chs. 4–5, and Benes, *In Babel's Shadow*.

[178] Thomas Grey, "Wagner," in Gracyk and Kania, *The Routledge Companion to Philosophy and Music*, 382. Grey phrases this question as a dialectic for Wagner between opera and symphony (ibid.).

[179] Grey, "Wagner," 384–5.

[180] Richard Wagner, "Oper und Drama," in *Richard Wagner: Dichtungen und Schriften*, ed. Dieter Borchmeyer, vol. 7, 10 vols. (Frankfurt a.M.: Insel Verlag, 1983), 9–370.

at a conception of drama that is itself music, rather than equivalent to the text, which helps him argue that music has (per Schopenhauer) a noumenal quality that reveals the will by way of manifestation in concrete art media.[181]

Wagner's views on rhythm remain quite consistent across his Schopenhauerian turn, as comparisons of his longest discussion in "Opera and Drama" (1851) and his essays on conducting and on Beethoven from 1869–70 demonstrate. In "Opera and Drama," Wagner examines the interaction of tone and articulation within the vowels and consonants of language: he imagines a *Tonsprache* (tone language) as an originary expression of emotional arousal in unarticulated vowel sounds and identifies it as the basis of melody.[182] These sounds are accompanied by naturally fitting gestures, which organize the tones into ordered temporal segments, that is, rhythm, which thus emerges organically from melody.[183] (The vocabulary of "naturalness" and "organicism" is Wagner's.) Applying spatial metaphors of internal and external to phonology, Wagner believes that while vowel tones could express inner feelings, language needed consonants to express external objects; their combination means that the resulting "language roots" (*Sprachwurzeln*) bore an iconographic relation to what was expressed, and their combination into alliterative verse bespoke affinities between words that shared sounds[184]. The emphasis placed on these root words shaped what would become a line of poetry, organizing it into groups and setting the limit on the line via the greater expulsion of breath required for emphasized syllables .[185] Wagner explains that these emphases are the source of all metrics, and scorns philologists for failing to understand meter properly: "How simple is the explanation and understanding of all meter, if we make the reasonable effort to return to the natural conditions of all human capacities for art, from which alone we can return to true artistic productivity!"[186] He narrates a fall away from innately expressive language, which can only be corrected by a return to alliterative verse that will generate strong and weak beats for melody, organizing sound into articulated sections that arise from the essence of language.[187]

In his 1869 essay on conducting, Wagner transfers the dichotomy between tone and articulation from language to a contrast between "held tone" and "figured movement" in music.[188] He uses this distinction to explain the difference

---

[181] "Following Schopenhauer, but resisting Hanslick, Wagner grants to music a kind of absolute or noumenal essence while insisting that, as a phenomenon or 'representation,' in Schopenhauer's terms, it will necessarily be conditioned by various ritual or discursive modes of human utterance" (Grey, "Wagner," 386).

[182] Wagner, "Opera and Drama," 218–9.

[183] Wagner, "Opera and Drama," 219. This disagrees with Schopenhauer's view that rhythm is imposed on tone from the other art forms.

[184] Wagner, "Opera and Drama," 221.

[185] Wagner, "Opera and Drama," 221.

[186] Wagner, "Opera and Drama," 223.

[187] Wagner, "Opera and Drama," 251ff.

[188] Wagner, "Über das Dirigieren," 92.

between the tempos of adagio and allegro not necessarily as matters of speed but of the difference between tone and rhythmical figuration: "Here the *adagio* stands opposite the *allegro* as the held tone to the figured movement. The held tone gives the law to the tempo adagio: here rhythm dissolves in the pure life of tone [*Tonleben*] that belongs only to itself and is sufficient in itself."[189] The expressiveness of tones accomplishes for an adagio tempo what in the allegro is the work of rhythm as the "variation of figuration."[190] The essay Wagner completes to mark the 100th anniversary of Beethoven's birth likewise establishes an opposition between unshaped, timeless tone or harmony and the plastic, visual, or spatial, with rhythm now as the mediating instance between them: "Through the *rhythmical* organization of his tones the musician comes into contact with the visual plastic world, specifically through the similarity of the laws according to which the movement of visible bodies reveals itself to our perception."[191] Arguing against Hanslick, Wagner disagrees that this analogy means music is defined by "pleasure ... in beautiful forms" and criticizes focus on architectonic musical structures ("rhythmisch[er] Periodenbau").[192] Instead, he suggests, Palestrina should be a model for a musical rhythm that is shaped by changes in harmony, rather than externally imposed symmetry; Wagner's own compositional practice, as we have seen, was used by metrical theorists as an example of precisely this kind of complex, non-symmetrical large-scale rhythmical structure.[193]

Westphal Turns to Modern Music

In a third stage of his career (following his work in comparative linguistics and classical philology), Rudolf Westphal engages directly with modern European (largely German) music, as the titles of two of his late works indicate: *Elements of Musical Rhythm with Particular Attention to our Opera Music* (1872),[194] and *General Theory of Musical Rhythm since J.S. Bach* (1880).[195] Westphal discusses Wagner in both, first as an analogy to the music of Aristoxenus' (somewhat belated Greek)

[189] Wagner, "Dirigieren," 92.
[190] Wagner, "Dirigieren," 92.
[191] Richard Wagner, "Beethoven," in *Beethoven/Über das Dirigieren* (Darmstadt: Wissenschaftliche Buchgemeinschaft, 1953), 22.
[192] Wagner, "Beethoven," 24.
[193] Rowell points out that Wagner "recognized ... the extraordinary effectiveness of long-held durations and extremely slow tempos in sustaining moods of intense feeling" and was a forerunner of "current musical tendency toward complex, extended passages of anacrusis and phrases that begin after the initial thesis (metacrusis)" (Rowell, "Time in the Romantic Philosophies of Music," 166).
[194] Rudolf Westphal, *Elemente des musikalischen Rhythmus mit besonderer Rücksicht auf unsere Opern-Musik* (H. Costenoble, 1872).
[195] Rudolf Westphal, *Allgemeine Theorie der musikalischen Rhythmus seit J.S. Bach* (Leipzig: Breitkopf und Härtel, 1880). Westphal views this work as the culmination of his career and sums up his work from classical philology (collecting and explaining Ancient metrical, rhythmical, and musical

era in its irregularity, which means Wagner's music will never be "volksmäßig,"[196] and in the latter as somewhat self-deluded, as Wagner (per Westphal) does not in fact compose melodies that are "infinite" or without rhythm and represents less of a break with the modern European opera tradition than he believes.[197] In both texts, Westphal asserts the fundamental similarities of Greek and modern musical rhythms, but the claims become much stronger in the later text: whereas in the *Elements of Musical Rhythm* he concedes "the study of Ancient rhythmics had led to the result, that the rhymical sense of the Ancients was essentially the same as the modern civilized peoples, without it being the case that every detail of the rhythmical compositions of Antiquity agrees with those of the modern world,"[198] in the *General Theory of Musical Rhythm* he insists that "rhythm with its laws has remained unchanging in music, from the earliest times of the Greeks to our modern day—not merely by and large, but in amazing agreement of the smallest details."[199] Twenty years before the end of the century, then, contentions that Greek and modern rhythms are essentially identical and accessible through modern music reach their peak.

Westphal notes that this agreement does not come about between Greek and modern *poetry*, but rather Greek poetry and modern music; this is because the modern poetry falls short of Greek rhythmical multiplicity.[200] He also holds that his understanding of the relation between musical and linguistic units in Greek rhythm and poetry revolutionized his work in metrics: "The connection between verse and musical period is my own discovery; only in the moment that I had found this relation was it possible for me to establish myself on a truly scientific standpoint [*auf einen wirklich wissenschaftlichen Standpunkt*] in the study of metrics."[201] Both volumes analyze the ways the material of language and the material of music fit together in rhythm. The "connection between verse and musical period" Westphal describes requires full agreement between language and rhythm, where sentence structure helps organize words into units with or on which rhythm can work (see, for example, section 14, "Logical Sections of Rhythmical Language. Smaller Syllable Groups and their Rhythmical Ictus").[202] As the mention of "ictus" in the section heading indicates, Westphal considers the fit between the two *rhythmizomena* from the small-scale syllabic to the larger-scale

---

texts) and comparative metrics (of modern and older languages, including German, Sanskrit, Persian, and Russian), which finally enable him to compare modern music to "Ancient practice" (III–IV).

[196] Westphal, *Elemente des musikalischen Rhythmus*, XXXV and 14.
[197] Westphal, *Allgemeine Theorie der musikalischen Rhythmus*, LIV–LV.
[198] Westphal, *Elemente des musikalischen Rhythmus*, XI.
[199] Westphal, *Allgemeine Theorie der musikalischen Rhythmus*, LIII–LIV.
[200] Westphal, *Allgemeine Theorie der musikalischen Rhythmus*, XII.
[201] Westphal, *Elemente des musikalischen Rhythmus*, XV.
[202] Westphal, *Elemente des musikalischen Rhythmus*, 17ff.

melodic, harmonic, or periodic.[203] Text, melody, and harmony cooperate to designate rhythmical units; recalling the quandaries of who counts what and how
that initiated the polemics between Hermann and Böckh, Westphal argues that
melody and harmony help determine the endings of metrical rows, whereas the
text can help distinguish larger units from one another.[204] Underscoring the affinities between types of organization, he compares the ends of musical-rhythmical
periods on the first, third, fifth, and seventh notes of the musical scale with a
period, a question mark, a question mark for an unanswerable question, and an
exclamation point, respectively.[205]

Westphal's analogy between cadences and punctuation foregrounds performance practice in a way that his earlier texts do not. Westphal first declares that
Bach is the composer "whose artistic sensibility is most congenial to those of
the Greeks"[206] and then states that musicians must understand Ancient rhythms
to play Bach correctly.[207] Westphal clarifies that Bach, like the Greeks, had an
innate feeling for the laws of rhythm which allowed him to arrive at the same
structures.[208] For this reason, the need for modern musicians to hear Greek
rhythms applies to all music: "So therefore let the rhythm of Greek art be heard
in our modern music."[209] He names awakening musicians' attention to rhythmical organization as a primary goal of *General Theory of Musical Rhythm since
J.S. Bach* and both there and in the *Elements of Musical Rhythm* he gives several hints at what the results might be. First, Westphal denies the role of the bar
line in designating metrical units: in modern music it is necessary for keeping the
orchestra together, but it does not indicate that the note following it receives the
strongest ictus.[210] Westphal calls for more nuanced execution of accents, noting
that "scansion and all-too-strong marking of ictus syllables" is poor practice both
in musical performance and poetic recitation; instead, performers should intensify the ictus/accent of important words across musical phrases.[211] Finally, he asks
performers to attend to moments of movement and stillness in large-scale periods, whose opposition creates an over-arching "accentuation principle" that will

---

[203] He points out that modern and ancient meter and rhythm attend to different components of
language: in modern prosody length is ignored and so note lengths can be freely assigned; in Ancient
prosody accent is ignored and so the ictus can be freely assigned (Westphal, *Elemente des musikalischen Rhythmus*, 25). Moreover, Westphal describes this difference in terms of freedom and constraint
that Nietzsche will also use: "The ancient, like the modern artist, has bound his own hands each in a
different way with regard to the freedom to rhythmicize and melodicize a linguistic text, the one in reference to the rhymical ictus, the other in relation to the length of time, and it is difficult to say whether
in Greek Antiquity or in the modern world the rhythmical artist is more independent from the natural
qualities of language" (Westphal, *Elemente des musikalischen Rhythmus*, 25).

[204] Westphal, *Elemente des musikalischen Rhythmus*, 132.

[205] Westphal, *Elemente des musikalischen Rhythmus*, 133.

[206] Westphal, *Allgemeine Theorie der musikalischen Rhythmus*, V.

[207] Westphal, *Allgemeine Theorie der musikalischen Rhythmus*, XIV–XVI.

[208] Westphal, *Allgemeine Theorie der musikalischen Rhythmus*, XX.

[209] Westphal, *Allgemeine Theorie der musikalischen Rhythmus*, LXV.

[210] Westphal, *Elemente des musikalischen Rhythmus*, XLII.

[211] Westphal, *Elemente des musikalischen Rhythmus*, 175–6.

mark the "rhythmic-musical period."[212] If modern musicians follow these guide-
lines, their performances will bring rhythm into clearer, more plastic, determinate
focus.[213]

Methods of Music Theory: Hugo Riemann

Hugo Riemann, today little known outside music theory, helped define the "canon
of subdisciplines" of the relatively new field of musicology, including "acoustics,
tone physiology and psychology, music aesthetics, practical music theory and
... music history."[214] His work enters into the problems of disciplinary identity
and *Wissenschaftlichkeit* I followed through the new philologies, comparative and
historical linguistics, and into classical philology across the nineteenth century.
When, therefore, Riemann makes the claim that in his experiments he can hear
the undertones of a note played on a grand piano, he is attempting "to accom-
plish the peculiar wedding of speculative philosophy and 'hard' natural science
that characterized the epistemology of Wilhelmine Germany."[215] That is, Riemann's systematic theories had deduced that undertones should exist in the sound
wave, and he attempts to confirm them empirically by way of experimentation.[216]
Riemann's work also emphasizes the turn toward performance-practical considerations I foregrounded in Westphal's works on musical rhythms. Riemann adds
composition-pedagogical issues, such that he is suspended between the "two main
concerns of the German nineteenth-century music-theoretical tradition: the preoccupation with pedagogy on the one hand, and the urge to find quasi-scientific
rules as a basis of a universal aesthetics on the other."[217] Finally, Nietzsche mentions Riemann in *Der Fall Wagner* and discusses him extensively in letters to Carl
Fuchs and Heinz Köselitz in the late 1880s; Nietzsche is critical of Riemann, but
several points of the Riemann's work will confirm Nietzsche's own philological
insights from fifteen years earlier.[218]

---

[212] Westphal, *Elemente des musikalischen Rhythmus*, 178.

[213] Westphal, *Elemente des musikalischen Rhythmus*, LXV.

[214] Alexander Rehding, *Hugo Riemann and the Birth of Modern Musical Thought* (Cambridge:
Cambridge University Press, 2003), 2. Rehding describes the commemorative activities surrounding
Riemann's death as indicating his enormous status and reports that his "theories of harmony and meter
suggested that the basic codes of music had finally been cracked" (Rehding, *Hugo Riemann*, 1).

[215] Rehding, *Hugo Riemann*, 35

[216] For more on the experiment, and Riemann's eventual revising of its claims, see Rehding, *Hugo
Riemann*, 19–26.

[217] Rehding, *Hugo Riemann*, 65.

[218] For a discussion of Nietzsche's reception of Riemann only in *Der Fall Wagner*, see Leslie David
Blasius, „Nietzsche, Riemann, and Wagner: When Music Lies," in *Music Theory and Natural Order
from the Renaissance to the Early Twentieth Century* (Cambridge: Cambridge University Press, 2001),
93–107. Blasius does not discuss Nietzsche's letters (those from 1886 did not appear in the *Kritische
Gesamtausgabe* until 2003).

Riemann's rhythmical theory expresses an ambivalence about philology and its relation to music: on one hand, he credits Westphal (and in particular Westphal's turn to Aristoxenus) as the source of his primary insights, while on the other, he rejects the importing of linguistic-metrical structures into music to explain rhythm. Thus in his essay "On Musical Phrasing," he reports that "the effect of Westphal's book has been horror over the undeniable fact, *that our rhythmical sense gropes along from bar line to bar line.*"[219] This realization forms the central point of Riemann's critique of the accentual theory (*Akzenttheorie*) of musical meter that had developed throughout the eighteenth and into the first decades of the nineteenth century, "whereby the idea of accented and unaccented syllables is transferred to musical tones."[220] The results, per Riemann, are performances that have abrupt changes in tone intensity and clunky phrasing, over-emphasizing individual measures and losing a sense of any structural-rhythmical whole.[221] Instead, at least in his work before 1900, Riemann calls for shading that leads to and from a dynamic climax across motifs not defined by the bar line: "The bar line is thus not a boundary post erected between tone groups that do not belong together in any tighter unity, but rather a dynamic representative of value [*Werthzeichen*], an indication of the note that follows it as the weightier, stronger of the group."[222] Echoing Wagner's attention to the "held tone" as the fundamental unit of music, Riemann explains that the essence of rhythm is an alteration of either "strength of tone" (i.e. volume) or speed; the most fundamental form is *legato*, not *staccato* notes with a pause after every tone.[223]

Because Riemann emphasizes the importance of duration rather than accentuation in determining metrical rhythm, he notes the difference between Ancient and modern poetic-metrical practice:

As is well known, the Ancient and modern handling of poetic meter differs especially insofar as the Ancient theory distinguishes longer and shorter syllables, the modern conversely strongly and weakly accented. The principles of modern

---

[219] Hugo Riemann, "Ueber musikalischen Phrasirung," in *Die Zukunft des musikalischen Vortrages und sein Ursprung,* ed. Carl von Fuchs (Danzig: A.W. Kafemann, 1884) , 12.

[220] William E Caplin, "Theories of Musical Rhythm in the Eighteenth and Nineteenth Centuries," in *The Cambridge History of Western Music Theory,* ed. Thomas Christensen (Cambridge: Cambridge University Press, 2002), 683.

[221] Caplin, "Theories of Musical Rhythm," 683.

[222] Riemann, "Phrasierung," 13–4. Caplin explains that after 1900 Riemann developed a different model of phrasing in which a question and answer structure between musical ideas creates moments of metrical strength at multiple levels (Caplin, "Theories of Musical Rhythm," 687); he also notes that both Riemann's phrasing models were and are rejected by the great majority of performers (691).

[223] Hugo Riemann, *Musikalische Dynamik und Agogik. Lehrbuch der musikalischen Phrasierung auf Grund einer Revision der Lehre von der musikalischen Metrik und Rhythmik* (Musical Dynamics and Agogics. Textbook of Musical Phrasing Based on a Revision of the Theory of Musical Meter and Rhythm, Hamburg: D. Rahter, 1884), 10.

poetic meter were transferred without further ado onto musical meter, and thus arose the frequently explained accentual theory.[224]

He proposes instead a system of "dynamic" and "agogic" accents, where the former are extended crescendo or diminuendo structures and the latter "an extension" of the tones in question as a form of emphasis.[225] Riemann's realization that accentual metrics in music project modern poetic meters onto music is what will appeal to Nietzsche, who extends the argument to Antique meters in his rejection of the theory of the ictus. Riemann, meanwhile, derives not only general recommendations for performance, but creates musical editions and editorial principles from his reconceived notion of musical meter in his *Catechism of Phrasing. Practical Instructions for Phrasing* (with Carl Fuchs).[226] They propose the use of the slur marking to denote phrase groupings (rather than legato tones), with slurs above the staff marking larger units and those beneath marking sub-units;[227] to mark "large-scale meter," they use an inverse caret ($^{\lor}$) at the bar line of heavier measures.[228] Despite their notational innovations, Fuchs's and Riemann's goal is not "to have the manner of phrasing we have established recognized as the only correct one" but rather "to awaken *an intensive demand* [Verlangen] *for clear cognition,* to make *phrasing to a matter of necessity.*"[229] Riemann and Fuchs thus call for the return to medium-specific metrical sensitivity in the face of inappropriate projection of accentual theory onto temporal structures—a call that Nietzsche will echo in his metrical texts.

A Schopenhauerian *Critique of Music*: Carl Fuchs

Carl Fuchs, Riemann's collaborator on the *Catechism of Phrasing,* is more critical of Westphal than Riemann is; indeed, Fuchs' two great enemies across his career are philologists (Nietzsche excepted) and Eduard Hanslick. In his *Preliminaries to a Critique of Music,* Fuchs turns to Schopenhauer to refute Hanslick, even though Schopenhauer's chapter on the "metaphysics of music" contains (according to Fuchs) numerous errors about music.[230] Nonetheless, Fuchs finds in Schopenhauer a philosophical system that moves past formalism to provide

---

[224] Riemann, *Dynamik und Agogik,* 50.
[225] Riemann, *Dynamik und Agogik,* 32.
[226] Hugo Riemann and Carl Fuchs, *Katechismus der Phrasierung. Praktische Anleitung zum Phrasieren* (Leipzig: Max Hesse's Verlag, 1886).
[227] Fuchs and Riemann, *Katechismus der Phrasierung,* 8–10.
[228] Fuchs and Riemann, *Katechismus der Phrasierung,* 15–6.
[229] Fuchs and Riemann *Katechismus der Phrasierung,* 17.
[230] Carl Fuchs, *Präliminarien zu einer Kritik der Tonkunst* (Leipzig: E.M. Fritzsch, 1871), 15–6. Fuchs thus rejects the basis of the affinities between Schopenhauer and Hanslick I followed Zöller in pointing out (see Zöller, "Schopenhauer,"128).

a valuation of music based on its psychological-affective effects.[231] Because in Schopenhauer "Gemüth" (meaning all of mind, soul, temperament, and feeling) is where the will manifests in human consciousness as feelings of pleasure or displeasure ("Lust oder Unlust"[232]), and *Gemüth* is the proper arena of response to music,[233] Schopenhauer's philosophy can serve as the basis for an account of what Fuchs calls the "metaphysical value" of music that transcends intellectual or physiological pleasure in its self-referential forms.[234] The metaphysical pleasure of music comes not from its sounds (Fuchs remarks "There is something in music that is not heard at all, and that is the best part"[235]) but because music "brings about an exercise of the will in the mastery over affective arousal of every kind through its will-free expression in tones."[236] This "exercise of the will" comes from the capacity of music to express and evoke emotion, schooling the hearer in his "subjection" of his will and desires to temporality, that is to the flux of emotional arousal; understanding desire to be temporary, he achieves "emancipation from the rule of feelings" resulting in "lightening of the burden of existence via the purification of the will."[237]

Rhythm plays a particular role in this exercise as itself a manifestation of the will: "So there is in rhythm a *will* that calls forth a type of movement: it is therefore a *metaphysicum* in music."[238] For this reason, the power and pleasure of form comes from the will, not the material arrangement itself.[239] Indeed, Fuchs sees rhythm as revealing the difference between the will and the intellect. He concedes a necessary role to the latter in artistic making in the forming and shaping of the will but insists on their different functions and roles.[240] Fuchs gives the example of the difference in music between one six-beat measure and three two-beat measures; while 1×6 and 2×3 are equal (=6) according to the intellect, in the latter "the rhythm means the *will* to group every three of six moments into a whole."[241] In addition to rhythm as a succession of moments of time, Fuchs adds (musical) meter (*Taktart*) and tempo to distinguish rhythm in art from rhythm in nature, and defines *Taktart* as the regular recurrence of differentiated accents.[242] Fuchs

---

[231] Fuchs, *Kritik der Tonkunst*, 8.

[232] Fuchs, *Kritik der Tonkunst*, 24.

[233] Fuchs, *Kritik der Tonkunst*, 27.

[234] Fuchs, *Kritik der Tonkunst*, 69. Fuchs compares Hanslick's aesthetics of music, which as I glossed above insists on the importance of auditory perception and the centrality of the material components in deriving aesthetic principles for music, to a "material" that "treats thinking as identical with the phosphorescence of the brain, because the former cannot happen without the latter" (Fuchs, *Kritik der Tonkunst*, 140).

[235] Fuchs, *Kritik der Tonkunst*, 143.

[236] Fuchs, *Kritik der Tonkunst*, 140.

[237] Fuchs, *Kritik der Tonkunst*, 139–140.

[238] Fuchs, *Kritik der Tonkunst*, 33.

[239] Fuchs, *Kritik der Tonkunst*, 135.

[240] Fuchs, *Kritik der Tonkunst*, 32.

[241] Fuchs, *Kritik der Tonkunst*, 32.

[242] Fuchs, *Kritik der Tonkunst*, 78.

proposes a variation of Riemann's critique of the bar line: in some musical styles, expressive accentuation aligns with the accentuation implied by the metrical structure, but in modern compositional and performance styles, the accent is placed expressively *against* the bar accent (*Takt-Accent*); he calls this the "meditative" style.[243] To convey the interaction of rhythm, meter, and tempo that makes rhythm artistic/aesthetic rather than merely a natural-acoustic phenomenon, Fuchs adopts the term "Drastik" from drama, where it refers to the liveliness of gesture and language; he thus emphasizes the expressive quality of rhythm in music and of music as such.[244]

Fuchs rejects, however, the expressivity of language mapped onto music in metrical structures:

> The only artistic phenomenon that shares with music the fact that its material is organized into successive measured quantities of time is Ancient poetry: in it, the time taken up by single syllables was regulated, albeit not with the full precision of our note values, and formed the basis of the metrical organization of verse, while in German poetry as is well known "long" and "short" are determined by the word accent, and therefore do not exist rhythmically at all[.][245]

Fuchs recognizes the analogy between quantitative meters and music (though even then the former are less precisely measured) but rejects German-language approximations of the "long" and "short" of classical meters. He credits Gottfried Hermann with creating a "scientific metrics" and raising interest in metrical theory but criticizes philologists in general for appealing to personal taste and, worse, using accentual structures as a crutch to support inadequate knowledge of Ancient meters.[246] Westphal, then, cannot be a "predecessor" of Riemann's except insofar as a "cloudy dawn" precedes a "bright midday," despite Riemann's own acknowledgment of his debt to Westphal.[247] Fuchs castigates the state of modern theories of musical meter: "We have knowledge of the note values, we have a false accentual principle—taken over from language—whose notation is the bar line, are proud of our 'natural feeling' ... and remain dependent ... on the subjective tastes of a few authorities."[248] Fuchs' work seeks to curtail precisely the cross-pollination between philology and music theory that I have traced in this section; in *The Future of Musical Performance*, he names as one of his goals "to erect a rampart and moat against the further intrusion of philologists into our territory and to show that the

---

[243] Fuchs, *Kritik der Tonkunst*, 72.

[244] Fuchs, *Kritik der Tonkunst*, 79.

[245] Carl Fuchs, *Die Zukunft des musikalischen Vortrages und sein Ursprung* (Danzig: A.W. Kafemann, 1884), 184.

[246] Fuchs, *Zukunft des musikalischen Vortrages*, 185.

[247] Fuchs, *Zukunft des musikalischen Vortrages*, 3.

[248] Fuchs, *Zukunft des musikalischen Vortrages*, 185.

attempts at filling gaps in our elementary knowledge and abilities through Greek metrics is entirely in vain."[249]

* * *

The years from Hermann's *Handbuch der Metrik* in 1798 to Fuchs' *Future of Musical Performance* in 1884 outline the tradition from which Nietzsche's thinking about meter and rhythm emerged in the 1870s and developed in the 1880s. The two questions I have traced throughout—1) How foreign or distant are the meters of past or other cultures? That is, can members of one culture imagine or understand, much less experience, the metrical achievements of another? 2) How do we study meter? Specifically, is metrics a science (*Wissenschaft*), and what does it mean to be "scientific" (*wissenschaftlich*)? Who measures what and how?—show that theorizing about meter continues to engage with central cultural, political, philosophical, and aesthetic questions. It shows, moreover, that not only the question of whether metrics is a science—and thus whether the measurements and what it measures are truly objective—but what a science is must always be negotiated within its cultural and historical contexts. The question of the accessibility of both past and foreign meters was not new to the nineteenth century, as my outlining of the hexameter debate in my first chapter showed; the shift from discussion of its implications for poetic practice (which went on quite happily writing German poetry in Greek meters and dozens of other forms) to disciplinary identity and *Wissenschaftlichkeit* arises in response to the development of new disciplines and the changes within both the university and German-speaking culture more broadly. Precisely because metrical theory—and, as we shall see in Nietzsche, practice—responds to those changes, it can illuminate the complex interplay between language, culture, and the body.

---

[249] Fuchs, *Zukunft des musikalischen Vortrages*, 3.

4

Nietzsche's Meters as Cultural Critique

On November 23, 1870, Friedrich Nietzsche (1844–1900) announced jubilantly to his friend Erwin Rohde, "On my birthday I had the best philological insight that I have ever had ... There is a new metrics that I have discovered, compared with which the entire modern development of metrics from G. Hermann to Westphal or Schmitt is an *error*."[1] Contemporary readers will recognize Nietzsche's characteristic modesty, but his interest in metrics and the names of his erring colleagues are likely unfamiliar, except to readers of my previous chapter. There, I analyzed the cultural, political, and epistemological stakes of the tradition Nietzsche challenges; in this chapter, I show that Nietzsche's work has three primary attributes that we should reclaim for thinking about meter and/in poetry. Before I embark on this agenda, however, a terminological caveat is in order: elsewhere in this book, I distinguish between meter and rhythm because the theorists I consider so do and because the terms activate different poetic and intellectual traditions. For Nietzsche, conversely, meter is quite simply the appearance of rhythm specifically in language (as opposed to music or dance). This view comes from his studies of classical philology, as I discuss below. Consequently, Nietzsche discusses what would generally be considered metrical forms—hexameter, alternating verse, trochees, etc.—using the vocabulary of rhythm. He also analyzes those phenomena together with features such as intonation and punctuation that might, in the twenty-first century, be discussed under the rubric of rhythm. But meter, as syllable patterning, shapes intonation and punctuation shapes syllable patterns, while all three can influence syllable stress and thus the realization of metrical rules—the distinction is once again not clear-cut. I follow Nietzsche's terminology in this chapter and refer mostly to *rhythm* rather than meter; as I argued in my introduction and as Nietzsche's work shows, the distinction itself is fluid and vexed.

Nietzsche's contributions to thinking about meter and rhythm are as follows. First, he emphasizes embodiment to a greater extent than his contemporaries and shows that and how bodily experience is always culturally and historically

---

[1] Nietzsche, Letter to Erwin Rohde, November 23, 1870. (http://www.nietzschesource.org/#eKGWB/BVN-1870,110). I cite Nietzsche's letters, his published texts, and many of his fragmentary notes from the digital critical edition of Nietzsche's works, Friedrich Nietzsche, *Digitale Kritische Gesamtausgabe Werke und Briefe (eKGWB)*, ed. Paolo D'Iorio (Paris: Nietzsche Source, 2009), http://www.nietzschesource.org/#eKGWB. Since many of the documents in the online edition are not translated, I give my own translations throughout the chapter except where otherwise marked.

Metrical Claims and Poetic Experience. Hannah Vandegrift Eldridge, Oxford University Press.
© Hannah Vandegrift Eldridge (2022). DOI: 10.1093/oso/9780192859211.003.0005

determined.² Second, he articulates the epistemological instability of thinking about meter and rhythm, undermining the self-satisfactions of *Wissenschaftlichkeit* (being scientific) claimed by much of nineteenth-century and some contemporary metrical scholarship. Third, Nietzsche foregrounds the inevitability but also the productivity of historical difference, attending to the ways in which particular cultures in their particular historical moments arrive at forms of expression that are both symptom and critique of their modes of being. These three attributes— attention to physiology, skepticism, and historical thinking—are not particularly news apropos *Nietzsche*. But, as with my reading of Klopstock's metrical theory and practice, I argue that Nietzsche's thinking about meter, as rhythm in language, illuminates aspects of our responses to patterned language that have disappeared from contemporary discussions of meter in particular and poetry in general.

My primary areas of investigation in this chapter are two even now marginalized facets of Nietzsche's career: his philological notebooks and his poetry.³ As several commentators have noted, there can be no firm distinction between Nietzsche as philosopher, rhetorician, poet, and philologist: whatever "philosophy" we find in Nietzsche cannot be separated from his handling of language, and a sense for the movement of language in and as thought is by his own lights the pinnacle of skills to be pursued by the philologist as well as the rhetor or poet.⁴

---

² This means that his discussion of the body in general disrupts any naturalized view of bodies as universally working a certain way, though his subsequent discussions of heartbeats, dance, and running do make assumptions about the pulse and the possibilities of movement. Moreover, having a view of the bodily experience as culturally-constituted hardly prevents discriminatory views of some bodies and cultures—in addition to his famously misogynistic and much-debated antisemitic statements, Nietzsche articulates horrifically racist positions, including that Black people do not feel pain as other races do and are thus not fully human. As with much of Nietzsche's philosophical and especially moralist work, there may be some debate about whether such statements are ironized, polemical, satirical, etc.— but trying to determine what Nietzsche "really meant" is by his own lights foolish. Nietzsche's modes of talking about meter and rhythm may offer a tool to direct the kind of textual-historical-cultural critique they evince at his own work, even as the textual examples I consider here do not include the direct racist, misogynist, and antisemitic statements elsewhere in his work. On Nietzsche's anti-Black racism, see William A. Preston, "Nietzsche on Blacks," in *Existence in Black: An Anthology of Black Existential Philosophy*, ed. Lewis R. Gordon (New York: Routledge, 1997), 165–72. On Nietzsche's antisemitism, misogyny, and relation to various other identity questions of his era, see Robert C. Holub, *Nietzsche in the Nineteenth Century: Social Questions and Philosophical Interventions* (Philadelphia: University of Pennsylvania Press, 2018).

³ Many of the obstacles outlined by Philip Grundlehner in one of the first extended treatments of Nietzsche's poetry still apply: Nietzsche's poems are almost always incorporated in other (prose) works; Nietzsche is critical of both poetry and poets; his poems invite biographical interpretations; and, finally, his poetry is of lower quality than that of, say, Goethe, Hölderlin, or Droste-Hülshoff. Philip Grundlehner, *The Poetry of Friedrich Nietzsche* (New York: Oxford University Press, 1986), xi– xiii. Grundlehner's final point is somewhat disingenuous, since there are many studies on poets who are not comparable in quality to three of the greatest lyricists ever to write in German. Some of Nietzsche's poems are surely better than others, but part of the difficulty is that Nietzsche puts pressure on categories such as lyricism, and especially anything that might resemble a lyric subject. It would exceed the scope of my interests here to establish criteria by which to determine which of his poems are of higher caliber than others; I focus on the ways in which the poems mobilize language to articulate and perform certain positions or points.

⁴ Thus in his *Encyclopedia of Classical Philology*, the notes for an introductory course he taught at the University of Basel, Nietzsche asserts "everything depends on the feeling for form [Formgefühl] for

Moreover, Nietzsche dissolves the boundaries between poetry, verse, lyric, and prose—in part because of his philological training, which gave him an "orientation to antique speech rhythms."[5] His prose texts, composed, edited, and re-composed from his enormous "reservoir of different kinds of notebooks," form a "deliberately recursive chain of commentaries on commentaries, prefaces, postscripts, and explanations."[6] Nietzsche's poetry, then, is the most direct and flagrant instance of his attention to the dynamics of language in all its metaphoricity and materiality, although prior scholarship has investigated similar claims in his work on and in rhetoric.[7] The three poems I consider in this chapter span his career: "To Melancholy" ("An die Melancholie," 1871) is one of the relatively few surviving poems from the 1870s, virtually all of which remained unpublished;[8] "Poet's Calling" ("Dichters Berufung") appears in the appendix of the second edition of *The Gay Science* (1887); and "Only a Fool! Only a Poet!" ("Nur Narr! Nur Dichter!") is the first of the *Dionysus Dithyrambs*, the last manuscript Nietzsche authorized before his mental collapse in 1889. All three are programmatic, in the sense that they discuss poets and poetry. The first two deploy and critique so-called "alternating verse," in which stressed and unstressed syllables alternate in either iambic or trochaic patterns, while the *Dithyrambs* are in free rhythms, anticipating the use of lineation for rhythmical-metrical effect in the twentieth century.[9]

Nietzsche's studies, published papers, and notebooks from his training and career as a professional philologist at the University of Basel are even more neglected than his poetry.[10] After studying at the Universities of Bonn and Leipzig

---

[5] perfected language." Friedrich Nietzsche, "Encyclopaedie der klass. Philologie," in *Nietzsche Werke. Kritische Gesamtausgabe*, vol. II.3 Vorlesungsaufzeichnungen (SS1870–SS1871) (Berlin: de Gruyter, 1993), 339–437, 393.

[5] Dieter Breuer, *Deutsche Metrik und Versgeschichte*, 4th ed. (Munich: Wilhelm Fink Verlag, 2008), 235.

[6] Christian Benne, "The Philosophy of Prosopopoeia," *The Journal of Nietzsche Studies* 47, no. 2 (July 6, 2016): 275–86, 275–6.

[7] On the philosophical work done by Nietzsche's language in his lyric and elsewhere, see Christian Benne and Claus Zittel, "Einleitung," in *Nietzsche und die Lyrik. Ein Kompendium.*, eds. Christian Benne and Claus Zittel (Berlin: de Gruyter, 2017), 1–8, 5. On rhetoric in Nietzsche's thought, see the introduction by Sander L. Gilman and Carole Blair in Friedrich Nietzsche, *Friedrich Nietzsche on Rhetoric and Language*, eds. Sander L. Gilman, Carole Blair, and David J. Parent (New York: Oxford University Press, 1989).

[8] Armin Thomas Müller, "Nietzsches Gimmelwalder Melancholie-Gedichte aus dem Sommer 1871," in *Nietzsche als Dichter. Lyrik—Poetologie—Rezeption*, eds. Katharina Grätz and Sebastian Kaufmann (Berlin: de Gruyter, 2017), 47–77, 49.

[9] Martin Opitz introduced alternating verse as the most natural to German in his *Buch der deutschen Poeterey* (1624); as I outlined in Chapter 1, the monotony of poorly executed iambic and trochaic verse forms was a primary motivation for the hexameter debate and Klopstock's metrical experimentation. On Nietzsche as a forerunner of Expressionist poetry in breaking the boundaries of inherited forms, see Dieter Breuer, *Deutsche Metrik und Versgeschichte*, 4th ed. (Munich: Wilhelm Fink Verlag, 2008), 231.

[10] James I. Porter and Christian Benne have done admirable work to remedy this neglect in the years since 2000; my debt to their texts is only partially represented by the number of references to each. See especially Porter, *Nietzsche and the Philology of the Future* (Stanford: Stanford University Press, 2000) and Benne, *Nietzsche und die historisch-kritische Philologie* (Berlin: de Gruyter, 2005).

(in addition to secondary schooling at Schulpforta, which gave him an excellent grounding in ancient languages and classical rhetoric), Nietzsche taught philology in Basel for ten years.[11] In general, Nietzsche's work in philology opens onto topics shared by his other writings: philology serves as "a conduit through which larger questions from adjacent areas of inquiry could be explored (chiefly philosophy, psychology, and culture, usually in this ascending order)."[12] Thus Nietzsche's interests in classical antiquity cannot be separated from his questions about subjectivity, history, and embodiment, and he draws on material from his philological notebooks to the end of his career.[13] Nietzsche's notebooks and courses on rhythm exemplify the ways in which his philological investigations are always involved in wide-ranging activities of cultural critique.[14] Rhythm and meter foreground questions of linguistic effectiveness, rhetoric, perception, and temporality in ways that Nietzsche will continue to draw on and that are shaped, even in their latest versions, by his earlier notebooks.[15] Meter and rhythm remain consistent concerns for Nietzsche, across (and against) the standard periodizations of his work into "early," "middle," and "late" phases; indeed, the thoughts in the rhythm notebooks call the very grounds of this periodization into question.[16] Both because of their centrality

[11] Nietzsche "lectured for a decade with mixed success at both the university and the local Pädagogium on themes ranging from early Greek philosophy, the Platonic Dialogue, and Aristotle's *Rhetoric* to Greek music drama, religious institutions, lyric poetry, Latin grammar, literary history, Aeschylus, Homer, and Hesiod." Anthony K. Jensen and Helmut Heit, "Introduction," in *Nietzsche as a Scholar of Antiquity*, eds. Anthony K. Jensen and Helmut Heit (London: Bloomsbury, 2014), xvii–xxii, here xxvii–xxviii. For an overview of what Nietzsche wrote on, presented, and published, as well as considerations of the reasons for his professional success at a relatively young age, see Joachim Latacz, "On Nietzsche's Philological Beginnings," in Jensen and Heit, *Nietzsche as a Scholar of Antiquity*, 3–26.

[12] James I. Porter, "Nietzsche, Rhetoric, Philology," in *Philology and Its Histories*, ed. Sean Gurd (Columbus: Ohio State University Press, 2010), 164–91, 165.

[13] Porter, *Nietzsche and the Philology of the Future*, 2–3.

[14] Porter, *Nietzsche and the Philology of the Future*, 128–130. Nietzsche's "burst of activity" on rhythmical topics included two courses dedicated entirely to Greek meter and rhythm, sundry remarks in other courses between 1869 and 1874, and the notebooks I discuss below, largely composed between 1870 and 1872 (ibid.).

[15] See Porter for an argument that rhythm relates to Nietzsche's "deepest lifelong concerns," including "thematics of musical and linguistic rhythm ... also those having to do with time, physiology, the analysis of quantitative and qualitative differences, agonal struggles with form, ancient and modern cultural history, and the history of criticism of the present" (Porter, *Nietzsche and the Philology of the Future*, 130). He adds, "The concepts and even the terms of the later reflections are all derived from this early phase, as is the tendency to surround the question of rhythm with philosophical perspectives, whereby rhythm tends to be viewed as 'symbolic of the drives'" (Porter, *Nietzsche and the Philology of the Future*, 128).

[16] "It is customary to divide Nietzsche's corpus into three distinct periods: an early first period of 1872–6 (*Birth of Tragedy* and the four *Untimely Meditations*), a second, middle period of 1878–82 (the free spirit trilogy comprising *Human, All Too Human, Daybreak* and *Gay Science*) and 1883–5 (*Zarathustra*) and a late, final period of 1886–8 (*Beyond Good and Evil* and onwards)." Keith Ansell-Pearson, "Friedrich Nietzsche: An Introduction to his Thought, Life, and Work," in *A Companion to Nietzsche* (Oxford: Blackwell, 2006), 1–21, 11. Ansell-Pearson notes that these divisions are not absolute, but the rhythm notebooks undermine even the grounds for the rough distinctions he draws (e.g. a pro-science, almost positivist perspective in the middle period, the emergence of the ideas about the will to power in the mid-1880s); as Porter points out we can trace a post-1873 shift "in genre and style" but not "method and object" (Porter, *Nietzsche and the Philology of the Future*, 25).

to Nietzsche's thinking about rhythm (thus for his career as a whole) and because of the sheer volume of text, they make up the bulk of my discussion here. I begin, however, with "To Melancholy," chronologically the earliest poem and one whose themes evoke *The Birth of Tragedy*, the work that effectively destroyed Nietzsche's academic reputation and led to his erasure from the history of philology.[17]

4.1   "To Melancholy" ("An die Melancholie")

In the summer of 1871, Nietzsche takes up themes and vocabulary that will subse-quently appear in *The Birth of Tragedy* in a forty-eight-line poem, "To Melancholy" ("An die Melancholie").[18] The poem praises the muse or goddess of melancholy as offering insight into the (Dionysian) "abyss of being" ("des Daseins Abgrund," l.16); in presenting these topics in a regular rhythmical form and thus channeling the horror of existence into a controlled surface, it seems to perform the interpene-tration of the Dionysian and the Apollonian in aesthetic production that Nietzsche identifies in *The Birth of Tragedy* as a function not only of tragedy but of the (tragic, dithyrambic) lyric.[19] But in its ironized tone (reminiscent of Heinrich Heine), in the circularity of the poetic program it narrates, and especially in its metrical prac-tice, the poem satirizes or parodies Schopenhauerian metaphysics and Nietzsche's revision of Schopenhauer as they will appear in *The Birth of Tragedy*. The poem describes itself as a delicate or even dainty plaiting of rhymes about the terrifying figure of melancholy, and its pedantic adherence to alternating iambs in eight-line rhyming strophes exaggerates what Nietzsche will later call the "unbearable" "tick tock" of German verse.[20] I have chosen "To Melancholy" to open my discussion of Nietzsche's thought on meter and rhythm because its thematic content anticipates the better-known Nietzsche of *The Birth of Tragedy*, even as its metrical strategies reduce the lofty claims of the later work to a monotonous tick-tock.

Writing about Writing

"To Melancholy" begins with a scene of writing; it then narrates a past-tense pro-cess of introspection and insight that melds the Schopenhauerian metaphysics

---

[17] On this reception and the consequences, see Latacz, "Nietzsche's Philological Beginnings," and James I. Porter, "Nietzsche's Radical Philology," in Jensen and Heit, *Nietzsche as a Scholar of Antiquity*, 27–50.

[18] http://www.nietzschesource.org/#eKGWB/NF-1871,15[1]. Hereafter I cite the online edition by line number.

[19] See *The Birth of Tragedy*, sections 5 and 6 (http://www.nietzschesource.org/#eKGWB/GT-5) as well as Bernhard Buschendorf, "Die Geburt der Lyrik aus dem Geiste der Parodie." Friedrich Niet-zsches Gedicht, 'An die Melancholie,'" in *"Jedes Wort ist ein Vorurteil": Philologie und Philosophie in Nietzsches Denken*, ed. Manfred Riedel (Köln: Böhlau, 1999), 105–30, 127.

[20] Letter to Carl Fuchs, presumed middle of April, 1886, http://www.nietzschesource.org/#eKGWB/BVN-1886,688.

of *The Birth of Tragedy* with canonical depictions of melancholy.[21] As several interpreters have noted, the lyrical speaker activates a two-sided tradition of melancholia representations as on the one hand pathological, detrimental to poetic productivity, and on the other hand revelatory, offering insight that leads to artistic production.[22] The speaker's narrative starts with the melancholic pose par excellence: sitting with head "bowed to [his] knee" as in in Dürer's *Melancholia I* (a print of which Nietzsche gave to Richard Wagner as a birthday present), before deploying an image that links the poem to *The Birth of Tragedy*: a vulture. Contrary to most classical sources, Nietzsche identifies the vulture as the bird that picks out Prometheus' liver, and he not only names Prometheus as one mask of Dionysus in Greek tragedy but chooses an image of Prometheus as the frontispiece for the work.[23] In the second and third strophes of "To Melancholy," the speaker continues to interlace themes and images from traditions of melancholic poetry with those anticipating the blending of Dionysian and Apollonian: the canonical contrast between interior reflection and outward inactivity (1.15), the "abyss of being" (1.16, "des Daseins Abgrund"), the *locus terribilis* in the mountains (ll.17, 22), and the association with barbarism or savagery (l. 18).[24]

While the second strophe apostrophizes the vulture in the second person as "you," in the third strophe the speaker turns his address to melancholy: "You spoke to me, incapable of deceiving humans,/ truly, with a horribly strict countenance."[25] Curiously, the next strophe depicts not speaking but showing, as the truth of melancholy reveals the interpenetration of life and death ("Qualvolle Gier, sich Leben zu erzwingen"/ "Torturous desire to seize life by force" [1.30]), the constant threat to self-contained individuality of the elemental natural world ("Rings athmet zähnefletschend Mordgelüst"/ "All around breathes a savage lust to murder" [1. 29]), and the erotically charged dialectic of pleasure and suffering ("der Lawine Lust"/ "the avalanche's desire" [1.28], Verführerisch"/"seductively" [1.31]).[26] This truth, disclosed in the landscape, shares with *The Birth of Tragedy* an emphasis

---

[21] The entire poem and translation by Grundlehner (*The Poetry of Friedrich Nietzsche*, 52–3) are in the appendix.
[22] See e.g. Buschendorf, "Die Geburt der Lyrik," 116–8 and Müller, "Nietzsches Gimmelwalder Melancholie-Gedichte," 50–1.
[23] See *Die Geburt der Tragödie* section 10 (http://www.nietzschesource.org/#eKGWB/GT-10); for the vulture as consuming Prometheus's liver, see *Die Geburt der Tragödie* sections 3 and 4 (http://www.nietzschesource.org/#eKGWB/GT-3, http://www.nietzschesource.org/#eKGWB/GT-4) See also Müller, "Nietzsches Gimmelwalder Melancholie-Gedichte," 57, and Buschendorf, "Die Geburt der Lyrik," 125.
[24] On the association of melancholy and insight see Müller, "Nietzsches Gimmelwalder Melancholie-Gedichte," 58–9 and 60; on the Dionysian as a kind of barbarism, see *Die Geburt der Tragödie* section 4 (http://www.nietzschesource.org/#eKGWB/GT-4).
[25] Ll. 23–4: "Du sprachst zu mir, unfähig Menschentrugs,/ Wahrhaftig, doch mit schrecklich strengen Mienen."
[26] All of Adela Sophia Sabban, "Zitternd und zuckend ein Preislied. Nietzsches Gedicht 'An die Melancholie,'" in Benne and Zittel, *Nietzsche und die Lyrik. Ein Kompendium*, 59–77, here 67, Müller, "Nietzsches Gimmelwalder Melancholie-Gedichte," 59, and Buschendorf, "Die Geburt der Lyrik," 126 make this point, Buschendorf the most directly apropos the Dionysian.

on the threatening energy of the will as it expresses itself in nature;[27] it culminates in the fifth strophe (with a shift into the present tense) in an epiphanic
moment of unification with nature in which the speaker modifies Schopenhauer's
Brahminic "Dies alles bist du" (All this you are) to "Dies Alles bin ich" ("All this
am I," line 33).[28] Already in the fourth strophe there are hints that "Dionysian
self-dissolution" occurs at the expense of (Apollonian) individuality;[29] previous
commentators have overlooked the hints of seduction to suicide in gazing off the
edge of a cliff, following the vulture's path, and especially the ambivalence of the
phrase "Qualvolle Gier, sich Leben zu erzwingen!" (l.30). The phrase could be
translated as "Torturous desire to seize life by force" (as Grundlehner does and
as most interpreters take it) but also as "horrible craving, to force life out of one-
self," depending whether the pronoun "sich" is dative or reflexive.[30] Anticipating
the function of art as making life bearable by way of combining abyss and beauty,
Apollonian and Dionysian, "To Melancholy" appears as a poetological poem in
which the speaker experiences the Dionysian "Urgrund" of all life and contains it
within an individual speaker and a poetic form.[31]

In keeping with its poetological elements, "To Melancholy" begins and ends
with a depiction of poetic productivity: in the first strophe, the poet asks to
be excused for sharpening his pen to write a hymn to melancholy rather than
adopting the classical melancholic pose. The final strophe, beginning with the
same words as the first ("Verarge mir es nicht"—"Do not reproach me" or, more
colloquially, don't hold it against me, l.1 and l.41), contrasts the awfulness of
melancholy with the delicacy of the poet's rhymes and his inept trembling and
twitching as he writes (so we assume) the poem we have just read.[32] Moreover,
the lines describing the sharpening of the poet's quill come after the writing (i.e.
the poem) has already begun.[33] This temporal complexity extends into the body of
the poem as well as framing the first and final strophes: the poem shifts to the past
tense to describe the poet's earlier conformity to the melancholic trope of sitting

[27] Buschendorf, "Die Geburt der Lyrik," 120.
[28] On the Schopenhauerian formula see Buschendorf, "Die Geburt der Lyrik," 121, and Müller, "Nietzsches Gimmelwalder Melancholie-Gedichte," 62.
[29] See Buschendorf, "Die Geburt der Lyrik," 123, and Grundlehner, The Poetry of Friedrich Nietzsche, 57.
[30] The latter is more consistent with eighteenth—and nineteenth-century usage; see Johann Christoph Adelung, "Erzwingen," in Grammatisch-kritisches Wörterbuch der Hochdeutschen Mundart mit beständiger Vergleichung der übrigen Mundarten, besonders aber der oberdeutschen (Vienna, 1811) and Jacob Grimm and Wilhelm Grimm, "Erzwingen," in Deutsches Wörterbuch von Jacob und Wilhelm Grimm. 16 Bde. in 32 Teilbänden (Leipzig, 1854–1961), Sp. 1104.
[31] Buschendorf refers to this as the "Apollonian reflection of the Dionysian abyss" (Buschendorf, "Die Geburt der Lyrik," 129). Müller also reads the poem as poetological but argues that the poet-speaker takes on the Dionysian function of making palpable a unity with nature; he thus neglects the importance of the Apollonian both in the poem and in The Birth of Tragedy (Müller, "Nietzsches Gimmelwalder Melancholie-Gedichte," 63).
[32] See Sabban, "Zitternd und zuckend ein Preislied," 64, and Buschendorf, "Die Geburt der Lyrik," 116.
[33] Sabban, "Zitternd und zuckend ein Preislied," 61.

sunken in thought (ll.4–32), then moves into the present in the fourth strophe to describe the simultaneously ecstatic and threatening (Dionysian) oneness with all of being (l.33).[34] It then remains in the present tense to return to the moment of writing described at the outset. The very lines that assert the epiphanic moment of unity revealed by melancholy slide into lines that distinguish between being affected by melancholy (sitting motionless) and writing;[35] whereas the topos of melancholy as a stimulant to writing exists in the tradition, the speaker focuses on the materiality of the act of writing in his unruly pen and messy ink ("The ink flows, the sharpened quill spatters" [l.47]), perhaps because the speaker is trembling as he stammers his song (l.45) and twitching rhythmically (l.46) in the iambs of the poem.[36]

The poem thus highlights its own formal and rhetorical handling of language in its attention to the materials of writing, its foregrounding of the ineptitude of oral speech, and its description of meter and rhythm as "twitching." Nietzsche's other notebook fragments from the years surrounding *The Birth of Tragedy* insist on the alignment of affect, body, and rhythm: "The movement of the mind/feelings [*Gemüth*] in an analogous bodily movement. This in turn is expressed in rhythm and the dynamic of the word."[37] But *The Birth of Tragedy* itself criticizes the specific type of rhythm and dynamic of the words Nietzsche uses in "To Melancholy": in the former, rhyme is a symptom of the theoretical-Socratic modern culture that derives even its poetic forms from intellectualized imitations.[38] In particular, the strophe form of "To Melancholy" was widely used in the nineteenth century and deployed especially for "longer apostrophes, contemplations, and images."[39] Nietzsche thus adheres to the cultural register of the form, but he deploys it so rigorously as to be pedantic, especially in the neat alignment of lineation and syntax in the first and last strophes and his perfect alternation of stressed and unstressed syllables.[40] The poem's sole decisive divergence from its metrical regularity occurs

---

[34] Sabban describes the complex temporalities of the poem as "making present the entanglement of past (what is narrated) and present (the now of the writer)" (Sabban, "Zitternd und zuckend ein Preislied," 61).

[35] As Sabban points out, it is precisely because the speaker is *not* fully possessed and immobilized by melancholy can he write the poem (Sabban, "Zitternd und zuckend ein Preislied," 66); whereas she reads the distancing of melancholy as enabling irony (Sabban, "Zitternd und zuckend ein Preislied," 66), I would contend that the irony is a defense mechanism to hold melancholy at bay and enable poetic productivity.

[36] Müller identifies the contrast between the melancholic tradition with the materiality of the ink as an ironizing strategy (Müller, "Nietzsches Gimmelwalder Melancholie-Gedichte," 66).

[37] Nietzsche, Nachgelassene Fragmente Winter 1870–1—Herbst 1872 (http://www.nietzschesource.org/#eKGWB/NF-1870,8[67]).

[38] Nietzsche, *Die Geburt der Tragödie,* section 18 (http://www.nietzschesource.org/#eKGWB/GT-18).

[39] Müller, "Nietzsches Gimmelwalder Melancholie-Gedichte," 55 refers to and cites H.J. Frank, *Handbuch der deutschen Strophenformen,* where "An die Melancholie" is listed as an example of form type 8.44 (H.J. Frank, *Handbuch der deutschen Strophenformen* [Munich: Hanser Verlag, 1980)], 665).

[40] Sabban, "Zitternd und zuckend ein Preislied," 62, claims that lines 18–20 deviate into some trochaic feet; I can follow this assertion only in the first word of line 18, "Unschön"; where normally the

in the fifth strophe's depiction of the unity of "I," nature, death and life: the speaker announces that he "thirsts for life, life, life!" in line forty, which in the German has only four stressed syllables and thus falls an iamb short.[41] The repetition of "Leben" and the dramatic alliteration it occasions once more foreground the lexical-material elements of language, a strategy Nietzsche deploys in repeating sounds and lexemes across the poem.[42] "To Melancholy," then, shows how Nietzsche uses meter both to support and to ironize semantic content, tying it more tightly than its metaphysical claims might allow to the materiality of language as sounds, words, and beats.

Parody

Several elements of the poem fit with an understanding of parody in the everyday or contemporary sense as an imitation of an earlier work or tradition that makes it laughable: the poet puts melancholy in place of a muse, but then asks her pardon for writing, and indeed it seems he can only write with melancholy at a safe distance; both sitting hunched on a stump (mistaken by the vulture for carrion) and spattered with ink, he presents a ridiculous figure.[43] But Nietzsche, by virtue of his attention to classical literature and to music, also uses a more nuanced conception of parody: in the fifth century BCE, parody referred to instances in which a speaker separated music and speech by deviating from standard linguistic rhythm, such that "the deviation of speech and rhythm or music created complex possibilities of alluding to various sources at once," without any necessary elements of humor or mockery.[44] Parody is thus analogous to musical *contrafactum*, in which a new text is laid over an existing musical setting[45]—as indeed Nietzsche stretches his own Apollonian and Dionysian metaphysics of art over the structure of the ruminative eight-line strophe in an innovative handling of received forms.

prefix "un-" would be stressed to emphasize the negation; however, since "schön" is the more semantically weighted syllable, it does sounds unusual but not incorrect to read "unSCHÖN" rather than "UNschön," particularly given the metrical conditioning Nietzsche has inflicted on his readers in the first seventeen lines.

[41] Sabban reads this as mimetic of the line's content: in falling short, it thirsts after its additional foot (Sabban, "Zitternd und zuckend ein Preislied," 124).

[42] This strategy likewise appears in his other work, in particular his lectures on ancient rhetoric, which call attention to the fact that even the loftiest of Schopenhauerian concepts, the will, is a word, a collection of sounds (Porter, "Nietzsche, Rhetoric, Philology," 190).

[43] Grundlehner, for example, reads the poem solely in this vein as a caricature of the Dionysian in *The Birth of Tragedy*. See Grundlehner, *The Poetry of Friedrich Nietzsche*, ch. 3, "Dionysus a Caricature: "An die Melancholie" ("To Melancholy").

[44] Benne, "The Philosophy of Prosopopoeia," 280. Buschendorf also remarks that from early on Nietzsche had an understanding of parody related to the antique or musical conception of the term (Buschendorf, "Die Geburt der Lyrik," 109).

[45] Benne, "The Philosophy of Prosopopoeia," 280-1. Benne points out further connotations of speaking in a role or mask and prosopopoiea that will become central to the later Nietzsche and to which I return below.

As Nietzsche read Schopenhauer in the mid-1860s, his conception of parody added comic and critical components as well as an insistence that nothing—including the parody and parodist—be spared from the parodic gaze.[46] "To Melancholy" exemplifies these features: it innovatively appropriates both the form and the images of earlier representations of melancholia as well as Schopenhauer's metaphysics and the Prometheus myth and it uses formal handling to call Nietzsche's own dichotomy between the Dionysian and the Apollonian united in lyric into question.[47] Crucially, this conception of parody does not mean that Nietzsche discards or invalidates the very themes and structures he will polemicize for in *The Birth of Tragedy*, nor does it mean that all of the ideas in the poem are ridiculous or unimportant. Indeed, because Nietzsche's more capacious notion of parody encompasses both creativity and critique, parody becomes a crucial poetic tool that enables modern writers to take up the cultural forms of their past to address their own cultural situation.[48] In "To Melancholy," Nietzsche can work through the mutual imbrication of creativity and destruction, form and formlessness, and their relation to nineteenth-century German tropes of melancholia without fully adopting or discarding them, while his use of meter helps sharpen his readers' ears for ambivalences and critiques of the poem's positions.

"To Melancholy" thus performs the implication of rhythmical-metrical practice in a complex form of cultural critique, one that inevitably calls itself into question and turns back on its own assertions—movements that the self-referential structures of metrical patterning by their nature enact. The poem emphasizes the interconnection of the bodily-material, the cultural, and the rhetorical in language. It does so not from a stable point of critique but from a necessarily circular epistemology that recognizes its own inevitable conditionedness. Rhythm, and meter as the appearance of rhythm in language, have a particular role to play in this process, one that Nietzsche worked out most directly in his notebooks and lecture courses on rhythm and meter in 1870 and 1871, and one that, I contend, stands less to revolutionize our understanding of Nietzsche than our understanding of meter in our own theoretical and epistemological moment.

---

[46] Buschendorf, "Die Geburt der Lyrik," 110–1. Buschendorf takes "An die Melancholie" as his central text because of Nietzsche's engagement with poetic tradition, the tension between the poem's artful construction and the directness or obviousness of its conceptual content, and its documentation of Nietzsche's practice of parody prior to his theoretical discussions of it (Buschendorf, "Die Geburt der Lyrik," 114).

[47] Buschendorf, "Die Geburt der Lyrik," 128–9.

[48] See Buschendorf, "Die Geburt der Lyrik," 129–30; Benne makes this point apropos the remark "incipit parodia" in the fifth book of *The Gay Science*. See Benne "The Philosophy of Prosopopoeia" and "Incipit parodia—noch einmal" (in Pelloni and Schiffermüller, *Pathos, Parodie, Kryptomnesie. Das Gedächtnis der Literatur in Nietzsches Also sprach Zarathustra*).

4.2 Rhythm Notebooks

Although I am emphasizing his singular contributions to an understanding of meter and rhythm that we should want to reclaim, Nietzsche does share several questions and tendencies with the philology of his epoch, and in particular its investigations of meter and rhythm, as I sketched them in the previous chapter. In addition to his era's interest in Schopenhauer and in music, Nietzsche shares the attention of nineteenth-century classical philology to the question of what units are meaningful in verse practice and how they should be measured and the tendency, from Westphal and Rossbach on, to follow Aristoxenus' distinction between rhythm and the materials it appears in. Nietzsche extends these debates in innovative directions as he connects them to his particular concerns. First, he focuses in far more detail than his predecessors or contemporaries on physiology and embodiment in both the performance and the experience of rhythm. Second, he enters an extended and complex argument against the rhythmical ictus as a projection of modern sensibilities onto ancient verse structures. Third, he builds on his arguments about embodiment and the ictus to investigate what, specifically, in ancient (as compared to modern) verse practice was expressive or mimetic of an ethos or affect. And finally, Nietzsche exhibits an exceptionally high degree of skepticism toward both disciplinary knowledge and language as such; he highlights the lenses through which modern scholars view antiquity and reflects consistently on the situatedness of his own and his contemporaries' claims to knowledge, with rhythm as a central example.

Nietzsche was well aware of how radical his proposals were, as indicated in the letter I cited at the beginning of this chapter announcing his discovery that the entire tradition of modern metrics is an error. A week later, he writes to update his former teacher, Friedrich Ritschl, about his studies, noting that he has "gotten properly entangled in the nets of rhythm and meter."[49] The results of these activities appear in four main sources: his lecture notes for a course on "Griechische Rhythmik" (Greek Rhythmics) in the winter semester of 1870/1871 (KGW II$_3$, 99–202); an untitled convolute of notes referred to as "Aufzeichnung zur Metrik und Rhythmus" (Notes on Meter and Rhythm, KGW II$_3$, 202–67); a planned publication, "Zur Theorie der quantitirenden Rhythmik" (On the Theory of Quantitative Rhythmics, KGW II$_3$, 263–80); and another set of notes, which Nietzsche titled "Rhythmische Untersuchungen" (Rhythmic Investigations, KGW II$_3$, 28–338).[50] The differences between each type of text,

---

[49] Letter to Friedrich Ritschl, December 30, 1870 (http://www.nietzschesource.org/#eKGWB/BVN-1870,117.

[50] I am grateful to Ximing Lu, who provided not only translations and transliterations of Greek and Latin sections of Nietzsche's lectures and notes—there exists as yet no annotated edition—but contextualization of the terms and classical sources. Any errors in these areas are mine. Nietzsche, when he gives transliterations from the Greek into the Latin alphabet, often uses somewhat non-standard

however, are less pronounced than these descriptions would suggest: Nietzsche generally begins from an established question and with a relatively clear structure, after which the texts develop (or devolve) into sketches, planned projects, or lists of questions.[51] In this section, I therefore treat Nietzsche's interests thematically, rather than by text or by the order in each text in which they appear, starting with the argumentative moves he has in common with his contemporaries and then showing how he extends those arguments to his own inquiries.

Distinctions and Units

Like most of the theorists he critiques (including Westphal, Rossbach, and Brambach), Nietzsche draws heavily on the fragments of rhythmical texts by Aristoxenus. His numbered sections in the lecture notes on Greek rhythmics follow the organization of Aristoxenus' *Elementa Rhythmica* quite closely (although Nietzsche's numbering stops about halfway through his text). More significantly, Nietzsche takes up Aristoxenus' distinction between rhythm and the *rhythmizomenon*, "the material to be formed, e.g. tone, language, marble" (KGW II$_3$, 103).[52] Rhythm itself is not equivalent to any rhythmizomenon or any appearance of rhythm in a rhythmizomenon. Instead (as Nietzsche glosses Aristoxenus for his students), rhythm is an arrangement of time units or *chronoi* that manifests as an alternation of movement (*kinesis*) and stillness (*eremia*) in the rhythmizomenon, as in the movement from tone to tone, syllable to syllable, dance arrangement to dance arrangement (KGW II$_3$, 104). Nietzsche insists that the units of each rhythmizomenon and the laws or rules for their combination and organization do not properly belong to "the abstract theory of rhythm" (KGW II$_3$, 144). Thus, for example, the division of syllables into feet is a problem for metrics (the discipline of combining rhythm with language), not rhythm (KGW II$_3$, 143). In Nietzsche's view, this means that the problems of where to divide melodies, dances, and poems (or, most often, their combination) into larger units such as cola and periods belongs to the practical problems of composing in rhythm, or *rhythmopoiia* (KGW II$_3$, 154); here he differs from his contemporaries, who attempted to designate rows, feet, or periods according to rhythmical laws. Nietzsche argues that ancient rhythmical and poetic practice are more distant than his colleagues hold,

---

versions, e.g. "rhythmopoiia" rather than "rhythmopoeia." I cite parenthetically using the abbreviations given above.

[51] On the construction of Nietzsche's teaching materials, see Porter: "Nietzsche's original, core lectures are the most organized and articulated of the lot, while later accretions lose sight of these initial contours" ("Nietzsche's Radical Philology," 28). Apropos the notebooks in general, Porter explains "the notes begin in sober philological fashion, but then modulate quickly into envisioned publications, while becoming more imaginative and in places fantastical" (ibid., 30).

[52] Compare KGW II$_3$, 101 with Aristoxenus, *Aristoxenus Elementa Rhythmica: The Fragment of Book II and the Additional Evidence for Aristoxenean Rhythmic Theory*, trans. Lionel Ignacius Cusack Pearson (Clarendon Press, 1990).

and although he concedes that using metrical theories or musical transmission can help illuminate the rhythmicist's missing work, the fact that we no longer perform or have records of ancient dance means modern philologists cannot identify large-scale rhythmical units with any certainty (KGW II$_3$, 207).

Both the emphasis on the body's movement in dance and the foregrounding of what remains inaccessible or unknown are characteristic of Nietzsche's thinking about rhythm. Physiology and uncertainty likewise shape his treatments of one of the more complicated concepts in Aristoxenus, that of the *chronos protos*, or first time unit, a pure unit of time distinct from any of the materials worked on by rhythm.[53] Because Aristoxenus distinguishes rhythm from the rhythmicized material, the *chronos protos* cannot be equivalent to a foot or a syllable, as most of the ancient metricists had held (KGW II$_3$, 104 and 293).[54] Instead, the *chronos protos* is the smallest time unit that can be grasped by perception;[55] Nietzsche defines it as "the moment of time, in which necessarily only *one* syllable *one* movement *one* tone can be given" (KGW II$_3$, 144). Because of this brevity and because of his attention to physiology, Nietzsche repeatedly argues against the widespread representation of the *chronos protos* by the eighth note of modern music, contending instead that it should be a sixteenth note: "We must take seriously the remark that it was not possible to speak more than one syllable in the *chronos protos*. If this is assumed to be 1/8, how lazy was the Greek tongue! And how slowly they ran!" (KGW II$_3$, 248–9). Instead, "the *chronos protos* a sixteenth note" (KGW II$_3$, 254). He adds that Aristoxenus' insistence that two *chronoi protoi* cannot make a foot or *Takt* also makes more sense if the *chronos protos* is a sixteenth note since (in the European musical practice of the 1870s) 2/16 is not considered a valid musical measure, but 2/8 is (KGW II$_3$, 259).

While sixteenth and eighth notes, like the *chronos protos*, are relative measures, Nietzsche suggests a tempo based on the pulse: given a heartbeat of sixty-four beats per minute (KGW II$_3$, 198), several formal features align with physiology.[56] First, each foot of a hexameter (one long and two short, i.e. four *chronoi protoi*) would be one heartbeat, an easily-felt quarter-note (KGW II$_3$, 197); second, at this speed, declaiming a tragedy would take approximately half as long as most

---

[53] See Aristoxenus, *Elementa Rhythmica*, 76ff.

[54] Nietzsche follows Aristoxenus' struggle to determine whether the *chronos protos* is an absolute/objective measure—say, one second—or if it is always relative. According to Nietzsche, Aristoxenus originally asserted the relative nature of the chronos protos but then tried to define it objectively, but for most of his discussions Nietzsche treats the *chronos protos* according to the discussion in the *Elementa Rhythmica* as a relative unit. See KGW II$_3$, 293.

[55] Porter, *Nietzsche and the Philology of the Future*, 132. Porter also refers to these units as "atoms of rhythm" (132) but he perhaps understates the degree to which Nietzsche's handling of Aristoxenus is consistent with that of his contemporaries in metrical theory.

[56] Elsewhere, in keeping with the relative rather than absolute nature of the *chronos protos*, Nietzsche does not set the beats per minute and instead only argues that "The heartbeat is = a double long that is = 4 [*chronoi protoi*]. Such a double long is represented in our music as a *quarter note*. Therefore the *chronos protos* is a sixteenth note" (KGW II$_3$, 259).

estimates, and it would easily be possible to perform a tetralogy on a single day (KGW II₃, 197).⁵⁷ He adds as supporting evidence that Greek is known to be a rapid language and that many of the foot names refer to running (e.g. "trochaios means running step!" KGW II₃, 197). Whether or not we accept Nietzsche's notation and tempo (four syllables per heartbeat of English or German is speaking very fast), what is significant here is the way Nietzsche takes distinctions and concerns of the most abstract rhythmical theories and extends them to great physiological specificity. No other theorist of meter in the nineteenth century calculates the number of seconds per tragedy based on the heartbeat; no other theorist of meter takes foot names so literally.

Embodiment and Physiology

Nietzsche also draws on dance to support his reinterpretation of the *chronos protos*: "How can the fundamental movement have been the eighth-note movement! One need only think of our ballet dancers!" (KGW II₃, 259) Using a familiar form of dance, he brings the constraints of the body into metrical performance practice. And indeed, Nietzsche defines the vexed term "Takt" or *pous* as coming from dance movement, arguing "that *foot* [der Takt] was originally based on dance: the singer is governed by *dance* (which was not a whirl, but a pleasant walk)."⁵⁸ Dance movement also helps explain the size of feet or measures, as "four orchestric movements of both feet are the largest that we can grasp as a unit" (KGW II₃, 154). His diagrams attempting to theorize what Aristoxenus calls *alogia*, slight irregularities in rhythm with an unclear source and effect, likewise draw on the movement of the body.⁵⁹ He marks not only long and short syllables but the rising and falling of the left and right feet (KGW II₃, 147), suggesting that the irregularity of the *alogia* comes from a slight slowing of the movement of the leg: "In a choral dance a retardation on a preparatory lifting [of the foot] quite natural. The leg stretched further forward" (KGW II₃, 151). To explain the numerous terminological confusions and reversals in ancient rhythmical and metrical theories, Nietzsche appeals first to the difference between conducting or keeping time (*Tactiren*) and dance (KGW II₃, 152, 320) and then to different types of conducting developed "for the eye" and "for the ear," that is, marked by audible beating of foot, fingers, or batons (KGW II₃, 319–20). Throughout, then, Nietzsche draws explanatory power from

---

⁵⁷ This would take between seven and eight hours, by Nietzsche's calculations (KGW II₃, 198 and 259).

⁵⁸ Friedrich Nietzsche, "Nietzsche: On the Theory of Quantitative Rhythm," trans. James W. Halporn, *Arion: A Journal of Humanities and the Classics* 6, no. 2 (1967): 233–43, 237. This is, he adds, an "important rule" (237).

⁵⁹ These calculated irregularities remain among the more perplexing features of ancient rhythmical theory. (See e.g. Porter, *Nietzsche and the Philology of the Future*, 153).

thinking about the way the body actually moves, as prescribed by historically-conditioned performance practices. His work provides a strikingly specific model for an understanding of meter's bodily effects that relies on cultural practice.

In deriving metrical structures and tempos from orchestrics, Nietzsche can link his ideas on the movements of the body and other physiological rhythms. After noting the origin of the names "trochee" and "iamb" in march steps, he adds, "Now we have a firm hold on the pulse" (KGW II$_3$, 157). This connection between pulse and gait grounds what he calls the "Kraft des Rhythmus" (force, energy, power of rhythm): "I suspect that the sensory force of rhythm consists therein, that two rhythms working upon each other determine each other, such that the more expansive organizes the narrower. The rhythmical movements of the pulse etc. (the gait,) are probably newly grouped by a musical march, just as the gait accommodates itself to the beat of the pulse" (KGW II$_3$, 322). Nietzsche recognizes that the gait and pulse are just two of the rhythms of the body: "And because the entire body contains innumerable rhythms, so through every rhythm there a direct attack is made on the body. Everything suddenly moves according to a new law: not in such a way, that the old laws no longer rule, but such that they are determined. The physiological ground and explanation of rhythm and its power" (KGW II$_3$, 322). A few pages later in the notes, Nietzsche gives a definition of life as "a continuous rhythmical movement of the cells" and explains the "influence of rhythm" in similar terms to its force as "an infinitely small modification of those rhythmical movements" (KGW II$_3$, 325).[60] These striking passages link rhythmical practice with the body all the way from gesture to microphysiology, treating artistic performance on a continuum with cellular movement.

This may seem to move in the direction of the scientism in thinkers I discussed in the previous chapter, such as Ernst Brücke and his *Physiological Foundations of New High German Metrics* (which Nietzsche considers [KGW II$_3$, 398]), or invite the methods of the contemporary scientific investigators of rhythm that I discuss in the next chapter. But contra a narrow scientism, Nietzsche insists on the importance of cultural practice (which changes historically) in the experience of rhythm. He recognizes that the exact proportions or schema are "only ideally present" as a structure against which we "measure our perceptions of the filling in of real times" (KGW II$_3$, 309). And this recognition leads him to give an account of the interaction between "nature" and a culturally-conditioned "symbolic realm": "Gradual conquering of nature by the symbolic realm, e.g. in the minor scale, but also in five-part measures, *alogia* etc. Here conceptualization/representation is already involved" (KGW II$_3$, 309). Nietzsche gives examples

---

[60] His definition uses terms reminiscent of the materialist Friedrich Albert Lange. On Lange as influential for Nietzsche's thought on rhythm, see Friederike Felicitas Günther, *Rhythmus beim frühen Nietzsche* (Berlin: de Gruyter, 2008); on Lange as offering a materialism of the body that Nietzsche could link with his own attention to the materiality of language, see Porter, "Nietzsche's Radical Philology," 169.

of artistic phenomena that seem relatively distant from nature: minor scales (a precise minor third cannot be derived from the division of strings), five-beat measures (counterintuitive for beings with even numbers of limbs), or *alogia* (which remains unexplained). These phenomena are not neutrally or naturally significant or effective, as I understand Nietzsche's contention (in Schopenhauerian terms) that "conceptualization/representation" (*Vorstellung*) is involved. Moreover, this suggests that there is no bodily *experience* that is directly natural, devoid of cultural shaping.[61]

As a result, both rhythmical practice and bodily response are subject to cultural formation, which is itself historically variable, as Nietzsche notes at the end of his section on the force of rhythm. There, he remarks that for the Greeks, harmony had not been incorporated into the symbolic realm and therefore was not an organizing force on either poetic-musical composition or the body (KGW II$_3$, 322). An analysis of rhythm that takes into account its bodily efficacy must also address what effects have been activated in or by the symbolic realm, and it must therefore consider the history of formal-material features' entry into that symbolic realm.

Ictus

Nowhere does Nietzsche enter a stronger argument for the fundamental historical differences in which formal features affect the body than in his polemics against the rhythmical *ictus*. Nineteenth-century metrical theory follows Gottfried Hermann's usage of the term, adapted from Richard Bentley's editions of Terence and Plautus, where "ictus" referred to the regular beat of the foot of ancient musicians accompanying verse.[62] Nietzsche seems largely to accept the presence of some kind of time-keeping percussion or conducting in ancient performance practice;

---

[61] *Bodies* may be determined by sheerly material-physical laws and processes, but as soon as *experience* is added, culture intervenes. Think of potty training: the process of digestion is mechanical, but recognizing the nerve and muscle responses as an urge to urinate or defecate and then releasing them on the toilet must be learned. As Porter remarks, just as Nietzsche holds that there is no language prior to or outside of rhetoric (Porter, "Nietzsche's Radical Philology," 173), there is no natural or neutral body outside language and culture, or at least not one that can ever be reached from within them (Porter, "Nietzsche's Radical Philology," 177).

[62] See Kristine Louise Haugen, *Richard Bentley. Poetry and Enlightenment* (Cambridge: Harvard University Press, 2011). "In the case of Terence and Plautus, Bentley claimed, any metrical account based on quantities alone missed the real principle of their verse, which he called its beat (ictus). This had been, quite literally, the regular beating of an ancient flute-player's foot throughout a poetic line, and it corresponded (Bentley said) to the metrically important syllables in the line, which the ancient actor emphasized through a 'raising' or 'heightening' of the voice (*arsis*)." The *New Grove Online* gives a contemporary definition: "A term which in prosody indicates the stress or accent schematically implied on a certain syllable of a foot or verse; hence, in music, it is a comparable stress or accent schematically implied on a certain beat of a bar, in a certain meter, whether or not this implication coincides with the stress or accent actually made. The term is also used in relation to conducting patterns, to describe the downbeat." Robert Donington, "Ictus," in *Grove Music*

he rejects, however, the association of the ictus with stress or accent. Because Hermann aligns the ictus with the force ("Kraft") that starts each row in his metrical theory and because Bentley identifies it with pitch accent, the ictus smuggles accentual features into quantitative verse, thus, per Nietzsche, projecting modern prosodic criteria backwards onto ancient poetry and performance practice.[63] Nietzsche's rejection of the ictus therefore also entails a rejection of any use of modern structures to interpret ancient rhythms, as for example when he castigates Königsberg philologist Karl Lehrs as the "primary representative" of the position that "the rhythmical feeling/sense [*Gefühl*] of all cultured peoples should be the same" (KGW II$_3$, 131). Echoing the language of his letters to Rohde and Ritschl, Nietzsche contends that the theory of the ictus has ruined the entire tradition of modern metrics and its systems: "All systems have up to now the fundamental flaw that they begin with the ictus. It can be shown how this *one* error called forth one system after another. What we need now is a new construction, with which we admittedly must renounce the desire to know everything."[64] Philologists must now attempt to conceptualize a set of compositional and performance practices far more distant from their own than previous theories have admitted.[65]

Nietzsche draws on several sources to explain how time, especially larger structures of time, was measured in ancient performance; appealing to Diomedes, Terentius Maurus, Horace, and Cicero, he suggests there were "Two means of marking time: visual or oral. The first (by raising and lowering of the hand or foot) marked full intervals, the second ... by an audible striking—marks only the boundaries of the parts of a measure and the beginning of all parts of a measure. The word ictus often appears in this context."[66] In the notebooks he explains more succinctly: "We find no trace of an *ictus of the voice*, but rather only a measuring of *times* through pedum et digitorum ictu [beat of the feet and fingers]. This is important" (KGW II$_3$, 229). The absence of any such rhythmical ictus means, for Nietzsche, that the macro-structural elements of Greek performance practice came from dance and were visual, not aural: "The measures of the ancients permits no *rhythmical* structure of periods. Measure [*der Takt*] for them was directed originally at the apprehensible spatial relations of the chorus, that is,

Online, accessed July 5, 2022, http://www.oxfordmusiconline.com.ezproxy.library.wisc.edu/view/10.1093/gmo/9781561592630.001.0001/omo-9781561592630-e-0000013699.

[63] See Porter, *Nietzsche and the Philology of the Future*, 135–6.

[64] This remark comes from the section on meter and rhythm in Nietzsche's *Encyclopedia of Classical Philology*, a kind of handbook or textbook for his introductory philology course, where he sums up some of his insights from the rhythm notebooks for non-specialist students. Nietzsche, "Encyclopaedie der klass. Philologie," 400.

[65] As I have argued elsewhere, Nietzsche is somewhat ambivalent about the absolute difference between ancient and modern meters; the arguments cited above conflict with his argument that "the extension of measures was not *essentially different* from ours" and his use of Wagner's *Tristan* (Act II Scene II) as an example. KGW II$_3$, 201. On this tension in Nietzsche, see Hannah Vandegrift Eldridge, "Towards a Philosophy of Rhythm: Nietzsche's Conflicting Rhythms," *Journal of Literary Theory* 12, no. 1 (2018): 151–170, https://doi.org/10.1515/jlt-2018-0009.

[66] Nietzsche, "On the Theory of Quantitative Rhythm," 237.

the higher-level rhythm was only *visible*, not audible" (KGW II₃, 225). Here, Nietzsche's attention to dance—the visual-spatial arrangements of the chorus—and his division of abstract rhythm from rhythmical composition meet to describe a performance practice very different from the regularly pulsed alignment of micro-and macro-structures in modern music or poetry.

One reason for this difference and for the ancient neglect of the rhythmical ictus is, according to Nietzsche, the much greater role of language in shaping Greek poetic and musical structures (KGW II₃, 159). Moreover, the importance of speech becomes a general principle: "In general one has to imagine everything purely musical very much in the service of the *word*" (KGW II₃, 172). In a fragment from the same time that anticipates the connection between philology and opera in *The Birth of Tragedy*, Nietzsche gives a description of Greek music:

> Greek music the most ideal, insofar as it did not take word emphasis, the agreement overall of the smallest peaks of the movements of the will in the word with the arsis, into account at all. It doesn't recognize musical accentuation at all: the effect rests on *time-rhythm* and *melody*, not in the rhythm of the *strong syllables*. The rhythm was only *felt*, it was not expressed in *emphasis/accentuation* [Betonung]. Rather they *emphasized/accented* [betonten] according to *conceptual content* [Gedankeninhalte]. Height and depth of the notes, thesis or arsis of the measure had nothing to do with this. On the other hand, the sense/feeling [Gefühl] for scales/modes and the *time rhythms* was developed to the finest extent. We can see in the talent for dance of this people its tremendous rhythmical ποικιλία [*poikilía*=variety, multiplicity]: meanwhile our rhythmical relations have a narrow schematism.[67]

This passage provides a description of Greek music and song that differentiates ancient and modern perceptual capacities and shows how ancient performance detached semantic or word accent from rhythmical organization. Using spaced letters (*Sperrdruck*) for emphasis (which I have represented using italics), Nietzsche pulls apart temporal structures (which properly belong to rhythm), pitch (part of melody), and musical accent (e.g. of stronger or weaker beats in a measure, marked by the rise and fall of conducting). I return to the question of why stressed syllables in words should express peaks of movements of the will below; for the moment, I want to note that Nietzsche contrasts Greek rhythmic flexibility, enabled by a separation of phonological components, with modern rhythmical schematism, perhaps the result of the alignment or conflation of ictus, accent, and rhythmical structure.[68]

---

[67] Nietzsche, posthumous fragment, 1871. http://www.nietzschesource.org/#eKGWB/NF-1871, 9[111]; all emphases Nietzsche's.

[68] This does not mean that there were no word accents in ancient Greek, but that those word accents were not organized as part of a metrical pattern. For a contemporary Classicist's discussion and confirmation, see Porter, *Nietzsche and the Philosophy of the Future*, 135–6.

Modern metrics makes most of its interpretive mistakes based on such con-flation between accent, ictus, rhythm, and meter, in ways that prompt further confusion between ancient and modern rhythmical practice. Noting modern the-orists' perplexity over the relation between ictus and accent, Nietzsche holds that "the situation is only surprising because we let high pitch, ictus, and primary sylla-ble fall together" (KGW II$_3$, 231). In the text on the theory of quantitative meters, he complains of a "very naïve confusion of accent and ictus in Bentley" and points out that moderns, assuming an audible ictus in the voice, struggle to understand the point of keeping time with the conducted ictus: "We actually did not under-stand at all why marking time was necessary, for we *considered the ictus* to be *part of the recitation*. The ancients knew nothing of this."[69] To modern theorists, visual conducting should be unnecessary, since the rhythmical structures should be audible in the volume and pitch of the voice. The conflation of accentual and time-measured rhythm in the ictus has misdirected the entirety of modern met-rics; the question, for Nietzsche, is how the modern notion of the ictus could come about from the shift from duration to accentual rhythms.

Nietzsche therefore undertakes to give an account of the development of accen-tual prosody; against Westphal and others, he rejects the idea that word accent and rhythmical accent coincided in some pre-Greek phase of poetry and subsequently separated (KGW II$_3$, 222). In several places he identifies the folk song and the Greek church hymn as the first appearances of accentual verse (KGW II$_3$, 206, 221) and reflects that the hymns' rule of "equal syllable count" is "a vestige of quantita-tive verses" (KGW II$_3$, 209). At first in relatively neutral terms, Nietzsche describes how strong emphasis of accented syllables in folk songs and Byzantine verse led to the vocalized ictus, which then became strong enough to place an accent on an unaccented syllable (KGW II$_3$, 226). In his last set of notes, however, Nietzsche depicts the same process in terms that echo Wagner's account of the compres-sion of the soul into the root syllables of Germanic words (see chapter 3.4.1), but with a precisely reversed normative valence. Nietzsche uses the vocabulary of decay and decline (*Verfall, zerfallen*) to describe the loss of the feeling or sense for time in language (*das Zeitgefühl beim Sprechen*) (KGW II$_3$, 307). The "spiri-tual life of the word" becomes concentrated in the accent, which "sucks all life into itself while everything around it withers," a process that Nietzsche describes in acoustic-physiological terms in the next sentence: "The words now express them-selves in explosions, the *physical tension* pressed into *one* point is therefore lacking in the other points. Thus arises a new type of rhythm, not a wave of changing times [*Zeitwechselwelle*] but a wave of *changing strengths* [*Stärkewechselwelle*]" (KGW II$_3$, 308). What the earlier notebooks express as alterations in the deploy-ment of prosodic-phonological components now appears as part of a fundamental speech-physiological and cultural-metaphysical shift.

---

[69] Nietzsche, "On the Theory of Quantitative Rhythm," 240.

Nietzsche's final narration of the change in prosody uses the most agonistic and simultaneously the most vitalist vocabulary: "At the very earliest stage, struggle between time- and tone-life [*Zeit- und Tonleben*]. Victory of the time-life [*des Zeitlebens*] over the tone-life [*das Tonleben*]. / Decline of the time-life and victory of the tone-life" (KGW II₃, 308). Using highly unusual terms, Nietzsche links prosodic features to forms of life;[70] the sheer energy of his narrative of struggle and life contradicts to some extent his account of the shift away from durational meters as loss, rather than a more elemental conflict between two forces.[71] Nietzsche begins to articulate an interest in both the shaping force of language (recall the passages on rhythm as "a direct attack on the body") and the forces that shape language; he closes his comparison of Greek and German rhythms by subsuming both under an artistic drive to creativity within language itself: "artistic drive in the creation of language. The Germanic peoples in the opposition of strongs and weaks, in connection with height and depth—the Greek of proportional times, in connection with high and low" (KGW II₃, 330). He recognizes language itself as codetermining the prosodic-phonological features deployed in bodily effective, culturally shaped forms and suggests a reciprocal relation between poetic practice, material elements of language, and bodily efficacy: "It is poetry [*die Poesie*] that views the existing language according to rhythmical time-proportions and establishes a feeling/sense [*Gefühl*] for them" (KGW II₃, 330). Although German/Germanic poetry and thus its shaping of language work very differently ("A quite different rhythmics is that of proportions of force [*Kraftverhältnisse*]"), "here too the infinite variety of nature is to be restrained by certain basic forms [*Grundformen*]," within which "once again the greatest dynamic multiplicity is allowed." (KGW II₃, 309). The technical question of whether the rhythmical ictus existed opens onto questions of historical difference, cultural techniques, and the impact of aesthetic production on a language.

Expression and Ethos

Having analyzed in detail how different phonological features of different languages become organized into metrical and rhythmical structures at different historical moments, Nietzsche likewise considers the way those features are

---

[70] "Zeitleben" and "Tonleben" do not appear in most dictionaries, and Nietzsche does not (as far as I have found) use them elsewhere. Wagner uses somewhat similar vocabulary in "On Conducting," imagining Beethoven chastising conductors not to ignore fermatas: "Then the life of the tone [Leben des Tones] should be sucked out until its last drop of blood." Richard Wagner, Über das Dirigieren", in *Beethoven/Über das Dirigieren* (Darmstadt: Wissenschaftliche Buchgemeinschaft, 1953), 69–140, 90.

[71] See Porter for an argument that this narrative is a "genealogy" in Nietzsche's sense, therefore not straightforwardly critical of historical change (Porter, *Nietzsche and the Philology of the Future*, 144); he argues that this reading is supported by the way the vitalist perspective complicates the narrative (Porter, *Nietzsche and the Philology of the Future*, 146).

deployed for expressive effect. Given the different phonological resources and cultural contexts, Nietzsche argues that Greek and German rhythms express different characteristics and achieve their respective kinds of expression differently. In particular, Greek rhythms (and thus poets and listeners) were attuned to differences in the size of metrical units, so-called *metabolē rhythmikē* (rhythmic change): "Fundamentally the [*metabolē*] is the primary means of rhythmical expression in the Greeks ... Our equal measure [*Takt*] is a naïveté compared to a finer execution. But it is an uncomfortable schematism" (KGW II₃, 260). Compared with ancient rhythmical practice, modern rhythms are both naïve and constraining; Nietzsche explains that for moderns the expressive force of music occurs in harmony, while for Greeks it was contained in rhythm, with rhythmical alteration as its primary means (KGW II₃, 135). Indeed, according to Nietzsche Greek music had no conception of harmony but instead perceived the spatial relations between tones: "In melody, too, one didn't perceive harmonic force, but the spatial differences from tone to tone as mimetic. The *height relations* of the tones, that is at bottom the differences in number, were experienced in their imitative force" (KGW II₃, 321). This is perhaps the most fundamental difference between Greek and modern artistic practice and thus perceptual faculties: whereas moderns attend to the alignment of harmony, rhythm, and melody in macro-structural units, Greek culture felt and deployed proportional relations of time, pitch, and dance.[72]

Thus Nietzsche can argue that "the philosophy of the Pythagoreans is the essence of antiquity become conscious. Their tremendous ability to enjoy proportions, to look at and to hear everything proportionally, is the most powerful characteristic" (KGW II₃, 321). And due to the differences in cultural perception, a "tremendous chasm" separates both affect and effect of Greek and German performance practice:

On the whole we see that our manner of performance is much more passionate .... For the Greeks it is the enjoyment of proportions of time, for us of excitations and alleviations. Here is a tremendous chasm. Here strong and weak, there short and long. We have the rigid mechanism of equal measures [*Taktgleichheit*]. In this respect the Ancients were much more sensitive: here our sense of time is coarse. Rhythm is "beat of the waves" [*Wellenschlag*]: every word is perceived immediately in speaking and hearing as a *group of times.*

(KGW II₃, 401)

---

[72] These differences likewise indicate how each culture perceives larger-scale elements: as I discussed, Nietzsche contends that dance movement established macrostructural rhythms in Greek practice, which were therefore visual not auditory (KGW II₃, 136), while for moderns harmonic structures enable large-scale compositional oppositions (KGW II₃, 137).

Greek sensitivity enables less dramatic but more fluid rhythms shaped by proportions of time; German insensitivity demands the rigidity of equal measures organizing monotonous alternations of strong and weak, which produces a less subtle, even over-dramatic performance practice. There are a number of ambivalences or contradictions in Nietzsche's account of both German and Greek rhythms and the chasm between them, as for example in the contrast between the fluidity he praises in ancient rhythms and the architectonic sense of spatial rhythm he derives from dance or in his discussion of types of Greek rhythms that are more affectively excited.[73] Nonetheless, Nietzsche consistently links the different phonological components organized in meter and rhythm to different capabilities of perception in different cultures.

Philology, Philosophy, Skepticism

The differences in perceptual capacity and the chasm they entail foreground the inevitable limits of philology as a discipline, and Nietzsche persistently calls attention to the ways philology and philologists are enmeshed in their own cultural situations and risk projecting their perceptions and norms onto the object of study.[74] In the planned article "On the Theory of Quantitative Rhythm," Nietzsche points out both the projection of modern rhythmical systems and the inevitable uncertainty of rhythmical investigation. He attacks the notion that we should "enjoy" ancient meters, in particular, remarking "my theory takes away much of the *pleasure* which the others offer. The others intend to make us *enjoy* the rhythmical schemes [Schemata]."[75] Nietzsche undertakes to "prove" that his contemporaries "have only *read into* ancient rhythms, on the basis of our modern habituation, what we then admire in them."[76] What the metrical theorist or the student admires is only a projection of his own imagination, which Nietzsche contends must be given up. Moreover, not only enjoyment but scholarly certainty are casualties of a more nuanced understanding of the differences between Greek and German rhythms: "According to my theory, in respect to individual rhythmical schemes there is no sure decision, only many possibilities. It is however very

---

[73] Rhythms that begin with a short syllable were more excited or emotional in their affect or "ethical effect" (KGW II₃, 112, also 237). Nietzsche points to ancient theorists' cautions that such rhythms, as well as excessive changes in rhythm, can be "pernicious and dangerous" (KGW II₃, 176). On the ways in which ambivalences in Nietzsche over the similarities or differences of Greek and German metrics, as well as the ways in which affective arousal versus control or constraint, interact with each other, see Eldridge, "Towards a Philosophy of Rhythm."

[74] On Nietzsche's practice of philology as skepticism, see especially Porter, *Nietzsche and the Philology of the Future* in addition to Porter, "Nietzsche's Radical Philology."

[75] Nietzsche, "On the Theory of Quantitative Rhythm," 234.

[76] Nietzsche, "On the Theory of Quantitative Rhythm," 234. Porter characterizes this awareness of projection as one element of Nietzsche's persistent focus on the subject rather than the object of knowledge (Porter, *Nietzsche and the Philology of the Future*, 8).

foolish to find in this a scientific setback (as Schmidt does against Westphal). We lack the ancient rhythmical taste, we lack ancient music [antike Melos]—how can we be infallible!"[77] In his lecture course he thus notes "The most important disputes *fundamental. My skepticism.* The demand a high one: to learn to enjoy a metrical schema. In our modern education nothing similar, one need only learn to beat a drum" (KGW II₃, 134). Nietzsche seeks to undo the self-congratulatory certainty of his discipline that only a more rigorous system is needed to understand and fully enjoy the systems of ancient metrics that, in his view, disparities in perceptual abilities across cultures render unreachable.[78]

Nietzsche's self-identified skepticism inflects both his pedagogy and his scholarship (in addition to, as is better known, his philosophy). He begins his *Encyclopedia of Classical Philology* by emphasizing the circularity of the enterprise, noting that *enkyklios* means "running in circles" (KGW II₃, 342). In keeping with his attention to historical situation, Nietzsche gives his students a history of philology as a discipline in several national or linguistic contexts (KGW II₃, 347ff.), and he also takes care to differentiate the questions, priorities, and methods of philology from comparative or historical linguistics (KGW II₃, 389 ff.). He credits linguistics in general for assisting philologists in breaking through the "rigid formalisms" of prior philology and, in terms that echo the language of Wagner's racism and national chauvinism, "We need above all the living view of language as the soul of the people" (KGW II₃, 390). (Unlike Wagner, Nietzsche does not view some languages as expressive of loftier souls than others, and the tensions in his account of the transition from durational to accentual prosody suggests he is interested less in which languages are best than in the revelatory power of rhetorical or literary form vis-à-vis culture.) Nietzsche notes further that philologists need historical grammar to understand different authors (KGW II₃, 396), but identifies a crucial difference: "Historical grammar has a quite different goal than *a feeling for style* [Stilgefühl]. It envisages the becoming of language. The finished language is only a moment, not even the most important. The older stages are far more instructive" (KGW II₃, 396). For philologists, however, "everything depends on the *feeling for form* [Formgefühl] *for the perfected language*" (KGW II₃, 393). The two remaining points of access to this feeling in the ancient world are, for Nietzsche, rhythm and rhetoric (KGW II₃, 394).

Rhythm, for Nietzsche, thus offers insight into the past sense for formal perfection and simultaneously underscores how far philology remains from full understanding: "Stylistically we are coarse empiricists: we know almost nothing of the rhythm of speech, of the periods, of the choice of *words*, the cadences of the sentences" (KGW II₃, 393–4). As the numerous project outlines and topic lists Nietzsche jots down in the notebooks indicate, moving past "coarse empiricism"

---

[77] Nietzsche, "On the Theory of Quantitative Rhythm," 235.
[78] See also Porter, *Nietzsche and the Philology of the Future*, 8–10.

will require a combination of cultural-historical study, phonological attention, and physiological acumen, joined in a "philosophy of rhythm": "important, that in the introduction the entire metrical task of the epoch is identified: careful observation of the rhythmical sensations [*Empfindungen*] still present in some peoples and a history of rhythmical sensation [*Empfindung*]. Following on that a philosophy of rhythm" (KGW II$_3$, 309).[79] Although Nietzsche never fully composed or published his proposed philosophy of rhythm, I suggest that the elements I have drawn out of his collection of lecture notes, sketches, plans, and outlines indicate its primary contributions. His nascent philosophy of rhythm emphasizes embodied experience as shaped by culture and history; it depicts the inevitability but also, perhaps, the productivity of cultural difference in the account of the ictus; it undermines the self-satisfied *Wissenschaftlichkeit* of philology and destabilizes the epistemological status of knowledge about meter and rhythm.

As I remarked, that Nietzsche attends to physiology and history and is skeptical is a familiar portrait of him as a thinker and writer; what I hope to have shown in the passages above is the degree to which his work on rhythm informs these characteristics from very early in his career and, more importantly, that studying rhythm and meter in the ways Nietzsche does shows how an account of bodily efficacy can take culture and history into account without succumbing to prescriptive universalism, to claims that certain phonological features always work in certain ways, or to scientized epistemologies. It is also worth noting that the rhythm notebooks unfold these arguments in ways that are more nuanced and less polemical than *The Birth of Tragedy*, where rhythm and its variations (rhythmic, rhythmical) appear only five times and are reduced to constituting the architectonic/Apollonian side of music.[80] Nietzsche's first book contains little trace of his work on rhythm, and its reception in the history of philology obscured his prior philological work. The notebooks—messy, contradictory, insightful, and provocative—thus offer an enormously rich and untapped resource for thinking through metrical claims and poetic experience. They show how verse practice extends all the way from micro-physiology to cultural critique, without reducing one to the other or forgetting the ways in which poetic practice is always historically situated, culturally determined, and bodily effective.

---

[79] Porter reads this remark as presaging Nietzsche's later ideas about rhythm as individuation and the Will to Power (Porter, *Nietzsche and the Philology of the Future*, 143).

[80] See for example *The Birth of Tragedy*, section 2 (http://www.nietzschesource.org/#eKGWB/ GT-2). Some of the last passages in the rhythm notebooks anticipate this presentation, including their final remark, which associates rhythm with beauty and individuation (KGW II$_3$, 338). On the disconnect between *The Birth of Tragedy* and the rhythm notebooks, see Héctor Julio Pérez López, "Die doppelte Wahrheit von Nietzsches Tätigkeit 1870–1872," *Nietzscheforschung* 2 (1995): 219–36. Because Pérez only cites limited sections from the rhythm notebooks and does not fully situate Nietzsche within nineteenth-century philology, he overestimates the conflict between Nietzsche's philology and philosophy, rather than simply between the approaches and missions of the two (sets of) works.

4.3 Between Philology as Science
and *The Gay Science* (1873–87)

Although Nietzsche does not dedicate any projects exclusively to the topic of rhythm in the years after the rhythm lectures and notes, rhythm and meter continue to appear in his letters, notebooks, and published works. In particular, rhythm shows up in his criticisms of culture, music, and writing. Rhythm and meter likewise take part in his theorizations of constraint as productive or generative. Finally, Nietzsche works out an account of human beings as "rhythm-creating creatures" that pertains to his renowned perspectivism and his notorious theories of the Will to Power. These themes will appear together in the poem "Dichters Berufung" (Poet's Calling) in the "Lieder des Prinzen Vogelfrei" (Songs of Prince Free-as-a-Bird) added as an appendix to the second edition of *The Gay Science*, which also reintroduces the topics of parody and paradox from "To Melancholy." Thus "Poet's Calling" brings together many key elements of Nietzsche's rhythmical thinking from the mid-1870s to the mid-1880s and performs them via its metrical-rhythmical practice. Before turning to the poem, I outline a few crucial moments from that thinking, organized according to the themes of critique, productive constraint, and perceptual force.

Critique

Perhaps the most significant impetus for Nietzsche's critiques through and about rhythm in the mid-1870s comes from his re-evaluation of Richard Wagner. In 1874, Nietzsche argues that Wagner's rhythmical practice is deceptive, noting that "the cessation of the larger rhythmical periods ... makes the impression of infinity, the ocean: but it is an artistic effect, not the regular law Wagner would like to make it."[81] By 1886, he extends the attack to romantic music in general in a fragment titled "On the physiology of art" that notes his need for music "to which one forgets suffering" and "to which one would like to dance."[82]

Nor do Nietzsche's critiques of rhythmical practice restrict themselves to music; he also chastises both writers and readers for inadequate attention to rhythm. In *Human, All Too Human*, Nietzsche remarks that good writers (of whom there are

---

[81] Nietzsche, posthumous fragment, 1874 (http://www.nietzschesource.org/#eKGWB/NF-1874,32[42]). On the ambivalences in Nietzsche's attitude to Wagner and the role Wagner played in his analyses of rhythm even in the 1870s, see Eldridge, "Towards a Philosophy of Rhythm,"157–8 and 162–3. On Nietzsche's attention to Eduard Hanslick (whom I discussed in the previous chapter) as shaping his critiques of Wagner, see ibid. and in addition Marc-Oliver Schuster and Christoph Landerer, "Die Musik kann niemals Mittel werden‹: Nietzsches Ästhetik und ihre Wurzeln bei Hanslick," *Österreichische Musikzeitschrift* 55, no. 6 (2000): 17–24.
[82] Nietzsche, posthumous fragment, 1886 (http://www.nietzschesource.org/#eKGWB/NF-1886,7[7])

few) change the rhythm of their writing out of "consideration for the rhythmical incapacity of current readers"; the writers "make it easier, insofar as they privilege better known rhythms."[83] In a fragment from 1884, Nietzsche denounces the "perpetual repetition — ∪ — ∪ etc. the rhythm of rhyme-poetry."[84] Perhaps surprisingly, given the anti-Wagner polemics from around the same time, he calls for "the freedom, that we have already reached in music through Richard Wagner!"— namely, "play with the most variable meters and occasionally the unmetrical," to be claimed for poetry.[85] Writing to Carl Fuchs in 1886 about his own earlier metrical studies, Nietzsche admits, however, that "our German poets 'in antique meters' thereby brought many rhythmical charms in to poetry that it lacked (the tick-tock of our rhyme-poets is terrible in the long run)" (BVN-1886, 688).[86] "Tick tock" (*Tiktak*) appears as Nietzsche's pejorative term for accentual verse; it describes the poetic speaker's coercion to meter and rhyme in "Poet's Calling." Rhythm and meter thus serve as avenues for Nietzsche's incisive cultural critiques, which in turn make them central to his "philosophiz[ing] with a hammer."

Productive Constraint

But in other passages from the same years, Nietzsche contends that the constraints meter and rhythm apply to thought and movement prove productive, anticipating the poem-generating effects of rhythm in "Poet's Calling" and extending the expressive functions of meter elaborated in the earlier notebooks. In *Human, All Too Human*, the section "How meter beautifies" echoes the arguments of *The Birth of Tragedy* but with ambivalent nuances ("Art makes the sight of life bearable through laying over it the veil of unclear thought") and with specific discussion of meter: "Meter lays a veil over reality; it leads to some artificiality of speech and unclarity of thought; by way of the shadow it throws on the thoughts, sometimes it hides, sometimes it emphasizes."[87] Meter becomes a kind of *chiaroscuro*, both obscuring and throwing into relief. Nietzsche's most direct theorization of productive constraint, in *Human, All Too Human II*, describes creativity within rules as "*Dancing in chains*": "About every Greek artist, poet, and writer we should

---

[83] Nietzsche, *Human, All Too Human*, 198 (http://www.nietzschesource.org/#eKGWB/MA-198).

[84] Nietzsche, posthumous fragment, 1884 (http://www.nietzschesource.org/#eKGWB/NF-1884, 25[172]).

[85] Nietzsche, *Human, All Too Human*, 198 (http://www.nietzschesource.org/#eKGWB/MA-198).

[86] Nietzsche, letter to Carl Fuchs, presumed middle of April, 1886 (http://www.nietzschesource.org/#eKGWB/BVN-1886,688.) Nietzsche adds, "I defended myself with hands and feet against the idea that for example a German hexameter had anything at all in common with a Greek one" and recalls his discovery of the "fundamental error" of all of modern metrics ("from Bentley to Westphal"); he describes the "rhythmical attraction" of ancient meters as consisting solely in "the time quantities and their relations" "and not, as in German hexameter, in the hop-sa-sa of the Ictus."

[87] Nietzsche, *Human, All Too Human*, 151 (http://www.nietzschesource.org/#eKGWB/BVN-1886,688).

ask: what is the *new constraint* he has imposed on himself and that he makes appealing to his contemporaries (so that he finds imitators)? For that which we call 'invention' (in metrics for example), is always such a self-imposed shackle."[88] Every additional constraint adds an additional creative possibility as it lets the artist make its deployment seem effortless; every engagement with inherited cultural forms offers a chance for the artist to show mastery of them. Strict meter and rhythm thus open up artistic possibilities. In *Beyond Good and Evil* Nietzsche appeals to "metrical constraint, the tyranny of rhyme and rhythm" "under which up until now every language has attained strength and freedom" as an analogy to help explain the relation between constraint and freedom in cultural formation; the analogy indicates the wider stakes of poetic practice.[89]

Knowledge and Perception

Finally, rhythm plays a fundamental role in Nietzsche's accounts of knowledge and perception, the philosophical rather than philological version of his skepticism and his celebration of epistemological uncertainty. In a series of fragments from 1885, Nietzsche reflects on the relation between thought, will, and perception; mentioning artists, critics, and philosophers, he arrives at the lapidary statement: "Man is a form-making and rhythm-making creature" ("Der Mensch ist ein Formen- und Rhythmen-bildendes Geschöpf").[90] The activity of form-making is necessary for experience or perception as such: "Without the transformation of the world into forms and rhythms there would be nothing 'the same' for us, that is, nothing recurring, thus also no possibility of experience and appropriation [*Aneignung*], of nourishment."[91] Without this shaping of the flux of stimuli into rhythmically formed, thus identifiable and recurring elements, the world would remain a blur of noises, lights, smells, etc. He emphasizes the skeptical point: we therefore have no access to any "in itself," since even perception is a formational act. But there is a productive element of self-discovery or self-knowledge, as "in this process man discovers his own strength [*Kraft*] as a resisting and even more as a determining strength."[92] The act of making rhythms reaches into perception and into the self-understanding of the human being; as the next set of fragments indicates, starting with its title, "The Will to Power/ Attempt/ at a new interpretation/ of all Occurrences/ By/ Friedrich Nietzsche," the activity of imposing a formal will on the world grants significance and power to the one who imposes

[88] Nietzsche, *Human, All Too Human*, 140 (http://www.nietzschesource.org/#eKGWB/WS-140).

[89] Nietzsche, *Beyond Good and Evil*, 188 (http://www.nietzschesource.org/#eKGWB/JGB-188).

[90] Nietzsche, posthumous fragment, 1885 (http://www.nietzschesource.org/#eKGWB/NF-1885,38[10]).

[91] http://www.nietzschesource.org/#eKGWB/NF-1885,38[10].

[92] http://www.nietzschesource.org/#eKGWB/NF-1885,38[10].

it.[93] Similar ideas regarding the creation of forms as defining the human appear as early as 1883, and the notion of perception as rhythmical alternation of stimuli emerges in Nietzsche's 1875 notes on and critique of Eugen Dühring's *The Worth of Life* (Der Werth des Lebens) (eKGWB/NF-1875,9[1]).

The role of rhythm and meter during these years in the arenas of cultural critique, productive constraint, and anthropological-epistemological investigation show that rhythm filtered into virtually all of Nietzsche's primary interests and concerns long after he ceased to write or lecture about it directly. Moreover, the ways rhythm appears in these areas demonstrate the degree to which the themes, questions, and provocations of Nietzsche's earliest work continued across his career. They show that Nietzsche's middle period likewise contributes to the vision of meter I have been arguing we should want to reclaim for modern thinking about patterned language. Because meter and rhythm give a bodily dimension to historically-inflected cultural critique, exert productive constraint on artistic work, and shape human perception, Nietzsche's discussions in the late-1870s to the mid-1880s give specific instances of meter's inevitable cultural particularity and physiological effectiveness.

4.4 "Poet's Calling" ("Dichters Berufung")

Idyll, Science, Cycle: Contexts

In turning to a reading of "Poet's Calling," I show how Nietzsche's thinking about rhythm and meter informs his poetic practice and how that poetic practice both performs and enriches his attention to the contradictions of rhythm. "Poet's Calling" appears in a collection of poems, the "Song of Prince Free-as-a Bird" ("Lieder des Prinzen Vogelfrei) published as an "appendix" to the second edition of *The Gay Science* in 1887. Nietzsche derived the title from the Provençal *gaya scienza* or *gai saber* of troubadour lyric, although neither the "Songs of Prince Free-as-a-Bird" in the second edition's appendix nor the "Prelude in German Rhymes" that opened the first edition imitate Provençal verse forms in any exact way.[94] His decision to frame the volume with collections of poetry raises the question once again of the relation between poetic and (perhaps?) philosophical discourse

---

[93] http://www.nietzschesource.org/#eKGWB/NF-1885,39[1]. For a reading of the Will to Power as the organization of units of force, and as such related both to Nietzsche's interest in Democritus' atomism and his work on rhythm, see James I. Porter, "Nietzsche's Theory of the Will to Power," in *A Companion to Nietzsche*, ed. Keith Ansell-Pearson (Oxford: Blackwell, 2006), 548–64.

[94] Sebastian Kaufmann, "'die letzte Entscheidung über den Text zwingt zum scrupulösesten ‚Hören' von Wort und Satz' – Textgenese und Druckgeschichte der *Fröhlichen Wissenschaft*," in *Friedrich Nietzsche: Die fröhliche Wissenschaft*, eds. Christian Benne and Jutta Georg (Berlin: de Gruyter, 2015), 7–18, here 15. https://www-degruyter-com.ezproxy.library.wisc.edu/document/doi/10.1515/9783110440300/html. Nietzsche lists troubadour verse types in a fragment from 1881, as Kaufmann points out.

as well as that of the relation between the collections and the remainder of the volume. Whereas Nietzsche's designation of the collections as paratexts—a "prelude" and and "appendix," respectively—seems to subordinate lyric to the prose sections, the structure of the volume suggests the *Songs* as a culmination or even self-correction of the book's arguments and tone[95]: the 383rd section of *The Gay Science*, labeled "Epilogue," challenges the "dark question mark" the speaker claims to have "paint[ed]" at the end of the book, as the "Spirits of [his] book" pounce on him and call for song and dance.[96] The "Songs of Prince Free-as-a-Bird" thus answer the demands of—and perhaps seem to be sung by—the book's spirits, in a continuation of the complicated play of roles, masks, textual allusions, and arguments that Nietzsche unfolds in *The Gay Science*.[97] In keeping with this play, the first poem of the collection addresses another poet in its title, "To Goethe," and picks up the highly unusual meter while satirizing the content of the final lines of *Faust II* (eKGWB/FW-Lieder-1).[98] As "Poet's Calling" shows, the "Songs of Prince Free-as-a-Bird" parody not just Goethe but the very idea of lyric poetry or a lyrical persona, once again in the sense of parody as a formal and thematic mode that speaks in masks, plays with forms, and destroys its own illusions.[99]

Rhythm as Compulsion

To ears sharpened by the more obvious formal parody of "To Goethe," "Poet's Calling" also takes on parodic contours. In combining the elements of a refrain, internal rhyme, a poet driven (nearly) mad by repeated sound, and a quasi-prophetic bird, Nietzsche re-forms Poe's proudly proclaimed original verse form in "The Raven" into the most common of German eight-line strophes: trochaic,

---

[95] On the structure of the volume presenting the *Songs* as culmination, see Sebastian Kaufmann, "'Verbessert', verlängert, zum Theil verkürzt, dieser Sammlung einverleibt.' Nietzsche's 'Rezyklierung' der 'Idyllen aus Messina' in den 'Liedern des Prinzen Vogelfrei,'" in Benne and Zittel, *Nietzsche und die Lyrik. Ein Kompendium*, 115–34, here 132.

[96] Heinrich Detering, "Stagnation und Höhenflug: 'Die Lieder des Prinzen Vogelfrei,'" in Benne and Georg, *Friedrich Nietzsche: Die fröhliche Wissenschaft*, 151–74, 155.

[97] On the use of masks as a performative instance of Nietzsche's perspectivism, and in addition on the function of the prose rhythms of *The Gay Science* in marking the multiplicity of voices in the text, see Christan Benne and Jutta Georg, "Einführung," in Benne and Georg, *Friedrich Nietzsche: Die fröhliche Wissenschaft*, 1–6. Detering advances the suggestion Prince Free-as-a-Bird is a mask for the "Spirits of the Book" (Detering, "Stagnation und Höhenflug," 154).

[98] Nietzsche, "Songs of Prince Free-As-A-Bird," *The Gay Science* (http://www.nietzschesource.org/#eKGWB/FW-Lieder-1).

[99] For the full poem and Grundlehner's translation, see appendix. Kaufmann notes the extension of mockery to "lyrical poetry as such" ("'verbessert', verlängert," 126) though he reduces parody to mockery rather than the more ambivalent play of forms I used Buschendorf and Benne to articulate apropos "To Melancholy."

with alternating weak and strong endings.[100] Like "To Melancholy," "Poet's Call-ing" begins in a scene of solitude in nature, and it, too, narrates the process of writing. "Poet's Calling" describes how its speaker, sitting "under dark trees" (l.2), hears a soft, "delicate" (*zierlich*) ticking that irritates him until he "speaks along in tick tock" (l.8) "like a poet" (l.7)—which, of course, the poem has done from its perfectly trochaic first lines.[101] The poem continues discussing poetic tech-niques, in particular "verse-making" (l.9), "syllable" (l.10), "saying" (*Spruch*, l.19), "image" (*Bild*, l.19), "rhyme" and "rhymes" (ll.20, 25), "verse" (l.22), "little saying" (*Sprüchlein*, l.33), "little word" (*Wörtlein*, 20), "line" (l.35), and of course "poet," a total of eleven times (ll.7, twice in 13, 15, 22, 23, 31, 38, 39, 45, and 48). Moreover, the speaker expresses a poor opinion of poets: first mocking tropes of inspira-tion and/as madness, as the speaker addresses himself, "is your head in such bad shape?" ("Steht's mit deinem Kopf so schlecht," ll.14) and then adding, "If things are bad with my head,/ Would they be worse with my heart?" (ll.42–3). By the fifth strophe, the speaker asks "Are poets—bad?" (ll.38). The previous line suggests that the poetic joys of regular rhythms please only "vicious rabble" (*grausam Gelichter*, ll.37), to whom the poets apparently belong.

"Poet's Calling" thus raises the question of why poets are "bad" and potentially insane; and the answer it gives is that they write in rhyme and rhythm. This cri-tique of rhyme and meter using rhyme and meter picks up Nietzsche's earlier vocabulary for denouncing accentual verse: line eight calls it *Tiktak*, which Niet-zsche described as "terrible" in the letter to Carl Fuchs I cited above,[102] and line ten repeats another term from the letter, "Hopsasa," modified to "hopsa" to fit the rhythm: "Syllable by syllable its hopsa leapt" ("Silb' um Silb' ihr Hopsa sprang)." Moreover, the poem suggests that poets are not particularly gifted in their deploy-ment of phonological-prosodic strategies: in a mix of hunting and compositional metaphors, rhymes dart onto images and sayings (l.19–20) and the poet stabs at slithering sounds to make them fit his verses (ll.21–2), which he patches together (ll.45–6). But the poem also gives the lie to this ineptitude, as the rhymes increase in complexity and number across its course, adding internal and broken rhymes on the word for poet, "Dichter":

---

[100] Numerous readers (Giulia Baldelli "Von Spechten und Lacerten: Nietzsches Auseinanderset-zung mit der Epigrammtradition in 'Dichters Berufung,'" in Benne and Zittel, *Nietzsche und die Lyrik. Ein Kompendium*, 173–90, and Christian Benne, "Incipit parodia—noch einmal," in Pelloni and Schiffermüller, *Pathos, Parodie, Kryptomnesie. Das Gedächtnis der Literatur in Nietzsches Also sprach Zarathustra*, 49–66) have noted the connection to Poe, although, as Thomas Forrer points out, the edition of Nietzsche owned did not include "The Raven." Given both how well-known the poem is and was and Poe's discussion of it in "The Philosophy of Composition," it seems highly probable that Nietzsche had read it, and it is hard to explain the similarities if he did not. See Thomas Forrer, "Rhythmische Parodie. Friedrich Nietzsches Gedicht Dichters Berufung," in *Der Witz der Philologie. Rhetorik-Poetik-Edition.*, eds. Felix Christen et al. (Frankfurt a.M.: Stroemfeld, 2014), 108–22.

[101] Baldelli points out the circularity of the poem's temporal structure ("Von Spechten und Lacerten," 173).

[102] http://www.nietzschesource.org/#eKGWB/BVN-1886,688.

Was nur schlüpft und hüpft, gleich *sticht der*
Dichter sich's zum Vers zurecht. (ll.21–2) (Whatever skips and
slips, just then the /poet stabs it into a verse)

...

"Doch der *Dichter*—Reime *flicht er*
Selbst im Grimm noch schlecht und recht. (ll.45–6) (Still the poet,
rhymes he cobbles/ in his wrath as best he can)

And both of these lines rhyme once more with *Dichter* in the poem's refrain, "—
'Ja, mein Herr, Sie sind ein Dichter'/ Achselzuckt der Vogel Specht." ("—'Yes, good
sir, you are a poet'/ Shrugs the woodpecker bird.," ll. 15–6, 23–4, 31–2, 39–40, and
47–8). The virtuosic use of enjambment (which also occurs between ll.9 and 10,
11–2, 19–20, and 27–8) suggests the poet's struggle to fit his sentences into lines,
while the extreme regularity with which Nietzsche realizes the metrical schema of
trochaic tetrameter recreates the tick-tock compulsion the poem complains of in
the woodpecker.[103]

Moreover, the strange layering of hunting metaphors with compositional struggles in the third and fourth strophes references, as Giulia Baldelli has shown,
a further instance of anti-rhyme polemic. Baldelli follows the poem's use of the
highly unusual Latinized word for lizards, *Lacerten* (rather than *Eidechsen*) to link
"Poet's Calling" to Goethe's *Venetian Epigrams* (where Goethe uses the word *Lacerten* to refer to the prostitutes of Venice), tying the critique of alternating verse in
"Poet's Calling" to the eighteenth-century debates about the adaptation of Greek
meters that I analyzed in the first chapter.[104] This tradition frequently condemned
German verse in iambs or trochees (with its alternating weak and strong syllables)
as monotonous, and rejected rhyme as a tool for insensitive ears, as compared with
the polymetrical verse of ancient Greek, including the distich traditionally used in
epigrams.[105] Nietzsche himself denounces modern adaptations of Greek meters as
being entirely different from their ancient counterparts; in "Poet's Calling," rhyme
itself takes on the attribute most commonly associated with the epigram, a sharpened satirical point or "Pointe," in lines twenty-five and twenty-seven as "Pfeil/e"
(arrows or darts).[106] And indeed, the poem's parodic nature, its self-staging as
an improvised poem, and its poetological meditation on the (here, mechanical

---

[103] Forrer describes this as "overfulfillment of the meter" and sees it as a reminder "that poetry,
especially German poetry, that orients itself to strophe forms, metrical patterns, and rhymes cannot
simply shed the magic of schematism" (Forrer, "Rhythmische Parodie," 117).

[104] Baldelli, "Von Spechten und Lacerten," 176. The erotic connotations are direct in "Poet's Calling"
as well, as the poet lodges his rhyme-arrows in "noble parts" of the lizard's bodies (ll. 27–9).

[105] See Chapter 1, Section 1.2.3 ("Latitudinarians").

[106] Baldelli also points to an epigram of Martial's (Goethe's model) that depicts a statue of Apollo,
god of poetry, hunting lizards (Baldelli, "Von Spechten und Lacerten," 179). She glosses the eighteenth-
century debate between Lessing and Herder over the satirical versus illuminating program of the
epigram (178).

and irritating) process by which poetry comes about are all among the features of different poets' and epochs' definitions of the epigram genre.[107]

"Poet's Calling" thus performs a complex double bind: it critiques the compulsion of rhyme and rhythm in using them; it condemns poets in poetry; it invokes tropes of inspiration, madness, and intoxication ("bezecht," l.30, "Trunkne Wörtlein" l.35) before attributing them to a monotonous mechanical ticking.[108] In laying out the drive to rhyme and meter as well as the suspect character of poets, the poem at once instantiates and parodies the views in one of Nietzsche's best-known passages about rhythm, the eighty-fourth aphorism of the second book in *The Gay Science*, called "Of the Origin of Poetry."[109] The aphorism analyzes the significant cultural functions fulfilled by poetry and in particular by rhythm: "Once people noticed that people remembered a verse more easily than unbound speech, they believed that they could likewise make themselves audible over greater distances through the rhythmical tick-tock; rhythmical prayer seemed to come nearer to the ears of the gods."[110] The power of rhythm is its ability to compel: "Rhythm is a compulsion; it arouses an unconquerable desire to give in, to join in; not only the steps of the feet, even the soul itself follows the measure."[111] The physical or physiological effects of meter as well its affective components that drove Nietzsche to seek a "philosophy of rhythm" in the notebooks here explain the cultural functions (and considerable power) of poetic language, which for "the old superstitious type of humans" conferred nearly god-like powers.

Moreover, the aphorism contends that the power of rhythm persists: "Even today, after millennia of combatting such superstition, even the wisest of us is occasionally made a fool of by rhythm, even if it is only in feeling a thought to be truer if it has a metrical form and trips along with a godly hopsasa."[112] The term for the leaping syllables in "Poet's Calling," "Hopsa," can shore up truth claims; and the aphorism ends by finding it humorous "that even now the most serious philosophers, so strict they otherwise are about all certainty, call on *poet's sayings* to give their thoughts strength and plausibility," when "it is more dangerous for a truth, when the poet agrees with it than when he contradicts it! For as Homer says: 'Poets lie a lot indeed!'"[113] Poets lie, and both per the aphorism and in "Poet's Calling" they do so with the help of rhyme and rhythm. The contradiction that "Poet's Calling" acts out, using flagrant and virtuosic strategies of rhyme and rhythm to

---

[107] Baldelli "Von Spechten und Lacerten," 180–1.

[108] Heinrich Detering reads this as a satirization of tropes of Romantic inspiration from nature (Heinrich Detering, "Stagnation und Höhenflug: 'Die Lieder des Prinzen Vogelfrei,'" in Benne and Georg, *Friedrich Nietzsche: Die fröhliche Wissenschaft*, in *Friedrich Nietzsche: Die fröhliche Wissenschaft*, 151–74, 160.

[109] Nietzsche, *The Gay Science*, 84 (http://www.nietzschesource.org/#eKGWB/FW-84).

[110] http://www.nietzschesource.org/#eKGWB/FW-84.

[111] http://www.nietzschesource.org/#eKGWB/FW-84.

[112] http://www.nietzschesource.org/#eKGWB/FW-84.

[113] http://www.nietzschesource.org/#eKGWB/FW-84.

critique what it performs, is thus a paradigmatic case of Nietzsche's use of parody as a self-exposure of the illusions of language.[114] Meter thus becomes a primary tool for this exposure, as it calls attention to the material unfolding of language in ways that are particular to the historical moment of the language in its culture and that move the bodies of the listeners.

4.5 "Only fool! Only poet!"

Like "To Melancholy" and "Poet's Calling," "Only fool! Only poet!" is a poem about poets; like them, it exhibits a complex and potentially circular temporal structure; it, too, is parodic in both the mocking/humorous and prosopopoeic senses. But there are several differences that raise problems for interpretation in general and for my discussion of rhythm in particular. First, the poem's argument articulates a paradox. Rather than depicting its own emergence in the writing process, "Only fool! Only poet!" makes a general statement about poets, specifically: poets lie.[115] Prior interpretations disagree as to how this statement should be read, either as self-debasement lacking the irony of the earlier poems or as ironizing those who critique poets as liars. Second, Nietzsche includes the poem in *Thus Spoke Zarathustra* under the title "Song of Melancholy" (*Lied der Schwermuth*) in addition to placing it at the start of the *Dionysus-Dithyrambs*; the differences in these contexts exacerbate the ambiguities of the poem's parodic and ironizing qualities. Finally, unlike either "To Melancholy" or "Poet's Calling," "Only fool! Only poet!" is in free rhythms, with irregular number of syllables and stresses per line and almost no rhymes. The poem thus raises the question of what kind of rhythm Nietzsche uses and what it has to do with the view of language in its self-contradicting investigation of lying poets. Asking what kind of rhythms Nietzsche uses and how they are implicated in questions of truth and lies, in turn, raises new possibilities for the types of bodily response that free rhythms (as opposed to tick-tock) evoke and highlights the skepticism that, I have argued, has been a central element of Nietzsche's thinking about rhythm, contrary to the epistemological self-satisfactions of his epoch's philological tradition.

[114] On both "To Goethe" and "Poet's Calling" as "exposing the poetic 'lie' of artists" and "inform[ing] the reader of the hypocrisies hidden in language, see Grundlehner, *The Poetry of Friedrich Nietzsche* 149, 164; Forrer ("Rhythmische Parodie," 110) and Sander Gilman ("Incipit Parodia: The Function of Parody in the Lyrical Poetry of Friedrich Nietzsche," *Nietzsche-Studien* 4 (1975): 52–74, 63) also note parody as a stylistic register that doesn't hide the illusions of language.

[115] On this argument, and on Nietzsche's predecessors in articulating the untruthfulness of poets (specifically Goethe and Heine), see Gerhard Kaiser, "Wortwelten, Weltworte. Die ersten beiden 'Dionysos-Dithyramben' Nietzsches," in *Augenblicke Deutscher Lyrik: Gedichte von Martin Luther bis Paul Celan*, by Gerhard Kaiser (Frankfurt a.M.: Insel Verlag, 1987), 300–52, 300.

Overview and Divergent Interpretations

The poem has three parts:[116] it begins with a speaker's address to his own heart, asking whether the heart recalls its longing for dew and evening when it was seared by the mocking voices of "blinding sun-glow-glances" (*blendende Sonnen-Gluthblicke* l.14): "do you remember, hot heart/ how once you thirsted/ for heavenly tears and dewdrops" (l.7–8). In the second (longest) section, the heart addresses itself in the voices of the sun, reiterating their mocking critiques of the poet as a lying fool (strophes II–VIII). The third section returns to the present and a scene of evening (using the same words as the first line, "In dimming air" [ll.1, 81]), this time narrating in the first person and in self-address using the lyrical speaker's own voice, rather than the voices of the sun beams.[117] Throughout the poem, the word "truth" (*Wahrheit*) takes on a multiplicity of valences (as desirable knowledge, as unreachable longing, as reified self-congratulation, as moral cudgel); the final lines explain that the poetic speaker is "singed and thirsty" "by a Single truth," *"that I should be banished/ from all truth! Only fool! Only poet! ..."* (ll.99–101, italics and ellipsis in original).[118] Several readers take this as a self-castigation on the part of the poet, who accepts the criticisms and punishment of the mocking sun beams in "pure self-parody as a means of self-examination and self-abnegation," abandoning the ironized distance that protected the poet in "Poet's Calling."[119] Others, however, see the poem as an affirmation of the poet's particular access to the linguistically-constituted nature of truth(s), internalizing the voices of his critics to overcome them and taking the fool of the title as a positive figure of identification.[120] In either case, rhythm might serve to support or to undermine the discursive-semantic statements, obliging us to ask either how such a self-abnegating figure manages to create such confident formations of language, or how the sheer rhythmical energy of some of the views parodied might seduce us to them nonetheless.

---

[116] For the full poem and Grundlehner's translation, see appendix.

[117] Kaiser and Wolfram Groddeck give very similar overviews of the poem's structure, voicing, and plot. See Kaiser, "Wortwelten, Weltworte," 306–8 and Christoph König, "'Ich bin dein Labyrinth...' Zur poetischen Klugheit in Nietzsches 'Dionysos Dithyramben,'" in Benne and Zittel, *Nietzsche und die Lyrik. Ein Kompendium*, 331–49, 339–41.

[118] The lines are in the first subjunctive mode, which can be used either as an imperative (as in the divine "Es werde ..."/ "let there be") or to express disbelief in indirectly reported speech; they are thus extremely difficult to translate: *"dass ich verbannt sei/ von aller Wahrheit!/ Nur Narr! Nur Dichter! ..."*

[119] Gilman, "Incipit Parodia." Philip Grundlehner subsumes the entire cycle of *Dionysus-Dithyrambs* under the rubric of "Poetic Nihilism," with "Only fool! Only poet!" as a paradigmatic example. (Grundlehner, *The Poetry of Friedrich Nietzsche*, 185). Sebastian Kaufmann likewise views the poem as an expression of "poetry-critical skepticism" that abandons the irony of "Poet's Calling." (Sebastian Kaufmann, "Heiterkeit, Heroismus, Sentimentalität. Nietzsche's Idyllen aus Messina und sein poetologisches Konzept der Idylle," in Grätz and Kaufmann, *Nietzsche als Dichter. Lyrik—Poetologie—Rezeption*, 95–119, 118).

[120] König, Groddeck, and Kaiser all follow this line of interpretation, as does Klaus Mönig, "Sie hätte singen sollen, diese 'neue Seele'—und nicht reden!' Nietzsche's späte Lyrik," in *Nietzsche als Philosoph der Moderne*, eds. Barbara Neymeyr and Andreas Urs Sommer (Heidelberg: Winter, 2012), 193–221, 199.

Nor does an appeal to the context of *Zarathustra* or the *Dionysus-Dithyrambs* settle the question. In the fourth part of *Zarathustra*, the speaker of the poem is a "magician" (*Zauberer*) who shares significant characteristics with Wagner; he sings the poem in Zarathustra's absence, seducing the "higher men" to melancholy and self-abnegation, only to be denounced by Zarathustra on his return. This would seem to support the reading that takes the identification of poets with fools and liars negatively; the identification must be overcome by Zarathustra as an example of the importance of the dialectic of self-overcoming, and absent this contextual dialectic, the poem would be purely negative.[121] But the contexts of *Zarathustra* and of the *Dithyrambs* are both more ambivalent: to begin with, Zarathustra ironically shakes the hands of each of the "higher men" on his return, suggesting that they should have been able to see an alternative interpretation of the poem without his input.[122] Moreover, in the section called "Of Poets" ("Von den Dichtern") in the second part of *Zarathustra*, Zarathustra both identifies himself as a poet and says that poets lie.[123] The poem itself suggests the association of the poet-fool-liar with several figures Nietzsche valorizes, in particular the panther (as companion to Dionysus in *The Birth of Tragedy*) and the eagle (associated with Zarathustra); on this reading, "the poet, who lies knowingly and knows in lying, who wants to and must lie, becomes the epitome of the highest human possibilities."[124] *Zarathustra* and the *Dithyrambs* share considerable material and several textual strategies, perhaps most strikingly the layering of masks and voices in formal arrangements that enable simultaneous negation or nihilism and Nietzschean "Ja-Sagen."[125]

Free Rhythms, Affect Rhythms, Sentence Rhythms

"Only fool! Only poet!," like the rest of the *Dionysus-Dithyrambs*, is in so-called free rhythms, in keeping with the genre's identity as a wild and unconstrained hymn, particularly one to Dionysus.[126] Nietzsche thus practices "renunciation

---

[121] Grundlehner, *The Poetry of Friedrich Nietzsche*, 199.

[122] See König, "Ich bin dein Labyrinth," 338.

[123] http://www.nietzschesource.org/?#eKGWB/Za-II-Dichter; see Michael Skowron, "Dionysische Perspektiven. Eine philosophische Interpretation der Dionysos-Dithyramben," *Nietzsche-Studien* 36, no. 1 (2008): 296–315, https://doi.org/10.1515/9783110192827.1.309.

[124] Kaiser, "Wortwelten, Weltworte," 313.

[125] On the adaptation of material associated with Zarathustra—both the novel and planned "Songs of Zarathustra"—and the formal combination of negation and affirmation, see Skowron, "Dionysische Perspektiven," 302. Kaiser points to the layering of voices in the *Dithyrambs* as evidence that the speaker appropriates the voices of the sunbeams (Kaiser, "Wortwelten, Weltworte," 324). On the layering of voices in *Thus Spoke Zarathustra* and the relation of speaking in masks to parody, see Benne, "The Philosophy of Prosopopoeia," 276.

[126] Nietzsche's title is both self-referential and tautological, per Wolfram Groddeck, *Friedrich Nietzsche. "Dionysos-Dithyramben,"* vol. 2. Die "Dionysos-Dithyramben." Bedeutung und Entstehung von Nietzsches letztem Werk, 2 vols. (Berlin: de Gruyter, 1991), XVIII.

of the 'tick tock' of rhyme and meter, renunciation of a regulating temporal-symmetry; rhythmical isolation of the single line, associative sequentialization of lines, limitation to the prosodically demanded accentual values in the sense of 'affect-rhythmics[.]"[127] Absent schematic patterning—though not absent meter, by Nietzsche's definition of meter as the specific appearance of rhythm in language—the question arises of what creates the rhythmical structures of "Only fool! Only poet!" Here Nietzsche's complaints about his readers offer some suggestions; in noting the importance of style in both poetry and prose, as well as their proximity, he laments, "there are so many secrets of rhythm, of sentence cadences, of which my readers know nothing."[128] He gives further indications in writing to Carl Fuchs's about Fuchs and Riemann's editions of Beethoven with careful phrasing (*Phrasirung*) markings (see chapter 3.4): in annotating "this animation, enlivening of the smallest parts of speech in music," he wishes that "you [Fuchs] and Riemann used the words that everybody knows from rhetoric: period (sentence), colon, comma ... question, conditional sentence, imperative—because the theory of phrasing is simply that which for prose and poetry is the theory of punctuation."[129] Nietzsche's remarks are highly ambivalent: while he criticizes the practice of phrasing as a sacrifice of macro-structures to micro-effects and a symptom of decadence, he closes by remarking that "you and Riemann are on 'the right path'—that is, the only one that still exists."[130]

I return to the implications of this ambivalence for Nietzsche's views of rhythm and language below; first, I follow his hints about attention to punctuation and sentence cadences, as well as the smallest components of language, to draw out the language-rhythmical (thus: metrical) structures of "Only fool! Only poet!" The poem's punctuation is idiosyncratic. It serves to organize repetition (as in the commas in repeated lists); particularly in question marks and exclamation points, it highlights the mocking and skepticism of the voices in the poem; the frequent ellipses (nine in 101 lines) forbid closure (seven of the nine are at strophe endings) and create ambiguity in the relations between units of discourse, especially following on other punctuation. Perhaps the poem's most striking feature is its repetitions on multiple scales: lines repeat across the poem (sometimes identically, sometimes with slight variations), and both words and sounds repeat across and within lines. For example, the poem's title, "Only fool! Only poet!" recurs exactly in

---

[127] Breuer, *Deutsche Metrik und Versgeschichte*, 242. Breuer reads this technique as pushing past the earlier parodies in alternating meters as part of an "urge toward a *true* statement, that is the expression of the impulse of life" (238), though he acknowledges that Nietzsche's dithyrambs proceed "*without* the certainty of speaking more truly in this form than in the parodic negation of conventional verse" (242). These assertions both undermine the potential of irony in "Only fool! Only poet!" and unjustifiably restrict Nietzsche's conception of parody.
[128] Letter to Heinrich Köselitz, April 19, 1887 (http://www.nietzschesource.org/#eKGWB/BVN-1887,834).
[129] Letter to Carl Fuchs, August 26, 1888 (http://www.nietzschesource.org/#eKGWB/BVN-1888,1096).
[130] http://www.nietzschesource.org/#eKGWB/BVN-1888,1096.

the twenty-fifth line; in line thirty-two it is modified by a switch to lower case, the introduction of spaced letters (*Sperrdruck*, a mark of emphasis, usually rendered in English as italics), and an ellipsis after its second exclamation point: "o n l y fool! o n l y poet! ..." At the end of the sixth strophe it becomes "you fool! you poet! ... (1.72)," and the poem's last line returns the capitalization to line twenty-five: "O n l y fool! O n l y poet! ..."

The repetition—in the title, at the end, and roughly in the middle of the poem—establishes a sense of framing that in fact runs contrary to the division of the poem into three parts of present, remembered/internalized speech, and return to the present, dynamizing its large-scale structures. The variations heighten readers' attention to punctuation and the smallest parts of speech; the spaced letters, especially, remind us that words are made up of letters on the page, foregrounding optical rhythms in a way that is new for Nietzsche's poetry but consistent with his attention in the rhythm notebooks to the visual patterning arising from dance.[131] Visual rhythm governs one of the most pronounced structures in the poem, a line that imitates the sudden dive of an eagle to attack a lamb:

> Dann,
> plötzlich,
> geraden Flugs
> gezückten Zugs
> auf L ä m m e r stossen,
> jach hinab, heisshungrich,
> nach Lämmern lüstern,
> gram allen Lamms-Seelen,
> grimmig gram Allem, was blickt,
> tugendhaft, schafmässig, krauswollig,
> dumm, mit Lammsmilch-Wohlwollen ... [ll.57–67][132]

The lines also exemplify several of Nietzsche's other strategies of repetition. First, the lines use sound repetition (here L, M, and G sounds) and word repetition across multiple parts of speech (as in lambs, lusting, the adjectival lamb-souls, lambs' milk and the alliterative "gram .../grimmig gram" [*woe .../grim woe*]). Second, line sixty-six gives a list of three adjectives ("virtuous, sheep-like, curly-wooled") that each fall into two parts (tugend-haft, schaf-mässig, kraus-wollig), anticipating the double composite of lambs'-milk-well-willing (or wishing). The

---

[131] Other instances of *Sperrdruck*: l.15 "t r u t h", l. 25 "t h a t", l. 50 "l y i n g", l.53 "h i s", l. 71 "y o u r", l. 74 "G o d a s s h e e p", l. 75 "t e a r", l.77 "l a u g h", l. 78, "t h a t, t h a t i s y o u r b l i s s", and all of lines ninety-nine and 100: "t h a t I s h o u l d b e b a n i s h e d f r o m a l l t r u t h !"

[132] "Then,/ suddenly/ in a straight flight/ dragged down/ pouncing on l a m b s , / steeply down, hotly hungry/ lusting for lambs/ woe to all lambs-souls/ grim woe to everything that looks/ virtuously, sheep-like, curly-wooled,/ stupid, with lambs-milk-well-wishing ..."

term joins two words that are themselves each two words (lamb, milk, well, wishing) and the placement in the line of "wooly" right above "willing/wishing" emphasizes the sonic similarity (wollig/wollen) of the signifiers for very different signifieds. Several other lines exhibit three-term lists, most strikingly "blissfully-mocking, blissfully-hellish, blissfully-bloodthirsty" (l.49),[133] while the practice of creating noun-noun composites (making it unclear which fulfills an adjectival, which a nominal role) occurs not only in the lambs-milk-well-wishing but in "God's-Columns" (l.36) "Virtue-Statues" (l.39), "Cats-Willfulness" (l.41), "Rose-Hanging-Mats" (l.87), "Truth's-Madness" (*Wahrheits-Wahnsinn*, l.81), "Day's-Longings" (l.92), and "lying word-bridges,/ ... Lie-Rainbows" (ll.28–9).[134]

And so on; one of the ways that the poem's sonic features coalesce into rhythm is the sheer density with which Nietzsche deploys them, creating not only repetition but expectation and its satisfaction, delay, or disruption. The combination of all of these effects creates a detailed and striking "linguistic topography," what Rüdiger Görner has called a "thought landscape" (*Denklandschaft*) consisting of "language rivers, clause contours, surveying points, rises and falls [*Hebungen und Senkungen*] in the topography of the language determined by meter or thought-rhythm[.]"[135] Rhythm in "Only fool! Only poet!" thus enacts the insight, at once celebration and critique, that the human world is always a word-world (*Wortwelt*); shaped by metaphors, sound associations, repetitions, and the pauses, hesitations, delays, accelerations, and trailings off notated by punctuation.[136] The "lies" of poets, as Nietzsche's 1874 essay "On Truth and Lies in an Extra-Moral Sense" anticipated, are just the expression of the inevitably linguistically-conditioned relation to perception and the world; recalling the remark that "Man is a form- and rhythm-making creature,"[137] poets and fools shape their language and thus worlds more vitally and energetically than those who, like the servants of truth in the middle of the poem, are "still, stiff, cold, smooth," and dishonest about their own inevitable perceptive and linguistic distortions.[138]

This all sounds rather triumphalist, compared with the vicious self-critiques internalized by the speaker. Moreover, it loses sight of the ambivalence in Nietzsche's discussions of the rhythms of his epoch in the letter to Carl Fuchs I cited

---

[133] Other examples: "clever, stealing, slinking" (l.17), "still, stiff, smooth, cold" (l.34), "stealing, slinking, l y i n g" (l.50), "downwards, evening-wards, shadow-wards" (l.94).

[134] Kaiser notes the double meanings of the noun-noun composites: "Truth's-Madness" as madness through truth and madness in pursuit of truth, and "Day's-Longings" as longing aroused by and also longing for day. Kaiser, "Wortwelten, Weltworte," 321.

[135] Rüdiger Görner, "Nur Narr, nur Dichter. Musikalität und Poetik," *Nietzsche-Studien* 41, no. 1 (2012): 43–57, https://doi.org/10.1515/niet.2012.41.1.43.

[136] Kaiser, "Wortwelten, Weltworte," 313. He adds, "The determination that life is only literature loses here the pejorative sense it has in Heine and takes on an epoch-making new meaning that represents a decisive German contribution to the self-understanding of European Symbolism" (313).

[137] Nietzsche, posthumous fragment, 1885 (http://www.nietzschesource.org/#eKGWB/NF-1885,38[10]).

[138] Kaiser, "Wortwelten, Weltworte," 347.

above. In a second letter written to Fuchs a few days later, Nietzsche begins without salutation, instead giving a title-like opening: "*On the keeping apart of ancient rhythm ('**time**-rhythm') from the barbarian ('**affect**-rhythm').*"[139] Nietzsche recapitulates in considerable detail the arguments he gave against the ictus in his rhythm notebooks, echoing his work from some eighteen years earlier at the twilight of his career. He concludes with a "Main point" (Hauptsache): "the two types of rhythm [accentual and quantitative] are *contrary* in their most primary purpose and origin."[140] These purposes return to the distinction between "affect rhythm" and "time rhythm" from the title-heading; Nietzsche explains that, in general, German puts accentual stress on the most semantically important syllable, or the "*affect-dominating* syllable."[141] As such, German performance of poetry heightens affect, to the point of being "pathological"; Greek performance, conversely, drew on rhythm as "a bridle applied to passion," in part due to the strong emotional arousal attributed to the rhapsode.[142] The concentration of all emotive force into the smallest units of language recalls Nietzsche's history in which the accent "sucks all life into itself while everything around it withers" (KGW II₃, 308). "Only fool! Only poet!" leaves undetermined whether the lying poet-speaker, having concentrated rhythmical effects into the smallest components of language, succeeds also in deploying larger-scale repetitive structures and in creating the rhythmical achievements commensurate to his epoch and culture, or whether he succumbs to the "pathology" of affect in words alone, absent both the macroformal proportional organization and the gestural efficacy of Greek rhythms.

* * *

The rhythmical practice of "Only fool! Only poet!" is thus both symptom and critique of its epoch. Such ambivalences are the necessary poetic corollary of Nietzsche's attention to the epistemological instability of language itself and thus, necessarily, any work on language, whether in philosophy, philology, or poetry. His emphasis on pathology and his instantiation of visual rhythms foregrounds bodily experience, and the differentiation between ancient aesthetic-ethical rhythms and modern pathological ones bears on the way in which bodily experience is always already culturally conditioned. Nietzsche's work on and in rhythm—in particular his attention to physiology, skepticism, and historical thinking—defies the narrow scientism of his epoch and, as we shall see, significant portions of twentieth- and twenty-first central metrical thinking. The same three attributes help show how any account of the physiological efficacy of rhythm and meter must be historically

---

[139] Letter to Carl Fuchs, presumed end of August, 1888 (http://www.nietzschesource.org/#eKGWB/BVN-1888,1097).
[140] http://www.nietzschesource.org/#eKGWB/BVN-1888,1097.
[141] http://www.nietzschesource.org/#eKGWB/BVN-1888,1097.
[142] http://www.nietzschesource.org/#eKGWB/BVN-1888,1097.

and culturally specific. Reading together Nietzsche's philology and poetry invites an approach to meter and poetic experience that is historically attuned, attentive to the body, and reflective of its own epistemological conditionedness. This approach is one that, I contend, contemporary thinking about patterns in language would do well to reclaim in order to articulate poetic experiences more fully.

5

From Meter to Media and Materiality

"Wollen wir also überhaupt weiterhin Metrik betreiben?" (Do we still want to pursue metrics at all?)[1] So begins a German history of meter from 1984 that is still widely used in 2022, demonstrating a dramatic change in the status of metrical theory as a field in the roughly 150 years between Nietzsche's studies and contemporary considerations of poetry. This chapter locates (roughly) contemporary arguments about metrics in a wider history of metrical claims, revealing both affinities and breaks with that history. I analyze these arguments in three almost entirely separate fields: first, historical overviews primarily designed for university or secondary school students; next, what is known in German Studies as "posthermeneutic" literary theory, which imports most of its concepts from information theory and mathematics; and, third, disciplines that study language and literature using quantitative and empirical methods. I highlight what is innovative and productive in each of them, adding contemporary approaches to the moments of eighteenth- and nineteenth-century metrical debates that, I argue, help us think about meter and poetic experience. At the same time, I note the shortcomings of each approach and the problems caused by their isolation from each other and literary studies as a whole.

I show how metrical histories or handbooks (the first area) helpfully underscore the multiplicity of traditions at work in German-language metrical practices and emphasize the degree to which poets appeal to and take up prior practices and traditions. They also, however, treat claims by past poets and theorists about the bodily and emotional effects of meter as errors to be corrected, cutting off metrical theory and practice from wider arguments about meaning, language, culture, and embodiment. Meter thus becomes merely of historical or intellectual interest. In my considerations of posthermeneutic literary theory, I note that its authors intensify the separation of meter and rhythm from meaning; moreover, since the terms of posthermeneutic analysis and its theoretical horizons are imported from the non-literary fields, posthermeneutic authors miss the contributions of literary history to the very questions they address. But posthermeneutic reading suggests innovative ways of looking at syllable patterns in its attention to the subtle ways in which techniques and technologies of producing, storing, and transmitting texts affect the texts themselves. Furthermore, the posthermeneutic focus on conflict between meaning and materiality illuminates elements of texts that do not fit

---

[1] Leif Ludwig Albertsen, *Neuere deutsche Metrik* (Bern: Peter Lang, 1984), 9.

Metrical Claims and Poetic Experience. Hannah Vandegrift Eldridge, Oxford University Press.
© Hannah Vandegrift Eldridge, (2022). DOI: 10.1093/oso/9780192859211.003.0006

neatly into conceptual interpretation. Finally, I demonstrate that quantitative or natural-scientific approaches to metrical theory and practice make a compelling contemporary case for the effectiveness of metrical practice for the emotions and in the body—something other contemporary accounts of meter and poetry often dismiss. These approaches likewise offer fine-grained tools and strategies for analyzing different levels of metrical organization, from the syllable to the word to the line to the strophe. But empirical approaches often operate with the false assumption that syllable patterns can be counted independently of cultural context or individual perception; as the previous chapters have shown, who counts what as which meter and why turns out to be a matter of combined individual practice, historical location, and aesthetic or political commitments.

Taken together, these areas—metrical handbooks, posthermeneutic theories, and empirical studies—provide tools and approaches for talking about the ways meter matters in the twenty-first century. But the isolation of metrical theory in these subfields reveals how far metrics in the late twentieth century has fallen from its privileged position in both eighteenth- and nineteenth-century scholarship. In the eighteenth century, metrical theory and practice explicitly expressed cultural and political value judgments and were central for projects of activating the "whole human"; that is, for developing and being effective for emotion and embodiment in addition to reason (see Chapters 1 and 2). By Nietzsche's career in the nineteenth century, these stakes had diminished somewhat, but meter still helped define the disciplines of philology and linguistics and their epistemologies; theorists of the 1840s through the 1870s also argued that understanding meter guaranteed or denied access to the valorized past cultures of Greece and Rome (see Chapters 3 and 4). In the late twentieth and early twenty-first centuries, by contrast, metrics seems hypertechnical or old-fashioned (or both). But as I show in Chapter 6, the contemporary poet and essayist Durs Grünbein brings together elements of all three contemporary strands in order to articulate and put into poetic practice the claim that meter remains central for poetic—and thus, in his view, human—experience. Grünbein's poetic practice and his reflections reveal how meter resists both ideological cooptation and reduction to natural-scientific data. In doing so, his work demonstrates the ability of metrical poetry to negotiate and perform the conflicts that shape contemporary language and subjectivity.

5.1 Literary History and Literary Theory

I turn first to approaches from literary history and literary theory, namely, the handbooks of meter and the posthermeneutic literary-theoretical texts characterized above. In the second part of the chapter, I divide my discussion of quantitative and empirical approaches into three main areas: linguistics, especially generative metrics, cognitive scientific and neuroscientific studies, and evolutionary accounts of art in general and verse in particular. Despite the challenges of handling this much material in a single chapter, I argue that one drawback of all three approaches is their isolation from one another, and I therefore attempt to begin a conversation between them.

Metrical Histories and Handbooks

There are two peculiarities of the metrical handbooks or histories I discuss here that would seem to make them uninteresting for analyzing the stakes of metrical debate in the twenty-first century. (These peculiarities might also explain why meter itself appears outmoded and pedantic.) First, they are relatively old, originally published in the 1980s and reprinted virtually unaltered in the years after 2000 in second through fifth editions.[2] Second, these metrical handbooks and histories represent themselves as being for pedagogical purposes, instructing secondary school and university students, and thus informing, rather than arguing; the goal is correctness or accuracy, not innovation or effectiveness. Further, the reprinting rather than rewriting of metrical handbooks indicates an assumption of historical stasis: it suggests (inaccurately, as we shall see) that neither metrical theory nor poetic practice is breaking new ground, but only choosing between a multiplicity of available options. This is a significant change from both the eighteenth and nineteenth centuries. In the eighteenth century, poets in general and Klopstock with particular virtuosity developed new meters by playing with Greek and Latin traditions, while in the nineteenth century vigorous debates about how various meters worked opened new theoretical terrain, which Nietzsche then expanded. The pedagogical focus of late twentieth-century handbooks and histories reveals what recent metrical theory takes as given, precisely because the authors believe themselves to be presenting information without argument. Specifically, their authors operate with the principle that the main reason to study meter is to avoid making mistakes; correctness or accuracy are the primary payoff in paying attention to patterns of syllables. Their metrical treatises do not see themselves as taking stances on canonical metrical-theoretical questions, such as the relationship between form and meaning or the emotional efficacy of metrical practice; instead, they want to help readers be correct.

Small wonder, then, that by the late twentieth century, metrical theory appears as a "traditionally unpopular object" to the extent that Dieter Breuer opens his 1981 *German Metrics and Verse History* with a section on "Scorn for Metrics" (Metrik-Verachtung).[3] Leif Ludwig Albertsen's 1984 *Modern German Metrics*

---

[2] See Renzo Caduff, "Sebastian Donat: Deskriptive Metrik. (Reihe Comparanda. Literaturwissenschaftliche Studien zu Antike und Moderne)," *Arcadia* 47, No. 1 (Juli, 2012), https://doi.org/10.1515/arcadia-2012-0014, 219.

[3] Dieter Breuer, *Deutsche Metrik und Versgeschichte*, 4th ed. (Munich: Wilhelm Fink Verlag, 1981).

begins with a paragraph "On the expected utility of metrics" (Über den zu erwartenden Nutzen der Metrik). Before posing the question I quoted to open this chapter, "Do we still want to pursue metrics at all?," Albertsen criticizes philosophical interpretations of metrical forms,[4] and indeed the *Historisches Wörterbuch der Philosophie* (Historical Dictionary of Philosophy) has an entry for rhythm (volume 8, R-Sc, 1992[5]) with several subentries but none for meter or metrics, while the *Ästhetische Grundbegriffe* (Fundamental Terms in Aesthetics, 2000) includes articles for rhythm and measure ("Maß") but not meter.[6] If in 1981 Breuer is optimistic that a new balance might emerge between formalist metrical theory and "the social-historical approach" to literature,[7] in 2012 Renzo Caduff laments that "innovative publications on metrics in general and German metrics in particular have been few and far between in the last few years."[8] Metrical theory and practice, at least in literary studies, no longer has any import for how we understand fundamental human faculties or dispositions, nor does it play a role in shaping disciplinary identities.[9]

Metrical histories and handbooks from the 1980s and 1990s, reprinted into the 2000s, share with their eighteenth- and especially nineteenth-century counterparts an interest in the historical and comparative development of metrical traditions as they appear or are adapted into Germanic languages.[10] Many, especially those that discuss multiple languages, begin from typologies of metrical systems based on which (combinations of) phonological elements are organized into patterns; for example, Mikhail Gasparov's *A History of European Versification* outlines traditions that count the number of syllables, syllable weight, vowel and/or syllable length, or combinations of numbers of syllables plus regulated placements of stress or length.[11] All the German handbooks, contrary to the metrical theories of the eighteenth century (and a few nineteenth-century outliers), agree that modern German has stressed and unstressed syllables, with syllable

[4] Albertsen, *Neuere deutsche Metrik*, 9.

[5] Angelika Corbineau-Hoffmann, "Rhythmus," in *Historisches Wörterbuch der Philosophie. R - Sc*, eds. Joachim Ritter and Karlfried Grunder (Schwabe Verlag Basel, 1992), 1026–33.

[6] Wilhelm Seidel, "Rhythmus," in *Ästhetische Grundbegriffe*, eds. Karl Barck et al., vol. 5, 7 vols. (Stuttgart: Metzler Verlag, 2003), 291–314.

[7] Breuer, *Deutsche Metrik und Versgeschichte*, 12–3.

[8] Caduff, "Sebastian Donat: Deskriptive Metrik," 219. Caduff views Donat's volume, which he is reviewing, as an exception.

[9] As I show below, both of these aspects appear in new ways in the approaches to metrical language based on the natural sciences, which, however, by and large ignore the history of metrical theory.

[10] Unlike their eighteenth- and nineteenth-century predecessors, they neither assume that German or European verse forms are universally effective nor read metrical patterns as revealing the essence of a nation, culture, or race.

[11] Mikhail L. Gasparov, *A History of European Versification*, trans. G.S. Smith and Marina Tarlinskaja, ed. G. H. Smith with Leofranc Holford-Strevens (Oxford: Clarendon Press, 1996), 3. Other examples are John Hollander's, *Rhyme's Reason*, 3rd ed. (New Haven: Yale Nota Bene, 2001), 4–5 and Alfred Corn's chapter headings in *The Poem's Heartbeat. A Manual of Prosody* (Brownsville, OR: Story Line Press, 1997). See also Christian Wagenknecht, *Deutsche Metrik. Eine historische Einführung*, 5th ed. (Munich: C.H. Beck, 2007), 20.

length (correlated to vowel length) playing at best a secondary role. They disagree, however, as to whether binary (weak versus strong) or multi-level (e.g.,
weak, medium-weak, medium-strong, strong) designations of stress are most useful. The conflict over which units are counted and whether they are of equal size,
which shaped so much of nineteenth-century metrical thinking (see Chapter 3),
continues into the mid-twentieth century in debates about isochrony, the idea
that metrical regularity comes from equal amounts of time (but potentially variable numbers of syllables or words) between stressed syllables.[12] In the nineteenth
and early twentieth centuries, some theorists hoped that isochrony measurements
would replace foot names (dactyls, trochees, etc.) imported from Greek and Latin.
By the 1980s and 1990s, however, linguists and metrical theorists agree that lines
with equal numbers of strong syllables do not have exactly equal time intervals
between those syllables, even as it makes the most sense to analyze some poetic
traditions as made of lines with a fixed number of strong syllables per line.[13] Taken
together, all of these different ways of counting different things reveal that there
is, as Albertsen remarks, no unified metrical system or theory that can encompass
the entirety of German verse practice.[14]

This recognition that different scansion systems—different ways of measuring
different phonological elements of language—are most illuminating for different poetic traditions, epochs, or poets is both characteristic for late-twentieth
and early-twenty-first century metrical theory and helpful for considering Durs
Grünbein, who writes in a wide range of meters and poetic forms, including free rhythms, haiku, alexandrines, Greek/Latin ode and hexameter forms,
and rhyming German folk styles. His oeuvre thus exemplifies the interaction
between a given language (here, German) and international cultural influences
that Gasparov foregrounds as characteristic of European versification: "The cultural influences that define the development of verse forms never operate in
isolation, but always in interaction. The relative strength of these influences is
determined, firstly, by the hierarchy obtaining in the prestige of cultural traditions ... and, secondly, by the degree of closeness of cultural contact."[15] Gasparov's
attention to multi-language interaction, (inter-)cultural contact, and the prestige
of various traditions helps him account for the copresence of multiple systems
of versification in a single language, potentially in the same era. Moreover, it

---

[12] See Albertsen, *Neuere deutsche Metrik*, 170–1, Breuer, *Deutsche Metrik und Versgeschichte*, 74–81, and Erwin Arndt, *Deutsche Verslehre*, 13th ed. (Berlin: Volk und Wissen Verlag, 1996), 25 and 50.

[13] To give an example, one *can* describe Goethe's "Erlkönig" as an irregular mix of two- and three-syllable feet (and one can call those feet trochees, iambs, dactyls, and anapests, if one likes), but doing so will not yield much regularity from line to line or verse to verse, whereas the description "four-line verses with four stresses per line" applies to the whole poem and distinguishes it from, say, four-line ode strophes. Hollander gives an even more extreme example in *Rhyme's Reason* of what he calls "pure accentual meter": In accentual *meter* it *doesn't matter*/ *Whe*ther each *line* is thin or *fatter*;/ *What* you *hear* (this *matters more*)/ Is *one, two, three, four.*" (Hollander, *Rhyme's Reason*, 21–2).

[14] Albertsen, *Neuere deutsche Metrik*, 16.

[15] Gasparov, *History of European Versification*, 294.

leads him to a nuanced understanding of the relation between the phonological features of a language (length, accent, pitch, etc.) and its metrical practices: "Some unsophisticated metrical primers tell us that a system of versification cannot exist in a language if the language does not provide it with a phonological basis. The situation is not quite so simple."[16] He gives the example of the persistence of quantitative metrics in Medieval Latin as proving that, at least for a "learned minority," "cultural traditions and influences are sometimes stronger than linguistic givens."[17] Which relations between phonology and meter are acceptable at which time will vary by culture, history, and individual poet or theorist.[18]

German meters, in the contemporary understanding, combine a phonology whose most prominent feature is accentuation with verse systems imported from Ancient and Romance languages.[19] Thus the entire convention of describing German verse as consisting of iambs, trochees, dactyls, anapests, etc., strictly speaking applies only to those verse types that are based on Greek or Latin forms, such as hexameter;[20] as Albertsen warns, transferring foot names to other traditions is a mere labeling convention and easily leads to misunderstanding.[21] Arndt, too, points out that adopting Greek and Latin foot names can prompt readers to make distinctions that are too absolute for German poetry.[22] Breuer sums up that readers of German poetry must know and recognize the Romance and antique traditions because they influenced poets and theorists, but he forbids any generalization from those traditions to "the *entire* history of German verse."[23] He adds that not only the imported syllable counting and durational rules but also the rules for determining "natural word accent"[24] in German are defined and applied differently throughout the German tradition[25]—as, for example, in the shift from German hexameters based on duration to those based on accent (which I traced in Chapter 1). History and tradition likewise help identify limit cases of verse lines, such as those marked visually rather than prosodically and the fluid boundary between free

---

[16] Gasparov, *History of European Versification*, 89.
[17] Gasparov, *History of European Versification*, 89.
[18] Gasparov sees this as a "struggle" between "the demands of the language" and those of the verse system (Gasparov, *History of European Versification*, 294). His colleague and translator, Marina Tarlinskaja, argues that the demands of the culture predominate over those of the language: comparing iambic pentameter by Pope, Byron, Shakespeare, Frost, and Donne, she uses statistical analysis to suggest that deviation from strict meter depends on the authorized canon of the day, not the difficulty of putting English vocabulary into iambs. Marina Tarlinskaja, "What Is 'Metricality'? English Iambic Pentameter," in *Formal Approaches to Poetry: Recent Developments in Metrics*, eds. Bezalel E. Dresher and Nila Friedberg (Berlin: De Gruyter, 2006), 53–74, 64.
[19] Breuer, *Deutsche Metrik und Versgeschichte*, 33.
[20] Wagenknecht, *Deutsche Metrik*, 39.
[21] Albertsen, *Neuere deutsche Metrik*, 33.
[22] Arndt, *Deutsche Verslehre*, 23–4.
[23] Breuer, *Deutsche Metrik und Versgeschichte*, 68.
[24] Breuer, *Deutsche Metrik und Versgeschichte*, 67.
[25] Breuer, *Deutsche Metrik und Versgeschichte*, 71.

verse and prose.[26] Unlike their earlier counterparts, metricists in literary studies from the end of the twentieth century do not attempt to arrive at a law of rhythm that applies to all metrical practice;[27] they likewise (unlike some nineteenth century and many twenty-first century natural-scientific metricists) emphasize the importance of understanding the historical context and individual commitments of poets in interpreting their metrical practice.

On the canonical topic of attributing semantic or thematic content to specific metrical forms, all of Albertsen, Arndt, Breuer, and Wagenknecht call for similar historical-contextual nuance. Albertsen asserts that there is no absolute, one-to-one relation between meter or content, foot type, or mood, but that because various poets have *thought* there was, could be, or should be, modern readers should be aware of past claims about form-content interaction.[28] In a similar vein, Arndt refers to the *Stimmungskraft* (mood or atmospheric force) that particular forms attain by way of tradition and notes that cultural conditioning is restrictive enough to prevent the content of a given verse form from being completely open at a given time.[29] Arndt suggests that poets can cite or reactivate older forms, creating a deliberate intertextual connection within which the verse form can play a signifying role; his example is the GDR poet Johannes R. Becher's use of alexandrines to evoke Andreas Gryphius's Baroque poetry on human suffering.[30] Breuer recalls the cooperation of meter and content as defining genres in antiquity,[31] while Wagenknecht puts the historical contextualization of form-content associations into practice. At the end of each section, titled after a verse type (e.g., "2. Meistersang, Kirchenlied, Knittelvers"[32]), he gives an overview that points out themes or topics associated with the form in question, as for example in his tracing

---

[26] Breuer lists "typeface, font size, letter spacing, line length, line order" as well as "types of page mirroring, color," and even "paper type, paper color, kind of binding, type of cut" and format as a whole as components that create visual ordering (Breuer, *Deutsche Metrik und Versgeschichte,* 24); Arndt notes the difficulty free rhythms pose to historical conceptions of verse (Arndt, *Deutsche Verslehre,* 14–5).

[27] Sebastian Donat's *Deskriptive Metrik,* which "understands itself as a new systematic attempt to create a simple but at the same time precise and differentiated description of all (or at least as many as possible) verse and poem forms" (Sebastian Donat, *Deskriptive Metrik,* Comparanda 15 [Studien Verlag, 2010], 7) is thus something of an anachronism; then again, its approaches are closer to those of linguistics—as the title's echo of "Generative Metrics" and Donat's interlocutors indicate. Donat, as well as figures like Gasparov and Tarlinskaja, makes clear that the differences between methods, epistemologies, and disciplines I outline here are not absolute.

[28] Albertsen, *Neuere deutsche Metrik,* 14.

[29] He gives the alexandrine as a "paradigmatic example for the way historical factors condition the possibilities for use of a verse form," noting its appearance in German in the seventeenth century as a verse with highly pathetic expressivity, adopted from Holland and France, while by the eighteenth century it became so strongly associated with courtly and erudite poetry that the poets of the *Sturm und Drang,* similarly interested in expressivity and pathos, rejected alexandrines as stilted, aristocratic, and artificial (Arndt, *Deutsche Verslehre,* 33–4).

[30] Arndt, *Deutsche Verslehre,* 35–6.

[31] Breuer, *Deutsche Metrik und Versgeschichte,* 34ff.

[32] *Meistersang* refers to the verse type of minstrel guild singers; *Kirchenlied* means "church song" or "hymn"; "Knittelvers" is a stressed and rhymed verse form AABB with four stresses per line, originating in the Middle Ages and popular in the German-language poetry of the fifteenth and sixteenth

of Goethe's use of Knittelvers to activate a stuffy, old-fashioned, almost parodic register in the beginning of *Faust*.[33]

Given the status of metrics in the latter decades of the twentieth century, it is not surprising that each author gives a justification for his (and his readers') attention.[34] To begin with, late twentieth-century metrical experts contend that studying metrical theory and practice helps to prevent errors in the interpretation of literary texts. Thus Albertsen describes "elements of metrics" as "a part of European cultural knowledge" necessary for historical and present understanding;[35] he adds, gesturing at wider claims, that at least some parts of "metrical knowledge" can lead the reader to "get more" out of literature, that is "to understand better that and how it can affect and sometimes still does affect him and others."[36] Wagenknecht, too, enters a plea for metrics as a way to "clear and correct understanding" of literary texts,[37] while Arndt, writing in the GDR, considers metrics part of the "museal education" (*musische Bildung*) he views as important to the "socialist educational program."[38] Although Breuer hints at wider stakes in hoping to overcome readers' forced choice between their "lively aesthetic experience of verse" and "cold metrical theory,"[39] on the whole, arguments that accuracy and understanding are the primary payoff of studying meter represent a significant deflation from the heady metrical-theoretical claims of the previous centuries. Indeed, as Albertsen's critique of those who link meter with "psychological primal rhythms"[40] indicates, for most scholars of meter in literary studies in the late twentieth century, anthropological-philosophical interpretations of metrical

centuries. (See Chris Baldick, "Knittelvers," in *The Oxford Dictionary of Literary Terms* (Oxford University Press, 2008), https://www.oxfordreference.com/view/10.1093/acref/9780199208272.001.0001/acref-9780199208272-e-631).

[33] Wagenknecht, *Deutsche Metrik*, 45–6.

[34] The male-gendered pronoun not only refers to the four authors I discuss here but is representative of German academia in both the 1990s and, to a lesser but still significant extent, today: according to the European Commission, 8% of university professors were women in 1995, 15% in 2006 ("Women Professors on the Increase in German Universities | News | CORDIS | European Commission," accessed July 5, 2022, https://cordis.europa.eu/article/id/28031-women-professors-on-the-increase-in-german-universities.). For a comparative study of gender disparities in German and American academia in the 1990s, see Stefan Fuchs, *Gender Disparities in Higher Education and Academic Careers in Germany and the United States*, Policy Report #7 (Washington, DC: American Institute for Contemporary German Studies, Johns Hopkins University, 1999). On race in the humanities in Germany, see Mahmoud Arghavan et al., *Who Can Speak and Who Is Heard/Hurt?: Facing Problems of Race, Racism, and Ethnic Diversity in the Humanities in Germany* (transcript Verlag, 2019).

[35] Albertsen, *Neuere deutsche Metrik*, 18–9.

[36] Albertsen, *Neuere deutsche Metrik*, 19.

[37] Wagenknecht, *Deutsche Metrik*, 7.

[38] Arndt, *Deutsche Verslehre*, 5. "Musisch"/ "museal" refers to "of the muses," that is, the fine arts and history, not exclusively to musical ("musikalische") education. This is one of relatively few places where Arndt's political-historical location in the German Democratic Republic obviously influences his argumentation; otherwise, his emphasis on social-historical effects contexts and effects of formal features aligns with that of the other authors I consider here. Since one of my leading contentions in this project is that metrical theory and practice are always shaped by (and shaping) cultural, political, and aesthetic commitments, I see Arndt as not significantly different from other metrical theorists.

[39] Breuer, *Deutsche Metrik und Versgeschichte*, 9.

[40] Albertsen, *Neuere deutsche Metrik*, 9.

practice are errors to be avoided and should ideally be replaced by more sober, historically informed accounts. Two hundred and fifty years after meter abandoned
genre poetics to play a central role in accounts of the lyric as an index of fundamental human capacities (see Chapter 1), claims that meter can yield insight into
species-defining human traits have shifted into natural-scientific approaches such
as neuroaesthetics, cognitive poetics, and evolutionary aesthetics.[41]

Posthermeneutics

The scholarship of the so-called posthermeneutic turn, a high tide of literary theory as media and cultural studies that emerged in the German academy around
the same time as Albertsen, Arndt, Breuer, and Wagenknecht were writing their
histories, is a somewhat unlikely place to consider metrics, since it has almost no
contact with metrical theory, history, or practice. Relatively unknown in the American academy (apart from media theorists who read German), "posthermeneutics,"
is not a unified school or defined methodology.[42] As the name "posthermeneutic"
(coined by the American Germanist David Wellbery in 1990) suggests, theorists
writing in a posthermeneutic vein challenge habits of interpretation that privilege semantic meaning and subordinate or neglect material and formal features.[43]
Instead, they foreground various kinds of "materiality" that support and, in their
view, condition, the transmission of information. In the 1988 volume *Materialities
of Communication*, which includes pieces by Friedrich Kittler, Niklas Luhmann,
Hans Ulrich Gumbrecht, and other authors associated with posthermeneutic
approaches, editor Ludwig K. Pfeiffer's introduction articulates an agenda and
a critique of interpretive practices: "We are looking for underlying constraints
whose technological, material, procedural, and performative potentials have been
all too easily swallowed up by interpretation habits. These habits have been over-
developed and have, to some extent, veered out of control."[44] This work thus

---

[41] Some scholars in those traditions would, of course, position themselves within "literary studies,"
thus conflicting with my characterization of "scholars of meter in literary studies in the late twentieth
century." To be fully precise I would have to describe the latter as "scholars of meter in literary studies in
the late twentieth century who do not avail themselves extensively of the methods of linguistics, brain
imaging, or cognitive science."

[42] On German posthermeneutics and American media theory, see especially the work of Geoffrey
Winthrop-Young, "The Kittler Effect," *New German Critique* 44, no. 3 (132) (November 1, 2017):
205–24, https://doi.org/10.1215/0094033X-4162322; Nicholas Gane and Geoffrey Winthrop-Young,
"Friedrich Kittler: An Introduction," *Theory, Culture & Society* 23, no. 7–8 (2006): 5–16, and John
Durham Peters, "Introduction: Friedrich Kittler's Light Shows," in *Optical Media: Berlin Lectures 1999*,
ed. Friedrich A. Kittler, trans. Anthony Enns (Cambridge: Polity Press, 2010).

[43] David E. Wellbery, "Foreword," in Friedrich Kittler, *Discourse Networks 1800/1900*, trans. Michael
Metteer (Stanford: Stanford University Press, 1990), vii–xxxiii, xii.

[44] Ludwig K. Pfeiffer, "The Materiality of Communication," in *Materialities of Communication*,
eds. Hans Ulrich Gumbrecht and Ludwig K. Pfeiffer, trans. William Whobrey (Stanford: Stanford
University Press, 1994), 1–12, 12.

examines devices and techniques that enabled and shaped a wide range of cultural artifacts, from the poems and novels of Johann Wolfgang von Goethe to the music of Jimi Hendrix to the hyperlinks in html documents. Considering these phenomena, posthermeneutic theorists turn away from analyzing "authors or styles associated with authors," and attend instead to "inconspicuous technologies of knowledge," such as "index cards, writing tools and typewriters," and/or to "discourse operators (e.g., quotation marks), pedagogical media ... and disciplining techniques (e.g. language acquisition and alphabetization)."[45] The precise relation asserted or denied between "materiality" and assorted kinds of content or meaning varies; at its most nuanced, posthermeneutic reading considers possible relations between material and semantic functions but rejects subordination of the former to the latter.[46]

In turning to posthermeneutic scholarship, I contend that it matters for how contemporary poets, scholars, and readers think about metrical theory and practice that the one of preeminent discourses in literary theory makes materiality and media its central terms, with meter occurring only occasionally and even then in a marginal role. In rare moments, meter appears as one type of materiality among others; the few passages I discuss below raise the tantalizing possibilities both that meter's relation to meaning and embodiment could complicate posthermeneutic stances and that posthermeneutic theory could add to the repertoire of approaches for understanding metrical experience.

Friedrich Kittler's treatment of meter in his discussions of romantic poetry is typical—or perhaps symptomatic—of the treatment of meter in posthermeneutic thought as a whole. Meter occasionally appears as one among several forms of materiality in literature, but without reference to the history of metrical forms and the complex ways in which they are imbricated in cultural norms. For example, in taking poetry as a pedagogical medium and disciplining technique for making certain kinds of subjects, Kittler points to the "psycho-pedagogy" initiated by Locke and Rousseau. He thus links romanticism's focus on sound and orality in lyric to a conception of the maternal voice that initiates the poetic subject into language in a contentless "play of sounds:" "Sounds melt with nature; noises murmur and whisper with the maternal voice, which induces harking [*horchen*] and not hearing [*hören*] in the infant. The matrix of motherly lullabies—which take the place of less complicated methods of quieting children—gives rise, at the border between speaking and sleeping, to a new lyricism that has existed ever since 'Wanderer's

---

[45] Bernhard Siegert, "Cultural Techniques: Or the End of the Intellectual Postwar Era in German Media Theory," *Theory, Culture & Society* 30, no. 6 (November 2013): 48–65, 50.

[46] This subtle version of posthermeneutic reading ("Lesen") is the one articulated in David Wellbery's programmatic "Interpretation vs. Lesen. Posthermeneutsiche Konzepte der Texterörterung" (in *Wie international ist die Literaturwissenschaft? Methoden- und Theoriediskussion in den Literaturwissenschaften: Kulturelle Besonderheiten und interkultureller Austausch am Beispiel des Interpretationsproblems, 1950–1990*, ed. Lutz Danneberg [Stuttgart: Metzler Verlag, 1996], 123–38).

Night Song,' by Goethe."[47] Kittler reads this program as a departure from erudite poetry and "the norms of verse theory" (*Normen der Verslehre*), and he notes (more or less correctly) of "Wanderer's Night Song" that "no traditional metrical scheme governs the lines."[48] Kittler then quotes snatches of other lullaby poems without noting that these *do*, in fact, have regular rhyme schemes and rhythmical patterning.[49] Instead, he attends to the noises ("rauschen") of nature that the snippets present.[50] Kittler makes meter fit his argument by claiming that it supports the pedagogical functions of lyrical orality around 1800 even as he has almost nothing to say about a variety of specific, differentiated functions of meter within different poetic techniques.

Kittler repeatedly appropriates Nietzsche's aphorism "Of the Origins of Poetry," which I analyzed in detail in the previous chapter, as an explanation for the powers of rhythm.[51] He reprises Nietzsche's arguments about effects and purposes of rhythmical speech, as poets "participate in the bloody task of making bodies hear and obey. Verses provide an instrument that fixes speech mnemotechnically, steers bodies rhythmically, and guards against disturbances in channels of discourse."[52] "The God of the Ears," a compact rumination on recording technology, sound engineering, madness, and Pink Floyd, exemplifies Kittler's habit of subsuming metrical practice to general questions of media and materiality while neglecting metrical theory and history. There, Kittler's central concern is how techniques for sound storage and amplification collaborate in and affect mental states and aesthetic production, and he deploys Nietzsche's aphorism as an early example of artificial amplification and storage techniques: "The simple secret of all poetic lyric is to tear words from oblivion [*Vergängnis*]. When the Greeks invented the hexameter, they had nothing else in mind. 'The rhythmic tick-tock' was meant to make

---

[47] Friedrich A. Kittler, "Poet, Mother, Child: On the Romantic Invention of Sexuality," in *The Truth of the Technological World: Essays on the Genealogy of Presence*, trans. Erik Butler (Stanford: Stanford University Press, 2013), 1–16, 5–6. For all his innovation around materiality and his challenge to subjectivity, Kittler's work unthinkingly adopts long-standing gender stereotypes, where the poetic subject is male and the woman is mother, who speaks only for or as nature and never for or as herself.

[48] Friedrich A. Kittler, "Lullaby of Birdland," in *The Truth of the Technological World: Essays on the Genealogy of Presence*, 31–44, 39. I say "more or less correctly" because, as Anne Holzmüller demonstrates, the poem, like its companion poem, "Wandrers Nachtlied I," activates the register of various religious strophe forms. See Anne Holzmüller, *Lyrik als Klangkunst. Klanggestaltung in Goethes Nachtliedern und ihren Vertonungen von Reichardt bis Wolf* (Freiburg: Rombach Verlag, 2015), 259–61.

[49] The poems are Goethe's "An den Mond," Joseph Freiherr von Eichendorff's "Nachts," Clemens Brentano's "Singet leise, leise, leise," and August Becker's "Da lieg ich nun des Nachts im Wald," all of which have multiple strophes (although Kittler cites only one, sometimes only a few lines) and alternating (iambic or trochaic) rhythms. In keeping with the posthermeneutic disinterest in meaning and interpretation, for Kittler it does not matter that several of the poems were embedded in novels, the others in lyric collections.

[50] Kittler, "Lullaby of Birdland," 40.

[51] For my reading of this aphorism, see Chapter 4.4. As with Kittler's reading of the romantic lyric, his observations are more or less accurate but undercontextualized and oversimplified in the interest of his overarching points.

[52] Friedrich A. Kittler, "Nietzsche (1844–1900)," in *The Truth of the Technological World: Essays on the Genealogy of Presence*, 17–30, 26.

certain discourses inescapable for human ears—and amplify them, over great distance, for the ears of the gods. (The ones are so forgetful, and the others so hard of hearing.)"[53] The appeal to Nietzsche in this context hints at a potential continuity or affinity between technological materiality and literary materiality, which might perhaps open a new approach to meter's canonical function as a mnemonic (and thus quasi-storage) device or a link between recording technology and the physiological acoustics of meter in the nineteenth century, but the history of metrics plays no role in Kittler's genealogies.

Perhaps the most consistent theme of Kittler's career is his accusation "that the humanities forgot how to count."[54] Whereas in the 1980s and 1990s he drew attention to the suppressed equations, devices, and algorithms that underlie projects such as poetry, at the end of his career Kittler turns to ancient Greece, finding a full synthesis of mathematics, music, and eroticism in the emergence of alphabetic writing.[55] And here, for the first time, meter seems poised to play a central role: Kittler follows the (highly controversial) theory of classicist Barry Powell in asserting that the Ancient Greek alphabet, unique in that it represents vowels as well as consonants, developed in order to record Homer's hexameters, since Ancient Greek meters relied on vowel length. In a 2008 lecture that compares Odyssey narratives from Homer to Kubrick, Kittler summarizes Powell: "To recite the hexameters of the *Iliad*, it is necessary to have invented and recorded vowels in writing; otherwise, no singer would know whether the syllables of the verses should be voiced long or short."[56] Kittler thus discovers late in his career that meter represents a small corner of the humanities that has remembered how to count, although he remains relatively uninterested in the complex histories of that counting.

Crucially, for Kittler, letters in Ancient Greece were used to represent not only sounds but also musical intervals and mathematical ratios in a Pythagorean unity of poetry, mathematics, and music as kinds of counting.[57] Kittler valorizes this unified use of the alphabet, which he opposes to the kludged-together system of "Roman letters, Hindu-Arabic numerals, and musical notation" of modern

---

[53] Kittler, "The God of the Ears," in *The Truth of the Technological World*, 45–56, here 54.

[54] John Durham Peters, "Assessing Kittler's *Musik und Mathematik*," in *Kittler Now. Current Perspectives in Kittler Studies*, eds. Stephen Sale and Laura Salisbury (Cambridge: Polity Press, 2015), 22–43, 29.

[55] On this turn, see Gumbrecht's afterword to a collection of Kittler's essays in translation (Hans Ulrich Gumbrecht, "Media History as the Event of Truth: On the Singularity of Friedrich A. Kittler's Works," in *The Truth of the Technological World*, 307–29, especially 318–9), and John Durham Peters' discussion of Kittler's last, unfinished work, *Music and Mathematics* (Peters, "Assessing Kittler's *Musik und Mathematik*," 22–43).

[56] Kittler, "In the Wake of the *Odyssey*," in *The Truth of the Technological World*, 275–89, 276. Peters gives a more scholarly summary of Powell: "Systematic vowel graphemes were invented to represent Greek poetic meter, which scans in intricate patterns of short and long vowels that are unwritable in the syllabic scripts of Semitic, Linear B or Egyptian hieroglyphs." (Peters, "Assessing Kittler's *Musik und Mathematik*," 31–2).

[57] Kittler, "Homer and Writing," in *The Truth of the Technological World*, 259–66, 264.

European notation.[58] As Kittler narrates a fall from this Pythagorean synthesis, which then initiates the shift from length-based to stress-based scansion, and from there to rhyme, he begins to sound not unlike a cultural-critical eighteenth-century metricist: "Latin discarded its grammar and forgot that poets like Virgil, following a Greek model, had endowed it with long and short metrical values," until "syllables were no longer measured out but rather separated into stressed and unstressed units. The place of metrical feet, then—because otherwise we barbarians would only speak in prose (like Molière's M. Jourdain)—was taken over by rhymes in late antiquity."[59] Kittler recasts the (imagined) originary Greek unity of the art forms—a topos of German aesthetics and metrics from the Enlightenment on—as a lost synthesis of sounds and numbers, of which hexameter is a last, echoing reminder. Kittler thus rehashes earlier metrical debates and topoi, but because he is oblivious to metrical history, he does so unawares. Moreover, compared to, say, the details of the hexameter debate, the specifics of metrical practice matter very little to Kittler; despite its apparent importance, hexameter is merely a shortcut to introduce sexualized women's voices in the singing of the sirens.[60]

The other moments in which posthermeneutic scholarship approaches questions of metrical patterning occur in the work of comparatist Hans Ulrich Gumbrecht.[61] Even when discussing poetic language directly, however, Gumbrecht dismisses the specific phenomena of meter as opposed to the overarching phenomenon of rhythm. Indeed, he almost always refers to rhythm in general and almost never to specific metrical forms or features. Gumbrecht argues against establishing any harmony between rhythm and meaning, despite the "and" in the title of his contribution to the *Materialities of Communication* volume, "Rhythm and Meaning" (*Rhythmus und Sinn*).[62] He also rejects Roman Jakobson's claim that there is an "association of 'rhythm' both with literature *and* with the body."[63]

---

[58] Peters, "Assessing Kittler's *Musik und Mathematik*," 33.

[59] Kittler, "In the Wake of the Odyssey," 280–1.

[60] John Durham Peters remarks that the connections between voice and eroticism persists across Kittler's career, along with a less sophisticated tendency in which Kittler "equates sexy women and music." Peters, "Assessing Kittler's *Musik und Mathematik*," 37. Peters' "assessment" concludes convincingly that the sexism and heterosexism of Kittler's linking of sex, mathematics, and music, together with his regressive philhellenism, ultimately damage *Music and Mathematics* as a whole.

[61] On Gumbrecht's career and the situation of his work in relation to hermeneutics, posthermeneutics, and what he calls a "non-hermeneutics," see Carsten Strathausen, "A Rebel Against Hermeneutics: On the Presence of Hans Ulrich Gumbrecht" (*Theory & Event* 9, no. 1 [March 27, 2006] https://doi.org/10.1353/tae.2006.0021) and Gumbrecht's interview with Ulrik Ekman, "The Speed of Beauty: Hans Ulrich Gumbrecht, Interviewed by Ulrik Ekman," (*Postmodern Culture* 16, no. 3 [2006] http://pmc.iath.virginia.edu/issue.506/16.3ekman.html).

[62] Hans Ulrich Gumbrecht, "Rhythm and Meaning," in *Materialities of Communication*, eds. Hans Ulrich Gumbrecht and Ludwig K. Pfeiffer, trans. William Whobrey (Stanford: Stanford University Press, 1994), 170–82. The text poses significant difficulties for comprehension, as it alludes to all of Jakobson, Paul Zumthor, Émile Benveniste, Aristotle, Niklas Luhmann, Edmund Husserl, Alfred Schütz, George Herbert Mead, Humberto Maturana, and Francesco Varela with minimal explanation in a mere thirteen pages.

[63] Gumbrecht, "Rhythm and Meaning," 171.

Per Gumbrecht, this association leads readers astray because whereas literature exists comfortably with the "frameworks of representation" in "'Western Culture'" (the use of scare quotes is Gumbrecht's), neither the body nor rhythm possesses "a primary representation dimension."[64] Via an equation of "literature," "meaning," and "representation," he posits that "a *constitutive tension exists between the phenomenon of rhythm and the dimension of meaning.*"[65] Because Gumbrecht brackets out questions of the relation between rhythm and meter and the cultural-historical usages of specific rhythms or meters, he ignores previous metrical theory and practice to claim that literary studies (operating within the realms of representation) lacks an adequate vocabulary to describe or analyze either rhythm or embodiment.[66] As both the eighteenth- and nineteenth-century debates about meter reveal (and as I discussed in Chapters 1 and 3), numerous theorists and poets have developed detailed vocabularies and phenomenologies to describe the relation between meter, rhythm, and meaning, which by no means invariably subordinate the meter and rhythm to meaning.

But Gumbrecht wants a definition of rhythm and an explanation of its function in abstraction from specific practice, and so he neglects this tradition, appealing instead to evolutionary biology and cybernetics to explain the canonical functions of rhythm as enhancing memory, creating or deepening emotion, and "coordinating" or synchronizing individual bodies.[67] In Gumbrecht's view, the grouping that occurs in rhythmical form as it unfolds in time provides an "explanation for [rhythm's] *memory-enhancing function*" by reducing the number of potential phonemes available to fit the pattern.[68] To explain the "affective" and "coordinating" functions of rhythm, Gumbrecht draws on the work of G.H. Mead and Humberto Maturana.[69] Using Mead, Gumbrecht describes the connection between the body and the utterance within the speaker as the source of rhythm's affective power: rhythm prompts involuntary bodily movements, overcoming the somatic control that developed across human evolution.[70] To explain the coordinating function of rhythm, Gumbrecht refers to Hugo Maturana's work on how living systems reproduce themselves and influence each other, creating a feedback loop between a system—such as an individual organism—and its environment.[71]

---

[64] Gumbrecht, "Rhythm and Meaning," 171.

[65] Gumbrecht, "Rhythm and Meaning," 171.

[66] Gumbrecht, "Rhythm and Meaning," 172.

[67] Gumbrecht, "Rhythm and Meaning," 172.

[68] Gumbrecht, "Rhythm and Meaning," 174, italics in original.

[69] Gumbrecht's turn to Maturana marks a shift in the kind of cybernetics or information theory that influences posthermeneutic scholarship: whereas Kittler focuses almost exclusively on earlier cyberneticists such as Claude Shannon and Warren Weaver (who analyzed electronic communication and machine systems), Maturana and later cyberneticists turn "from physics to biology as the paradigm for system analysis" and consider living organisms as well (Winthrop-Young, "Silicon Sociology, or, Two Kings on Hegel's Throne?" 411).

[70] Gumbrecht, "Rhythm and Meaning," 178.

[71] Gumbrecht, "Rhythm and Meaning," 178. For an introduction to Maturana that explains his ideas about living organisms and systems more carefully than Gumbrecht does, see Maureen L. Leyland,

Further, when the organisms in the feedback loop and the loop itself begin to be influenced by their mutual interaction, the feedback loop itself becomes self-referential.[72] These multiple feedback loops explain the "coordinating" function of rhythm as, on a second or meta-level, organizing the organism's organizations. The fact that, in Gumbrecht's view, only the self-referential level of feedback loop is accessible to representation explains why only certain elements of rhythm—those that are related to meaning—have played a role in literary studies.[73] It is worth pausing again to note the degree to which Gumbrecht—like Kittler and other posthermeneutic authors—draws his conceptual framing from non-literary discourses; he succumbs to the view that literary history reveals relatively little about literature and the literary use of language.

Finally, metrical structures appear briefly in Gumbrecht's 2003 *The Production of Presence: What Meaning Cannot Convey.*[74] "Presence," in Gumbrecht's understanding, refers to a range of phenomena or experiences that cannot be explained as *about* anything in particular, but rather give an impression that something "comes out of nowhere" and usurps both space and attention.[75] He suggests that modern culture has shifted away from presence to meaning, which is representational and reducible to semantic information. Contending that all cultures have elements of both presence effects and meaning effects, Gumbrecht wants to reclaim the elements of presence culture in modern life, and he identifies poetry as the best example of the interaction between presence and meaning. Moreover, he refers (unusually, for him) specifically to metrical and other phonological features: "Poetry is perhaps the most powerful example of the simultaneity of presence effects and meaning effects—for even the most overpowering institutional dominance of the hermeneutic dimension could never fully repress the presence effects of rhyme and alliteration, of verse and stanza."[76] But as part of his critique that literary studies has historically failed to engage with the presence dimensions of poetry, Gumbrecht dismisses lists of formal repertoires and metrical features as "long, boring, and intellectually pointless,"[77] thus banning discussion of syllable patterning and its embodied, cultural, and aesthetic significance from his consideration of presence effects. Gumbrecht's work might, I suggest, offer insights into the ways metrical patterning works in contact with but not solely determined by semantic meaning, creating a more complicated picture than one in which form imitates content or in which their relation is a mere scholarly projection.

"An Introduction to Some of the Ideas of Humberto Maturana," *Journal of Family Therapy* 10, no. 4 (January 1988): 357–74, https://doi.org/10.1046/j.1988.00323.x.
   [72] Gumbrecht, "Rhythm and Meaning," 179.
   [73] Gumbrecht, "Rhythm and Meaning," 182.
   [74] Hans Ulrich Gumbrecht, *The Production of Presence. What Meaning Cannot Convey* (Stanford: Stanford University Press, 2003).
   [75] Gumbrecht, *Presence*, 113.
   [76] Gumbrecht, *Presence*, 18.
   [77] Gumbrecht, *Presence*, 18.

But because Gumbrecht refuses to take detailed account of meter and its histories, his thinking falls short of this possibility.

In focusing on Kittler and Gumbrecht, I have analyzed the relatively rare moments in which posthermeneutic scholarship takes notice of meter and rhythm. The focus on material techniques of linguistic production, transmission, and storage will be central for Grünbein, and the resistance of all kinds of materiality to being coopted for ideological ends is perhaps the primary ethical and provocative gesture of his writing. But there are also a number of moments where posthermeneutic theorizing *could* talk about meter, yet *doesn't*. For example, what would happen if Kittler's focus on the binary codes of computing confronted the binary codes of strong and weak syllables? Is meter not itself a kind of "time-axis manipulation," long before the sound-recording technologies Kittler sees as capable of inscribing the real?[78] Adding thinkers from other strains of German posthermeneutic literary and media theory, might meter be a paradigmatic example of the fluidity and interplay in Niklas Luhmann's form-medium distinction (or a refutation of the distinction)?[79] Is meter a medium in the sense used by media philosopher Dieter Mersch, who emphasizes the performative qualities of media and sees aesthetic objects as their most productive realizations?[80] Or do certain metrical practices work to *de*medialize language, reversing the process of becoming-media outlined by literary scholar Joseph Vogl?[81] And so on. These questions are examples of the kind of investigations that might open up if posthermeneutic literary studies and its twenty-first century exponents were to take metrical claims seriously. Although posthermeneutic scholarship as it exists has fallen short of these possibilities and has lost sight of meter in its theories of "materiality," the way posthermeneutics analyzes not how only theories but devices and technologies produce texts could illuminate what kinds of equipment and notation systems shape our contemporary understandings of metrical patterning.

---

[78] On Kittler's theories of time-axis manipulation, see Sybille Krämer, "The Cultural Techniques of Time Axis Manipulation: On Friedrich Kittler's Conception of Media," *Theory, Culture & Society* 23, no. 7–8 (December 2006): 93–109, https://doi.org/10.1177/0263276406069885.

[79] For a critique of the form-medium distinction, see Michael Schlitz, "Form and Medium: A Mathematical Reconstruction," *Image & Narrative* III, no. 2 (6) (2003): online. (http://www.imageandnarrative.be/inarchive/mediumtheory/michaelschiltz.htm).

[80] See Dieter Mersch, "Wozu Medienphilosophie? Eine programmatische Einleitung," *Internationales Jahrbuch für Medienphilosophie* 1, no. 1 (1. Januar, 2015), https://doi.org/10.1515/jbmp-2015-0103, 21 and Dieter Mersch, "*Meta/Dia*: Two Different Approaches to the Medial," *Cultural Studies* 30, no. 4 (July 3, 2016): 650–79, https://doi.org/10.1080/09502386.2016.1180751, 659–6, here 668–671.

[81] In a discussion of Galileo's telescope as turning polished glass lenses from mere material into a medium, Vogl outlines the characteristics of media and their historical becoming: "No such thing as a medium exists in any permanent sense. That media denaturalize the senses and allow their historicization; that media can be understood as self-referential, world-creating organs; that media are defined by the anesthetic space they produce—these might form the outline of a framework in which the history of media is constituted in nothing more and nothing less than the mere events of a discontinuous becoming-media." (Joseph Vogl, "Becoming-Media: Galileo's Telescope," *Grey Room* 29 (October 2007): 14–25, https://doi.org/10.1162/grey.2007.1.29.14.,22-23).

5.2 Quantitative and Natural-Scientific Approaches

Posthermeneutic scholarship and the approaches I examine below share an interest in bridging the humanities and the natural sciences. Gumbrecht closes "Rhythm and Meaning" with the suggestion that attending to materialities of communication "could ultimately help alleviate the schism between the natural sciences and the humanities" (182), while Kittler's attention to counting and computing, at its best, shows the mutual influencing of literary, cultural, and technological production. Posthermeneutic and empirical approaches differ enormously, however, in their aims, methodologies, and epistemologies, as their theoretical underpinnings indicate: whereas the posthermeneutic turn draws primarily on the poststructuralism characteristic of Derrida, Foucault, and Lacan for its theoretical grounding,[82] the natural-scientific approaches I consider here draw on the hypotheses of structuralist and proto-structuralist poetics and linguistics, attempting to offer empirical validations of the ideas of theorists like Jakobson, Shklovsky, and Mukarovsky.[83] Posthermeneutics analyzes the techniques of science and of literature with one and the same (cybernetic, systems-focused) vocabulary, whereas the approaches I discuss below apply the methods, devices, and conceptual resources of the natural sciences to the analysis of literature and its effects. The materiality of the medium of language becomes the material of phonemics and phonetics or the materialism of brain science, while the careful poststructuralist analysis of techniques of knowledge production shifts into an embrace of the natural-scientific epistemologies of hypothesis, data collection, and proof.[84]

Linguistics

Linguistics, at least in the variants I consider here, occupies an ambiguous status between the humanities and the natural and social sciences: phonologists draw on metrical patterning as data and metrical theorists appeal to phonological rules in an effort to explain deviations or irregularities in metrical practice. In the 1980s, when Kittler, Gumbrecht, and company are investigating meter as one cultural technique among many for bodily-effective amplification and transmission of language, and while Albertsen, Arndt, Breuer, and Wagenknecht are warning against forcing scansion systems from one culture onto verse practices of another, the

---

[82] David E. Wellbery, "Foreword," in *Discourse Networks 1800/1900* by Friedrich Kittler, viii.

[83] This is particularly pronounced in work from the Department of Language and Literature, Max Planck Institute for Empirical Aesthetics in Leipzig (https://www.aesthetics.mpg.de/en/research/department-of-language-and-literature.html).

[84] Wellbery sees this move as anticipated in Kittler: "The unified and unifying *Geist* of Hegel has long been replaced by the functional multiplicity of Broca's brain and maintains its ghostly afterlife only in hermeneutic philosophy and literary criticism." (Wellbery, "Foreword," xxix).

linguistic subdiscipline of generative metrics works to identify precise rules under-girding language and represent how those rules work not only at the level of the word or syllable but across multiple levels of syntax and discourse. Modeled on the methodological approaches of generative grammar, generative metrics attempts to identify a set of rules that will encompass all metrically permissible lines and reject all non-metrical lines. In doing so, it brings a fine-grained and detailed atten-tion to the line as a unit of language that considers words and their arrangement into larger syntactic and semantic units. It does so, moreover, in ways that are not distorted by importing foot names or structures from languages that work very differently from the ones under consideration.[85]

At least some generative approaches, however, share the drawback of asserting an unjustified epistemological certainty about which phonological units deter-mine which lines count as metrical, making metrics a matter of purely objective rules rather a complex interaction of language, culture, and individual author or reader as an embodied subject. In this respect, some generative metricists start to sound very similar to their nineteenth century predecessors, who strove to make metrics a true science (see Chapter 3). Others, however—including Bruce Hayes, Gilbert Youmans, and Marina Tarlinskaja—derive nuanced accounts of the episte-mological status of normative or statistical versus absolute rules, reflecting on the interrelation between individual poetic practice, phonological elements, and cul-tural conventions.[86] In each case, it is important to note that generative metricists have very different agendas from either the histories of prosody or literary theo-rists I discussed in the previous sections of this chapter: generative metrics seeks to identify how metrical lines work as language on a fairly abstract level, using close analysis of single lines to identify parameters for forms (e.g. iambic pentame-ter), periods (Elizabethan England), or authors (Shakespeare versus Johnson). In its focus on the line, generative metrics has less to say about the interactions of stanzas, strophes, or other larger-scale verse forms.

Generative metrics develops several modes of representing metrical lines, and these metrical trees and grids help to show how metrical rules draw on higher level structures such as the phonological phrase. For the sake of space, I focus

---

[85] Primarily English—which works similarly to German in assigning strong and weak syllable positions—but also Finnish (see Kristin Hanson and Paul Kiparsky, "A Parametric Theory of Poetic Meter," Language 72, no. 2 [1996]: 287–325), German (e.g. Achim Barsch, *Metrik, Literatur und Sprache. Generative Metrik zwischen empirischer Literaturwissenschaft und generativer Phonologie* [Braunschweig: Friedrich Vieweg & Sohn Verlagsgesellschaft], 1991) and, in Nigel Fabb and Moritz Halle's monumental *Meter in Poetry: A New Theory*, (Cambridge, UK; New York: Cambridge Univer-sity Press, 2008), all of English, Spanish, Italian, French, classical Greek and Latin, Sanskrit, classical Arabic, Chinese, Vietnamese, and Latvian.

[86] I am grateful to Natalie Gerber for pushing me to articulate a more nuanced account of the differ-ences in approach and epistemology between different generative metricists. This section, especially, owes an immense debt to her careful reading on mechanical, organizational, and informational levels, as does the chapter as a whole. Any remaining over-simplifications or errors are mine, not Gerber's.

here on the mode of representing phonological stress known as a metrical "grid," which Hayes describes as "a set of marks arranged in columns over the syllables of an utterance, with the higher columns designating greater degrees of stress."[87] Moreover, the grid can be refined into levels that mark the highest stresses of an utterance, as in the following example, where parentheses mark the beginning of a unit, from Nigel Fabb and Morris Halle's *Meter in Poetry: A New Theory* (they shift Haye's markings to beneath the line):

```
        Pléasure néver is at hóme"
        (*   *    (** (**  (*   0
        (*        *  (*   *(  1
        (*             *(     2
           *                  3[88]
```

Literary-historical metrics would generally represent the line / x / x / (with / representing a stressed, x an unstressed syllable), which it would then describe as trochaic tetrameter with a dropped final syllable. Fabb and Halle, however, argue that meter measures the "groupings" they mark with parentheses and not the total number of syllables per line. Each group is determined by the presence of a strong syllable at the level of stress in question; thus level 0 in the example above consists of four groups, level 1 of three, level 2 of two, and level 3 of one.[89] As my discussions of metrical theory in the eighteenth and nineteenth centuries have shown, and as the metrical histories I cited in Section 1 of this chapter remark explicitly, different scansion systems may be illuminating of different features or types of verse. The generative metrical grid helpfully and precisely identifies multiple levels of prominence and the ways in which they group syllables according to the phonology of a language, rather than according to an imported system of foot names.

From the inception of the field, however, its practitioners grapple with the status or kind of rule (or sets of rules) that the generative approach produces. In an article that articulates the epistemologies of generative theories with a high degree of reflection, Gilbert Youmans, a founder of the discipline, expresses frustration with attempts to find universal rules that can describe all metrical lines:

> The debate among metrical theorists has reached something of an impasse. Any formally rigorous theory of meter is bound to identify a certain residue of verse lines as exceptions. Consequently, metricists in every camp have been able to cite

---

[87] Bruce Hayes, "The Prosodic Hierarchy in Meter," in *Rhythm and Meter*, eds. Paul Kiparsky and Gilbert Youmans, 201–60 (San Diego, CA: Academic Press: 1989). https://doi.org/10.1016/B978-0-12-409340-9.50013-9, 225.

[88] Fabb and Halle, *Meter in Poetry*, 6.

[89] Fabb and Halle, *Meter in Poetry*, 4–5.

numerous counterexamples to rules proposed by their opponents, while equally numerous violations of their own rules are dismissed as random exception. New kinds of evidence are needed, then, if the debate is to continue productively.[90]

This passage is based on the idea that what "metrical debates" are about or produce are "formally rigorous theor[ies] of meter," whose apparent function is "identifying" verse lines—implicitly, as metrical or nonmetrical, correct or incorrect, rules or exceptions. Next, such exceptions are considered a problem, because they make up "counter-examples" for a given "formally rigorous theory of meter" and thus provide ammunition for opponents, which in turn are opposed to "random exception[s]." Finally, the passage calls not just for new evidence but for new *kinds* of evidence.

Youmans proposes using "poems themselves" as the "new kinds of evidence" in question, specifically by looking for places where lines of verse depart from standard syntax and checking the effects of the deviation on the metrical pattern.[91] Once again, the ideal for a theory of meter is the ability "to account for all metrical inversions successfully, using the simplest possible set of 'rules.'"[92] Different generative metricists use poetic manuals and previous metrical histories in different ways as they work to determine such rules; Youmans, who uses a Renaissance English corpus, cites late 1500s and early 1600s manuals for poetic composition as "contemporary testimony" about what types of syntactical inversion were allowed.[93] He returns to the problem of how to determine whether a line that deviates from the metrical rule proposed by a given theorist provides counter-evidence for the theory or whether it can be dismissed as "transmission error" or "poetic oversight," as previous generative metricists such as Morris Halle, S.J. Keyser, and Paul Kiparsky had suggested.[94]

In addition to accounting for deviations from metrical rules, on Youmans' account a successful metrical theory should also provide reasons why some kinds of lines that should be metrical never occur in verse practice, beyond dismissing them as a kind of "performance constraint."[95] Youmans casts the problem in explicitly epistemological terms: between claims of random error and performance constraint "generative metrics risks becoming both irrefutable and unprovable—i.e. empirically vacuous."[96] The standard for success for a theory of meter in generative metrics is high: universal applicability, parsimony, and empirical verifiability.

[90] Gilbert Youmans, "Generative Tests for Generative Meter," *Language* 59, no. 1 (1983): 67–92, https://doi.org/10.2307/414061,67.
[91] Youmans, "Generative Tests for Generative Meter," 67.
[92] Youmans, "Generative Tests for Generative Meter," 69.
[93] Youmans, "Generative Tests for Generative Meter," 68.
[94] Youmans, "Generative Tests for Generative Meter," 70-1.
[95] Youmans, "Generative Tests for Generative Meter," 72.
[96] Youmans, "Generative Tests for Generative Meter," 72.

Without recapitulating Youmans' tests of two theories of meter in detail, I focus here on the kind of evidence he enters for the success of each theory and the epistemological status of both evidence and success in his generative-metrical approach.[97] Looking at the effects of syntactic inversions in Shakespeare's *Hamlet* and his *Sonnets*, Youmans notes that most inversions are metrically necessary by both theories' rules, which he moreover notes are quite similar, given that what is necessary under one theory is "almost always" obligatory or at least statistically preferred under the other.[98] Youmans concludes that Paul Kiparsky's theory accounts for more syntactical abnormalities than Morris Halle and S.J. Keyser's, and thus that, with a few revisions, Kiparsky provides a satisfactory account of Shakespeare's verse. But the topic of revisions returns to the question of the epistemological status of rules for determining whether a line is metrical or unmetrical; noting that one can go on tweaking rule systems indefinitely but with "rapidly diminishing returns," Youmans suggests "that the boundary between metrical and unmetrical lines is 'fuzzy' rather than exact."[99] This in turn alters the task of generative metrics: instead of coming up with one single set of binary rules that define metricality, "the goal of metrics should be to formulate a suitable definition of 'degrees of metricality,' rather than an arbitrary distinction between metrical and unmetrical lines."[100] In a striking shift, Youmans suggests a focus on whether or not a rule is "normative," meaning whether poets seem to correct their lines "to conform with" it.[101] Following a detailed analysis of two of the most sophisticated generative metrical theories of his day, then, Youmans ultimately turns to poetic practice as the decisive measure of the success of a proposed metrical rule.

At its most nuanced, work on meter in linguistics shares Youmans' reflectiveness about what degrees of proof may be available for certain types of metrical claims as well as his attention to poetic practice in its historical realization. But as the field develops, its practitioners tend to claim a stronger primacy of phonology and to strive to make metrical rules categorical (binary metrical/non-metrical) rather than statistically descriptive. In the German-speaking academy, Achim Barsch departs from earlier theorists' attention to specific metrical traditions and

---

[97] Youmans compares Halle and Keyser's "stress maximum principle" (SMP) versus Kiparsky's "monosyllabic word constraint" (MWC). He explains the two rules as follows: "Briefly stated, the SMP prohibits stress maxima from occupying odd-numbered metrical positions in iambic verse. (A stress maximum is defined as any fully stressed syllable flanked by two unstressed syllables in the same syntactic constituent.) The MWC is a comparable but different constraint: roughly, stressed syllables are prohibited in odd positions unless (a) the stress is on a monosyllabic word, or (b) it is preceded by a phrase boundary (i.e. by a potential caesura)." (Youmans, "Generative Tests for Generative Meter," 67).

[98] Youmans, "Generative Tests for Generative Meter," 73.

[99] Youmans, "Generative Tests for Generative Meter," 91.

[100] Youmans, "Generative Tests for Generative Meter," 91.

[101] Youmans, "Generative Tests for Generative Meter," 91. He contrasts the statistical/normative rule that "stressed syllables in polysyllabic words NORMALLY occupy even-numbered positions [in iambic pentameter]" with the categorical "stressed syllables in polysyllabic words occupy even-numbered positions [in iambic pentameter]" (Youmans, "Generative Tests for Generative Meter," 90; emphasis in original).

individual variation between poets to assert without qualification "that the metrical system is determined by the prosodic system of the language in question."[102] As generative metricists begin to argue that prosodic-phonological components, not cultural traditions or individual practices, determine meter, the differences between particular linguistic traditions (say, German versus English) become less important; Barsch concludes that the task of a "metrical grammar" is to provide "abstract metrical schemata as structural descriptions of linguistic utterances (here read: lines of verse)."[103] Linguistic studies of meter thus move from statistical norms of historical practice to abstract schemata, and from there to universal linguistic and potentially cognitive structures.[104]

Fabb and Halle, perhaps most strikingly, go beyond identifying what components of metrical practice a grid can illuminate to contend that their grid system not only describes but determines which lines are metrically "well-formed":

> The central claim of this study is that every well-formed line of metrical verse consists not only of the syllables and phonemes that determine its pronunciation, but also of what we have called a metrical grid, i.e., a pattern, which though not pronounced, determines the perception of a sequence of syllables as a line of metrical verse, rather than as an ordinary bit of prose.[105]

This unpronounced "central claim" sounds rather like a twenty-first century version of Carl Fuchs' remark that "there is something in music that is not heard at all, and this is the best part";[106] a deep, inaudible structure determines verse, and in particular whether or not verse is well-formed.[107] Fabb and Halle insist that syllables and phonemes are controlled by something that is not pronounced and also reject the importance of word boundaries and semantic units in verse.[108] Moreover, the particularities of epochs' and poets' handling of stress and patterning

---

[102] Barsch, *Metrik, Literatur und Sprache*, 15. All translations from Barsch are mine. Much of the work in generative metrics I cite is written in English and refers to the English iambic pentameter tradition, but as the work from cognitive and evolutionary approaches shows, the internationalization of linguistics as a quantitative science brings with it the dominance of English-language scholarship, while the phonologies of English and German work quite similarly. (On the latter point, in a volume comparing intonational systems, see Dafydd Gibbon, "Intonation in German," in *Intonation Systems. A Survey of Twenty Languages*, eds. Daniel Hirst and Albert di Cristo [Cambridge: Cambridge University Press, 1998], 78–95, especially 94).

[103] Barsch, *Metrik, Literatur und Sprache*, 53.

[104] There are, of course, exceptions and nuances to be noted here, which depend partly on which linguists one describes as generative metricists. As Youmans' work shows, numerous authors do attend to cultural, individual, and historical variation, as do linguists such as Marina Tarlinskaja and Kristin Hanson.

[105] Fabb and Halle, *Meter in Poetry*, 11.

[106] Carl Fuchs, *Präliminarien zu einer Kritik der Tonkunst* (Leipzig: E.M. Fritzsch, 1871), 143, my translation. For a discussion of this remark, see Chapter 3.

[107] In fairness to Fabb and Halle, they do not assert that "well-formed" necessarily means "good" in a broader aesthetic sense, though neither do they work out the relation between well-/ill-formed verse and poetic quality.

[108] Fabb and Halle, *Meter in Poetry*, 11.

disappear. The universality of "*every* well-formed line of metrical verse," if it is indeed achieved, comes at the cost of a very high level of abstraction.[109]

This level of abstraction, and the universal claims it allows, enables generative metrics to suggest species-wide cognitive hypotheses about the way meter might respond to human mind-brain structures. In *Meter in Poetry*, Fabb and Halle suggest that their metrical grids "constitute the data to be accounted for by a future theory of human cognition."[110] This suggestion rests on ideas Fabb worked out in an earlier discussion of "literary form" (e.g., lines, rhymes) in relation to "linguistic form" (e.g., words, syntax). He hypothesizes that because literary form is based on linguistic form, which in turn is based on "mental structures," by studying literary form "we can therefore study the mind."[111] Meter is the paradigmatic case of such (perhaps) cognitively-grounded literary form because "metrical form is one of the few areas of literary linguistics where there may be some involvement of specialized cognitive mechanisms: thus the possibility of metrical verse may be based on aspects of human cognitive structure, just as the possibility of language is based on aspects of human cognitive structure."[112] By 2013, literary scholar Natalie Gerber can argue on the basis of a nuanced overview of the advantages and drawbacks of both traditional and generative metrical approach that "insights from generative metrics are foundational to our ability to pinpoint rhythmic structures in language and by extension to appreciate how rhythmic structures in verse, particularly metrical verse, involve cognitive expectations about certain prosodic patterns."[113] The task for literary studies is thus to give "interpretive significance" to "generative metrical analysis,"[114] with the ultimate goal of an interdisciplinary "aesthetics of prosody" that uses "scientific methods to explain the psychological, neuronal and socio-cultural basis of aesthetic perceptions and judgments."[115] Accordingly, I turn

---

[109] For a discussion of Fabb and Halle's theory that recognizes its explanatory power within specific limits, as well as a critique from the perspective of the history of generative metrics, see Bruce Hayes, "Meter in Poetry. Nigel Fabb, Morris Halle, Cambridge University Press, Cambridge (2008)." *Lingua* 120, no. 10 (October 1, 2010): 2515–21, https://doi.org/10.1016/j.lingua.2010.04.001.

[110] Fabb and Halle, *Meter in Poetry*, 9.

[111] Nigel Fabb, *Linguistics and Literature: Language in the Verbal Arts of the World* (Oxford: Blackwell, 1997), 2–3. "Mental structures" as a term does not make clear whether such "structures" are cognitive or neurophysiological, innate or acquired, culturally specific or species universal, though Fabb holds that humans are "born with" such structures. On the danger of linking linguistic and mental structures, see John E. Joseph, *Language, Mind and Body: A Conceptual History* (Cambridge University Press, 2018), especially 191–6. Joseph's critiques are addressed largely at Noam Chomsky, whose "generative grammar" provides a model for the "generative metrics" of Fabb and Halle.

[112] Fabb, *Linguistics and Literature*, 50.

[113] Natalie Gerber, "Stress-Based Metrics Revisited: A Comparative Exercise in Scansion Systems and Their Implications for Iambic Pentameter," *Thinking Verse* III (2013): 131–68, 132. Gerber acknowledges the need to account for historical convention and individual variation (142) as well as "reasons to balk at the generative metrical approach," including "its technical complexity, its relative inutility for pedagogy, and its apparent rejection of temporal concerns" (146), but believes that its ability to account for a high level of detail in a systematic way compensates for these disadvantages (162).

[114] Gerber, "Stress-Based Metrics Revisited," 164.

[115] Gerber, "Stress-Based Metrics Revisited," 165.

in the next section to approaches that apply empirical tests of several kinds to metrical phenomena and the responses they elicit.

Cognitive Poetics and Neuropoetics

The best work in the cognitive and neuroscientific vein of metrical studies is attentive to claims made about the functions of poetry in the "long tradition of research including classical rhetoric, esthetics and poetic theory, formalism and structuralism, as well as current perspectives in (neuro)cognitive poetics" that has "investigated structural and functional aspects of literature reception."[116] Much can go wrong in the interpretive process that connects brain electricity measurements with arguments about functions of meter, and in some sense the studies in question are not telling us anything particularly new, since, as this book has demonstrated, arguments that poetry in general and meter in particular affect bodies, emotions, and minds have drawn on contemporaneous natural scientific knowledge since (at least) the eighteenth century. We might reasonably ask what either a literary scholar or a reader of poetry ought to do with the information that the N400 brain electricity peak is associated with metrically unexpected events, or that rhyme and compactness diminish clarity but increase aesthetic liking.[117]

But neuroscientific and cognitive approaches also restore the idea—which contemporary metrical handbooks and literary theory typically reject—that meter in particular does something to and for listeners and readers. These approaches do so using a set of tools that help focus attention on fine-grained formal features both independently of and in interaction with semantic meaning, contra the separation between meter and meaning asserted by metrical histories and the complete severing of meter and meaning in posthermeneutic literary theory. In what follows, I therefore outline the promises and pitfalls in the development of this approach in the years from the 1980s to the present as preparation for Grünbein's attention to brain science (and his confrontation of science with aesthetics). I thus index the claims made about syllable patterning in a rising area of study in the late-twentieth and early-twenty-first century.

---

[116] Arthur M. Jacobs, "Neurocognitive Poetics: Methods and Models for Investigating the Neuronal and Cognitive-Affective Bases of Literature Reception," *Frontiers in Human Neuroscience* 9 (April 16, 2015), https://doi.org/10.3389/fnhum.2015.00186.

[117] Claims made in Peter Praamstra and Dick F. Stegeman, "Phonological Effects on the Auditory N400 Event-Related Brain Potential," *Cognitive Brain Research* 1, no. 2 (April 1, 1993): 73–86, https://doi.org/10.1016/0926-6410(93)90013-U, Christian Obermeier et al., "Aesthetic Appreciation of Poetry Correlates with Ease of Processing in Event-Related Potentials," *Cognitive, Affective, & Behavioral Neuroscience* 16, no. 2 (April 1, 2016): 362–73, https://doi.org/10.3758/s13415-015-0396-x, and Winfried Menninghaus et al., "Rhetorical Features Facilitate Prosodic Processing While Handicapping Ease of Semantic Comprehension," Cognition 143 (October 1, 2015): 48–60, https://doi.org/10.1016/j.cognition.2015.05.026, respectively.

At the same moment as metrical histories are rejecting arguments for psychological and physiological efficacy of meter, natural-scientific approaches are reconstructing those arguments using cognitive psychology and neuroscience; at the moment in which posthermeneutic literary theory turns *post*structuralism into "a set of instruments productive of knowledge,"[118] the authors I consider here return to the Russian formalist forerunners of structuralism with new instruments to test its hypotheses empirically. There are multiple kinds of tools for such empirical tests, and in what follows I analyze studies that use several of them, showing both the useful ways in which many empirical studies of meter yield highly precise attention to meter's physiological efficacy and some of the problems and limitations of empirical approaches.

To do so, it is helpful to see how the proposals of structuralism—in particular, Russian formalism—turn into cognitive or neurophysiological hypotheses. First, empirical studies take up Roman Jakobson's view that what makes an utterance poetic its calling attention to its own characteristics as an utterance, and that, furthermore, the ways in which the utterance calls attention to itself (e.g. through parallelism) contribute to ambiguity in the message.[119] This view fits with two further structuralist positions: Jan Mukařovský's suggestion that poetic language deliberately *foregrounds* certain components of language (e.g. intonation) against the default background of the standardized language and Victor Shklovsky's notion of art in general as defamiliarizing or estranging us from the everyday and especially from everyday language.[120] These ideas appear in so-called cognitive poetics and later in neurocognitive poetics in the hypothesis that art reception, in particular reception or processing of literature and poetry, "exploits, for aesthetic purposes, cognitive (including linguistic) processes that were initially evolved for non-aesthetic purposes" by first activating and then disrupting these processes.[121] Most practitioners of cognitive poetics or neurocognitive poetics recognize that although poetry (likely) makes use of cognitive processes, it also operates according to literary norms and practices that develop within and across cultures, epochs, and individual authors' practices.[122]

---

[118] Wellbery, "Foreword," viii.

[119] See Roman Jakobson, "Closing Statement: Linguistics and Poetics," in *Style in Language*, ed. T.A. Sebeok (Cambridge: Cambridge University Press, 1960), 350–77.

[120] See Jan Mukařovský, "Standard Language and Poetic Language," in *Linguistic and Literary Studies in Eastern Europe*, eds. Josef Vachek and Libuše Dušková, vol. 12 (Amsterdam: John Benjamins Publishing Company, 1983), 165, https://doi.org/10.1075/llsee.12.11muk and Victor Shklovsky, "Victor Shklovsky: 'Art as Technique,'" in *Twentieth-Century Literary Theory: A Reader*, ed. K. M. Newton (London: Macmillan Education UK, 1997), 3–5, https://doi.org/10.1007/978-1-349-25934-2_1.

[121] Reuven Tsur, *Toward a Theory of Cognitive Poetics, Second, Expanded and Updated Edition*, 2nd ed. (Brighton: Sussex Academic Press, 2008), 4–5.

[122] Thus Tsur notes that "a major assumption of the present cognitive approach is that literature does have important operational principles that cannot be exhausted in terms of cognitive science" (Tsur, *Cognitive Poetics*, 3).

But these structuralist-formalist hypotheses conflict with a second set of proposals regarding aesthetic processing, largely derived from the visual arts. In particular, this work suggests that aesthetic pleasure or liking is associated with features that ease cognitive processing, such as contrast between figure and ground, repetition, and symmetry.[123] On this hypothesis, metrical patterning might create contrasts between regularity and irregularity, repeated relationships of syllables, and symmetry between lines or strophes, making poetic language *easier* to process and thus aesthetically pleasurable. Moreover, any of these hypotheses—of self-referentiality, ambiguity, defamiliarization, or ease of processing—might be investigated either at the level of subjective reporting, objective response, or neurophysiological processing. Hence some studies ask participants to rate features such as liking, sadness or joy, poeticity, ambiguity, or clarity, while other studies measure microsecond differences in time taken to read manipulated lines. Still others use brain electricity measurements associated with semantic or metrical irregularities to identify how strong the effects of each were on cognitive processing. Particularly as the field develops, studies using subjective tests (such as ratings) call for additional objective measuring as next steps or combine types of tests to see if their results align.[124] As with much work in cognitive science and neuroscience, researchers struggle to design experiments whose approaches do not distort the results, and to link data collected back to the hypotheses about poetry and the brain, given the complexity of both.

One of the earliest efforts (in 1983) to explain the structures of poetry with reference to the particularities of the human brain begins by announcing that it "brings together an old subject, a new body of knowledge, and a new scientific paradigm which have not previously been associated with one another."[125] As we have seen from the association of meter with the physiology of emotion in the eighteenth century and with new understandings of acoustics and the perception of sound in the nineteenth, the affiliation of poetry with the latest work in physiology is not so new as the authors, Frederick Turner and Ernst Pöppel, would suggest; their innovation is the use of "the findings of that intense study of the human brain which has taken place in the last few decades" and the framework for understanding the experience of time developed by the International Society for the Study of Time.[126] Turner and Pöppel designate the line as the "fundamental

---

[123] Rolf Reber, Norbert Schwarz, and Piotr Winkielman, "Processing Fluency and Aesthetic Pleasure: Is Beauty in the Perceiver's Processing Experience?," *Personality and Social Psychology Review: An Official Journal of the Society for Personality and Social Psychology, Inc* 8, no. 4 (2004): 364–82, https://doi.org/10.1207/s15327957pspr0804_3.

[124] One might well question or critique the use of terms like "subjective" and "objective" here, where the former refers to consciously articulated judgments or response, while the latter refers to (as far as we know) unconscious and uncontrolled responses measured without any report from the individual.

[125] Frederick Turner and Ernst Pöppel, "The Neural Lyre: Poetic Meter, the Brain, and Time," *Poetry* 142, no. 5 (1983): 277–309, 277.

[126] Turner and Pöppel, "The Neural Lyre," 277.

unit of metered poetry" and discover by timing metered lines in Japanese, Chinese, English, Ancient Greek, Latin, French, and German that the time to read each line takes "nearly always from two to four seconds to recite, with a strong peak in distribution between 2.5 and 3.5 seconds."[127] The authors suggest that this temporal constraint matches the memory-processing capacities of the brain, though they are careful to note that the "shared biological underpinning" of cross-cultural verse characteristics is not genetically determined and restrictive but rather is "derived from the structure of the human auditory cortex and the brain in general" in such a way that those structures and the characteristics they support give rise to a wide range of cultural and expressive possibilities.[128]

Turner and Pöppel, writing in 1983, make several argumentative moves that shape subsequent cognitive and neuroscientific approaches to metrics: they insist on empirical testing of data (here of line lengths); they claim cultural universality for their findings; they suggest a biological advantage to various metrical features, and they view their work as arguing against or discrediting certain types of literary theory, whether cast as poststructuralist or postmodern. For Turner and Pöppel, the evolutionary uses of meter are themselves an argument against "postmodernist criticism": they contend that metrical regularity reflects "our species' special adaptation" of seeking or expecting "more order and meaning in the world than it can deliver; and that those expectations may constitute, paradoxically, an excellent survival strategy."[129] Consequently, they enter a quasi-evolutionary critique of "postmodernist criticism of moral and philosophical idealism" as counter to "the apparent facts about human neural organization."[130] They suggest that human beings find aesthetic beauty inherently brain-rewarding because it activates complementary activity in both hemispheres of the brain,[131] a kind of twentieth-century rewrite of the harmony of the faculties. Their work thus returns, some two hundred and fifty years after the emergence of aesthetics as the study of human capacities for sensation and perception, to the idea that the way poetry works reveals something fundamental about the way human consciousness works; it likewise succumbs to some of the same problems (polemicism, unreflective universalism, and oversimplification of poetic practice).

Many subsequent authors move away from proposals about where in the brain poetry and meter are processed to measurements of brain electricity as indicating types of response. These measurements come from electroencephalography, in which electrodes attached to the skull measure the strength of electric responses

[127] Turner and Pöppel, "The Neural Lyre," 286.
[128] Turner and Pöppel, "The Neural Lyre," 290.
[129] Turner and Pöppel, "The Neural Lyre," 304.
[130] Turner and Pöppel, "The Neural Lyre," 304. This also entails a polemic against free verse poetry. For a discussion of the affiliation between arguments for formally constrained poetry and conservative ideology, see Thomas B. Byers, "The Closing of the American Line: Expansive Poetry and Ideology," *Contemporary Literature* 33, no. 2 (Summer 1992): 396–415.
[131] Turner and Pöppel, "The Neural Lyre," 283–4.

to stimuli, called "event-related potentials" (ERPs).[132] Work in the course of the 1980s begins to tease out which types of responses occur following what kinds of stimuli: visual versus aural, phonological versus semantic, automatic versus consciously directed. (Of course, these responses may not and likely do not often happen separately but may be layered over one another.) These examinations focus primarily on one particular reaction, the so-called N400 response, a brain electricity response (or "component") that happens around 400 milliseconds after a stimulus and is associated with language processing.[133] For example, in a key early study, Michael Rugg measured ERPs in an experiment that "required subjects to discriminate between rhyming and non-rhyming visually presented pairs of letter strings."[134] Because some of the items in the "pairs of letter strings" were not words but still elicited the brain response to unexpected stimuli, the results suggest that the N400 "does not seem to depend on linguistic processing at the semantic level for its modulation."[135] In a subsequent experiment, Rugg and Sarah Barrett worked to distinguish whether the larger N400 magnitude came from disrupting expectations based on orthography or on phonology; their results confirmed the role of phonology in producing a greater N400 amplitude.[136] One final study, in a laboratory affiliated with the Max Planck Institute for Psycholinguistics that Grünbein visited, used recorded rather than written words to show that "the auditory N400 is sensitive to phonological variables," and, moreover, that this effect occurs even when subjects are given a task not related to phonology, suggesting that the N400 response does not require conscious attention to phonology.[137]

These studies and the questions they answer are, of course, quite distant from the more complex questions about the effects of meter, which may rest on an

[132] For an explanation of how EEG techniques were developed and how ERP measurements began to be correlated with particular stimuli, see Steven J. Luck, *Introduction to the Event-Related Potential Technique* (MIT Press: Cambridge, 2014), especially Chs. 1–3.

[133] A "component" refers to "an underlying neural response that sums together with other neural responses to produce the observed waveforms at the scalp electrodes" (Luck, *Introduction to the Event-Related Potential Technique*, 354). For an account of how the N400's association with semantic meaning was discovered, see Luck's discussion with Marta Kutas, one of the experimenters (Luck, *Introduction to the Event-Related Potential Technique*, 115). The original experiment is in M. Kutas and S. A. Hillyard, "Reading Senseless Sentences: Brain Potentials Reflect Semantic Incongruity," *Science* 207, no. 4427 (January 11, 1980): 203–5, https://doi.org/10.1126/science.7350657.

[134] Michael D. Rugg, "Event-Related Potentials and the Phonological Processing of Words and Non-Words," *Neuropsychologia* 22, no. 4 (January 1, 1984): 435–43, https://doi.org/10.1016/0028-3932(84)90038-1, 435.

[135] Rugg, "Event-related Potentials," 435.

[136] Michael D. Rugg and Sarah E. Barrett, "Event-Related Potentials and the Interaction between Orthographic and Phonological Information in a Rhyme-Judgment Task," *Brain and Language* 32, no. 2 (1987): 336–61, https://doi.org/10.1016/0093-934X(87)90132-5.

[137] Praamstra and Stegeman, "Phonological Effects." Praamstra and Stegeman summarize their findings: "Phonological effects are manifested in the auditory N400 in much the same way as its visual counterpart. A crucial difference is the fact that phonological effects on the auditory N400 are present even when phonology is not task relevant. In our view, this represents the most promising finding, as it might indicate a sensitivity of the N400 to phonological processes that are, presumably, performed automatically in comprehending spoken words" (Praamstra and Stegeman, "Phonological Effects," 84). Grünbein relates his visit to a conference of the Max Planck Institute for Psycholinguistics in Nijmegen,

interaction of semantics, phonology, and visual perception of written words and line endings, not to mention the cultural contexts and individual variations that natural-scientific paradigms strive to control for or excise in their experimental design. Their progression follows the careful building up of tools to understand— preliminarily, in fragments—how the human brain reacts to speech sound and language, which later work begins to extend into experiments on the hypotheses about self-referentiality, ambiguity, defamiliarization, or ease of processing of meter and poetry. Thus by 2012, Kathrin Rothermich, Maren Schmidt-Kassow, and Sonja A. Kotz could investigate metrical and semantic regularity with attention to the way meter may help or impede information processing. They found differing response patterns for semantically and for metrically unexpected words, but the spike in brain electricity in response to words that were semantically but *not* metrically unexpected was smaller than that for words that were both semantically and metrically unexpected, suggesting that although the two domains are processed differently, metrical regularity leads to easier processing of semantically unexpected words.[138] Summing up, the authors explain: "Regularity leads to prediction, and prediction impacts the ease of information processing," and, in particular, "that regular metric patterns facilitate information processing."[139] These remarks recall parts of the cognitive fluency hypothesis, since they make the argument that characteristics (like meter) associated with art make processing easier. Rothermich and colleagues, however, focus exclusively on ease of processing without considering its effect on aesthetic liking. Their study brings together brain activity data, the interaction between semantic meaning and metrical effect, and suggestions about how poetic language and everyday language are processed in the brain. In doing so, it demonstrates in detail the fit between various poetic features—specifically meter—and the way the (presumably neurotypical) human brain responds to language.

Several approaches investigating responses to poetry in general and formal structures such as meter in particular note the significant shared inquiry between literary studies and cognitive studies, noting for example that "attempting to link poetic structure and its potential aesthetic and emotional effects is one of the central concerns in literary studies, but more recently also in cognitive research."[140] (Significantly, the research team included authors from both disciplines, from the Max Planck Institute for Human Cognitive and Brain Science in Leipzig and

with whose members Praamstra published papers, in Durs Grünbein, "Katze und Mond," in *Galilei vermißt Dantes Hölle und bleibt an den Maßen hängen. Aufsätze 1989–1995* (Frankfurt a.M.: Suhrkamp Verlag, 1996), 55–60, 56.

[138] Kathrin Rothermich, Maren Schmidt-Kassow, and Sonja A. Kotz, "Rhythm's Gonna Get You: Regular Meter Facilitates Semantic Sentence Processing," *Neuropsychologia* 50, no. 2 (January 2012): 232–44, https://doi.org/10.1016/j.neuropsychologia.2011.10.025, 232.

[139] Rothermich et al., "Rhythm's Gonna Get You," 242.

[140] Christian Obermeier et al., "Aesthetic and Emotional Effects of Meter and Rhyme in Poetry," *Frontiers in Psychology* 4 (2013), https://doi.org/10.3389/fpsyg.2013.00010, 1.

the Institute of Comparative Literature at the Free University of Berlin.) In order to test the hypothesis that meter and rhyme affect emotion and aesthetic liking, the researchers created modified versions of metered and rhyming poetry in German to create metered and non-rhyming, non-metered and rhyming, and non-metered and non-rhyming versions for both words and non-words.[141] In a significant departure from eighteenth-century aesthetics, especially, the authors attempt to control for (read: remove effects of) words and their meanings. Whereas Klopstock celebrates the mutual interference of semantic and formal features as a great advantage for the poet specifically in order to arouse emotion in readers, the authors here worry that "if structural features interact with lexico-semantic content of poems, this would falsify the proposition put forward by the cognitive fluency theory that structural features are important contributors to aesthetic liking and emotional responses per se."[142] As a solution, they separate "emotional responses" ("as it is known that the valence of a word can influence emotional responses to it") and "aesthetic liking rating," proposing that the latter "should be rather unaffected, as it should only capture the stylistic quality of the stanzas"[143]—hence the creation of variations in word and non-word stanzas.

The study participants rated each stanza for "liking, intensity, perceived emotion, and felt emotion";[144] the study thus used subjective reporting to measure reader responses. In measuring "intensity," subjects were told to "assess the strength of the emotional response to the stanza,"[145] which was separated from "perceived emotion" (was the emotion in the poem positive or negative?) and "felt emotion" (very negative to very positive).[146] The results found "a significant main effect of meter" and of rhyme in the liking ratings; in general the effects of rhyme were stronger than those of meter, although as the researchers remarked the use of a single stanza may privilege rhyme, since it is more apparent in only four lines, versus the metrical regularity of a multi-stanza poem.[147] The authors note that, as expected, "lexicality, meter, and rhyme interact and influence perceived emotion ratings,"[148] but more granular examination of the data revealed a significant effect only of rhyme on perceived emotion ratings across the word and non-word stanzas. Moreover, "this effect was stronger for pseudo-word stanzas than for real-word stanzas suggesting that lexicality indeed affects the emotional response to poetry.

---

[141] The authors describe their procedure on pages 3–4; a table with all eight versions of one of the stanzas appears on 4 (Obermeier et al., "Aesthetic and Emotional Effects," 3–4).

[142] Obermeier et al., "Aesthetic and Emotional Effects," 3. See Chapter 2 Section 3.1 for Klopstock's celebration of the "illusion" (Täuschung) by which sounds seem not to signify but to *be* emotions.

[143] Obermeier et al., "Aesthetic and Emotional Effects," 3.

[144] Obermeier et al., "Aesthetic and Emotional Effects," 3.

[145] Obermeier et al., "Aesthetic and Emotional Effects," 3.

[146] Obermeier et al., "Aesthetic and Emotional Effects," 3.

[147] Obermeier et al., "Aesthetic and Emotional Effects," 5.

[148] Obermeier et al., "Aesthetic and Emotional Effects," 7.

Possibly, rhyme exhibits a stronger influence on felt emotion if there is no meaning that can interfere with its effect."[149] Conversely, the authors were surprised to find that non-metered, non-word stanzas "elicited more positively perceived emotions than metered pseudo-word stanzas," and fall back on the possibility of a "perceived parallel between form and content (the absence of metrical structure somehow 'matching' the chaotic impression of the pseudo-words)."[150]

The fact that even when no meaning is present researchers appeal to an affinity between sound and meaning to explain their results foregrounds the difficulty of separating the levels of meaning, meter, and rhyme. In addition, the study design that creates ideal conditions to analyze effects of rhyme but makes meter less pronounced shows how hard it is to tease out formal effects that interact by design in poetry. It might be the case that natural scientific techniques simply need to build up their tools to analyze meter in more pre-existing poems, although the next study conducted by Obermeier's group sought to link the simplified stimuli with ERP events, not to study more complex stimuli.[151] One further experiment by many of the same researchers identifies rhyme, meter, and brevity (in German *Prägnanz*, pithiness) as particularly important poetic features and attempts to look at their effects both separately and in combination.[152] But the study design uses single-sentence proverbs rather than poems, precisely because the authors found that poems were too complex to isolate and re-combine rhyme, meter, and brevity.[153] Bringing more attention to bear on potential disconnects between formalist and cognitive science hypothesis, their work recognizes the conflict between a Jakobsonian thesis that poetic features inhibit comprehension and the cognitive fluency hypothesis that formal features ease processing; it ultimately suggests that aesthetic speech involves inhibited processing in some domains and fluency in others.[154] The authors also note the need for approaches that take reader expectations into account.[155]

But the difficulty in bringing natural-scientific methods to bear on formal features of language as they are actually used in poetry may indicate an irresolvable incompatibility between natural-scientific epistemologies and poetic practice. It is of course crucial to examine formal or structural elements of poetic language individually in order to make scientific claims about what they do, but it is fair to wonder whether doing so removes what is specifically poetic, namely, the

---

[149] Obermeier et al., "Aesthetic and Emotional Effects," 7
[150] Obermeier et al., "Aesthetic and Emotional Effects," 7
[151] Obermeier et al., "Aesthetic Appreciation," 1.
[152] Menninghaus et al., "Rhetorical Features Facilitate Prosodic Processing," 48–60.
[153] Menninghaus et al., "Rhetorical Features Facilitate Prosodic Processing," 49.
[154] "To our knowledge, the present study is the first to show that fluency and disfluency effects can be measured with regard to both the very same sentences, the very same rhetorical target features, and even the very same dimensions of aesthetic evaluation (here beauty and *praegnanz* attributions)" (Menninghaus et al., "Rhetorical Features Facilitate Prosodic Processing," 56).
[155] Menninghaus et al., "Rhetorical Features Facilitate Prosodic Processing," 56.

simultaneous effects of all of meter, rhyme, alliteration, etc., as they support, conflict, or otherwise interact with semantic meaning, which itself may include metaphor, allusion, paradox, etc. Meter, given its connection to particular cultural traditions or associations, may be even more difficult to study, given the difficulty of controlling for readers' prior exposure, different languages spoken, varying experiences performing music or dance, all of which might well influence affective and even bodily responses to meter. It is also significant that the studies I have considered here examine only the simplest and most standard types of metrical patterning in German: alternating weak and strong syllables. Ode strophes or hexameters would likely not register as metrical at all, to say nothing of investigating the rhythmical strategies of poetry like Nietzsche's in free rhythms. There are, I think, good reasons to be skeptical about whether natural-scientific approaches will be able to tell us much about how we respond to the specific effects of poetry in their interaction with one another, with history, and with meaning—that is, as we encounter them in the poems we care about. Nonetheless, I have presented these studies at length both because Grünbein is attentive to their claims—indeed, one of them cites him as coining the term "factor N400" "as a general proxy for ... 'brainphysiological attention catchers'"[156]—and because they persistently call attention to the affective and physiological impact of meter, an argument that other in the twenty-first century approaches neglect or reject.

Evolutionary Aesthetics

The final natural-scientific approach to meter I analyze makes perhaps the most direct case for the significance of meter as fulfilling central functions for humans as a species, based on their evolutionary development. Evolutionary aesthetics, in its early phases, attempted two lines of argument. First, its practitioners suggested that various human art practices serve a competitive function in the essential evolutionary processes of sexual selection and reproductive success by engaging the attention of members of the opposite sex.[157] Alternatively, some theorists contended that art practices serve a non-competitive function in creating social cohesion between members of a species or sub-group.[158] These claims have by and large not held up, and were, moreover, not particularly media-specific, with volumes focusing on various forms of narrative and ignoring differences between,

---

[156] Jacobs, "Neurocognitive Poetics," 12–3.

[157] This is the view held by Brian Boyd, Joseph Carroll, and Jonathan Gottschall and the contributors to their anthology, *Evolution, Literature, and Film A Reader* (New York: Columbia University Press, 2010).

[158] See for example David S. Miall and Ellen Dissanayake, "The Poetics of Babytalk," *Human Nature* 14, no. 4 (1 December 2003): 337–64, https://doi.org/10.1007/s12110-003-1010-4.

say, novels and film.[159] More recently, claims about the specific evolutionary function of art have been replaced by accounts that make claims about the relation between poetic features of language and the pre- and proto-languages that preceded *homo sapiens'* development of full language, thus connecting poetic features to species-defining characteristics.

One primary contribution of evolutionary aesthetics as a whole is that it returns questions of art's function and central human significance to literary studies. Winfried Menninghaus, writing from the perspective of a literary scholar urging others to take up evolutionary perspectives, notes that the refusal of literary studies in almost all of its current forms (at least in 2008) to take up investigations of function or use of art is an exception rather than the rule in the history of aesthetics.[160] As my first chapter showed, for figures like Gottsched, Baumgarten, Breitinger, Sulzer, and Herder, meter frequently occupied a central position in accounts of the origins of art from fundamental human physiological and mental characteristics such as control of the voice and hands, articulation with tongue and teeth, emotional vocalization, cognitive abstraction, and group communication (see Chapter 1, Section 1.3), while Nietzsche's aphorism "On the Origins of Poetry" makes a similarly robust argument for functions of art (see Chapter 4, Section 4.4). Menninghaus goes so far as to question "whether evolutionary theory has developed any hypotheses at all that were not already represented in traditional poetics, rhetoric, and aesthetics," suggesting that evolutionary theories of art would do well to be more aware of and make use of historical work on art's functions to sharpen their categories of inquiry.[161] He proposes that evolutionary aesthetics should pay more detailed attention to the interpretation of specific works while literary studies should stop ignoring potential functions of art, and he concludes that evolutionary theory should be taken seriously in literary studies for its demonstrated successes in explaining extremely complex phenomena.[162]

Shifting from art more generally to language and poetry in particular, David Miall and Ellen Dissanayake propose several functions for poetic qualities of speech, especially meter and pitch: using analysis of "one minute of spontaneous babytalk with an eight-week infant," they argue that "the poetic texture of the mother's speech—specifically its use of metrics, phonetics, and foregrounding—helps to shape and direct the baby's attention, as it also coordinates the partners' emotional communication."[163] They suggest that "use of short, simple (one- or

---

[159] For a critique of arguments based on sexual competition and on social cohesion, see Steven Pinker, "Toward a Consilient Study of Literature," *Philosophy and Literature* 31 (2007): 162–78, especially 170–2. Pinker also notes the lack of specificity about art media (Pinker, "Toward a Consilient Study of Literature," 174).

[160] Winfried Menninghaus, *Kunst als Beförderung des Lebens. Perspektiven transzendentaler und evolutionärer Ästhetik* (Munich: Carl von Siemens Stiftung, 2008).

[161] Menninghaus, *Kunst als Beförderung,* 55.

[162] Menninghaus, *Kunst als Beförderung,* 60.

[163] Miall and Dissanayake, "The Poetics of Babytalk," 337.

two-syllable) words or phrases that are frequently repeated encourages a repetitive regulating meter around which elaborate melodic, dynamic, and rhythmic variations are interwoven,"[164] noting that the approximately three-second intervals of speech accord with Turner and Pöppel's data on line length (discussed above). Miall and Dissanayake propose that these features function as "foregrounding" and "coordinating attention" between mother and infant: "Overall, it is the resources provided by meter—from 4 to 5 stresses per line down to 2 or 1, together with the variations provided by tempo and pitch, that offer the basic aural instruments for the mother to either sustain, respond to, or reengage the baby's attention."[165] On an individual-psychological level, this furthers mother-baby bonding that, they hypothesize, "attunes cognitive and affective capacities in ways that provide a foundation for the skills at work in later aesthetic production and response."[166] Miall and Dissanayake move from the individual to species level, contending that their "stylistic analysis of babytalk for its metrical and phonetic features reveals an elementary poetics that, in turn, contributes to understanding the deep-rootedness, if not the origin of human aesthetic and emotive responses to the temporal arts."[167] The connection between babytalk and poetic features suggests powerful communicative and affective functions for meter, and the analysis the authors provide models detailed attention to metrical patterning. But Miall and Dissanayake's move from individual to species risks mapping particularities of mother-baby bonding in one culture and one temporal moment onto narratives of the species development; as Kittler's work in "Mother-Poet-Child" demonstrated, the idea that the mother's voice should instantiate affective and soothing connections between child, parent, and world is not a timeless given but rather developed in its European version in the late eighteenth and early nineteenth centuries.

The analysis of "poetic features" and meter in an everyday communicative situation has the advantage of emphasizing the communicative power and the ubiquity of linguistic patterning: we are exposed to and influenced by organizations of syllables all the time. It can, however, seem quite distant from the virtuosic and highly controlled use of strong and weak syllables in poetic practice. Brian Boyd, writing in 2012, acknowledges that much "literary evolutionism" has focused on narrative and neglected verse, a trend he seeks to remedy by turning to Shakespeare's *Sonnets*.[168] Boyd abandons the idea that verse is an adaptation, suggesting instead that it relies on a "human passion for nonnarrative pattern"[169] that prompted the development of verse in "cultures around the world,"[170] with line endings determined

[164] Miall and Dissanayake, "The Poetics of Babytalk," 343.
[165] Miall and Dissanayake, "The Poetics of Babytalk," 347.
[166] Miall and Dissanayake, "The Poetics of Babytalk," 337.
[167] Miall and Dissanayake, "The Poetics of Babytalk," 340.
[168] Brian Boyd, *Why Lyrics Last. Evolution, Cognition, and Shakespeare's Sonnets* (Cambridge: Harvard University Press, 2012), 3.
[169] Boyd, *Why Lyrics Last*, 4.
[170] Boyd, *Why Lyrics Last*, 11.

by the poet as the only constant across those cultures.[171] Because verse, in this argument, evolves to fit human cognitive capacities, it "makes a unique appeal to attention."[172] Moreover, this account offers a nuanced view of the relation between meter and meaning, noting that meter is not entirely separable from sense but also is not reducible to it, either: "We can be intuitively or explicitly aware of the metrical template and can hear the stresses that the actual syllables in a line need, but not know why the combination of sounds, words, phrases, and emerging sense and feeling and their variations from the template seem to dance, strut, or stumble."[173]

The physiological effectiveness of meter and rhythm both underscore their relation to fundamental species capacities and suggest a further evolutionary function in creating group bonds. Adding detail to this idea, Boyd proposes that the rhythmical patterning can support "emotional attachment and physical entrainment," which "links us to one another," making meter central to social cohesion.[174] Menninghaus notes that the capability to follow a rhythm is a capacity unique to humans among primates: while human children can follow an external beat either in movements or in vocalizations from a very young age, non-human primates cannot do so at all.[175] He goes so far as to suggest that meter is species defining: "*Homo sapiens* is—also—*homo metricus*," and adds that "capabilities for highly variable synchronization of bodies, movements, and song might well be a central prerequisite for embodied social cohesion mechanism."[176] Numerous scholars working on evolution and literature trace the power of meter to its roots in pre-linguistic affective expression in prehistoric human evolution. These authors—including Christopher Collins as well as Boyd and Menninghaus—argue that metrical and other prosodic components of language come from the way prehistoric humans communicated before the development of full language, a kind of "proto-language" that relied on gesture and expressive sounds.[177] Individuals repeat this development in their acquisition of language, and so metrical speech both calls up the affective language of infancy[178] and creates a "living link with our phylogenetic past" that "derives its special properties from its powers to actualize these older, deeper cognitive levels that still remain within us."[179]

---

[171] Boyd, *Why Lyrics Last*, 16.
[172] Boyd, *Why Lyrics Last*, 18.
[173] Boyd, *Why Lyrics Last*, 38.
[174] Boyd, *Why Lyrics Last*, 19–20.
[175] Winfried Menninghaus, *Wozu Kunst? Ästhetik nach Darwin* (Berlin: Suhrkamp Verlag, 2011), 179.
[176] Menninghaus, *Wozu Kunst?*, 179.
[177] Christopher Collins, *Paleopoetics. The Evolution of the Pre-Literate Imagination* (New York: Columbia University Press, 2013), 107–8. Collins differentiates "pre-language," a "minimal level of communication that a highly social, tool-making, hunting/gathering genus of primates would require," including "expressive vocalization," from "proto-language," a "symbolic code of syntaxless speech composed of clearly articulated phonemes that many assume to have been a transitional phase between pre-language and full language" (107).
[178] Menninghaus, *Wozu Kunst?*, 215.
[179] Boyd, *Why Lyrics Last*, 140.

These accounts rely on the most recent understandings of *homo sapiens'* development as a social and language-using being to provide detailed suggestions about the way meter activates inborn and species-defining structures in the human brain and supports social behavior that then further developed brain structures through the need for complex communication. As such, they return meter to a share of the anthropological importance that it attained in the eighteenth century, making a strong case that to understand meter is to better understand ourselves. At the same time, however, they share some of the drawbacks of their earlier counterparts: the great majority of the time, the authors' metrical claims do not undertake any detailed analyses of particular works, whether metrical, poetic, literary, or other art forms. Boyd's focus on Shakespeare's *Sonnets* is a happy exception, but he underplays the importance of culture and individual poetic style: the focus on species-universal cognitive capacities can elide the intra- and inter-cultural interactions in which poets respond to their predecessors and contemporaries.

Moreover, focus on the species-level can lead authors to overlook their own cultural situatedness, prompting the kind of universalizing from the behaviors of (European) cultures to humanity as a whole for which the Enlightenment has justly been critiqued. Work on the evolution of cultural techniques such as meter from human perceptual and cognitive capacities must take into account the role of cultural context in shaping not only metrical practices but physiological responses to them.[180] One model for such work, which I can touch on only briefly, studies music in rhythm, in particular examining the role of "generic constraint and selected cultural particularities in shaping rhythmic prototypes."[181] The authors (Rainer Polak, Nori Jacoby, Timo Fischinger, Daniel Goldberg, Andre Holzapfel, and Justin London) note that while speech research reveals that "phonemic perception varies with the linguistic context," "it is often assumed that rhythmic prototypes tied to the simplest integer ratios (1:1 and 2:1) will be identical across cultures," ratios that some arguments tie to brain mechanisms.[182] Instead, they

---

[180] As I noted in my introduction, claims about meter's relation to human physiological and cognitive capacities are prone to ableism, assuming that bodies and minds work the same way and have the same attributes. For an account that reads cognitive literary studies and disability studies together to challenge and enhance both, see the work of Ralph Savarese, especially his interview with Lisa Zunshine (Ralph James Savarese and Lisa Zunshine, "The Critic as Neurocosmopolite; Or, What Cognitive Approaches to Literature Can Learn from Disability Studies: Lisa Zunshine in Conversation with Ralph James Savarese," *Narrative* 22, no. 1 (January 2014): 17–44, https://doi.org/10.1353/nar.2014.0000) and his contribution to *The Oxford Handbook of Cognitive Literary Studies* (Ralph James Savarese, "What Some Autistics Can Teach Us about Poetry," *The Oxford Handbook of Cognitive Literary Studies*, January 1, 2015, https://doi.org/10.1093/oxfordhb/9780199978069.013.0020.). Savarese suggests that poetry, in particular formally complex poetry, can help make a bridge between the ways (some) autistics and neurotypicals process language. My thanks to Natalie Gerber for bringing Savarese's work to my attention.
[181] Rainer Polak et al., "Rhythmic Prototypes Across Cultures: A Comparative Study of Tapping Synchronization," *Music Perception: An Interdisciplinary Journal* 36, no. 1 (September 1, 2018): 1–23, https://doi.org/10.1525/mp.2018.36.1.1, 1.
[182] Polak et al., "Rhythmic Prototypes Across Cultures," 1.

argue, "humans' learning of rhythmic categories is a dynamic and ongoing process, one that may occur during the span of a single laboratory experiment as well as an entire lifetime," and moreover "a growing body of cross-cultural research finds both linguistic and music-cultural backgrounds to influence rhythm perception and processing."[183] The study compared musicians in different cultural contexts (Mali, Bulgaria, and Germany) and with training in different musical genres (folk or European classical music) and found that while the simplest rhythmical ratios (2:1 and 1:1) were easily recognized and replicated, more complex ratios (such as 3:2 or 4:3) varied by culture and genre.[184] In short, some responses seem universal, some seem culturally specific.

The authors also note the caveat that merely because a feature or behavior is universal does not mean that it is innate or genetically determined.[185] Moreover, the study presents (and performs) a powerful argument for the need for cultural knowledge in study design to avoid systemic biases that universalize the practices of one culture while also stigmatizing data about another, thus distorting the results of investigations.[186] They make this case in terms that reflect on some of the epistemological differences between humanistic and natural-scientific modes of investigation:

> Identifying hypothetically culture-specific variations in perceptual systems requires detailed knowledge of the specific musical environments to be studied. It will often require a sensitive adjustment of experimental parameters to evoke effects of cultural familiarity that could easily be overlooked in the context of the ever-pressing scientific striving to minimize variables for the sake of control. Thus, however large the methodological and epistemological differences between the sciences and the humanities may be, understanding the role of culture in human perception and cognition will be hard to achieve without their collaboration.[187]

This degree of reflection on what "understanding the role of culture in human perception and cognition"—and, I would want to add, perhaps also understanding human culture—requires offers the kind of collaboration between differing approaches that, I contend, has largely been absent from the twenty-first century discussions of meter.

* * *

[183] Polak et al., "Rhythmic Prototypes Across Cultures," 2.
[184] Polak et al., "Rhythmic Prototypes Across Cultures," 13–4.
[185] Polak et al., "Rhythmic Prototypes Across Cultures," 16.
[186] Polak et al., "Rhythmic Prototypes Across Cultures," 16.
[187] Polak et al., "Rhythmic Prototypes Across Cultures," 16.

Returning to the question I cited to open this chapter—*do we still want to pursue metrics at all?*—I hope to have shown that by bringing the insights of literary history, posthermeneutic theory, and empirical investigations together, there remains much to be gained from thinking with and about meter in the twenty-first century. Bringing the three fields together reveals why posthermeneutic and natural scientific approaches need the specifics of metrical history; how the posthermeneutic arguments about meter as a cultural technique become far more convincing when they are more specific about the practices and the cultures in question; and how metrical handbooks suffer from rejecting arguments about the physiological and emotional effects of meter. Read together, they show the importance of paying attention to all of the complexities of the way meter relates to meaning; they underscore the way species characteristics and cultural histories interact; they remind us that patterned language was our first language. Durs Grünbein, as I will show in the next chapter, brings together the disparate strains of metrical history, posthermeneutic literary theory, and natural-scientific analyses both in his essayistic writing on meter and in his poetic practice, offering one more approach to understanding meter and poetic experience.

6

Shaping Time, Forming Subjectivity

Grünbein's Meters

In the previous chapter, I showed how attention to meter has, in the late twentieth and early twenty-first centuries, dispersed into pedagogical handbooks, literary theorizations of materiality and media, and quantitative or natural-scientific approaches. Despite important insights in each of these areas, the lack of contact between them has led to the view that meter is old-fashioned and metrical theory is pedantic. By contrast, Durs Grünbein puts metrical tradition, attention to materiality, and interest in natural science back together. Although he occasionally addresses his recombination of these themes explicitly, more interestingly and more often he executes or enacts their mutual imbrications by way of a number of poetic strategies, including polyphonic poems that engage specifically with multiple voices across historical epochs, dramatic monologue or "role" poems (*Rollengedichte*), use of natural-scientific vocabulary and images, and a career-long attention to the physical-material body.

Meter, as physiologically effective and trans-historical yet historically shaped, becomes a central technique for Grünbein to investigate contemporary subjectivity as embodied, linguistic, and historically inscribed for several related reasons. First, because meter creates modes of coherence that are not based on argumentative agreement, metrical texts can hold together contradictory ideas or standpoints, particularly conflicting views about subjectivity. Second, because meter forms and shapes time, it organizes what Grünbein characterizes as an overwhelming flux of experience into palpable and memorable forms. These forms, moreover, enable the layering of different voices, epochs, and standpoints (returning to point one), which brings the organization of time and the organization of ideas into relation. Finally, metrical forms are linguistically, culturally, and historically shaped, but they are experienced in the body; on Grünbein's account, meter brings together individual, cultural, and evolutionary time.

In this chapter, I show how Grünbein makes these claims in ways that challenge prevailing late-twentieth and early-twenty-first century views about meter, as I analyzed them in the previous chapter. Seeing how meter works in Grünbein's poetics reveals the ways attention to metrical theory and practice both illuminates the interplay between language, culture, and the body and also opens up new realms of poetic experience. I begin by introducing Grünbein briefly, since he is much less well-known outside Germany, before turning to his poems and essays.

Metrical Claims and Poetic Experience. Hannah Vandegrift Eldridge, Oxford University Press.
© Hannah Vandegrift Eldridge, (2022). DOI: 10.1093/oso/9780192859211.003.0007

In keeping with his wide range of interests and the status of metrical theory as a standalone discipline in the twenty-first century, Grünbein does not write metrical treatises or rhythmical investigations in the manner of Nietzsche or Klopstock; instead, his remarks on meter are distributed through—and integral parts of—his reflections on poetry, language, and embodied subjectivity.

Grünbein, born in Dresden in 1962 into what was then East Germany, shares several characteristics with German lyric from the 1990s to the present, while he is in other respects atypical. Like his many of contemporaries, including (for example) Raoul Schrott, Thomas Kling, Ulrike Draesner, and Brigitte Oleschinski, Grünbein takes a detailed interest in science, technology, and media.[1] Grünbein's polyphonic overlapping of voices, subject positions, and time periods puts him in line with other 1990s poets and especially those of the East German avant-garde in Prenzlauer Berg, Berlin, where he took part in performance art happenings and published some of his work in the art books of visual artists (in part to avoid the censorship facing literary publications).[2] But Grünbein does not apply strategies of "aggressive linguistic experimentalism" (as in Kling) or "intermedial collage" (as in Draesner) to his handling of multiple voices and temporalities;[3] rather, he tends to collect disparate voices into a "fragile but still recognizable world of subjective expression" within which a biographical poet-subject is one among several personae.[4] Moreover, Grünbein—and here he is especially unusual amongst his contemporaries—begins to collect the images, arguments, and perspectives into increasingly controlled and prominent historical forms, including hexameter, rhyming iambic and trochaic verse, and sonnets.[5]

This shift, with associated moves toward more canonical/traditional subject positions, has found a mixed reception in both literary criticism and literary studies. Grünbein was anointed *the* poet of unified Germany in the 1990s and designated representative of his generation, in part because of his rejection of the tenets of socialism and his avoidance of the Stasi scandals that plagued other Prenzlauer Berg poets, which made him an ideal projection screen ("Projektionsfläche") for

---

[1] See for example Karen Leeder, "The Poetry of Science and the Science of Poetry: German Poetry in the Laboratory of the Twentieth Century," *German Life and Letters* 60, no. 3 (2007): 412–29 and Erk Grimm, "Mediamania? Contemporary German Poetry in the Age of New Information Technologies: Thomas Kling and Durs Grünbein," *Studies in 20th Century Literature* 21, no. 1 (1997): 275–301. Anna Ertel points out that using images and insights from anatomy, medicine, and neuroscience in the lyric has been a tradition at least since Gottfried Benn (Anna Ertel, *Körper, Gehirne, Gene. Lyrik und Naturwissenschaft bei Ulrike Draesner und Durs Grünbein* [Berlin: de Gruyter, 2011], 5).
[2] See Hinrich Ahrend, *"Tanz zwischen sämtlichen Stühlen": Poetik und Dichtung im lyrischen und essayistischen Werk Durs Grünbeins* (Würzburg: Königshausen und Neumann, 2010), 42 and Grimm, "Mediamania," 281.
[3] Ian Cooper, "Direction, Disruption, Voice. Durs Grünbeins 'Historien' and 'Neue Historien'," *Germanic Review* 84, no. 2 (2009): 99–121, 100.
[4] Ahrend, *Tanz zwischen sämtlichen Stühlen*, 38–9.
[5] On his use of inherited forms as unusual for contemporary German lyric, see Aniela Knoblich, *Antikenkonfigurationen in der deutschsprachigen Lyrik nach 1990* (Berlin: de Gruyter, 2014), 135ff.

literary-critical anxieties surrounding reunification.[6] This reputation has deflated, particularly since 2000, with several of Grünbein's later volumes criticized for conservatism and mannerism. As with my discussion of Nietzsche and to some extent Klopstock, I am not making an argument for the undisputed quality of all of Grünbein's work; some poems and volumes are better than others; some are interesting failures; some are interesting because of what they say and not what they do. The poems I have chosen here show what writing in and thinking about meter can do when thinkers and readers bring it back into contact with interest in the effects of poetry on the body and history on language.

Like many of his contemporaries, Grünbein develops theoretical or poetolog-ical positions in response to historical changes and medial conditions.[7] While his essays, interviews, and poems are often illuminating of one another, they are equally often mismatched.[8] Grünbein typically refuses to come down decisively on a single position; rather, he plays them against each other and reflects through the possibilities of each, as he himself explains in 2008 interview: "I often see myself in this deadlock between two positions. It's impossible for me take flight into a position because I rejected its opposite. But I don't want to stay between them, I want to play through both of them. And then I notice that there's a sta-bility there, albeit a precarious one."[9] Olav Krämer describes this as Grünbein's career-long project of interrogating "systems of coordinates" for making sense of the contemporary world and human beings in it, including the "systems" of psychology, philosophy, anthropology, neuroscience, individual biography, and poetic tradition as efforts to orient the poetic subject.[10] Previous readers, however, have missed that meter—old fashioned, mannered, pretentious, and vital—is cen-tral to these projects because it can enact the coalescence of voices, claims, and moments into poetry that is effective and memorable because of its shaping of time.

---

[6] See Fabian Lampart, "Der junge Dichter als Sphinx. Durs Grünbein und die deutsche Lyrik nach 1989," in *Schreiben am Schnittpunkt. Poesie und Wissen bei Durs Grünbein*, eds. Kai Bremer, Fabian Lampart, and Jörg Wesche (Freiburg: Rombach Verlag, 2007), 19–36.

[7] See Stephan Pabst, *Post-Ost-Moderne. Poetik nach der DDR.* (Göttingen: Wallstein Verlag, 2016), 27. He notes that since many poets, including Grünbein, abandoned the ideas (or ideologies) of the East German state before its fall, there is an asynchronicity between the ideological and political ends of the GDR (20). On the fall of the wall as the point of departure for Grünbein's poetological self-investigations, see Ahrend, *Tanz zwischen sämtlichen Stühlen*, 369.

[8] On the essays from the late 1980s and early 1990s, see e.g. Thomas Irmer, "Durs Grünbein," in *Deutschsprachige Lyriker des 20. Jahrhunderts*, eds. Ursula Heukenkamp and Peter Geist (Berlin: Erich Schmidt, 2007), 711–21. On the ambivalences in *Schädelbasislektion*, see Hermann Korte, "Zivilisa-tionsepisteln. Poetik und Rhetorik in Grünbeins Gedichten," in *Die eigene und die fremde Kultur. Exotismus und Tradition bei Durs Grünbein und Raoul Schrott*, ed. Dieter Burdorf (Iserlohn: Institut für Kirche und Gesellschaft, 2004), 79–95, 81–2.

[9] Durs Grünbein and Hans-Jürgen Heinrichs, "Gespräch mit Durs Grünbein," *Sinn und Form* 1 (2008): 47–66, 57. My translation.

[10] Olav Krämer, "Ich und Welt. Durs Grünbeins Zyklus 'Niemands Land Stimmen' und sein Gedicht 'Nach den Satiren I," *Jahrbuch der deutschen Schillergesellschaft* 48 (2004): 348–74, here 372–3.

6.1 Meter and Poetry in the Brain

Grünbein uses meter to support his arguments that poetry has immediate effects on the body and specifically the brain, arguments that he outlines using some of the neuroscientific work on language processing that I glossed in the previous chapter. His account of how poetry works directly on the body recalls Klopstock's contentions that the movement of verse reaches and affects hearers before they understand its content (see Chapter 2), albeit with a twentieth-century neurophysiological twist: "The poem, ideally, presents/performs [*vorführen*] thinking in a series of physiological short circuits."[11] This process picks out certain moments within the (post) modern "mass of noises" that are etched in memory as an "engram," the term Grünbein appropriates from neuropsychology to describe biochemical or biophysical brain changes in response to (in his description, auditory) stimuli.[12] "Engram" for Grünbein names a kind of writing on and in the brain, an immediate connection between poetry and physiology. Grünbein leaves undetermined whether this immediacy happens in the poet's processing of stimuli, which then turn into poetry, or in the hearer/recipient of poetry, or in both; he collapses the productive/receptive distinction to emphasize bodily efficacy.[13] His arguments, at least in the early phases of his career, also erase the distance between causing a brain response and having an effect in the body, which enables him to establish a neuro-poetics whose seamless unity of physiology and experience he will question in his later work.

Grünbein develops a neurophysiological account of why some sounds, images, or words are more poetically (thus physically) effective than others, and his key term for this effectiveness is "resistance." He reflects that "resistance is probably the beginning and end of all writing, at least a reliable sign that, physically speaking, there is a fight going on against something like gravity, something like emptiness[.]"[14] Noting the technical sense of "resistance" as a "measure for the hindrance that an electric conductor opposes to the current" ("Katze und Mond," 56–7), he explains aesthetic resistance in terms of brain electricity: the EEG responses that the experimenters I discuss in Chapter 5 use to track brain responses to

[11] Durs Grünbein, "Drei Briefe" (Three Letters), in *Galilei vermißt Dantes Hölle und bleibt an den Maßen hängen. Aufsätze 1989–1995* (Frankfurt a.M.: Suhrkamp Verlag, 1996), 40–54, 41. All translations from this essay are mine. Subsequent citations in text as ("Drei Briefe," [page number]).

[12] On Grünbein's appropriation of the term from Karl Lashley, see Alexander Müller, *Das Gedicht als Engramm. Memoria und Imaginatio in der Poetik Durs Grünbeins* (Oldenburg: Igel Verlag Wissenschaft, 2004).

[13] See Müller, *Das Gedicht als Engramm*, 72–3. Ertel also notes the collapsing of the distinction between production and reception (Ertel, *Körper, Gehirne, Gene*, 225).

[14] Durs Grünbein, "Katze und Mond," in *Galilei vermißt Dantes Hölle und bleibt an den Maßen hängen. Aufsätze 1989–1995*, 55–60, 56. All translations from this essay are mine. Subsequent citations in text as ("Katze und Mond," [page number]).

semantically and metrically unexpected events.[15] During a visit to the Institute for Psycholinguistics in Nijmegen, Grünbein reports learning that the EEG response to the (unexpected) phrase "the cat catches the moon" has a much greater amplitude than the response to the (expected) phrase "the cat catches the mouse" ("Katze und Mond," 57). The N400 factor, the EEG response whose amplitude the lab measured, becomes Grünbein's measure for the effectiveness of poetry because it indicates "a giant's leap over lexical divides" ("Katze und Mond," 57).[16] Unlike many of the researchers whose work I discussed in the previous chapter, however, Grünbein does not take an interest in the differences or similarities of brain electricity responses to semantically and metrically unexpected events. Instead, the studies provide him with a brain-based theory of poetry as disrupting ordinary cognition through "sensory/sensual difficulty" ("Drei Briefe," 56).[17]

Meter initially seems less important in this process; Grünbein appears to focus on semantically unexpected combinations of words, especially in metaphors. He claims that specific types of verse, such as alliterative verse or free verse, are "secondary forms" that support the presentation of unexpected images ("Drei Briefe," 52). But his poetry suggests otherwise: in contrast to his very first poems, Grünbein's poems from the years in which he writes these essays (roughly 1990–4) begins to use striking metrical forms. The approaches to meter I discussed in the previous chapter and to which Grünbein refers in his essays—in particular, here, those drawing on linguistics and the natural sciences—make a direct case that metrical detail likewise has a role to play in the physiological and affective effectiveness of a poem, even as neither Grünbein nor natural-scientific metrics work out every stage of the links between brain response and embodied poetic experience.

[15] See Chapter 5, Section 5.2, "Cognitive Poetics and Neuropoetics" and (discussed there) Peter Praamstra and Dick F. Stegeman, "Phonological Effects on the Auditory N400 Event-Related Brain Potential," *Cognitive Brain Research* 1, no. 2 (April 1, 1993): 73–86, https://doi.org/10.1016/0926-6410(93)90013-U; Michael D. Rugg, "Event-Related Potentials and the Phonological Processing of Words and Non-Words," *Neuropsychologia* 22, no. 4 (January 1, 1984): 435–43, https://doi.org/10.1016/0028-3932(84)90038-1, 435; Michael D. Rugg and Sarah E. Barrett, "Event-Related Potentials and the Interaction between Orthographic and Phonological Information in a Rhyme-Judgment Task," *Brain and Language* 32, no. 2 (1987): 336–61, https://doi.org/10.1016/0093-934X(87)90132-5; and Kathrin Rothermich, Maren Schmidt-Kassow, and Sonja A. Kotz, "Rhythm's Gonna Get You: Regular Meter Facilitates Semantic Sentence Processing," *Neuropsychologia* 50, no. 2 (January 2012): 232–44, https://doi.org/10.1016/j.neuropsychologia.2011.10.025.

[16] On the identification of N400 amplitude as a response to lexical stimuli, see Chapter 5, Section 5.2. and Steven J. Luck, *Introduction to the Event-Related Potential Technique* (MIT Press: Cambridge, 2014), 115.

[17] Ahrend notes the affinity of Grünbein's theory of resistance with Shklovsky's approach to art as defamiliarization (Ahrend, *Tanz zwischen sämtlichen Stühlen*, 104–5).

"Biological Waltz"

"Biological Waltz," the first poem in a cycle called "Mensch ohne Großhirn" (Human without a Cerebrum), indicates in its title the combination of biological poetics with formal-musical presentation:

Biologischer Walzer[18]

Zwischen Kapstadt und Grönland liegt dieser Wald	x x/x x/x x/x /
Aus Begierden, Begierden die niemand kennt.	x x/x x/x x/x /
Wenn es stimmt, daß wir schwierige Tiere sind	x x/x x/x x/x /
Sind wir schwierige Tiere weil nichts mehr stimmt.	x x/x x/x x/x /

Steter Tropfen im Mund war das Wort der Beginn	x x/x x/x x/x x /
Des Verzichts, einer langen Flucht in die Zeit.	x x/x x/x/x x /
Nichts erklärt, wie ein trockener Gaumen Vokale,	x x/x x/x x/x x/x
Wie ein Leck in der Kehle Konsonanten erbricht.	x x/x x/x x x/x x /

Offen bleibt, was ein Ohr im Laborglas sucht,	x x/x x/x x/x /
Eine fleischliche Brosche, gelb in Formaldehyd.	x x/x x/x/x x/x x
Wann es oben schwimmt, wann es untergeht,	x x/x/x x/x /
Wie in toten Nerven das Gleichgewicht klingt.	x x/x/x x/x x /

Fraglich auch, ob die tausend Drätchen im Pelz	x x/x x/x/x x /
Des gelehrigen Affen den Heißhunger stillen.	x x/x x/x x/x x/x
Was es heißt, wenn sich Trauer im Hirnstrom zeigt.	x x/x x/x x/x /
Jeden flüchtigen Blick ein Phantomschmerz lenkt.	x x/x x/x x/x /

Zwischen Kapstadt und Grönland liegt dieser Wald	x x/x x/x x/x /
... Ironie, die den Körper ins Dickicht schickt.	x x/x x/x x/x /
Wenn es stimmt, daß wir schwierige Tiere sind,	x x/x x/x x/x /
Sind wir schwierige Tiere weil nichts mehr stimmt.	x x/x x/x x/x /

---

[18] Durs Grünbein, *Gedichte. Bücher I–III* (Frankfurt am Main: Suhrkamp Verlag, 2006), 315. Ellipsis in original.

Biological Waltz[19]

Between Cape Town and Greenland there is this forest
  Of desires, desires nobody knows.
    If it is true that we're difficult creatures
      We're difficult creatures because nothing's still true.

Steady drops in the mouth, the word was the onset
  Of renunciation, a long escape into time.
    Nothing explains how a palate that's dry can vomit
      Vowels, a leak in the trachea consonants.

What's it doing in the specimen glass, this yellow ear,
  A fleshy brooch afloat in formaldehyde.
    When it floats to the top, or when it sinks,
      Balance starts ringing like nerves that have died.

Can the thousand little wires in its fur
  Sate the ravenous ape who's so quick to learn?
    What if sorrow's exposed in cerebral currents?
      A phantom pain steers every fleeting gaze?

Between Cape Town and Greenland there is this forest
  ... Irony, sending the body into the woods.
    If it's true that we're difficult creatures
      We're difficult creatures because nothing's still true.

The poem's most striking feature is its meter. In keeping with the title "waltz," the poem is made up of five four-line verses containing three three-syllable units with the emphasis on the last syllable (x x /) followed by a two-beat unit, again with the emphasis on the last syllable (x /): x x / x x / x x / x /. It more or less makes sense to call the three-syllable units anapests (although of they are, of course, German and not Greek anapests).[20] The straightforward diction, frequently colloquial tone, and easily perceptible meter belie the verse technique required to sustain an anapestic meter and keep it from sliding into other rhythms across the course of an entire poem. Numerous other interpreters have, of course, noted the poem's metrical structure, but their interpretations merely note in general that a triple rhythm is appropriate for a waltz.[21] In following Grünbein's metrical strategies into considerably more detail, I contend that seeing how the poem's meter works

[19] Durs Grünbein, "Biologischer Walzer/Biological Waltz," trans. Andrew Shields, *Poetry Magazine*, November, 1998. Ellipsis in original.
[20] Anapests in durational meters are feet of four time-units where one unit is twice as long as the other two, more like 2/4 than the German anapest's 3/8—not a waltz at all.
[21] See e.g. Leeder, "The Poetry of Science and the Science of Poetry," 425; Alexander Bormann, "Im Dickicht des Nicht-Ich. Durs Grünbeins Anapäste," in *Signaturen der Gegenwartsliteratur. Festschrift für Walter Hinderer*, ed. Dieter Borchmeyer [Würzburg: Königshausen und Neumann, 1999], 171–84).

reveals the traditions Grünbein activates and modifies (and the virtuosity involved in doing so). It also demonstrates which bodily effects he seeks to achieve. Finally, attention to the interaction between micro-structural and macro-structural form shows that the poem performs one way in which the recursive structures of meter organize time, in the case of "Biological Waltz" the evolutionary time of the human development of language, into a memorable sequence of sounds and story.

Grünbein establishes the pattern in the first strophe without any irregularities; to reinforce the lines as units, he has them coincide with semantic-syntactic boundaries, and even the enjambment between "dieser Wald/ Aus Begierden" (this forest/ Of desires) falls at the beginning of a prepositional phrase (the lines would feel very different if the line break fell before "Begierden" instead of "aus": "dieser Wald aus/ Begierden," "this forest of/ Desires"). Moreover, the chiastic structure of the poem's refrain places the repeated word "sind" ("are") at the turning point of the argumentative "if ... because ..." structure. Since single-syllable words like "wenn" (if), "es" (it), "stimmt" (holds true), "daß" (that), "wir" (we), "sind" (are), "weil" (because), "nichts" (nothing), and "mehr" (more or still) in the final two lines of the first and last strophes have ambiguous emphasis in German (as in English), Grünbein has to use multi-syllabic words, especially in the first two lines, to establish the pattern, which then becomes strong enough to classify the monosyllables as fitting into the pattern, even when ordinarily the personal pronoun "wir" (we) might be emphasized more than "sind" (are) as potentially more significant/informative.

Grünbein's meter works hard to maintain its distinctiveness: anapests in German can easily start to sound like amphibrachs (x/x), or the emphasized last syllable can start to sound like the beginning of a unit/foot/measure, yielding a dactylic structure (/xx) that would evoke German hexameters (and thus epic rather than dance).[22] The structure Grünbein deploys, however, helps us hear the first two syllables as the start and not the end of the foot by inserting the shorter (two-syllable) unit at the end of each line to create a slight pause, which is particularly clear when it aligns with syntax or punctuation (e.g. **nie**mand **kennt**./ Wenn es **stimmt** ...; stressed syllables in bold.) He is, further, careful to use the metrical schema with no irregularities in the first verse before varying it slightly in the second, third, and fourth. These variations have partly to do with the use of multi-syllable words, which have fixed stress designations based on the most grammatically salient portions of the words (stem vs. prefix/suffix, compound word components, etc.). Words like "Konso**nan**ten," "Lab**or**glas," or "Formalde**hyd**" don't fit into the meter, and the irregularities prevent the repetitions from lapsing into monotony.

---

[22] On "evoking" meters rather than imitating them, see my discussion of Grünbein's self-styled "coming *after*" various poetic modes below; on the difficulties and different ways of creating hexameter in German, see Chapter 1, Section 1.2, "The Hexameter Debate, 1730–1780."

The final verse returns to a perfect fit between the metrical pattern and the words; it also repeats much of the first verse's vocabulary. The repetition and return suggest that the title "waltz" refers not only to the small-scale meter but to the macrostructural movement of the poem. In addition to velocity and triple meters, the movement of the waltz involves turning and returning, which appear both in the return of the diction of the first strophe in the final strophe and in the circular structure of the final sentence of each. That sentence—"Wenn es stimmt, daß wir schwierige Tiere sind/ Sind wir schwierige Tiere weil nichts mehr stimmt"—uses the sole first-person pronoun in the poem, and organizes three units "stimmt," "wir schwierige Tiere," and "sind" symmetrically around the line break. The off-rhyme between "sind" and "stimmt" is the only one in the poem; Grünbein's highly unusual choice to deploy a prominent meter in unrhymed verse once again puts the focus on syllable pattern (and perhaps explains the need for careful marking of line endings at the beginning of the poem to clarify that pattern).

Both meter and macro-structure are difficult to tie to the semantic content of the poem: does the ease of the waltz meter belie the status of human beings as "difficult animals" (schwierige Tiere)? Does the rapid and dizzying turning of the dance reflect the disorientation of the talking and learning ape? The tension between different elements and structures that are held together but not fully resolved by poetic form underscores the way in which attending to meter reveals the productive conflicts in Grünbein's work—the "deadlock between two positions" that he "plays through." Conversely, looking at Grünbein shows how metrical forms can both challenge and adapt the projects of late-twentieth—and early-twenty-first—century poetry and attempts by evolutionary aesthetics to explain its development.[23]

"Biological Waltz" narrates Grünbein's version of the development of human language—a version that, because it occurs in poetic form and not in a scientific journal or poetic-theoretical article, draws out the difficulties, hitches, and contradictions of that process. In keeping with Grünbein's theory of poetry as resistance, the poem creates unusual or unexpected images—the depiction of a severed ear as a "fleshy brooch" in its formaldehyde solution is particularly striking. The poem links language to physiology in several places: "the word" comes from dripping saliva, and vowels and consonants are vomited or leaked from the palate and the trachea. Human beings (or who/whatever "we" are) appear as "difficult animals" ("schwierige Tiere"; Shields translates "difficult creatures," presumably to keep the meter) and teachable apes with a ravenous appetite, defined by drives and reflexes using metaphors of electricity ("wires" for nerves, "brain current" to describe the mental state of sadness). The poem adopts a skeptical, lightly ironic tone about

---

[23] For a more detailed account of evolutionary aesthetics and its projects, in particular their relation to poetry and verse, see Chapter 5, Section 5.2., "Evolutionary Aesthetics."

both the achievements of the teachable ape and the insights of natural science, suggesting that neither can satisfy or control the desires of the human-inhabited world (between Cape Town and Greenland). The gestures toward uncertainty in "nichts erklärt" (nothing explains) "offen bleibt" (it remains open) and "fraglich auch" (also questionable) underscore the poem's skepticism.[24] It suggests that human beings pay for their achievement of language with the loss of "the instinctual unity with the world that belong to ... animal being, with the result that 'nichts mehr stimmt.'"[25]

"Biological Waltz" demonstrates that and how the acquisition of language seems to alienate the speaker from its animal body (making it a "difficult animal"/ "schwieriges Tier"), while the language runs up against its limits in the body. Rather than a linear development from pre-language (gestures combined expressive cries or vocalizations) to proto-language (use of sounds as words but without syntax or grammar) to full language (words as signs and full syntax/grammar), Grünbein creates a poetic and self-referential story of language, desire, knowledge, and sound.[26] With the poem's meter, he activates poetry's connections to the affective inheritances of pre- and proto-language, as articulated in evolutionary aesthetics, where meter and rhythm create a "living link with our phylogenetic past"[27]—and he does so in order to articulate the limits and frustrations of language itself.

Meter and Memory

Grünbein continues his argument that meter links the poem to the physiological body through creating bodily experiences of time and memory in the essay "My Babylonish Brain," originally published in 1995.[28] In it, Grünbein intro-

---

[24] The poem is thus more careful about the equation of neurophysiology and experience than Grünbein's essays occasionally are. As Gabriele Dürbeck notes, "The skeptical beginnings of each line emphasize that previous explanations have failed to achieve any authoritative answers, neither an explanation of the human capacity for language, nor an explanation of the unconscious through anatomical dissection, nor any illumination of the connection between brain currents and the contents of consciousness through the generation of an EEG" (Gabriele Dürbeck, "'Wenn es stimmt, dass wir schwierige Tiere sind.' Anatomie und Anthropologie in Durs Grünbeins 'Mensch ohne Großhirn,'" Zeitschrift für Germanistik 19, no. 1 [2009]: 133–45, 139).

[25] Karen Leeder, "The Poetry of Science and the Science of Poetry: German Poetry in the Laboratory of the Twentieth Century," German Life and Letters 60, no. 3 (2007): 412–29, 426. See also Ertel, Körper, Gehirne, Gene 184–5.

[26] On the development of language and for more detailed definitions of language, pre-language, and proto-language, see Christopher Collins, Paleopoetics. The Evolution of the Pre-Literate Imagination (New York: Columbia University Press, 2013), 107–8.

[27] Brian Boyd, Why Lyrics Last. Evolution, Cognition, and Shakespeare's Sonnets (Cambridge: Harvard University Press, 2012), 140.

[28] Durs Grünbein, "My Babylonish Brain," in Eskin, The Bars of Atlantis. Selected Essays, trans. Michael Hofmann, 59–71 (New York: Farrar, Straus and Giroux, 2010). The German title is "Mein babylonisches Hirn," which translates equally well to "My Babylonian Brain," despite Hofmann's choice of "Babylonish" (Durs Grünbein, "Mein babylonisches Hirn," in Galilei vermißt Dantes Hölle und

duces more detailed considerations of metrical practice than in his prior essays. He begins with a presentation of poetry as physiological and adds that it can preserve "the singular, the ideography of primary experience" against the flux of everyday language and the rush of stimuli in daily experience ("My Babylonish Brain," 18-9). Moreover, meter becomes a means for supporting memory's resistance:

> Perhaps the best poems, the most enigmatic compositions are written against overstimulation, as a way for memory to draw breath under the barrage of sense impressions. In its effort to oppose the mere passage of time, to pause in the wastes of information ... memory's best ally is the red thread of the disject line, metrically scanned.
>
> ("My Babylonish Brain," 61-2)

Meter, for Grünbein, helps preserve impressions and images from rapid decay by making them memorable, compacted and preserved in lines that resonate in the brain.[29] Meter also, however, organizes and preserves multiple layers of time *within* a poem: "The meters, whatever they are, take time with them, postponed time ... dialectically offered time, time in which palimpsests unroll, transhistorically running time" ("My Babylonish Brain," 60). Poetry is thus polyphonic and palimpsestic *by way* of meter.[30] The specific ways Grünbein takes up metrical tradition appear, I argue, in his poetry; in his essays, he focuses on meter in general as a tool to preserve images *across* time and to organize time *within* a poem.

Grünbein returns to the vocabulary of engrams and inscription of memory in the brain and uses prosody to link the individual with the species across its evolution: "From the very beginning, poetry was a function of memory, and it is its prosodic character that creates the link between the individual voice coming out of a mortal body and the narratives of the species standing over the waters and moving through cities and landscapes" ("My Babylonish Brain," 62). Meter and rhythm bring together individual, cultural, and evolutionary time: "In the variety of rhythms, the in the shuffle of images, the imagination of one individual is

---

bleibt an den Maßen hängen, 18-33). The phrase is mysterious: Grünbein introduces it as an updating of Baudelaire: "Now, at the end of the twentieth century, it's perhaps time to adapt Baudelaire's phrase, the 'Babylonish heart': the new passionless arena, a place of chillier pleasures, is the Babylonish brain" ("My Babylonish Brain," 68-9), but I have not been able to find a reference to a "Babylonian heart" in Baudelaire, although there are references to Babel and Babylon in several of his poems (and of course to hearts in dozens). Subsequent citations in text as ("My Babylonish Brain," [page number]).

[29] This argument about the fit between meter and the brain echoes the claims of Pöppel and Turner on the fit between line length and active memory (see Chapter 5, Section 5.2. and Frederick Turner and Ernst Pöppel, "The Neural Lyre: Poetic Meter, the Brain, and Time," Poetry 142, no. 5 [1983]: 277-309).

[30] Knoblich, Antikenkonfigurationen in der deutschsprachigen Lyrik nach 1990, 34-5.

synchronized with the world perception of all—as long as such things are handed on. Whatever guise the words adopt, from hexameter epic to chatty free verse, the decisive factor is the energetic relation between memory and poetry" ("My Bablyonish Brain," 62). Metrical forms thus reinforce the fit between poetry and memory (poetry and the brain), helping poetry create a "present beyond death and this side of chronological time" ("My Babylonish Brain," 62). Although meter is only one among the "elements" a poem may employ in making language and image memorable, meter's relation to and organization of time makes it particularly powerful. For Grünbein, meter turns time into part of the body in memory, as the poem "penetrates the nethermost spaces of memory" and "becomes a chunk of embodied time" ("My Babylonish Brain," 65). On Grünbein's account, then, poetry has the task of preserving individual idiosyncrasy and perception, transmitting them to and standing in polyphonic dialogue with others (both poets and readers), and in doing so resisting the flow of time by shaping it.[31] Meter is poetry's most powerful tool for doing this, and the importance of meter for organizing temporality and its positive contribution to memory reappear throughout his poetics. Moreover, Grünbein's deployment and adaptation of particular meters in his poetry reveals a high degree of attention to formal resonances across poetic traditions, suggesting that his choices activate specific registers of organizing time.

6.2 Temporality, Antiquity, Prosody

Grünbein's poetry takes up metrical forms in varying ways. In addition to the flagrant and virtuosic meter of "Biological Waltz," Grünbein writes numerous poems that adapt, evoke, or modify meters from Greek and Roman poets. As I have argued throughout this book and as examining both the eighteenth and nineteenth centuries has shown, there can *be* no cross-cultural, trans-historical definition of (say) hexameter or ode forms. Both in the eighteenth and nineteenth centuries, the thinkers and poets I have discussed have shown that what counts as which meter for whom is always a matter of cultural contestation and involves complex aesthetic and political stakes. Grünbein's poems using or evoking antique meters are no different. Although his use of antique or canonical forms has been criticized as artificial and depoliticized, his engagement with those forms is not a flight or a turning away from the present.[32] Grünbein repeatedly foregrounds his writing as coming *after* in his poem and volume titles.[33] Moreover, "nach" used this way

---

[31] See Müller, *Das Gedicht als Engramm*, 116.

[32] See Michael von Albrecht, "Nach den Satiren. Durs Grünbein und die Antike," in *Mythen in nachmythischer Zeit. Die Antike in der deutschsprachigen Literatur der Gegenwart*, eds. Bernd Seidensticker and Martin Vöhler (Berlin: de Gruyter, 2002), 101–16.

[33] For example "Nach den Fragmenten" (After the Fragments), "Nach den Satiren" (After the Satires), "Nach Hadrian," "Europa nach dem letzten Regen" (Europe after the Last Rains), and "Mediationen nach Descartes" (Meditation after Descartes). See Pabst, *Post-Ost-Moderne*, 320–1.

suggests "in the manner of," emphasizing that Grünbein engages with but does not inhabit the territory of his predecessors. Consequently, his poems in quasi-antique meters do not seek to escape or transcend history but represent a complex engagement with the present that layers multiple temporalities.[34]

Forms of Coming *After*

Grünbein's use of canonical forms adds a further layer to the questions of meter, body, and poetry. Although odes or hexameters may be more difficult to hear for contemporary readers accustomed to rhyming stanzas or free verse, antique meters still group and organize time to make "a chunk of embodied time" ("My Babylonish Brain," 62). Moreover, metrical patterning itself provides a model of Grünbein's relation to past poetic time: meter, as a recursive or self-reflexive temporal structure, can perform the kind of complex relationships between different temporal moments or processes in ways that non-metrical text can only describe. As Grünbein argues in "My Babylonish Brain," meter (the "prosodic character") of poetry mediates between the singular, finite, mortal individual and the species ("My Babylonish Brain," 65); his poems "after" antique meters do so by way of their participation in and modification of metrical history, which in turn makes the narration of history (as time) metrical. Moreover, because canonical forms have strong associations with particular genres and thus (in antiquity) particular themes, Grünbein's adaptations of those forms foreground questions of the relation between meter and meaning. But because Grünbein sometimes evokes the genres and sometimes transgresses their thematic and formal norms, the relation between metrical pattern and semantic meaning appears far more flexible and complex than the approaches I considered in the previous chapter, where the authors either attempt to sever meter from meaning or to pin metrical patterning down as supporting or disrupting semantics.[35]

Significantly, Grünbein rarely uses inherited forms in their most canonical or recognizable versions. Instead, he introduces irregularities or combines formal features that do not normally belong together (such as rhyme in loosely hexametric

---

[34] Ulrich Kellner, "'Zwischen Antike und X.' Zur Poetologie Grünbeins," in *Zwischen Globalisierung und Regionalisierung. Zur Darstellung von Zeitgeschichte in deutschsprachiger Gegenwartsliteratur*, eds. Martin Hellström and Edgar Plate (Munich: Iudicum, 2008), 41–52, 42.

[35] As I discuss in Chapter 5, most metrical histories and handbooks see the relation between meter and meaning as at best a cultural invention (Section 5.1. "Metrical Histories and Handbooks"), while posthermeutic literary theory denies any connection between material and meaning (Section 5.1., "Posthermeneutics") and natural-scientific approaches try both to test them separately and check whether meter disrupts or facilitates cognitive processing (Section 5.2., "Cognitive Poetics and Neuropoetics").

verse).[36] Most readers are content to say (or cite each other saying) that numbers of Grünbein's poems "evoke" antique forms without clarifying how they do so or explaining the difference between evoking (say) a distich and being one.[37] Grünbein's theories of metrical patterning as shaping time to transmit and preserve language in the body invite us to pay closer attention to his almost-regular forms, seeing where the patterns shift or break down and how their doing so directs attention and preserves sounds in memory. I turn to a reading of the poem "Aporie Augustinus (Über die Zeit)" and analyze its metrical strategies in detail to show how meter shapes time in a poem that takes time and meter as its theme.

The poem "Aporie Augustinus. (Über die Zeit)" ["Aporia Augustine. (On Time)"][38] is, like numerous poems in the volume *Nach den Satiren* (After the Satires), a persona poem, this time in the voice of Augustine of Hippo.[39] It addresses Augustine's friend Alypius, who was baptized with him in 387 AD.[40] As its parenthetical subtitle, ("On Time" or "About Time") indicates, "Aporia Augustine" grapples with the question of Book 11 of the *Confessions*: "So what *is* time?"[41] As Michael Eskin points out, several lines of the poem refer to or translate almost directly from Augustine.[42] It also draws on Augustine's rhetorical features or strategies, in particular repetition and strings of questions.[43] Moreover, the poem presents other poetic treatments of temporality and transience, memory and forgetting. Finally, it balances metrical consistency and variety by establishing a basic, three-syllable pattern that appears in lines of varying lengths, verses of between one and seven lines, and occasionally fragmentary or irregular line lengths over

---

[36] Michael von Albrecht notes that the mixture of forms, including short stories, dialogues, and ethical reflections, is characteristic of antique satire, and notes in addition that Grünbein, like Horace, occasionally satirizes those forms (von Albrecht, "Nach den Satiren. Durs Grünbein und die Antike," 104). Korte notes that Grünbein's play with history extends "to verse construction, to meter, to rhetorical flourishes" (Hermann Korte, "Habemus poetam. Zum Konnex von Poesie und Wissen in Durs Grünbeins Gedichtsammlung 'Nach den Satiren'," ed. Heinz-Ludwig Arnold, *Text + Kritik*, 153 [2002]: 19–33, here 22–3).

[37] See, in addition to Knoblich, Olaf Krämer's remark that Grünbein's "Nach den Satiren I" uses "free variation on the hexameter of Juvenal's satires" (Krämer, "Ich und Welt," 363).

[38] I cite the German original by line number from "Aporie Augustinus (Über die Zeit)" in Durs Grünbein, *Nach den Satiren*, Frankfurt: Suhrkamp, 1999, 33–6. The English translations are cited from "Aporia Augustine (On Time)" translated by Michael Eskin. Copyright © 2013 by Upper West Side Philosophers, Inc., New York. Used by permission, pages 33–6. English phrases cited in-text without annotations are mine. For the entire poem with Eskin's translation, see the appendix.

[39] I avoid the term "dramatic monologue" because many of Grünbein's poems in other voices, like "Aporia Augustinus," address a contemporary of the persona by name and are thus not monologic. On the persona poems in *Nach den Satiren*, see Cooper, "Direction, Disruption, Voice," 111.

[40] Michael Eskin, "Denkbilder. Zu einem Motiv bei Durs Grünbein," in *Bildlichkeit im Werk Durs Grünbeins*, eds. Christoph auf der Horst and Miriam Seidler (Berlin: de Gruyter, 2015), 141–62, 154.

[41] Augustine, *Confessions*, ed. and trans. Carolyn J.B. Hammond, Volume II: Books 9–13, Loeb Classical Library 27 (Cambridge: Harvard University Press, 2016), 217.

[42] Eskin, "Denkbilder," 141.

[43] To give one particularly striking example, continuing from the passage I cited above, "So what is time? Who can explain this simply and briefly? Who can understand it, even by serious thought, sufficiently to express the idea in words? In ordinary speech, what is easier or more familiar for us to talk about than time? And we definitely understand it when we speak of it, and we also understand it when we listen to someone else talking about it. So what is time?" (Augustine, *Confessions*, 217).

its ninety-seven lines. This combination of uniformity and variety exemplifies one way in which meter can not only represent but unfold different experiences of time: as recurring (say, in one day after another), as different (linearly unfolding from year to year), or as self-referential (in deja-vu, or events like anniversaries, memories, or flashbacks). To see how these multiple layers of time work in meter requires detailed analysis.

The poem begins with three verses of four lines of between two and four loosely dactylic feet (/ x x). This initiates the pattern that the rest of the poem will continue and disrupt:

Die brennende Hornhaut im Salzschaum	x/x x/x x/x
Im Tuffstein die Augenhöhlen, Alypius,	x/x x/x/x x/x x
Das Meer das dein Wort schluckt—	x/x x/(/x)
Nichts was du kennst, ist die Zeit.[44]	/ x x/x x /

In addition to introducing the addressee of the poem, Alypius, the first verse establishes two patterns: first the loosely triplet meter, either /x x or x x /, and, second, the listing of loosely connected objects or images whose identity with time the last line negates. Grünbein here deploys semantic and metrical patterning or repetition simultaneously; later in the poem, he will play different kinds of repetition off each other to create contrast.

The second verse continues the pattern with slight alterations, as images of multiple domes and curves (taken from Book 11, chapter 23[45]) enclose one another:

Die Wölbung des Himmels, den Schädel	x/x x/x x/x
Umfassend, die Hände in Hohlform	x/x x/x x/x
Über der kreisenden Töpferscheibe—	/ x x/x x/x/x
Nichts was du siehst, ist die Zeit.[46]	/ x x/x x /

In these lines, the things that time is *not* foreground a fragmented bodily materiality: corneas, eye sockets, hands, and skulls never quite come together into a single body. The last line of each verse (the third ends "Nichts was du hörst, ist die

---

[44] "The cornea burning with salt foam,/ The eye sockets deep in the tuff, Alypius,/ The word-drowning sea—/ Time isn't something you know" (1–4). Eskin's translation alters the verse-closing formula, in particular, to preserve the meter (TIME isn't SOMEthing you KNOW); the original is closer to "Nothing that you know is time," or "Time is nothing that you know."

[45] "I once heard from a certain learned person that the movements of the sun and moon and stars are themselves times; but I did not agree. Why, then, would the movements of all physical objects not be times as well? And moreover, if the lights in the heavens were to fail, while a potter's wheel kept turning, wouldn't there be time by which to measure those rotations, and to state either that they were all the same size fractions of time ...?" (Augustine, *Confessions*, 235).

[46] "The vault of the sky that encloses/ The skull, the hands cupped over/ The spinning pottery wheel—/ Time isn't something you see" (5–8).

Zeit"; "Time isn't something you hear") reinforces both the rhetorical and metrical pattern, since its meter does not vary across the three beginning verses.

Grünbein then picks up this repeated line ("Time isn't something you _____") as the transition to the next four verses, each with four longer lines whose dactylic quality (/ x x) and relative length (between five and eight stresses) suggest hexameter without conforming fully to any established German variant of the meter. This is a paradigmatic example of the way Grünbein uses canonical forms' flexibility to hint at their cultural connotations. Hexameters were used in the ancient world for epic storytelling that mediates cultural memory, and in the baroque early modern periods for philosophical poetry in the elegy and epigram genres. Because hexameter typically is not identical from line to line thanks to the canonical rule that one "long" syllable can replace two "short" syllables or vice versa, and because German typically substitutes stress for syllable length, almost any line with a mixture of three-syllable and two-syllable feet with a variable number of stresses per line and no other obvious features like rhyme can "evoke" hexameter in German. Blending German and Greek conventions, in another example of coming *after* rather than being *in* an antique form, Grünbein divides his quasi-hexameter into four-line groups/verses (there are no verse or strophe groupings in Classical hexametric verse). In keeping with the hexameter-*like* form, the images of the four long-line irregular triple-meter verses call up the late-Roman milieu that Grünbein favors because (in his view) it has significant similarities with his own era.[47]

Turning the negating verse-endings of the previous section into the beginning of the new verse-type, the fourth strophe begins with the word "nothing" (*Nichts*):

Nichts was du fassen kannst, ist sie. Kein Brusthaar,	$/ \, x \, x \, /x \, (x \, / \,)/x \, (x/\,)/x$
Das nach dem Baden gezupft wird, und keine Tafel,	$(/x) \, (x/\,) \, x/x \, x/x \, x/x/x$
Die in den Stadien die Runden anzeigt beim Wagenrennen.	$(/x) \, x \, x/x \, x/x \, (/x)(/x) \, x/x/x$
Weder die Greisenstirn noch die rosa Fingerbeeren des Kindes.[48]	$/x \, x/x \, (/x) \, (/x) \, x/x/x/x \, x/x$

---

[47] In particular the attributes of urbanity, belatedness, and decadence. Grünbein develops this portrayal in his essay "Schlaflos in Rom. Versuch über den Satirendichter Juvenal" (Sleepless in Rome. Essay on the Satirical Poet Juvenal), in *Antike Dispositionen. Aufsätze* (Frankfurt a.M.: Suhrkamp Verlag, 2005), 328–68, 335. See also von Albrecht, "Nach den Satiren: Durs Grünbein und die Antike," 101–16.

[48] "Nor something you will ever grasp. No chest hair/ You pluck after bathing, no billboard/ Announcing the rounds of the chariot race in the stadium./ Neither the brow of the old man, nor the pink finger pulps of the child" (13–6).

Using the physical-material body (growing of hair, aging foreheads, or youthful finger pads) and city activities (the scoreboard for chariot races) as measurements, the speaker continues to insist that his interlocutor cannot grasp or measure time (line seventeen); the lines in this section repeat the negative indirect article "kein" (none of or not one), in addition to "auch nicht" (also not), "weder ... noch" (neither ... nor), "nichts" (nothing), "doch" (but/yet), supporting the argumentative and conversational tone. Grünbein also aligns punctuation or at least syntax with line endings throughout almost the entire poem, which heightens its affinity to ordinary speech and makes the few exceptions prosodically striking. The poem now extends the quasi-hexameter meter's reference to the epic genre to the semantic content, as it references epic themes and poets: the "number of governments, wars in a lifetime" (20), "seafarers ... routes to Troy ... way home" (22–3), and "Gods ... Heroes ... Homer" (27–8), although the epic themes are lightly mocked by description of the "groaning of the heroes in Homer's limp ears" (Eskin translates "welk" to faded, which sounds less foolish but makes less sense to describe ears). Grünbein uses meter, then, to execute his project of belated "coming after," in which altered versions of canonical meters evoke canonical themes at an ironized distance.

The seventh verse breaks with what has come before in several decisive ways: first, it establishes a distinction between past and present within the narration of the poem by using the word "yesterday" and the past tense; second, it uses the pronoun "I" for the first time in the poem; third, it calls attention to language by considering the *words* used to mark time; fourth, it shifts from negation to questioning in striving to understand time; and finally, it interrupts the even line lengths of the prior verses:

Gestern habe ich angefangen mit zuzuhören, Alypius.	/ x/x x/x/x x/x/x x/x
Aus jedem Satz sprang ein Wort, das mich älter zurückließ.	/(x/) x/x x/x x/x x/x
Irgend ein *Bald*, ein *Nicht mehr*, ein *Von altersher*.	/ x x/x (/x) (/x) x/ / x x
Da war dieses Noch...	x/x x /
Dieses Schon...	x x /
Dieses Einst...	x x /
Und nichts davon ist die Zeit.	(x/) (/x) x/x x /
Was aber ist sie?[49]	/ x x/x

[49] "Yesterday I began listening to myself, Alypius./ Words leapt out from each sentence leaving me older./ Some *soon* ...some *no more* ...some *of old*./ As if there were only direction in speaking, no standstill./ There was the *still* ... / The *already*... / The *once*.../ Time, though, is none of all that./ But what is it then?" (29–35; I am counting the short lines as independent lines, although as the printing suggests they function like a single line broken up.)

In contrast to the controlled, almost smug negations of the previous strophes, the speaker describes his (presumably, given the identification of Augustine) own listening and aging, breaking a single line into baffled adverbial phrases printed across three lines (this still… this already … this once …") and finishing with a question that trails off before completing the rhythmical pattern the prior verses established:/x x/x, not/x x/x x/. Precisely because Grünbein has established strong regularity in the prior six strophes (even line lengths, triple meters), the divergence here underscores that this is a turning point in the poem.

The last line shares its meter with the last line of a Sapphic ode strophe (/ x x/x), evoking antiquity more precisely and, in the genre and thematic connotations of the Sapphic ode (at least in the German context), mortality and finitude.[50] The poem's next verse discusses meter and mortality explicitly, asking whether time is "Ein Gedicht aus den Tagen des Plinius, in falschen Metren,/ Das vom Verliebt-sein handelt, und die zwei sind längst tot,/ Und es kommt dennoch ein Lied an, ein Herzton, ein Schauder?" (38–40)[51] The reference to "Plinius" could indicate Pliny the Elder or Pliny the Younger, but "false meters" perhaps suggests the latter, who announces in a letter that the verses he sends are merely "hendecasyllabics, in accordance with the measure in which the verses run," rather than "epigrams, eclogues, or … sonnets."[52] Pliny the Younger thus rejects the strict association of verse type and content, which would, in the poetics of antiquity, make the meters "false." In the remainder of the section (verses X to XII), consisting of further long-form lines with between five and seven lines per verse, the speaker continues the pattern of questioning around loosely defined themes. Grünbein never allows the poem or the reader to settle into a straightforward, mimetic relationship of metrical form to content.

In the thirteenth verse the verse pattern changes again, returning to three-line verses but this time with more irregular line lengths despite the continuation of the basic three-syllable unit. The speaker identifies the preceding questions as "Fragen … die ich mir selbst oft gestellt hab" (*questions that I have often asked myself*), referring them to his own past. In the next verse (the fourteenth), the poem cites almost directly from Augustine's *Confessions* Book 11, chapter 20: "Who is going to tell me that there are not three times (as we learned when we were children, and then taught our children)—past, present, and future—but only the present, for the other two do not exist?"[53] Using italics to underscore the focus on language, the poem rephrases:

---

[50] On German Sapphics, see Winfried Menninghaus, *Hälfte des Lebens. Versuch über Hölderlins Poetik* (Frankfurt a.M.: Suhrkamp Verlag, 2005).
[51] "A poem from Pliny's day, in uneven meters,/ About being in love, and the two are long dead,/ And still, a song does arrive, a heart sound, a shudder?" (38–40).
[52] Pliny the Younger, *The Letters of Caius Plinius Caecilius Secundus: The Tr. of Melmoth, Revised and Corrected with Notes and a Mem. by F.C.T. Bosanquet* (Bell, 1878), 127.
[53] Augustine, *Confessions*, 225.

Drei Arten Gegenwart sind in dir aufgespart.   //x/x x/x x/x x

Die eine heißt *Gestern*, die andere *Heute* und   x/x x/x x/x x/x x/x x/x
   Morgen die dritte.

Sie alle sind rege in dir, nur in dir, nirgendwo   x/x x/x x/(/x) x// x x /
   sonst.[54]

Continuing the section's close connection to the *Confessions*, the next verse (also
three lines of variable lengths) rejects the suggestion of "mortal astrologists" that
time is movement of the stars or phases of the moon.[55] The question of how measuring time is different from measuring space returns several verses later along
with the three-line irregular length format, creating formal continuities within or
against which the metrical variations and the different kinds of question and tone
stand out as salient, attracting readerly attention and preventing monotony across
the almost 100 lines of the poem.

The sixteenth and seventeenth verses take up the topic of poetry and meter more
directly than any others in the poem. Line sixty-eight begins with the conjunc-
tion "or": "Oder Gedichte mit wechselndem Versfuß...." (Or poems with varying
meters ... [68]). Syntactically, "or" suggests a continuation or connection of the
question that ends the previous verse, "What do they measure, when they measure the phases of the moon?, "*Or* [when they measure] poems with changing
meters ..." But the rest of the strophe shifts from questions to description and from
Augustine to a different interlocutor, Horace:

Oder Gedichte mit wechselndem Versfuß, zum   / x x/x x/x x/x x/x x /
   Beispiel Horaz.

Zwischen "*Lydia, schläfst du?*" und "*...Erz*   x x/x x/x x/x x/x
   überdauernd"

Eilt sein Vers hin und her, die geschäftige   (x/) x/x x/x x/x x/x
   Zunge—

Zwischen Schamhaar und Ewigkeit.[56]   x x/(x/) x/x x

The quotations—doubly marked by punctuation and italics—are from Horace's
odes, which do in fact use a wide variety of meters and are credited with (and
take credit for) importing Greek ode forms into Latin. Moreover, Grünbein takes
both quotations from odes that portray the passing of time and its consequences:
the first, ode twenty-five in Book I, addresses a woman whose beauty is fading and

---

[54] "Three kinds of presence are held in reserve within you./ One is called *yesterday*, another *today*,
and *tomorrow* the third./ They all are alive within you, only in you, nowhere else" (62–4).
[55] "I once heard from a certain learned person that the movements of the sun and moon and stars
are themselves times; but I did not agree" Augustine, *Confessions*, 235.
[56] "Or poems with varying meters—Horace, for instance./ Between '*Lydia, are you sleeping?*' and
'*more lasting than bronze*'/ Scurries his verse, that sedulous tongue—/ Between pubic hair and eternity"
(68–71).

whose suitors no longer call "Lydia, are you sleeping?" (*Lydia dormis*). The second quotation comes from the final ode in the third book, which begins by announcing that the speaker has erected "a monument more lasting than bronze" through his poetry.[57]

The speaker in Horace's ode claims immortality thanks to his metrical achievements: "I shall be spoken of where the violent Ausidus thunders and where Daunus, short of water, ruled over a country people, as one who, rising from a lowly state to a position of power, was the first to bring Aeolian verse to the tunes of Italy."[58] The meter in Grünbein's lines, however, does not follow any ode form exactly; in a further example of his *almost*-adaptation of antique meters, the four-line verse with unequal line lengths (of sixteen, thirteen, thirteen, and eight syllables, respectively) looks more or less like an antique ode in its basic outlines but does not correspond to either of the forms of the odes cited (I.25 is a Sapphic ode, III.30 in the first Asclepiadic meter[59]), nor to any of the standard Greek or Latin ode forms or their German adaptations. This almost-but-not-quite underscores the temporal and linguistic differences between Grünbein and the historical figures of Augustine and Horace while once again preventing a seamless overlap of meter and theme. Horace's combination of vulgar and lofty themes appears condensed into a single image, the "sedulous tongue" that, like his verse, hurries "between pubic hair and eternity" (ll.70–1); the speaking, eroticized tongue is perhaps the strongest link between poetry and bodily materiality.[60] In these lines, the metrical references are formal and thematically implicit, as "ode" in both English and German need not necessarily refer to the particular metrical forms of Horace, Alcaeus, or Sappho.

In the next verse, meter once again becomes an explicit theme, as Grünbein turns from Horace back to Augustine and to the question of syllable length:

> Einmal kurz, einmal lang sind die Silben, und   x x/x x/x x/x (/x) x x /
>   der sie spricht,
> Dehnt die Zeit und wird selbst gedehnt,   /x/x x x/x// x x/x /
>   rafft sie und wird gerafft.[61]

---

[57] Horace, *Odes and Epodes*, ed. Niall Rudd, vol. 33, Loeb Classical Library (Cambridge: Harvard University Press, 2004), 71 and 217, respectively.

[58] Horace, *Odes and Epodes*, 217.

[59] Horace, *Odes and Epodes*, 13.

[60] The lightly ironic, humorous tone, which occurs throughout "Aporie Augustinus" and especially in its final images, is more characteristic of Grünbein, Horace, and Juvenal than Augustine's urgency and religious appeals. Korte notes the Juvenalian tone of sarcasm and stoicism occasionally interrupted by moments of pathos (Korte, "Habemus poetam," 24).

[61] "Long, short, short, long are the syllables, and the one who recites them,/ Drawing out time, being drawn out himself, contracting it, being contracted" (72–3).

Augustine refers in several passages to syllable length as a potential measure of time;[62] in one of the most detailed and complex paragraphs, he wonders whether time measurement must be relative and compares it to measurement in space:

> Do we use a shorter time to measure a longer one in the same way as we do a cubit to measure a crossbeam? This is apparently how we use the length of a short syllable to measure the length of a long syllable and to describe the latter as double. In the same way we measure the length of poems by the length of lines, and the length of lines by the length of feet, and the length of feet by the length of syllables, and the length of long syllables by the length of short ones.[63]

Augustine's perplexity results from the fact that all of the time measurements seem to rely on each other and are subject to variation in pronunciation or performance ("it is possible that a shorter verse can be sounded over a more generous length of time, if it is pronounced in a protracted manner, than a longer one if it is pronounced in a more clipped fashion"[64]). He intensifies these questions several pages later, noting that measuring all the syllables in a flow of verse against a defined short syllable is impossible to do objectively or exactly, and, moreover, that since sounds pass away, not the sounds themselves but the memory of the sounds is what sense perception compares and measures.[65]

Augustine's meditation on syllable measurement leads him to the conclusion that "Within you, O my mind, I measure times."[66] Meter measures time in the mind's memory, a statement fully in keeping with Grünbein's theories of metrical efficacy in "My Babylonish Brain"; following his interest in physiology, Grünbein turns the Augustinian "mind" that measures time into a fleshy "brain." In the essay, as I discussed above, Grünbein describes metrical patterning as a way of resisting the overwhelming flow of transient stimuli and does not distinguish between different meters as creating different kinds of resistance. In "Aporia Augustine," we can see how the *specific* metrical practice of the poem makes time palpable and memorable by way of its organization into patterns and variations that never settle into a one-to-one relationship between meter and meaning but keep their possibilities shifting and open. The poem's varying meters also help layer different organizations of temporality and different times or eras on top of each other; Grünbein's poetic gymnastics with non-linear time become possible through meter.

Grünbein picks up the conflation of space and time before linking time and verse once more:

---

[62] See e.g. Augustine, *Confessions* 203, 235–7, and 255.
[63] Augustine, *Confessions*, 243.
[64] Augustine, *Confessions*, 245.
[65] Augustine, *Confessions*, 245.
[66] Augustine, *Confessions*, 249.

In jede Richtung reicht Raum, aber Zeit ist die   / x x/x x/x x/x x/x
    Klammer,
Die nach vorn spannt die Stirnen, die Deichseln   x x/x x/x x/x x/x /
    und jedes Lied,
Das in Strophen zerfällt wie ein Menschenleben   x x/x x/x x/x/x x/x/x
    in Anekdoten.[67]

The possibility that a poem could fall apart into its strophes and a life into unconnected anecdotes echoes Grünbein's depictions of the overwhelming flow of meaningless noise, events, and images—that is, the phenomenon of sheer transience that poetry strives to resist by preserving time in memory. In the next verse, the speaker links time directly to memory, describing it as "first appearance, then soon memory, fed by expectation" (80), adding "Strange, Alypius/ When no one asks, I think I know just what it [time] is. If you ask, though, / Nonsense is all I come up with" (83–4). Both passages allude once again to the *Confessions*[68] before some of the most negative images of the poem, in which time is described as "a sickness to death," and a "voiceless choir" in an "empty amphitheater," "with mouth cavities black with outrage and pain" (84–6). The poem calls its own strategies for creating cohesion—both thematic and metrical—into question, raising the possibility that meter cannot prevent the poem from falling apart under its own weight.

After a final, urgent Augustinian question, "*Sind hundert Jahre Gegenwart eine lange Zeit?*,"[69] isolated in italics on a single line (87), the poem deflates, shifting to vulgarity seemingly not so much out of irony as exhaustion ("I'm sleepy, Alypius. What did you say?" [88]). The last strophe describes time as the rope that a donkey eats and then excretes (89, herausscheißt), which its owner then untangles and feeds to it again (90–1). Because of the first line's question ("what did you say?"), the description seems to come from Alypius, although its grammar does not indicate either direct or indirect quotation. Metrically, lines trail off, from the sixteen syllables in line eighty-eight to ten in line ninety-two; in one of the only exact correspondences between meter and thematic content, this trailing off seems to exemplify exhaustion, coming to a stop.

The last line, isolated as a single-line verse, seems to follow from the homophony between donkey ("Esel") and riddle ("Rätsel") rather than any logical connection: "Zeit is kein Rätsel, Alypius. Vergiß es." ("Time is no riddle, Alypius. Forget it." 94). Its scansion is ambiguous: if the name "Alypius" can be squeezed into three syllables (a-LYP-ius) rather than four (A-lyp-i-us), it reiterates the three-syllable

---

[67] "Space branches out in every direction, but time is the bracket/ That stretches the foreheads ahead, the drawbars, each song/ Breaking up into strophes like the life of a man into so many scenes" (78–80).

[68] See Augustine, *Confessions*, 253 and 217.

[69] "*Is one hundred years of presence a long time?*" (87), "Is the current century a long time?" (Augustine, *Confessions*, 221).

pattern once more (/ x x/x x/x x/x), whereas the more standard German pronunciation of four syllables dissolves that pattern (/ x x/x x/x x x/x). The poem itself
seems to perform the productive tension or balance between two conflicting possibilities: either a repetition or an interruption. Since the poem itself has called
forgetting and remembering, patterns and their disruption into question, both
through its thematic content and its complex layering of metrical associations,
it seems to foreclose its own final command, superimposing multiple positions,
voices, and syllable patterns in a large-scale investigation of meter and temporality.

As the discussions of time, meter, poetic forms, and memory in "Aporia Augustinus" show, Grünbein typically addresses antiquity by way of engagement with
particular thinkers rather than any extended discussion of metrical theory. (In this
respect he is different from Klopstock or Nietzsche.) His essays follow a similar
strategy, analyzing individual poets not prosody, but at the same time, Grünbein's
claims about those poets, their use of language, and their meters continue the
themes of preserving images against transience and organizing time through verse.
Grünbein sees late Roman poetry, excluded from earlier German receptions of
antiquity as decadent and formally inferior to earlier Greek and Roman works, as
particularly suited to the contemporary world. Part of this fit, Grünbein explains,
comes from Juvenalian poetry's transgression of earlier poetic norms, particularly
metrical rules: "The perfect measures of yesterday provoked the conscious violation of rules by the historically younger—how could it be otherwise? They wrote
more prosaically now, more undisciplined, more direct in expression, less enam-
ored of form, unconcerned about meter and diction."[70] The resulting poetry is a
series of "moments of fixed presentness" ("Schlaflos in Rom," 335) which Juvenal combines with exceptional density and vividness, preserving "a maximum of
sensory information that without him would have disappeared without a sound
[sang- und klanglos] in the underworld of the torrents of time" ("Schlaflos in Rom,"
337). Grünbein sees several of the canonical criticisms of Juvenal—as stilted or
degenerate—as a function of the vigor of his satire, whose uneven hexameters and
enjambment ("hüpfende[r] Zeilensprung") bespeak the poet's frustration. Neither the violation of rules nor metrical irregularity indicate a rejection of meter,
however: for the transgression to be felt the norm must continue to be active,
and Grünbein's own metrical practice suggests the importance of tension between
pattern and variation.

Both the criticisms leveled at Juvenal and the description of his poetry as presenting a vivid and provocative concatenation of contemporary detail echo char-
acterizations of Grünbein's poetry by Grünbein himself and by others. Moreover,
Grünbein theorizes the means by which those details are preserved against the flux

---

[70] Grünbein, "Schlaflos in Rom," 334. All translations mine. Subsequent citations in text as ("Schlaflos in Rom," [page number]).

of time as inherent to the forms and structures of language. Latin, in his assessment, possesses particular capacities of preservation, and its forms underscore its continued fascination:

> Latin fascinates lovers of language up to the present day. It seems as if we had here a lingua universalis, to which the lyric meters are so intrinsic that they emerged merely out of the self-contemplation of the language. The meters formed the flexible scaly armor that held the eloquent [*redegewandt*] bodies turned in speech [*in die Rede gewandten*] together, with their contradictory passions.[71]

Meter holds the conflicting drives of poetic speech together, and part of Grünbein's attraction to Latin and to ancient meters is the necessary relation between the shape of language and the shape of verse, which creates a kind of universality.[72] Crucially, this universality derives from a particular engagement with time; Grünbein opposes the "timeless, eternal, eschatological single word" fetishized by poetry and philosophy to his practice of "entering, albeit hesitatingly, once more into the temporal order of speaking."[73] He adds, "the poem, for me, is a structure that allows a temporal orientation in different layers [*Schichten*]."[74] Meter plays a central role in this ordering, both in antiquity and for "we moderns."[75] The varying meters and strophe forms in "Aporia Augustinus" thus appear as strategies for layering multiple, potentially conflicting temporalities, images, and investigations.[76]

Shaping Syllables, Shaping Time

Poetry's handling—shaping, organizing, layering—of time likewise remains central to Grünbein's considerations of modern poets and his own poetry. He articulates poetry's capacity to orient human subjects *in* time *through* meter most clearly in a speech on literature and music, "Accented Time."[77] In both English and German ("Betonte Zeit"), the title uses terms shared by music and metrical theory, and Grünbein begins by reflecting on the similarities and differences between

---

[71] Grünbein, "Zwischen Antike und X," *Text + Kritik* 153 (2002): 68–71, 69. (Between Antiquity and X. All translations mine.)

[72] Grünbein, "Zwischen Antike und X," 69.

[73] Durs Grünbein and Heinz-Norbert Jocks, *Durs Grünbein im Gespräch mit Heinz-Norbert Jocks* (Köln: DuMont Buchverlag, 2001), 44.

[74] Grünbein and Jocks, *Gespräch*, 44.

[75] Grünbein and Jocks, *Gespräch*, 67.

[76] Olaf Krämer describes the layering of temporalities through rhythm and meter as productive use of "discrepancy between different temporal orders and rhythms" (Krämer, "Ich und Welt," 366).

[77] Durs Grünbein, "Accented Time," in Eskin , *The Bars of Atlantis. Selected Essays*, trans. Andrew Shields (New York: Farrar, Straus and Giroux, 2010), 116–31. Subsequent citations in text as ("Accented Time," [page number]).

music and poetry. In particular, the two share the centrality of sound, and the fact that "the perception of sound always precedes the quest for meaning" ("Accented Time," 118). But Grünbein enters an argument for the less spectacular methods of poetry against modern "overstimulation" by music, photography, and film; conditioned by these more overwhelming art forms, "most people find a plain epigram, a haiku, a line by Hölderlin so feeble and bland, so unspectacular" ("Accented Time," 123). Note that Grünbein refers, in haiku and epigram, specifically to highly regulated syllabic forms; he makes the contrast between meter and spectacle even stronger in the next sentence: "Whoever expects the art to overwhelm him externally with the force of thunder, whoever prefers the brutal methods of cinema-cum-Wagner to the modest amphibrach, will never get his money's worth from poetry. For such a person, every metrical foot is lame" ("Accented Time," 123).[78] Using the canonical metaphor of prosody as gait, Grünbein uses meter as a stand-in for poetry as such, as opposed to music.

Although the two share a "groundedness in time" ("Accented Time," 123), poetry, per Grünbein, remains more honest about its own temporality and finitude: "the fact ... that a structure of words is far more likely [than music] to remain true to human mortality and not to bury it under a flood of sound is certainly not the worst of poetry's characteristics" ("Accented Time," 126). Both poetry and music, however, "are about transforming neutral time—be it physical, historical, geological, or even, more generally, planetary—into shaped, individualized time, into the discontinuum of *accented time*" ("Accented Time," 127). Grünbein describes the capacity of metrical organization to translate time into a human measure or scale:

> In poetry, too, intervals (here understood as the distance between successively sounding syllables) determine the relationship to time. As time—infinite, manifold, and sweeping—increasingly inundates the individual, what can the poem do but break it down into endless moments? Time cannot be grasped or negotiated with, but it can be given accents. If its measure cannot be taken, it can at least be translated into our measure.
>
> ("Accented Time," 126)

In this passage, poetry's material-acoustic features appear in specifically metrical terms, as the "distance between successively sounding syllables," which Grünbein analogizes to pitch-based temporal relations in music by way of the term "intervals."

---

[78] Like his eighteenth—and nineteenth—century counterparts, Grünbein uses an ableist characterization of mobility difference as metaphorical deficit; curiously, he shifts the location of that deficit (here, incompetence) from the poet (think of Gottsched's complaints about "limping hexameter") to the hearer (whose expectation of the spectacular makes the metrical foot "lame").

Here, instead of imagining time etched into brain physiology, Grünbein claims that metrical organization coordinates infinite time to human measures:

> And few measures, discounting the measurements of physics, are better designed for such work than the measures of verse. They provide us with the modest norm that we, as individuals aware of our finitude, can hold up to the supreme measures of time. Allowing ourselves to be guided by the modulations of our voice and vouchsafing our entire spiritual existence to it, we transform time into a transparent fabric of stressed and unstressed moments.
>
> ("Accented Time," 126)

Despite the acknowledgment that the "measures of physics" might also be suited to the translation of time into a human scale, in this passage the "measures of verse" mediate between the finitude of the individual and "the supreme measures of time." Meter becomes a figure for the organization of time as such. In the "successively sounding syllables" that become "a transparent fabric of stressed and unstressed moments," the prosodic-phonological features (stressed and unstressed syllables) of German serve as the differentiation and segmentation of time across "our entire spiritual existence." Paradoxically, the modesty of metrical norms and transience enables the momentary suspension of human finitude: "Poems are pauses in dying, at least on paper" ("Accented Time," 126).[79] The finite measures of meter enable the layering and simultaneity of past and present, which poetry combines with semantic meaning to become "a memento suspended over the abyss of existence" in which "for the duration of a few breaths, the brain defies its own transience" ("Accented Time," 127). Any defiance of transience is necessarily temporary; permanent suspension of temporal decay would aim at the "timeless, eternal, eschatological single word" that Grünbein rejects in favor of risking speaking in time.[80]

I turn to Grünbein's essays on several modern German authors to add detail to his account of how meter and rhythm become means of resistance to the meaningless flow of time.[81] In remarks on Friedrich Nietzsche and Rainer Maria Rilke, among others, Grünbein emphasizes the materiality, even plasticity of language, which, he contends, these authors make uniquely palpable—as corporeally tangible as the physical body. Grünbein asserts that Nietzsche "knew all there was to

---

[79] Anna Dabrowska notes that poetry and music, per Grünbein, share the capacity to escape transience; she notes Grünbein's "admiration of the magical force of rhythm." (Anna Dabrowska, "Die Dichtung von Durs Grünbein und die Musik," in *Authentiziät und Polyphonie. Beiträge zur deutschen und polnischen Lyrik seit 1945. Für Gerhard R. Kaiser zum fünfundsechzigsten Geburtstag*, ed. Jan Volker Röhnhart [Heidelberg: Winter, 2006], 225–36, 226).

[80] Grünbein and Jocks, *Gespräch*, 44.

[81] Hinrich Ahrend notes that Grünbein's essays from the late 1990s and early 2000s continue the tendency to work out Grünbein's poetic positions by way of engagement with other authors (Ahrend, *Tanz zwischen sämtlichen Stühlen*, 145).

know—since Goethe and Schopenhauer, Hölderlin, Kleist, and Heine—about the style, syntax, rhythm, and tempo of linguistic expression."[82] Grünbein's admiration for Nietzsche's ability to use lineation, alliteration, repetition, and punctuation to evoke a particular voice eventually brings Nietzsche's prose close to poetry, and leads Grünbein to a definition of poetry that highlights "the concentration on what is essential, perception according to rhythm and measure" ("The Thinker's Voice," 239). Grünbein notes "by the way, one of the best justifications for meter in verse comes from Nietzsche. He calls it 'dancing in chains' and suggests that there might possibly be techniques to help one to reach beyond himself through a discipline of expression" ("The Thinker's Voice," 241)· Nietzsche's description of verse as "dancing in chains" occurs in the and is the title of the 140th aphorism in the second book of *Human, All Too Human*, where Nietzsche theorizes the productivity of poetic constraint;[83] for Grünbein, verse disciplines expression and thus helps reach beyond the barriers of the individual.

Indeed, Grünbein describes the emergence of poetic genres—defined in part by their metrical forms—as responses to the status of poets as "exiles within society."[84] Varying poets use varying strategies "to rely on themselves for guidance" ("The Poem and Its Secret," 86) and thus create different forms and genres:

> One poet polished his tender, bucolic verse for so long he ended up inventing his own meter. Another wrote noble hymns to the winners at the Olympic Games because athletic male bodies filled his nights with wet dreams. And yet another worked off his desire for the obscene in bawdy comedies. Thus were the meters created—asclepiad, sapphic, alcaic, amphibrach, iambus, trochee, anapest. Thus did the genres emerge, competing with each whenever they could.
>
> ("The Poem and Its Secret," 86)

The combination of poetry and eroticism continues from "Aporie Augustinus," this time linked to the praise of (male) athletic bodies and the raunchy love plots of comedy. The passage does not give any detailed discussion of genre functions or the different possibilities of each meter; quite in contrast to the genre poetics of classical antiquity (and parts of modern German classicism), meter here is a matter of individual reflection and self-reflexivity. Grünbein continues playing his central themes of bodily materiality (here in eroticism), memory (as the poets "recollect

---

[82] Durs Grünbein, "The Thinker's Voice," in Eskin, *The Bars of Atlantis. Selected Essays*, trans. John Crutchfield, 228–45, here 230. Grünbein's attention to Nietzsche is partly a matter of the occasion: his acceptance of the Friedrich Nietzsche Literature Prize in 2004. Subsequent citations in text as ("The Thinker's Voice," [page number]).

[83] See Chapter 4, Section 4.3, "Between philology as science and *The Gay Science* (1873–1887)."

[84] Durs Grünbein, "The Poem and Its Secret," in Eskin, *The Bars of Atlantis*, trans. Andrew Shields, 82–91, 85. The German is in Durs Grünbein, "Das Gedicht und sein Geheimnis," in *Gedicht und Geheimnis. Aufsätze 1990–2006*, (Frankfurt a.M.: Suhrkamp Verlag, 2007), 84–95. Subsequent citations in text as ("The Poem and Its Secret," [page number]).

themselves"), and the temporality of meter off of one another as he ranges across an exceptional breadth of interlocutors and predecessors.

Grünbein admires Rainer Maria Rilke's meters in particular, noting that Rilke is "utterly undervalued"[85] and pointing out that Rilke shares with Nietzsche an usually robust sense of poetry's bodily efficacy: "Throughout his life, and notwithstanding the very few exceptions (including the *Duino Elegies*), Rilke's conception of poetry was identical to that of Nietzsche. Poetry is a kind of a rhythmical tick tock."[86] In Rilke, this efficacy comes from what Grünbein calls "a mimetic smoothness that borders on the corporeal," arousing a "eurhythmic [pull] (or alternatively a knee-jerk reaction), [an agreement of synchronous resonances]" ("A Little Blue Girl," 211, translation modified in brackets). The degree to which Rilke's verse fits and follows movements of the body creates its effects in the hearer's body, in a collapsing of production and reception. In terms that recall Klopstock's focus on movement (*Bewegung*) and verse as dance (see Chapter 2), Grünbein describes Rilke's work as a "compendium" of "movement sketches transposed into language" with "choreography, the structuring measure" as its primary poetic technique ("A Little Blue Girl," 211). As both Grünbein and Rilke know, these "sketches of movement" are not always or only graceful choreography but also involuntary creaturely shivers and twitches, which they realize mimetically in poetic form.

If meter correlates with the movements of the body, its underscoring by rhyme in the great majority of Rilke's poems ties the choreography of meter to time made plastic and palpable: "Rhyme is a chunk of time made comprehensible [*greifbar*], and therein lay for eons its necessity, until one day we changed our minds. It's still unclear whether this was done out of idleness or anarchy, for reasons aesthetic or sociological" ("A Little Blue Girl," 224). Grünbein himself, of course, is amongst those who eschew rhyme in much of his poetry, but his description of its effectiveness echoes the assertions about meter from Augustine that make their way into "Aporia Augustinus." Moreover, rhyme aids in the experience of time that the poem puzzles over: "Every rhyme is, in its own fashion, limited—a quality, by the way, it shares with time, which we mortals experience only as tightly rationed, and not with space" ("A Little Blue Girl," 224). The centrality of temporality for poetry in Grünbein's view makes meter and rhyme—which often serves to underscore meter as it recurs more obviously than metrical patterns—crucial to his projects of (re)shaping time, layering voices, and balancing conflicting views and voices.

---

[85] Grünbein and Heinrichs, *Gespräch*, 57.

[86] Durs Grünbein, "A Little Blue Girl," in *The Bars of Atlantis. Selected Essays*, trans. John Crutchfield, 209–27, 224. (German: Durs Grünbein, "Ein kleines blaues Mädchen," in *Gedicht und Geheimnis*, 135–54.) The passage continues by noting Nietzsche's ambivalence about meter's bodily efficacy: "The philosopher spoke of a magical serpent and conjured up the terrible image of something that slowly constricts itself" (ibid.).

6.3 Meter, Materialism, and Metaphysics: *Descartes' Devil* and *On Snow*

In work on Descartes from the years between 2000 and 2010, Grünbein applies his poetic project of polyphony and multivocal conflict to perhaps the central question of modern philosophy (and, he will argue, poetry): what kind of subjectivity do humans possess, and how is it known and expressed in language? In particular, do human beings possess a mind in a body, or is "mind" a byproduct of bodily (brain electrical/chemical) activity? Grünbein poses this debate as a conflict between contemporary neuroscience and rationalist philosophy, both of which he then elaborates as more nuanced and more similar than their opponents acknowledge. As Grünbein discusses these questions with increasing directness in his essays ("meditations") on Descartes, he writes less and less about the shaping and organizing of time in and as poetic form. But his verse novel *Vom Schnee, oder Descartes in Deutschland* (2003, *On Snow, or Descartes in Germany*) exemplifies the way metrical practice can layer temporalities, voices, and positions. It also takes overlaps, dialogues, and differences between historical periods and their narration as one of its themes. To close this chapter, I first discuss the debates about subjectivity in Grünbein's Descartes essays—where Grünbein provides the clearest analysis of the kind of subjectivity and language use he hopes poetry can achieve. I then turn to detailed metrical consideration of *Vom Schnee* to show how poetic meter can go beyond the essayistic unfolding of debates about subjectivity because of meter's shaping of and by time, language, culture, history, and the body.

Descartes' Devil

Grünbein articulates his interest in Descartes and the basis of Cartesian thinking for a theory of poetry in *Der cartesische Taucher. Drei Meditationen* (*Descartes' Devil: Three Meditations*), published in 2008. The essays offer a useful summation of the themes Grünbein values in Descartes; at the same time, their arguments call attention to moments in *Vom Schnee* where Grünbein's use of poetic forms and, in particular, verse practice can exploit oppositions and preserve paradoxes that the essays later smooth over in attractive and stylized prose. In *Descartes' Devil*, Grünbein discovers in Descartes a productive point of entry into his own central questions of poetry, the metaphysical subject, the material body, and how they interact.[87] As so often, Grünbein finds his own questions addressed by an interlocutor, using Descartes' life and works to think through "deadlock between two

---

[87] Christoph auf der Horst, "Durs Grünbein, Descartes und die Neurologie: Kennt Grünbeins Psychopoetik einen *embodied cognition*-Ansatz?," in auf der Horst and Seidler, *Bildlichkeit im Werk Durs Grünbeins*, 190.

positions"—specifically dualist versus non-dualist understandings of body, mind, and brain—that Grünbein identifies as his own particular poetic approach.[88] Following late-twentieth-century reconsiderations of Descartes, Grünbein emphasizes the ambivalences in Descartes' dualist philosophy, in addition to Descartes' interest in the natural sciences as practices of careful observation and the emergence of his method from dreams and visions.[89] In Descartes, Grünbein finds a theory of poetry that is at once material and metaphysical, imagistic and theoretical, in part because the baroque world Descartes inhabited was not yet marked by any disciplinary separation between the study of the human and the study of nature.[90] Consequently, Grünbein's engagement with Descartes includes and recasts neuroscience, medicine, and the natural sciences. In taking Descartes as the "hero" of his projects, Grünbein works to show the one-sidedness of both dualism (in which body and mind are separate) and contemporary monism (in which mind reduces to matter and consciousness is an accident of brain reflexes).[91]

Perhaps most importantly for Grünbein, Descartes' theory of poetic production in particular challenges any absolute body-mind dualism: Descartes advances an anthropological theory of poetry as an expression of the arousal of animal spirits as "mediators" between body and soul.[92] Grünbein articulates his search for a Cartesian poetics early in the first "meditation": "The question at the heart of these meditations is that of the connection between the Cartesian revolution and the paradoxes and problems of modern poetry."[93] This revolution, which made the human being saying "I think" the center of the philosophical universe (*Descartes' Devil*, 23), turns out to have significant poetic consequences on Grünbein's account. Grünbein touches briefly on the theme of temporality as he gives a definition of "modernity" as "a phenomenon bespeaking the contemporaneity of the non-contemporaneous, a point of intersection of many disconnected

---

[88] Grünbein and Heinrichs, *Gespräch*, 57.

[89] See e.g. Judith Ryan's remark that Grünbein enters into a "dialogue with Descartes about the value and meaning of natural science and also about dualism and monism" (Judith Ryan, "Spurlose Frühe. Durs Grünbeins *Vom Schnee* und das Problem der Wende," in *Weiterschreiben. Zur DDR-Literatur nach dem Ende der DDR*, eds. Holger Helbig and Katrin Felsner [Berlin: Akademie Verlag, 2007], 164) and Bernadette Malinowski and Gert-Ludwig Ingold's claim that what fascinates Grünbein is that Descartes' philosophy, "that claims it has erected the firm foundations of all certain scientific knowledge," emerges from "the spirit it itself denies: the spirit of the visionary, dreamlike, imaginary-imagistic, poetic" (Bernadette Malinowski and Gert-Ludwig Ingold, "'... im andern dupliziert.' Zur Rezeption cartesischer Erkenntnistheorie und Naturwissenschaft in Durs Grünbeins *Vom Schnee oder Descartes in Deutschland*," in *Schreiben am Schnittpunkt*, 271–306, here, 274).

[90] Walter Erhart, "Literaturwissenschaft und Physik. Aus Anlass von Durs Grünbeins *Vom Schnee oder Descartes in Deutschland*," in *Literaturwissenschaft—interdisziplinär*, eds. Lothar van Laak and Katja Malsch (Heidelberg: Synchron, 2010), 119.

[91] See Urs Büttner, "Erkenntnisse des Schnees. Grünbeins cartesische Anthropologie und Ästhetik," in auf der Horst and Seidler, *Bildlichkeit im Werk Durs Grünbeins*, 174.

[92] Tanja van Hoorn, "'Keine Tiergeister im Schnee.' Grünbeins Descartes Idee," *Zeitschrift für Germanistik* 21, no. 2 (2011), 292.

[93] Durs Grünbein, *Descartes' Devil. Three Meditations*, ed. Michael Eskin, trans. Anthea Bell (New York: Upper West Side Philosophers, Inc, 2010), 23. Subsequent citations in text as (*Descartes' Devil*, [page number]).

historical progressions and evolutionary leaps that have nothing in common but the one effect of shooting beyond the events that occasioned them into a supra-temporal sphere" (*Descartes' Devil*, 15). The multiple simultaneous temporalities that puzzled the speaker of "Aporia Augustinus" and that called for the full reper-toire of metrical practice and strategies in Grünbein's earlier essays are now packed into a half-sentence of definition; their unruliness and unfolding will become central to *On Snow* in a way that *Descartes' Devil* glosses over.

In order to claim Descartes as the initiator of an anthropological poetics that makes the body-mind dualism productive by both activating it and challenging it, Grünbein must defend the philosopher from the charge of being a narrow rationalist. He appeals to recent Descartes scholarship and to arguments from the philosophy of language that draw on more-or-less-contemporary neuroscience to combat this criticism in Descartes and in early rationalist philosophy as a whole, noting "not only in the work of Descartes' successors—great thinkers such as Arnold Geulincx, Nicolas Malebranche, and Leibniz—do we find many an in-between nuance and many a sign of a healthy both/and approach" (*Descartes' Devil*, 97).[94] Grünbein finds evidence for Descartes' "healthy both/and approach" in the philosopher's other projects, for instance the treatise on meteors ("deal-ing with everything that moved around the earth at a certain distance from it, shone brightly, or loomed close in the form of vapors ... and complemented by an almost painfully meticulous description of the nature of salt, the causes of winds, and the shapes of snowflakes" [*Descartes' Devil*, 51]) and his interest in anatomy and dissection as well as poetry and painting. Grünbein's attention to Descartes' natural-scientific projects finds a continuity between philosophical metaphysics and physics, optics, and medicine, making Descartes a precursor of Grünbein's own combinations of poetry and the material body and material world. Since meter is perceived and becomes intelligible in the body but produced and analyzed in cultural-historical and poetic contexts, a conception of subjectivity as neither fully dualist nor fully non-dualist opens the possibility that meter might be espe-cially equipped to represent or perform the paradoxes of that subjectivity—even as Grünbein does not address this possibility directly.

Instead, he argues that poets, philosophers, and scientists cannot simply aban-don the problem of the relation between body and mind. Using the disagreements between contemporary neuroscientists such as Antonio Damasio and Benjamin Libet, Grünbein advances a view of Descartes as a qualified dualist attuned to the interactions between "psyche and physis."[95] He suggests that the monist position

---

[94] On Grünbein's dismantling of both natural-scientific and traditional philosophical accounts of Descartes as a narrow rationalist, see auf der Horst, "Durs Grünbein, Descartes und die Neurologie," 195–6.

[95] auf der Horst, "Durs Grünbein, Descartes und die Neurologie," 194, 198.

asserting the "unity of matter" passes as good form but is held in bad faith, as we continue to act like dualists "in psychology and everyday life" (*Descartes' Devil*, 70). Some qualified version of mind-body dualism is, per Grünbein, not only more plausible than monism (which can explain "why rosebuds, calcareous sponges, crocodiles, and anthropoid apes evolve from [matter], but not what suddenly produces a creature that can paint self-portraits and compose polyphonic motets" [*Descartes' Devil*, 70]) but "rooted deep within language" (*Descartes' Devil*, 97) and poetically productive. Grünbein shows us how poetic practice—I argue, metrical practice in particular because of the peculiarities of meter—can show us something about what it means to be the sort of anthropoid ape that produces self-portraits and motets.

Grünbein foregrounds the way language pushes us toward dualism, and thus focuses several moments of his inquiry on the linguistic or grammatical gestures of Descartes' philosophy: "In Descartes' work, for the first time since Plato and Augustine, thinking dares to speak in the first person singular, to say 'I' again. Descartes marks the beginning of the autobiography of the modern mind" (*Descartes' Devil*, 24).[96] For a poet, the *Discourse on Method* raises the question of the extent to which the "I" of the *cogito* depends on—is created by—language: "Since 'to think' is not an intransitive verb such as 'to rain' ..., it always already refers to an object. Moreover, it also automatically summons the grammatical subject. This means that Descartes' *I think, therefore I am* is, above all, well-oiled grammar" (*Descartes' Devil*, 87). Precisely the self-encounter of the I in language that occurs in the *Discourse* brings the philosophical "I" and the poetic "I" together: "The poetic 'I,' whose element, if anything is language. It proceeds from language, feeds on it, moves in it like a fish in water. In short, it owes to language everything it will ever be. There is no poetic 'I' outside language" (*Descartes' Devil*, 87). Both, for Grünbein, are constitutive of a more-or-less dualist subjectivity with doubts about its own dualism on which both poetry and philosophy depend. In *Vom Schnee* Grünbein depicts the emergence of this subject in the genesis of the *Discourse*.

Grünbein also notes differences between the poetic and philosophical subjectivities:

[96] *Pace* Grünbein's assertion about "the modern mind" in general, this philosophical subject and its quandaries emerge from a particular (white, male, upper-middle class) position, as philosophers such as Charles W. Mills, Arnold Farr, and Paul Mecheril have pointed out from a Black critical perspective. Grünbein's insistence on Descartes' particular interests and activities that go beyond the purely rationalist detached philosophical subject is in fact compatible with efforts to de-universalize the subject. See Charles W. Mills, *Blackness Visible: Essays on Philosophy and Race* (Ithaca, NY: Cornell University Press, 1998), Arnold Farr, "Wie *Weiß*sein sichtbar wird. Aufklärungsrassismus und die Struktur eines rassifizierten Bewusstseins," in *Mythen, Masken und Subjekte. Kritische Weißseinsforschung in Deutschland*, eds. Maureen Maisha Eggers et al. (Münster: Unrast Verlag, 2005), 40–55, and Paul Mecheril, "Der doppelte Mangel, der das Schwarze Subjekt hervorbringt," in Eggers et al. *Mythen, Masken und Subjekte. Kritische Weißseinsforschung in Deutschland*, 73–9.

While the cognitive "I" is born of the mastery of the world, emerging from the methodical processes of collecting, calculating, measuring, and structuring reality, the poetic "I" is completely immersed in intuition ... The poetic "I" could thus be described as a global positioning system that smuggles mind into verse, while the senses are busy perceiving the world. In the act of perception, however, both modes of subjectivity are as close as identical twins.

(Descartes' Devil, 87)

In his history of the lyric I (beginning in Pharaonic Egypt), Grünbein explicitly links subjectivity and verse practice, tracking the formal behavior of the lyric I as analogous to the struggles of the subject: "In Descartes' time, for instance, [the lyric I] barricades itself behind pompous metrical forms, oscillating between melancholy, ardent religiosity, and frivolity" (*Descartes' Devil*, 88), while in the era of Baudelaire and Mallarmé, "we see a largely disintegrated poetic 'I,' permanently hidden among the intricate harmonies of free-floating syllables. In its most ethereal moments, it seems to articulate the unconscious of language itself" (*Descartes' Devil*, 89). The particular moment of the baroque, with its combination of metaphysical poetry and materialist philosophy (*Descartes' Devil*, 12) is ideally suited to the conflict between mind and material. Instead of being "disintegrated" as in the free verse and calligrams of Mallarmé, the baroque poetic I with all its contradictions is gathered into elaborate verse forms—like the alexandrines Grünbein deploys in *Vom Schnee*.

Descartes' letters to Elisabeth of Bohemia begin, in Grünbein's reading, to offer an "anthropologically-based poetics" that links the lyric I to the body because the impulse to write poetry comes from the influence of the animal spirits on the brain: "And I think that the humor for making verses proceeds from a strong agitation of the animal spirits, which cannot but entirely confuse the imagination of those who do not possess a well-ordered brain, while merely slightly exciting those who are strong and disposing them toward poetry" (cited *Descartes' Devil*, 15). According to Grünbein, this quotation is the "seed for a whole theory of the imagination based on the physiology of the brain" (*Descartes' Devil*, 17), a merging of mental phenomena (imagination) and brain activity (excitation). Descartes thus "pav[es] the way for a for an anthropologically-based poetics" (*Descartes' Devil*, 15) that encompasses both monism and dualism, metaphysics, and materialism in a relation where mind and brain are both separate and connected.

For Grünbein, using the toy called Descartes' Devil both as his title and as his leading metaphor for the relation between the "I" and the brain, poetry shows that

the body is the mind's field of expressivity, not its cage. Something haunts its interior, be it the much feared ghost in the machine: a stubborn creature, for sure, that plays on the body as if on a musical instrument. Descartes' jumping devil in the bottle plays "I" in me and uses my brain for its ideas. But I will probably never catch it, for the body is always there, thrusting itself into the foreground with all its might. They are inseparable, yet never identical, whichever way you look at it.

(*Descartes' Devil*, 101)

This is a much more nuanced picture of the relation between brain, mind, and body than the simple equation of brain effects with bodily experience in Grünbein's earlier poetics. Poetry, here, has the ability to probe and explore this inseparable non-identity using the resources of poetic form, or, as Grünbein asks toward the end of the essay, "Must one become an artist to get one's money's worth with this dualism?" (*Descartes' Devil*, 101). This dualism—which, it is important to note, does not conform to the narrowly rationalist picture of Descartes because it insists on the mutual influencing of body and mind—may well prove productive for poetry. What I show in what follows is that poetry proves capable of displaying both ghost and machine—metrical practice, indeed, becomes a figure for their inseparable non-identity.

On Snow

Vom Schnee oder Descartes in Deutschland (*On Snow, or Descartes in Germany*) marks Grünbein's first extended foray into Cartesian territory; unlike the "meditations" published five years later, *Vom Schnee* maintains the attention to role played by time and memory in the constitution of any poetic or philosophical subject. Grünbein applies multiple genre designations and descriptions to his text: "a narrative poem," "a verse novella," "a work of lyrical stereoscopy" (because "the overlapping between different layers of thought should create a spatial effect in the reader's head"), "a picture puzzle," "thought music," "philosophical conversation," "or—nothing more than a snow-ball fight in verse."[97] As I noted above, *Vom Schnee* shares numerous themes with *Descartes' Devil*—in particular attention to Descartes' biography and his natural-scientific as well as philosophical pursuits. But at the same time the poem preserves and explores "extreme positions in the critique of knowledge, while the essay, as a published lecture on poetics, seeks a balance" between those extreme positions.[98] I argue that Grünbein's verse practice enables not only the exploration of extremes but also a complex layering of temporalities, fictional and non-fictional figures or characters, and voices in a single text.[99] *Vom Schnee* thus brings together the questions of time, memory, and

---

[97] Durs Grünbein, "Vom Schnee," *Zeitschrift für Germanistik* 21, no. 2 (2011): 256, my translations.
[98] Büttner, "Erkenntnisse des Schnees," 175.
[99] Carlos Spoerhase argues that *On Snow* shows how poetic anachrony involves a "highly intricate 'dialectic' of historical anchoring and historical unmooring" (Spoerhase, "Über die Grenzen der Geschichtslyrik: Historischer Anachronismus und ästhetische Anachronie in Durs Grünbein's Werk, am Beispiel seiner Arbeiten über Descartes," *Zeitschrift für Germanistik* 21, no. 2 [2011], 276).

subjectivity that drifted apart in *Descartes' Devil*; in the poem, it is clear that both dualist and monist views of subjectivity share the challenge of maintaining fragile coherence of the "I" across time and in the overwhelming flood of information and sense experience. Because meter shapes time and creates coherence without insisting on noncontradiction, it makes such coherence of self and experience possible in poetic language, at least for the space of a poem.

At least apparently, the bulk of the poem (thirty-one of forty-two numbered sections; much of the scholarship refers to these as "Cantos," but Grünbein does not) takes place in the winter of 1619, during which Descartes was confined by snow to winter quarters in what is now Bavaria and during which he later claimed to have had the experience of insight and vocation that gave rise to the cogito and the *Meditations on the First Philosophy*. Within that outline, however, the poem anticipates Descartes' investigations on optics, reflects on the problem of dualism and Elisabeth of Bohemia's objections to Descartes' position, ponders the relation between animals and humans, and hints at Descartes' investigations of emotion.[100] The final ten sections describe the room after Descartes' departure, the end of the Thirty Years' War, Descartes' decision to move to Sweden at the request of Queen Christina, and his death in the winter of 1650. Although the poem repeatedly gestures toward Descartes' works, it is anything but a "versified philosophical treatise"; instead, Grünbein restores Descartes' "liveliness and corporeality," as he repeatedly ties Descartes' works to moments of experience rather than ratiocination.[101]

These hints, along with panorama-like commentary on the Thirty Years' War, baroque culture, other scientists, and Dutch painting,[102] occur through Grünbein's use of and confusion between not only a narrator figure who blurs the distinctions between narrator, character, and author, but other characters or voices who explicitly announce their own fictionality. After a color print of Anthonis van Dyck's *Sketch of a Burning Hut*, a paragraph from the *Discourse on* Method translated into German, and an epigraph from Horace (*"Dissolve frigus ... "*), the confusion over speaker and addressee begins in the first verse lines: with no quotation marks or identifying features, a speaker addresses Descartes: "Monsieur, wacht auf! Es hat geschneit die ganze Nacht." (Monsieur, wake up. It has snowed all night.)[103] The

[100] Ryan, "Spurlose Frühe," 172.
[101] Wilhelm Große, "Descartes/Grünbein oder Das Dreieck aus Philosophie, naturwissenschaftlichem Denken und Literaturpoesie. Anmerkungen zu Durs Grünbein's *Vom Schnee oder Descartes in Deutschland*," *Literatur im Unterricht* 6, no. 5 (2005): 222. See also Barbara Naumann's remark that "In the poem, at least, Cartesian rationality is depicted as an open process. In the 'I think' moments of embodiment, of confusion and disorientation come through against the intentions of its assertions" (Barbara Naumann, "Gewalt der Sprache. Nietzsches Descartes-Kritik, Grünbein's Descartes," in *Die Literatur der Literaturtheorie*, ed. Boris Previšić [Bern: Peter Lang, 2010], 133–144).
[102] Irmer, "Durs Grünbein," 720.
[103] Durs Grünbein, *Vom Schnee, oder Descartes in Deutschland* (Suhrkamp, 2003) . In what follows I cite the German text by section or number followed by line number within the section, e.g. 1.1) All translations are mine.

"you" form used is the archaic formal "Ihr"; given the formal address, by the next section the speaker seems to be revealed as Descartes' servant, Gillot. In the second section, a speaker introduced using quotation marks addresses Gillot directly: "'Gillot, bist dus?'" (Gillot, is that you? 2.1). But by the fifth section it becomes clear that the poem includes all of a narrator, Descartes, Gillot, and a maid from next door, Marie, with whom Gillot appears to carry on an affair; all of these figures eventually appear to speak in the first person both with and without marking by quotation marks, italics, and other punctuation.

Moreover, the poem explicitly introduces questions of reality and fictionality. Section 18, titled "Solitude" begins "In Wirklichkeit ... war er allein" (In reality ... he was alone, 18.1, suspension points in original). It thus suggests that Gillot is a figment of Descartes' imagination or a mask for Grünbein's narratorial/authorial voice. In that case, it becomes impossible to say who has an affair with "Marie"—who, however, announces point-blank in the last section of the first part, "Es gab mich nie. Ich bin von Kopf bis Fuß erfunden./ Man kennt nur ihn. Von mir schweigt jede Chronik" (31.51–2).[104] As Michael Eskin remarks, "What Grünbein does is play history and fiction, life and literature off against each other to produce a veritable charade of historical-biographical displacement and onomastic casting in which the reader loses his bearings as if in a hall of mirrors."[105] This fluidity between author, characters, and narrator, history and fiction likewise blurs the boundaries between temporal epochs, that is, between the winter of 1619–20, the various publication dates of Descartes' works, the Peace of Westphalia in 1648 (section 34 is titled "Der Westfälische Frieden"), and Grünbein's post-modern poetic world and contemporary culture around 2003.[106] All of these strategies exemplify Grünbein's persistent assertion that poetry engages paradigmatically with temporality and history, bringing different voices and times into contact without universalizing or absolutizing them.

What holds all of this—voices, figures, times, topics—together in *Vom Schnee* is, as the title suggests, snow. The first lines announce the newly fallen snow and the

---

[104] "I never existed. I am invented from head to foot./ People only know him. Every history is silent about me." On one hand, Marie's stubborn insistence on her fictionality is legible as critique of class and gender as determining who can be the protagonists of poetry, philosophy, and history (Descartes not Gillot; Descartes not Marie). On the other hand, Marie only speaks for herself in a few lines, and her contribution to the story is as love object and sexual being—that is, the roles to which women are typically relegated in white male European narratives. (In later sections, the virginal princess Elisabeth who so discomfits Descartes rounds out the virgin/whore dichotomy.) Overall, Grünbein's focus on eroticism hovers uneasily between insistence on the importance of embodiment and sense experience, generalized provocation to intellectual decorum, and the objectification of women.

[105] Michael Eskin, "Descartes of Metaphor. On Durs Grünbeins 'Vom Schnee,'" in *Schaltstelle. Neue Deutsche Lyrik im Dialog*, ed. Karen Leeder (Amsterdam: Rodopi, 2007), 163–79, here 168.

[106] Große notes this point (Große, "Descartes/Grünbein," 226); Steffen Martus and Claudia Benthien mention the "suspicion" this raises that "Grünbein means us and then again does not mean us, when he speaks of Descartes and his time. This is especially the case when the topic is general mentality—and cultural-historical dispositions" Steffen Martus and Claudia Benthien, "Schnee von gestern—Schnee von heute: Die 'Wiederkehr der Frühen Neuzeit' bei Durs Grünbein," *Zeitschrift für Germanistik* 21, no. 2 (2011): 241–55, 248.

unidentifiable speaker calls attention to the empty white surface as a tabula rasa, a field for geometric abstraction (say, a Cartesian plane), and a blank paper: "Von Frost geputzt der Zeichentisch—ein idealer Boden/ Für den *Discours*, Monsieur. Allez! Für die Methode" (1.59–60).[107] Snow becomes the "material pre-condition for the insight into anthropology and aesthetics that Grünbein lets his Descartes achieve,"[108] clearing the ground for ratiocination and abstracted, undisturbed perception. The poem analogizes "the white ground, the white bed, and the white sheet of paper" as "the sites that fill up with objects, out of which a world as object and an I as a perceiving world-constituting instance emerges."[109] But the later sections also call into question the new beginning of 1619, as Grünbein returns to the dreams about poetry and writing that are suppressed in the *Discours*;[110] sometimes the snow seems to baffle reason and disrupt perception,[111] as when Descartes and Gillot walk for an afternoon and become disoriented (sections 9–15). The material qualities of snow and snow as material are also important: Descartes draws an analogy between snow and the "materie subtile" whose existence he posited as mediating between mind and body,[112] and as Grünbein notes in *Descartes' Devil*, Descartes was the first to observe and record the six-sided structure of snowflakes.[113]

The salient characteristics of snowflakes and snow—small, six-pointed structure that piles up over multiplicitous terrains, a material that fills in the gaps and holds different times and themes together—apply equally to Grünbein's verse practice in *Vom Schnee*. Several commentators note his use of alexandrines as appropriate to the baroque setting of the poem and to the presentation of polarities or oppositions, in keeping with the poetic counterpoint of materialism and metaphysics, rather than the essay's harmonization between them.[114] Canonically, alexandrines, as adapted from the French tradition to German, are twelve-syllable lines with alternating weak and strong syllables and a pronounced caesura. Both because of the relatively long line-length and the caesura, they are associated with complex, philosophical themes and with argumentative presentation of antitheses.[115] The

---

[107] "The drafting table cleaned by frost—an ideal ground/ For the *Discours*, Monsieur. Allez! For the method."

[108] Büttner, "Erkenntnisse des Schnees," 164.

[109] Große, "Descartes/Grünbein," 226

[110] Ryan, "Spurlose Frühe," 177.

[111] Büttner, "Erkenntnisse des Schnees," 170.

[112] Bernadette Malinowski and Gert-Ludwig Ingold, "'... im andern dupliziert.' Zur Rezeption cartesischer Erkenntnistheorie und Naturwissenschaft in Durs Grünbeins *Vom Schnee oder Descartes in Deutschland*," in *Schreiben am Schnittpunkt*, 271–306.

[113] He cites Descartes as saying "A single observation that I made of hexagonal snowflakes in the year 1635 was the origin of my treatise on the subject of snow" (Grünbein, *Descartes' Devil*, 54).

[114] See e.g. Große's remark that the six-footed alexandrine is "*the* verse of the baroque epoch" (Große, "Descartes/Grünbein," 221).

[115] See e.g. Hauke Kuhlmann and Christian Meierhofer, "Descartes à la Grünbein. Philosophiegeschichtliche und erkenntnistheoretische Implikationen von *Vom Schnee oder Descartes in Deutschland*," *Zeitschrift für Germanistik* 21, no. 2 (2011): 308–20, 317.

six strong syllables of the German alexandrine correspond, of course, to the six-sides of snow-flakes, as Descartes described them in 1635.[116] Grünbein, echoing the manifold different patterns of crystals within the six-sided unity, uses different caesura placements, irregularities, and rhyme schemes across the poem.

On the macroformal level, the poem is strongly regular: each section is numbered and has a title; each consists of seven strophes that, with only four exceptions in the entire poem, have ten lines each. Reflecting once again the combination of uniformity (the white surface that obliterates difference) and variety (the unique shapes of snowflakes), Grünbein deploys three primary rhyme schemes in his ten-line strophes, then which then vary slightly:

1) unrhymed except for a final rhyming couplet (xxxxxxxxaa);
2) a pattern that divides the strophe into a set of six and a set of four lines (abcabcdede);
3) a pattern that loosely evokes *Kreuzreim* (ababcdcdee).

He frequently combines different rhyme schemes within the seven-strophe sections, a strategy that, together with variations on those schemes or combinations of them (e.g. xxxxxxabab or abbacdecde), prevent monotony despite external regularity. Rhyme here serves as a kind of flag for the interplay of regularity and difference, since the more subtle differences in metrical pattern may go unnoticed. There are, of course, multiple potential relations of rhyme to meter when both are present, such as emphasis or support, undermining, distracting, etc. Characteristically, Grünbein uses all of these in various locations; I consider the organization of rhyme as part of a metrical scheme or verse practice as a whole.

The rhyme scheme patterns also contribute to the overlapping of speakers and temporalities. The text begins in rhyme scheme 1 (xxxxxxxxaa), used by the ambiguous speaker who opens the scene, then shifts into rhyme scheme 2 (abcabcdede) when dialogue notated with quotation marks begins in the second section, "Das Murmeltier" (the groundhog; in German, "to sleep like a ground-hog" means "to sleep like a log"). But 1 reappears in the fourth strophe of section three, "Ein Kaff bei Ulm" ("A Backwater Near Ulm"), which also uses quotation marks to indicate (apparently) direct speech between Descartes and Gillot. To give an even more striking example, in the tenth section, called "Landschaft mit Zeich-ner" ("Landscape with Draughtsman"), Descartes and Gillot are depicted walking through the winter landscape; the first strophe uses rhyme scheme 2 (abcabcdede) and consists of dialogue (marked with quotation marks) between the two. The second strophe describes Descartes and Gillot externally in a voice that, with the

---

[116] Martus and Benthien note the affinity between six-footed verse and six-sided snowflakes, but it would be more accurate to describe the verse as "hexagonal" rather than "hexametric," as they do, since hexameter has six feet in Greek meters but *not* six stressed syllables (Martus and Benthien, "Schnee von gestern—Schnee von heute," 252).

introduction of a narratorial "I" in the third strophe, identifies itself as contemporary: "Ich seh sie noch. Was sind schon drei-, vierhundert Jahre?" (10.21; I see them still. What are three, four hundred years?"). As the text zooms out, but before the contemporary "I" emerges, the rhyme scheme shifts to pattern 3 (ababcdcdee); forbidding the simple separation of voices, it continues into the next strophe as the poem returns to dialogue between Gillot and Descartes.

Grünbein uses regular rhyme and meter to balance unity and multiplicity; against this background, the four exceptions to the ten-line strophe structure are strong departures, but ones that are not particularly noticeable given the volume of text in the first place. I have not found them mentioned in any of the scholarship on the poem, but I find it unlikely that they are errors/accidents on Grünbein's part; when the lines are so regularly grouped it would be hard to lose track of even one of them in a strophe. (Surely one can count to ten as many times as necessary.) Each of sections seven, nine, and thirty-three has one strophe with an extra (eleventh) line, while section twelve has a strophe with twelve lines. I take these deviations as hints or invitations to scrutinize these sections as a whole, asking whether they are anomalous in other ways. Of the four, section nine, "Winterspaziergang" (Winter's Walk), clearly uses a metrical exception to mark a semantic shift: its third strophe contains a line of forty-five periods or dots inserted at the midpoint for a total of eleven lines, with the insertion marking the point at which Descartes and Gillot leave their quarters and go into the winter landscape:

> "Und wohin gehts?" "Den Schleichweg dort zur Meierei,
> Vorbei am Friedhof, dann hinaus und Wald und Flur."
> ....
> "Gott, wieviel Schnee." (9.25–7)[117]

The section closes on a view of a distant figure moving around in the snow, perhaps a hint at an distant observer as a stand-in for Grünbein or the reader: "Was treibt ihn um, beweglich wie im Satz die Letter?" (9.65, What impels him, as movable as the letters in a sentence?, or "as movable as the letters in typesetting"). The letter-like person or figure observed—and observing—from a distance indicates a slight re-balancing introduced by metrical irregularity. The extra line marks the shift in location of the internal figures and thus a shift in the relation between the narration and what it narrates from immersion to meta-reflection.

The seventh section, "Selbstportrait als leerer Teller" ("Self-Portrait as an Empty Plate"), describes the uncanny effects of a broken mirror, both as the blank silver backing plate stares into the room and in Descartes' loss of visual confirmation of his existence. Anticipating "I think, therefore I am," the speaker—associated with

---

[117] "And where will we go? Along the back way to the butcher's/ Past the cemetery, then out to the woods and fields."/ .... / "God, what a lot of snow."

Descartes through his descriptions of his appearance—seems to comfort himself: "Ich weiß genau, ich bin. Auch wenn er mich verschluckt/ Mit Haut und Haar." (7.11–2)[118] But the next strophe, which has eleven lines, seems more unsettled by the sudden disappearance of the mirrored face; its absence initiates rumination on image, brain, and material:

> Und doch, es schmerzt. Wundherde, Eingeweide sind,
> Zahnhälse, freigelegt, kaum schauriger als dies.
> Jetzt gähnt ein Tisch, ein Teller blinkt, wo sonst die Stirn
> So unerforschlich leuchtete—mein eigenes Gesicht.
> Es ist nur Glas, scheints. Und doch droht es dir: verschwinde.
> (7.21–5)[119]

Not being able to see his face is an experience comparable with physical pain; objects, perhaps reflected in the shards of glass on the floor, take the place of human features. The strophe closes with its extra line, which asserts the shifted balance of power between material and mind or human:

> Brutal,
> Ein Zacken Glas, hält die Materie über dich Gericht
> *Sub specie aeternitatis*—aus dem Hinterhalt. (7.29–31)[120]

Matter passes a secret or unanticipated judgment, as pointed as a shard of glass, on the "you" that seems to speak to itself here. It ambushes the "I," accustomed to seeing its "Bild, die Psyche, tief verzweigt" (7.5; image, the mind, deeply branched) represented as whole by the portrait in the mirror. Moreover, the rhyme scheme (abcdabcdede') does not fit any of the main patterns and the last (extra) line only barely manages to rhyme between "Brutal" and "halt," leaving line eleven doubly unmoored.

After this destabilization—marked by the extra line that lays claim to the eternal/universal perspective—section 7 shifts as a whole. The addressee changes from an apparently self-soliloquizing "du" (you, informal) to the formal "Ihr" (you, formal) addressed from outside: "Merkt Ihr was, Philosoph?" (7.33; Do you notice something, philosopher?). By the fifth strophe, the speaker distinguishes between a "you" and a "me" separated by increasingly distant epochs: "Der Abstand wächst. Von Euch zu Euch, von Euch zu mir." (7.42, The distance grows. From you to you, from you to me.) Descartes, the philosopher, grows increasingly distant from

---

[118] "I know exactly that I am. Even if it swallows me/ Head, hair and all."

[119] "And yet it hurts. Nodules, Entrails/ Exposed roots of teeth, are hardly more dreadful than this./ Now a table gapes, a plate blinks, where normally the forehead/ Gleams so inscrutably—my own face./ It is only glass, it seems. But still it threatens you: disappear."

[120] "Brutal,/ A jagged glass, matter executes judgment over you/ *Sub specie aeternitatis*—out of an ambush."

Descartes, the living person, as well as from the narrator of "three, four hundred years" (10.21) later, for whom his subject risks becoming "auflöst ganz in Schrift" (7.69; entirely disintegrated into writing)—though whether Descartes' writings or Grünbein's remains unclear. Here, then, the metrical irregularity of the eleventh line—an unexpected lump or fissure under the snowy alexandrine regularity—marks the fracture between speakers and temporalities, in a central instance of Grünbein's use of meter as time management. Moreover, the metrical performance of a lump or gap in time is initiated by a disruption in the visual perception of the self as a coherent image in the mirror. The fracturing of subjectivity in the fracturing of glass disrupts metrical time.

The twelfth section, "Querelen" (Quarrels), makes clear that metrical divergences do not always represent temporal disruptions, because it remains within a single temporality but toggles rapidly between spatial perspectives. The section begins zoomed in on Descartes and Gillot ("Descartes" and "Gillot"), still walking in the snow and noting the rapidly encroaching evening, as the narrator measures silence in seconds, then the tempo of steps, noting that "Das Zählen gilt nicht" (12.8; Counting does not hold true, or even "counting doesn't count"). Time as a theme, nonetheless, begins the next strophe, which zooms out rapidly to a series of world-historical but small moments or actions happening at the same time ("Zur selben Zeit," 12.11): the death of the last aurochs (12.11–2), the fashion of lace collars (12.12–3), the cashing of the first check (12.14–5), etc. The third strophe, with its extra lines, seems to extend the same themes—it turns to astronomical discoveries, noting that thanks to the latest algebra, "Alles hat/ jetzt seine Ordnung, seine Formel, sein Gesetz." (12.24–5; everything now/ has its order, its formula, its law.) Turning from heavenly calculation to earthly navigation, lines 6–10 of the strophe describe the settler colonialist theft of Manhattan.[121]

The two "extra" lines, eleven and twelve of the strophe, personify history as a being moving on a path and in the oceans:

> Auf krummen Wegen, zukunftssüchtig geht, Geschichte.
> Und doch ist Land, in manchem Menschenhirn, in Sicht.
> (12.31–2)[122]

---

[121] The poem describes the theft as a purchase in terms that are themselves settler-colonialist, referring to the territory stolen from the Lenape by Dutch settlers as "ein Stück Indanerland (Manhattan) in der Neuen Welt" (A piece of Indian land [Manhattan] in the New World, 12.30). Grünbein does not disassociate the poem's speaker from its subject's European colonialist perspective, and elsewhere he exhibits a classically white German fascination with Native Americans as exoticized other that ignores the role of German settlers in colonial genocide. See e.g. his title "Der Indianer des Geistes. Bagatellen über das Leben des Philosophen Pascale" ("The Indians of the Mind/Spirit. Bagatelles on the Life of the Philosopher Pascale"), *Zeitschrift für Ideengeschichte* 2, no. 1 (2008): 69–84.

[122] On crooked paths, addicted to the future, history walks./ And yet land is in sight in some human brains.

Navigation, human cognition, and history merge in a kind of tag added to the strophe, underscored by the rhyme scheme: the first ten lines of the strophe follow pattern 3, ababcdcdee, with the final two lines tacked on at the end and rhyming with each other, ff. One might expect a perspective or narrative shift after this conclusion, but the fourth strophe echoes the second in depicting personal-impersonal acts and the state of world history: people lean on one another (12.33), cut one another's throats, laugh (12.34), horses and camels die (12.40), and the Thirty Years' War continues, as "alles streitet sich um einen Gott, den keiner kennt" (12.41, and everything argues about a God that no one knows). The irregularity occurs at the most general presentation of the section's themes, the widest point of expansion from Descartes' and Gillot's walk out to the paths of history shaped as much by the quarrels of nameless individuals as by those of science and nations. By its end, the section returns to the walkers, embarking on a quarrel of their own as a disagreement over whether to walk toward the mill or turn back culminates in Descartes' offense at Gillot's description of him as "Der Philosoph—/Ein Eisblock" (12.63–4, the philosopher—/a block of ice).

The final strophe with an additional line occurs in the second part of the novella in section 33, after Descartes has left his winter quarters (and presumably Gillot, though we never hear what happens to him; section 32 describes Marie as pregnant). The section takes time as its theme in the title, "Zwischen den Jahren" (Between the years), and opens with a verbatim repetition of the first three words of the divergent lines of section 12: "*Auf krummen Wegen*, Zeit, im Taumelgang kommt sie voran" (33.1, on crooked paths, time, in a staggering gait, it moves along; my emphasis). By way of this narration of the passage of time, the section arrives by the end of its first strophe at the publication of Descartes' *Principia* in 1644, dedicated to Elisabeth of Bohemia. The remainder of the section imagines a dialogue between Elisabeth and Descartes in which the former voices her objection to Descartes' dualism on the grounds that it should not be possible for the immaterial soul to move the material body, which eventually prompted him to posit the existence of the "materie subtile" that Grünbein aligns with snow in his poem.[123] In the poem's version of their disagreement, Elisabeth frames her damning query with almost parodic modesty, while Descartes seems hindered in answering both by the fact that his dualism genuinely cannot answer the question and by a hesitation to adduce examples of sexual attraction to the virginal princess to whom he appears attracted.

Thus Elisabeth, having described herself as "das dumme Unschuldslamm" (33.25, the silly innocent lamb), asks (in quotation marks),

---

[123] On Elisabeth's biography, philosophical interests, and correspondence with Descartes, see Lisa Shapiro, "Elisabeth, Princess of Bohemia," in *The Stanford Encyclopedia of Philosophy*, ed. Edward N. Zalta, Winter 2014 (Metaphysics Research Lab, Stanford University, 2014), https://plato.stanford.edu/archives/win2014/entries/elisabeth-bohemia/.

"Sagt mir nur eins: wie kann es sein, daß unsre Seele—
Immateriell, der Stimme gleich—den rohen Körper lenkt,
Der protzt mit Fleisch und steht im Fett und dehnt sich
        aus?"(33.31–3)[124]

A voice in italics—perhaps the narrator, perhaps Descartes' own memory, since it speaks in the past tense—goads the philosopher: "*Gebt zu, Monsieur, die Frage fuhr Euch an die Kehle*" (33.34, *Admit it, Monsieur, the question went for your throat*), who answers evasively that the soul is "a fluidum" (33.36) and that body and soul are "a couple" (33.40). The conversation expands to religion and to different philosophical systems; in the sixth strophe Descartes rejects the peregrination of souls, remarking that "Man lebt nur einmal—jetzt" (33.58, we live only once—now), a position Elisabeth identifies as Epicurean. In the seventh strophe, with its eleventh line, Descartes compares Christianity with Stoicism and notes Elisabeth's withdrawal from court life as an act of self-preservation. Her answer—"Ist es nicht besser, sich zu lösen/Von allem, was da buhlt und stirbt und blind gebiert?" (33.69)[125]—leaves Descartes stammering, unable to say what he "knows" (that skin desires touch). Instead, he mutters "vom Guten was, von Urangst als dem Bösen" (33.71, something about good, about primal fear as what's evil), sputtering onto an additional line that, the rhyme scheme makes clear, does not advance the argument but merely repeats accepted morality as well as the previous rhyme: abcabcdedee.

My tour through the line length irregularities in *On Snow* foregrounds the numerous and complex ways that meter takes up the themes Grünbein pursues in his Descartes projects—the relation between mind and body, the puzzles of subjectivity—and in his work as a whole—temporality, memory, and the challenge of their coherence. One could, of course, suggest other interpretations for the deviations, or one could find other types of irregularities—say, lines with unusual numbers of stressed syllables, or unusually high or low numbers of syllables; metrical practice, as I attempted to show in Klopstock and Nietzsche as well, is most interesting and productive when it cannot be fully systematized or entirely semantically exhausted. My primary assertion in discussing *On Snow* and Grünbein's work as a whole is that meter makes a claim on or a demand for our attention, and that following this attention illuminates both the way we use language and the way we experience poetry.

* * *

[124] "Tell me just one thing: how can it be that our soul—/ Immaterial, like the voice—controls the coarse body,/ That flaunts its flesh and sits in fat and spreads itself out?"
[125] "Is it not better to detach oneself/ From everything that vies and dies and blindly gives birth?"

What Grünbein shows us, I contend, is that attention to the way meter works—as a cultural force in language and the body, as a mode of grasping and organizing time, as a technique for layering distant voices and holding together contradictions we seem unable to do without—reveals the continued impact and importance of meter for poetry. Moreover, the detailed theorizing about and attention to meter his work demands can, as I hope to have shown, prompt an expanded experience of poetry as simultaneously material and meaning-bearing, formal and cognitive, historically-shaped and species-wide.

Epilogue
Metrical Experience

Drawing on the metrical thinking from three centuries that I have examined in the preceding pages, I conclude by describing the suggestions this thinking provides for a contemporary understanding of what meter is and what it does. As the previous six chapters have shown, precisely what meter *is* depends who you ask and what they are trying to say about language, poetry, and those who speak, read, and write it. In consequence, I do not and cannot give an absolute and universal definition; only a flexible and variable description. Meter consists of patterns of syllables that interact with other structures in language such as rhyme, lines, strophes, or repetitions as well as alliteration, assonance, consonance, and other sonic structures. "Metrics" has historically referred and continues to refer to this interaction, not exclusively to syllables. Rhyme, lines, strophes, and repetition emphasize that although many of the features poets and theorists use to compose metrical patterns are inherent to a given language, for example accent, volume, pitch, and timing, the ways meter organizes those characteristics come from and help establish cultural and individual conventions or traditions. (And what is "inherent" to any language on the phonological as well as grammatical levels changes over time and depending where and by whom the language is spoken.)

Meter thus combines fundamental sense perception—predominately but not exclusively hearing—with complex cultural structures; whether writing or speaking, it comes from embodied subjects and its effects register in the body (though not the same way in every body). Because of this combination, metrical practices remain closely linked to particular poems in their individual, cultural, and historical contexts. In all of the eighteenth, nineteenth, and twentieth to twenty-first centuries, the detailed analyses of who talks about meter in what disciplines and why has shown that what counts as which meter is not a matter of objective phonological measurement, even when poets or theorists say that it is. Metrical theory and practice rest on culturally specific norms and ambitions; those norms and ambitions work with and on bodily perception and characteristics of language.

For that reason, metrical thinking is an ideal place to investigate the relations of language, culture, and the body as they shape human subjects. This is the central "metrical claim" of my title: we learn important things about language and thinking as they happen in bodies and minds and cultures by looking at meter.

In particular, the highly specialized use and discussion of meter in various cultures and eras yields crucial insights about language and how human beings use it. Language is not merely a vehicle for the transmission of information, and communication goes far beyond the informational content of words and syntax. All the qualities and characteristics of spoken and written language can be appropriated for either deliberate or unconscious expression of political commitments, aesthetic values, individual idiosyncrasy, and sheer pleasure in the play with sounds—communication involves openness to all of those expressions, as they interact with semantic meaning in innumerable ways.

Because meter rests on the combination of cultural convention, language characteristics, and bodily perception, analyzing metrical theory and practice reveals cultural, philosophical, aesthetic, and political norms. Thus, the eighteenth-century metrical theories in my first chapter express anxiety about the role of German as a literary language coupled with an effort to expand the conception of both human language use and human subjectivity. Using metrics as both tool and example, these theories challenge the idea that language is merely the translation of ideas into arbitrary signs and the position that subjectivity is determined solely by reason. Meanwhile, in the nineteenth century, questions of where and how to study meter underscore the cultural shifts that prompted the creation of new academic disciplines and the reorganization of the university. Metrical practice, conversely, participates in a sense of belatedness and distance from the past that produces a plurality of metrical forms, which in turn do not play a role in the newest developments in philosophy, psychology, or natural science.

By the late twentieth century, the study of meter has almost disappeared, either relegated to historical handbooks for students of poetry, absorbed into pockets of literary theory, or deliberately isolated from other formal and semantic poetic effects in natural-scientific studies of poetry's effects on the brain. Despite this, late-twentieth-century and contemporary poets continue to use meter in unexpected and sometimes provocative ways. It is more difficult to diagnose a cultural moment without the benefit of hindsight, but the current status of meter and metrics perhaps reflects the distance of much academic discussion of poetry from cultural practice (nursery rhymes, internet poems, songs, protest chants, prayers, tweets ...), literary studies' skepticism of claims about "the human" following decades of high theory, and a general cultural positioning of science and data as the only genuine sources of knowledge.

This is the cultural state I have attempted to challenge, first by demonstrating that meter and metrics have not always been as isolated from cultural, political, and aesthetic concerns as much of the twenty-first century believes them to be and, more importantly, by showing how Klopstock, Nietzsche, and Grünbein make metrical practice central to their poetry and thus all of the questions and projects—cultural, critical, corporeal, individual, political, historical, linguistic, human—their poetry embodies and performs. Because meter takes up these projects differently not only in each poet but in each poem, I cannot abstract rules about what meter does even for each poet, much less all three of them; instead, I re-emphasize a few central tendencies and bring the three thinkers into contact with one another by drawing out similarities between them.

All three of Klopstock, Nietzsche, and Grünbein share an interest in meters from other cultures, especially but not only ancient Greek and Latin. Whereas Klopstock's interest comes from his efforts to create a future for German-language literature whose metrical and poetic feats can rival those of its predecessors, Nietzsche's and Grünbein's metrical investigations and poetic revivifications of classical forms take part in complex projects of situating the present in relation to the past. Moreover, all three poets go beyond superficial assertions about the physical effects of meter and appropriate the natural-scientific ideas and vocabularies of their respective times. Thus Klopstock's poetics use the developing understanding of human nerves as a physiological location of emotion to help him articulate his account of meter as movement of language that moves the body.[1] Nietzsche, meanwhile, attends to newly emerging cellular biology and tools for measuring human physiology, including heart rhythms and speech movements.[2] And Grünbein studies and adapts neuroscience and neurophysiology to describe poetry's effects in the brain; he incorporates their vocabulary not only in his essays but in his poems themselves, placing poetry and natural science on an equal footing as providing insight into embodied subjectivity, cognition, and language use.[3] Their interests in past metrical practice and natural science underscore the way meter brings language, cognition, culture, and embodiment together in historically particular ways.

Given the historical particularity of metrical theory and practice, it is not surprising that Klopstock (1724–1803), Nietzsche (1844–1900), and Grünbein (b.1962) offer different—but compatible—insights about meter. Klopstock develops a theory and terminology of metrical expressiveness from his own poetic experimentation. That terminology challenges the idea that the emotional or physiological effects of any given meter must be the same wherever and however the meter is used. Instead, Klopstock both articulates and, in his poetry, demonstrates that the same metrical pattern can work differently depending on its semantic content and its broader formal context. Authors and readers create a mutually influencing interaction in which meaning directs attention to certain metrical features, which in turn evoke emotion and affect the body, thus deepening and

---

[1] See e.g., Carsten Zelle, "Klopstocks Diät—das Erhabene und die Anthropologie um 1750," in *Wort und Schrift: Das Werk Friedrich Gottlieb Klopstocks*, eds. Kevin Hilliard and Katrin Kohl, Hallesche Forschungen 27 (Tübingen: Niemeyer, 2008), 101–27, 113.

[2] See e.g. Christian J. Emden, *Nietzsche's Naturalism: Philosophy and the Life Sciences in the Nineteenth Century* (Cambridge: Cambridge University Press, 2014).

[3] See e.g. Anna Ertel, *Körper, Gehirne, Gene. Lyrik und Naturwissenschaft bei Ulrike Draesner und Durs Grünbein* (Berlin: de Gruyter, 2011).

moving beyond the semantic content. The categories Klopstock creates and the ways they focus attention open the possibility of talking about meter and meaning without demanding either absolute agreement or complete separation, allowing for a more flexible and nuanced account of poetic experience as sense-making in and as sound.

Nietzsche, writing some 120 years after Klopstock, uses his philological work and poetic practice to argue that meter comes from and works on a body that is always both physiological and cultural. This account challenges the idea, widespread in twenty-first-century studies of meter, that the physical effects of meter must be universal because they rest on species characteristics, and thus the misconception that the impact of meter must *either* be cultural-particular or physiological-universal. Nietzsche's notebooks and poetry show how any account of the physiological account of the efficacy of rhythm and meter must itself be historically and culturally specific; there cannot be any pre-cultural experience of embodied subjectivity or of meter. Because of this tight interweaving of culture, history, and the body, Nietzsche's thinking about meter and his poetic practice offer a complex and self-reflexive cultural critique: the ways readers or hearers respond to different kinds of patterns in language are both symptoms of and, potentially, challenges to the culture that moves these bodies in this ways with this language at this time. Furthermore, Nietzsche's historical consciousness means that he deliberately highlights the way his own writing, too, remains situated in, conditioned by, and symptomatic of its culture and history, even as he critiques them. His metrical critique has no objective, ahistorical standpoint from which to articulate the interaction of the bodily-material and the cultural-historical in meter, and it thus calls his readers to attend to their own conditionedness and the ways meter might disrupt it.

Durs Grünbein, writing in the last years of the twentieth century and the first years of the twenty-first, rejects the view that meter is archaic or merely historical; instead, metrical forms respond to particular struggles of postmodern subjectivity in Grünbein's—our—era. That subjectivity faces the difficulty of positioning itself in respect to both the modernist and the modern past as well as the growing attention to evolutionary time scales and the narratives of development they undergird. Further, postmodern subjectivity is itself composite and disharmonious, aware of its own contradictions and its relation to the past. This conflict is intensified since the subject itself subscribes both to materialist positions—in which consciousness is merely a side-effect of brain activity—and to dualist positions, in which the "I", though not independent of bodily reflexes, is at least not fully determined or created by them. Finally, the postmodern "I" finds itself threatened by the overwhelming volume (in the sense of both "noise" and "quantity") of experience. Because Grünbein, too, recognizes that meter merges culture and physiology and because its forms can create a coherence or cohesion that does not require noncontradiction, he finds in meter a central resource for addressing the polyphony and occasionally paradox of the contemporary lyrical "I." Moreover, because meter organizes time, he holds that it both assists memory in holding on to elements of the flux of experience by giving them a shape and also offers a way of interweaving or layering past and present that connects them in a non-linear, non-teleological way.

All three poets show that although the way we think about meter and the way we experience it are shaped by our cultural and historical moment, theories and experience are not fully *determined* by culture and history—and thus both ideas about and experiences of meter can change. Paying attention to meters—strange meters, simple meters, complex meters, meters from different languages, meters from our own languages—opens up the possibility of new, different, or surprising experiences of poems, songs, stories, chants, rituals, and sounds. I hope, in my readings of Klopstock's, Nietzsche's, and Grünbein's poems, to have shown that paying attention to meter can enhance the experience of a poem, either by way of heightened sense-experience or by deepened cognitive understanding of allusions or traditions. But meter might not do this; we might be unmoved by a meter, or find it mannered, or monotonous or simply not hear it at all. Conversely, meter might lead us into a poem that we found strange or unexpected—and, because meter comes from the interaction of language, culture, and subject, potentially into understanding of or resonance with a different language, culture, or person. My call to use the terms, ideas, and examples of Klopstock, Nietzsche, and Grünbein is thus an invitation into metrical—poetic—experience.

Poems and Translations

Der Bach[1]

```
x / x / x / x x /,
x x / x / x / x x /
/ x /, / x x /, / x /,
/ x x /, / x x /.
```

Bekränzt mein Haar, o Blumen des Hains,
Die am Schattenbach des luftigen Quells
Nossa's Hand sorgsam erzog, Braga mir
Brachte, bekränzt, Blumen, mein Haar!   [4]

Es wendet nach dem Strome des Quells
Sich der Lautenklang des wehenden Bachs.
Tief, und still strömet der Strom; tonbeseelt
Rauschet der Bach neben ihm fort.   [8]

[Inhalt, den volle Seel', im Erguß
Der Erfindung, und der innersten Kraft,
Sich entwirft, strömet; allein lebend muß,
Will es ihm nahn, tönen das Wort.]   [12]

Wohllaut gefällt, Bewegung noch mehr;
Zur Gespielin gab dem Herzen ich sie.
Diesem säumt, eilet sie nach; Bildern folgt,
Leiseren Tritts, ferne sie nur.   [16]

[So säumet, und so eilt sie nicht nur:
Auch empfindungsvolle Wendung beseelt
Ihr den Tanz, Tragung, die spricht, ihr den Tanz,
All ihr Gelenk schwebt in Verhalt.]   [20]

Mir gab Siona Sulamith schon
An der Palmenhöh den röthlichen Kranz
Sarons. Ihr weiht' ich zuerst jenen Flug,
Der in dem Chor kühn sich erhebt.   [24]

Nun rufet seinen Reihen durch mich
In der Eiche Schatten Braga zurück.
Hüllte nicht daurende Nacht Lieder ein,
Lyrischen Flug, welchem die Höhn   [28]

Des Lorberhügels horchten; o schlief
In der Trümmer Graun Alcäus nicht selbst:
Rühmt' ich mich kühneren Schwungs! tönte, stolz
Rühmt' ichs, uns mehr Wendung fürs Herz,   [32]

---

[1] Friedrich Gottlieb Klopstock, "Der Bach," in *Oden*, eds. Horst Gronemeyer and Klaus Hurlebusch, vol. 1, 2 vols. (Berlin: de Gruyter, 2010), 270–5.

Als Tempe's Hirt vom Felsen vernahm!
Und der Kämpfer Schaar am Fuß des Olymp!
Als mit Tanz Sparta zur Schlacht eilend! Zevs
Aus des Altars hohem Gewölk!   [36]

Der grosse Sänger Ossian folgt
Dem Getön des vollen Baches nicht stets!
Ferne, zählt Galliens Lied Laute nur;
Zwischen der Zahl, schwankt und dem Maaß   [40]

Der Britte; selbst Hesperien schläft!
O sie wecke nie die Sait' und das Horn
Braga's auf! Flögen sie einst deinen Flug
Schwan des Glasoor, neidet' ich sie!   [44]

Nachahmer, wie Nachahmer nicht sind,
Du erwecktest selbst, o Flaccus, sie nicht!
Graue Zeit währet' ihr Schlaf! O, er währt
Immer, und ich neide sie nie!   [48]

Schon lange maß der Dichter des Rheins
Das Getön des starken Liedes dem Ohr;
Doch mit Nacht decket' Allhend ihm sein Maaß,
Daß er des Stabs Ende nur sah.   [52]

Ich hab' ihn heller blitzen gesehn
Den erhabnen, goldnen, lyrischen Stab!
Kränze du, röthlicher Kranz Sarons, mich!
Winde dich durch, Blume des Hains.   [56]

The Brook

Crown my hair, o leaves of the grove,
That by the shady brook of the cool spring
Nossa's hand carefully grew, Braga brought
To me, crown, flowers, my hair!   [4]

The sounds of the lute turn towards the streams
Of the spring, the wafting brook.
Deep, and still streams the river, enlivened
By tones, the brook murmurs forth beside it.   [8]

[Content, which the full soul in its outpouring
Of invention, and of the innermost force
Creates for itself, streams; but being alive
The word must resound if it will approach.]   [16]

Euphony pleases, movement still more
To the heart as a playmate I gave her
She tarries and hurries after it; images
she follows in soft steps, at a distance.   [24]

[Not only does it tarry so, hurry so
But also turn full of feeling ensouls
Its dance, speaking bearing, its dance
All its joints sway in relation.]   [28]

To me already Siona Sulamith gave
The ruddy wreath of Saron on the
Palm grove. To her I dedicated first
That flight, that rose boldly in chorus.   [32]

Now he calls his ranks back through me,
In the oak's shadow—Braga.
If perpetual night did not cover
Songs, of lyrical flight, that belonged   [36]

To the heights of the laurel hill, if only
Alcaus did not sleep in the grey ruins:
I would boast bolder vigor! Ringing, proud
I would boast of it, for us more turns for the heart   [40]

Than Tempe's shepherd heard from the cliffs!
And the warriors throng at the foot of Olympus
Hurrying as if to a dance to the battle with Sparta!
Zeus from the altar's high clouds!   [44]

The great singer Ossian followed
Not always the soundings of the full brook!
Distant, Gaul's song counts only sounds;
Sways between the numbers and measure   [48]

Of the Briton; even Hesperia sleeps!
O if only the strings and the Horn of Braga never
Awoke her! Had she flown your flight,
Swan of Glassor, I would envy her!   [52]

Imitators of all imitators,
You your self, Flaccus, could not awaken her!
The dusk of time preserves her sleep! Oh, it lasts
For always and I shall never envy her!   [56]

Long already did the poet of the Rhein measure
The soundings of the strong song by ear;
But night hid from him perfect harmonious measures,
So that he only saw the ends of the staves.   [60]

I have seen it flash brighter,
the sublime, golden, lyrical verse!
Crown me, you ruddy wreath of Saron,
Entwine yourselves there, flowers of the grove.   [64]

Sponda.[2]

x / x / x / x x /,
x x / x / x / x x /,
/ x /, / x x /, / x /,
/ x x /, / x x /.
Der deutschen Dichter Hainen entweht
Der Gesang Alzäus und des Homer.

---

[2] Friedrich Gottlieb Klopstock, "Sponda," in *Oden*, 243–5.

Deinen Gang auf dem Kothurn, Sophokles,
Meidet, und geht Jambanapäst.   [4]

Viel hats der Reize, Cynthius Tanz
Zu ereilen, und der Hörer belohnts;
Dennoch hielt lieber den Reihn Teutons Volk,
Welchen voran Bragor einst flog.   [8]

Doch ach verstumt in ewiger Nacht
Ist Bardiet! und Skofliod! und verhallt
Euer Schall, Telyn! Triomb! Hochgesang,
Deinem sogar klagen wir nach!   [12]

O Sponda! rufet nun in dem Hain
Des ruinentflohnen Griechen Gefährt,
Sponda! dich such' ich zu oft, ach! umsonst;
Horche nach dir, finde dich nicht!   [16]

Wo, Echo, wallt ihr tönender Schritt?
Und in welche Grott' entführtest du sie,
Sprache, mir? Echo, du rufst sanft mir nach,
Aber auch dich höret sie nicht.   [20]

Es drängten alle Genien sich
Der entzückten Melodie um ihn her.
Riefen auch, klagten mit ihm, aber Stolz
Funkelt' im Blick einiger auch.   [24]

Erhaben trat der Daktylos her:
Bin ich Herrscher nicht im Liede Mäoons?
Rufe denn Sponda nicht stets, bilde mich
Oft zu Homers fliegendem Hall.   [32]

Und hörte nicht Choreos dich stets?
Hat er oft nicht Sponda's schwebenden Gang?
Geht sie denn, Kretikos tönt's, meinen Gang?
Dir, Choriamb, weich' ich allein!   [36]

Da sang der Laute Silbergesang
Choriambos: Ich bin Smintheus Apolls
Liebling! mich lehrte sein Lied Hain und Strom,
Mich, da es flog nach dem Olymp.   [40]

Erkohr nicht Smintheus Pindarus mich
Anapäst, da er der Saite Getön
Lispeln ließ? Jambos, Apolls alter Freund,
Hielt sich nicht mehr, zürnt', und begann: [44]

Und geh nicht ich den Gang des Kothurns?
Wo..Baccheos schritt in lyrischem Tanz:
Stolze, schweigt! ha, Choriamb, töntest du,
Daktylos, du, tönt' ich nicht mit?   [48]

Der schönste Päon eilte daher
Didymäos, leichtgewendet:
Flögen Thyrs' und Dithyramb schnell genug,
Risse sie nicht ich mit mir fort.   [52]

Ach, Sponda! rief der Dichter, und hieß
In den Hain nach ihr Pyrrichios gehn.
Flüchtig sprang, schlüpft' er dahin! Also wehn
Blüthen im May Weste dahin.   [56]

Denn, Sponda, du begleitest ihn auch
Der Bardiete vaterländischen Reihn,
Wenn ihn mir treffend der Fels tönt, und mich
Nicht die Gestalt täuschte, die sang.   [60]

15 (Skofliod) in der Sprache der Angeln und Sachsen das Lied des Dichters, noch ohne Musik, Sangliod, mit Musik.

16 (Triombon) Trompete, nach einem sehr alten Glossar.

16 (Hochgesang) Hymnus zu Otfrieds Zeiten.

30) (der Daktylos) Dieser Fuß / x x. Hier folgen auch die übrigen, welche in der Ode vorkommen: Choreos / x. Kretikos / x /. Choriambos / x x /. Anapäst x x /. Jambos x /. Bacheos x / / . Didymäos < x x / x >. (Die anderen Päone sind: x / x x, / x x x, x x x /.) Pyrrhichios < x x >.

44 (lispeln ließ) Das Wort, wodurch Pindar den Klang der Leyer ausdrückt, besteht aus zwey Anapästen. Elelyzomena.

51) (Didymäos) Dieser Fuß heißt nach Apollo so. Wenn man ihn mit dem Anapäste so verbindet: x x / x, x x /. und so mit dem Daktyle: / x x, x x / x. so wird die metrische Bewegung etwas dithyrambisch.

Spondee

From the German poets' grove flows
out the song of Alkaios and Homer
Shun your tread on the cothurn,
Sophocles, and tread iambanapests.   [4]

There are many charms in overtaking
Cynthius' dance, and it rewards the hearer;
Nonetheless Teuton's folk keeps to the set
At whose head Bragor once flew.   [8]

But ah, in eternal night have
Bardiet and Skofliod fallen silent
And your sound, Telyn, Triomb, died away
Hymn-song, even for you we lament!   [12]

O spondee! now in the grove calls
From ruins escaped, the Greek's companion,
Spondee! I seek you too often, alas, in vain
Listen for you, finding you not!   [16]

Where, echo, does her ringing step flow?
And in what grotto did you steal her away,
language, from me? Echo, you call softly after me
But you too she hears not.   [24]

All the spirits of delighted melody
Thronged hence around him,
Called too, lamented with him, but pride
Glittered too in some of their looks.   [28]

Dactylus entered, sublime:
Am I not ruler in Mäoons song?
Call then Spondee not constantly, form me
Often to make Homer's flying resound.   [32]

And did not Choreos always hear you?
Has he not often Spondee's floating gait?
Does she go then, Kretikos boasts, in my steps?
For you, alone, Choriamb I step aside.   [36]
Then did Choriambos sing the sounds
Silvery song: I am Smintheus Apollo's
Favorite! To me, did grove and river teach,
Me, his song, so it flew to Olympus.   [40]

Did not Smintheus Pindar choose me,
Anapest, as he let the string's singing
Whisper? Iamb, Apollo's old friend
Held back no more, grew cross, and began;   [44]

And do I not walk the tread of the kothurn?
Where..Baccheus stepped in lyrical dance:
Proud one, be silent! Ha, Choriamb, when you sound
Dactyl, you, do I not sound too?   [48]

Turning swiftly Didymäus hastened
Hence, and Päone as well:
If Thyrsis and Dithyramb fly fast enough,
Did not we wrest him along with us?   [52]

Ah, Spondee! cried the poet, and bade
Pyrrichios to seek her in the grove.
Swiftly he sprang, slipped away! Thus blow
Blossoms in May on the west wind.   [56]

For Spondee, you accompanied too
The Bardiet's fatherlandish dance,
When the cliff rang truly, and the form
That sang did not trick me.   [60]

15 (Skofliod) in the language of the Anglo-Saxons the song of the poet, still without music; Sangliod, with music.

16 (Triombon): trumpet, according to a very old vocabulary.

16 (Hochgesang) hymn in Otfried's time.

30) (the dactyl) This foot / x x. Here follow the others too, which appear in the ode: Choreos / x. Kretikos / x /. Choriambos / x x /.
Anapäst x x /. Jambos x /. Bacheos x / /.
Didymäos < x x /x >
(The other paions are: x / x x, / x x x, x x x /.) Pyrrichios: < x x >.

44 (let whisper) The word, with which Pindar expresses the sound of the lyre, consists of two anapests. Elelyzomena.

51) (Didymäos) This foot is called so after Apollo. If it is combined with anapests like this: x x / x, x x /. or with the dactyl: / x x, x x / x. then the metrical movement becomes somewhat dithyrambic

"An die Melancholie"[3]

Verarge mir es nicht, Melancholie,
Daß ich die Feder, dich zu preisen, spitze,
Und daß ich nicht, den Kopf gebeugt zum Knie,
Einsiedlerisch auf einem Baumstumpf sitze.
So sahst du oft mich, gestern noch zumal,
In heißer Sonne morgendlichem Strahle:
Begehrlich schrie der Geyer in das Thal,
Er träumt vom todten Aas auf todtem Pfahle.   [8]

Du irrtest, wüster Vogel, ob ich gleich
So mumienhaft auf meinem Klotze ruhte!
Du sahst das Auge nicht, das wonnenreich
Noch hin und her rollt, stolz und hochgemuthe.
Und wenn es nicht zu deinen Höhen schlich,
Erstorben für die fernsten Wolkenwellen,
So sank es um so tiefer, um in sich
Des Daseins Abgrund blitzend aufzuhellen.   [16]

So saß ich oft, in tiefer Wüstenei
Unschön gekrümmt, gleich opfernden Barbaren,
Und Deiner eingedenk, Melancholei,
Ein Büßer, ob in jugendlichen Jahren!
So sitzend freut' ich mich des Geyer-Flugs,
Des Donnerlaufs der rollenden Lawinen,
Du sprachst zu mir, unfähig Menschentrugs,
Wahrhaftig, doch mit schrecklich strengen Mienen.
Du herbe Göttin wilder Felsnatur,   [24]

Du Freundin liebst es nah mir zu erscheinen;
Du zeigst mir drohend dann des Geyer's Spur
Und der Lawine Lust, mich zu verneinen.
Rings athmet zähnefletschend Mordgelüst:
Qualvolle Gier, sich Leben zu erzwingen!
Verführerisch auf starrem Felsgerüst
Sehnt sich die Blume dort nach Schmetterlingen.   [32]

Dies Alles bin ich — schaudernd fühl' ich's nach —
Verführter Schmetterling, einsame Blume,
Der Geyer und der jähe Eisesbach,
Des Sturmes Stöhnen — alles dir zum Ruhme,
Du grimme Göttin, der ich tief gebückt,
Den Kopf am Knie, ein schaurig Loblied ächze,

---

[3] Friedrich Nietzsche, "An die Melancholie," posthumous fragments July 1871 (http://www.nietzschesource.org/#eKGWB/NF-1871,15[1]).

Nur dir zum Ruhme, daß ich unverrückt
Nach Leben, Leben, Leben lechze!   [40]

Verarge mir es, böse Gottheit, nicht,
Daß ich mit Reimen zierlich dich umflechte.
Der zittert, dem du nahst, ein Schreckgesicht,
Der zuckt, dem du sie reichst, die böse Rechte.
Und zitternd stammle ich hier Lied auf Lied,
Und zucke auf in rhythmischem Gestalten:
Die Tinte fleußt, die spitze Feder sprüht —
Nun Göttin, Göttin laß mich — laß mich schalten!   [48]

Gimmelwald.
(Sommer 1871).

"To Melancholy"[4]

Do not reproach me, Melancholy,
That I sharpen my quill to extol you;
And that I, [ ] my head bowed to my knee,
Sit like a hermit on a tree stump.
You saw me often in this pose, especially yesterday,
In the morning rays of the hot sun:
Greedily the vulture screamed into the valley,
He dreams of carrion on a stake.   [8]

You erred, foul bird, even though I
So like a mummy, rested on my log!
You did not see my eye that blissfully
Is still rolling proud and arrogantly back and forth.
And though my eye, exhausted by the far-off banks of
Clouds, did not steal to your height,
For that it sank all the deeper in order to
Illuminate the abyss of being with lightning flashes.   [16]

Thus I sat often in the deep wilderness,
Hideously bent, like a savage at a sacrifice,
My mind on you, Melancholy,
A penitent, though of youthful years!
Thus sitting I enjoyed the vulture's flight,
The thundering course of rolling avalanches—
Incapable of deceiving men, you spoke to me,
Truthfully, though with terribly stern expressions.   [24]

---

[4] Philip Grundlehner, *The Poetry of Friedrich Nietzsche* (New York: Oxford University Press, 1986), 52–3. Grundlehner's translation does not attempt the meter or rhyme, with the result that the poem sounds far more earnest than it does in German, even as Grundlehner argues that it is a caricature of the Dionysian. He does, however, preserve the diction and most of which words and images appear on each line.

You harsh goddess of the wild Alpine nature,
Mistress, you love to appear near me;
You show me then the vulture's course
And the laughter of the avalanches in order to repel me.
All around breathes a savage lust to murder:
Torturous desire to seize life by force!
Seductively there on a rigid cliff
The flower longs for butterflies.   [32]

All this am I—shuddering I feel it all—
The allured butterfly, the lonely flower,
The vulture and the rapid, icy brook,
The groaning storm—all these redounded for your honor,
You grim goddess, to whom, bowed down deeply,
My head upon my knee, I moan a fearful panegyric,
Only for your honor, that I steadily
Thirst for life, life, life!   [40]

Do not reproach me, evil deity,
That I plait rhymes delicately around you,
You terrifying phantom—whomever you approach trembles
And quivers when you extend your evil right hand.
And trembling here I stammer song upon song,
And twitch in rhythmic forms—
The ink flows, the sharp quill [spatters],
Now goddess, goddess, let me—let me rule!   [48]

[Gimmelwald,
(Summer 1871).]

Dichters Berufung[5]

Als ich jüngst, mich zu erquicken,
Unter dunklen Bäumen sass,
Hört' ich ticken, leise ticken,
Zierlich, wie nach Takt und Maass.
Böse wurd, ich, zog Gesichter, —
Endlich aber gab ich nach,
Bis ich gar, gleich einem Dichter,
Selber mit im Tiktak sprach.   [8]

Wie mir so im Verse-Machen
Silb' um Silb' ihr Hopsa sprang,
Musst' ich plötzlich lachen, lachen
Eine Viertelstunde lang.
Du ein Dichter? Du ein Dichter?
Steht's mit deinem Kopf so schlecht?

---

[5] Friedrich Nietzsche, "Dichters Berufung," *Die fröhliche Wissenschaft* 2, Lieder des Prinzen Vogel-frei (http://www.nietzschesource.org/#eKGWB/FW-Lieder–2).

— "Ja, mein Herr, Sie sind ein Dichter"
Achselzuckt der Vogel Specht.   [16]

Wessen harr' ich hier im Busche?
Wem doch laur' ich Räuber auf?
Ist's ein Spruch? Ein Bild? Im Husche
Sitzt mein Reim ihm hintendrauf.
Was nur schlüpft und hüpft, gleich sticht der
Dichter sich's zum Vers zurecht.
— "Ja, mein Herr, Sie sind ein Dichter"
Achselzuckt der Vogel Specht.   [24]

Reime, mein' ich, sind wie Pfeile?
Wie das zappelt, zittert, springt,
Wenn der Pfeil in edle Theile
Des Lacerten-Leibchens dringt!
Ach, ihr sterbt dran, arme Wichter,
Oder taumelt wie bezecht!
— "Ja, mein Herr, Sie sind ein Dichter"
Achselzuckt der Vogel Specht.   [32]

Schiefe Sprüchlein voller Eile,
Trunkne Wörtlein, wie sich's drängt!
Bis ihr Alle, Zeil' an Zeile,
An der Tiktak-Kette hängt.
Und es giebt grausam Gelichter,
Das dies — freut? Sind Dichter — schlecht?
— "Ja, mein Herr, Sie sind ein Dichter"
Achselzuckt der Vogel Specht.   [40]

Höhnst du, Vogel? Willst du scherzen?
Steht's mit meinem Kopf schon schlimm,
Schlimmer stünd's mit meinem Herzen?
Fürchte, fürchte meinen Grimm! —
Doch der Dichter — Reime flicht er
Selbst im Grimm noch schlecht und recht.
— "Ja, mein Herr, Sie sind ein Dichter"
Achselzuckt der Vogel Specht.   [48]

Poet's Calling[6]

Recently, as I sat under dark trees
to refresh myself,
I heard a ticking, a quiet ticking,
prettily, as according to beat and measure.
I became angry, made grimaces—
finally, however, I gave in,
until I, just like a poet,
spoke in that ticktock myself.   [8]

[6] Grundlehner, *The Poetry of Friedrich Nietzsche*, 159–60. Modifications in brackets.

As I kept making verses
and syllable upon syllable jumped [a-hopping],
I had to laugh suddenly, laughed
a quarter-hour long.
You a poet? You a poet?
Has your head become that sick?
— "Yes, good sir, you are a poet,"
shrugs the woodpecker bird.   [16]

Whom am I awaiting here in the bushes?
For whom am I lying in ambush like a robber?
Is it a maxim? An image? In a moment
my rhyme pounces on it.
Anything that runs and leaps, immediately
the poet sticks it appropriately into a verse.
— "Yes, good sir, you are a poet,"
shrugs the woodpecker bird.   [24]

Rhymes, I think, are just like arrows?
See the kicking, the tremor, the jumping
when the arrow penetrates into the noble parts
of the lizard's little body!
Ah, you'll die of it, poor wretches,
or you'll stagger as if you're drunk!
— "Yes, good sir, you are a poet,"
shrugs the woodpecker bird.   [32]

Poorly executed [sayings] made in haste,
Drunken little words, how crowded together you are!
Until you all, line upon line,
hang on the ticktock chain.
And there is a horrible rabble
that *likes* this all? Are poets—sick?
— "Yes, good sir, you are a poet,"
shrugs the woodpecker bird.   [40]

Are you [mocking], bird? Do you mean to [joke]?
If I'm so bad off in my head,
couldn't it be even worse with my heart?
Fear, oh fear my rage!—
Yet the poet—even in his fury
he still weaves his rhymes as well as he can.
— "Yes, good sir, you are a poet,"
shrugs the woodpecker bird.   [48]

Nur Narr! Nur Dichter![7]

Bei abgehellter Luft,
wenn schon des Thau's Tröstung

[7] http://www.nietzschesource.org/#eKGWB/DD-Narr. My line numbering omits the title and blank lines.

zur Erde niederquillt,
unsichtbar, auch ungehört
— denn zartes Schuhwerk trägt
der Tröster Thau gleich allen Trostmilden —
gedenkst du da, gedenkst du, heisses Herz,
wie einst du durstetest,
nach himmlischen Thränen und Thaugeträufel
versengt und müde durstetest,   [10]
dieweil auf gelben Graspfaden
boshaft abendliche Sonnenblicke
durch schwarze Bäume um dich liefen
blendende Sonnen-Gluthblicke, schadenfrohe.
"Der W a h r h e i t Freier — du? so höhnten sie
nein! nur ein Dichter!
ein Thier, ein listiges, raubendes, schleichendes,
das lügen muss,
das wissentlich, willentlich lügen muss,
nach Beute lüstern,   [20]
bunt verlarvt,
sich selbst zur Larve,
sich selbst zur Beute
d a s — der Wahrheit Freier?...
Nur Narr! Nur Dichter!
Nur Buntes redend,
aus Narrenlarven bunt herausredend,
herumsteigend auf lügnerischen Wortbrücken,
auf Lügen-Regenbogen
zwischen falschen Himmeln   [30]
herumschweifend, herumschleichend —
n u r Narr! n u r Dichter!...
Das — der Wahrheit Freier?...
Nicht still, starr, glatt, kalt,
zum Bilde worden,
zur Gottes-Säule,
nicht aufgestellt vor Tempeln,
eines Gottes Thürwart:
nein! feindselig solchen Tugend-Standbildern,
in jeder Wildniss heimischer als in Tempeln,   [40]
voll Katzen-Muthwillens
durch jedes Fenster springend
husch! in jeden Zufall,
jedem Urwalde zuschnüffelnd,
dass du in Urwäldern
unter buntzottigen Raubthieren

sündlich gesund und schön und bunt liefest,
mit lüsternen Lefzen,
selig-höhnisch, selig-höllisch, selig-blutgierig,
raubend, schleichend, l ü g e n d liefest...   [50]

Oder dem Adler gleich, der lange,
lange starr in Abgründe blickt,
in s e i n e Abgründe...
— oh wie sie sich hier hinab,
hinunter, hinein,
in immer tiefere Tiefen ringeln! —
Dann,
plötzlich,
geraden Flugs
gezückten Zugs   [60]

auf L ä m m e r stossen,
jach hinab, heisshungrig,
nach Lämmern lüstern,
gram allen Lamms-Seelen,
grimmig gram Allem, was blickt
tugendhaft, schafmässig, krauswollig,
dumm, mit Lammsmilch-Wohlwollen...

Also
adlerhaft, pantherhaft
sind des Dichters Sehnsüchte,   [70]
sind d e i n e Sehnsüchte unter tausend Larven,
du Narr! du Dichter!...

Der du den Menschen schautest
so G o t t als S c h a f —,
den Gott z e r r e i s s e n im Menschen
wie das Schaf im Menschen
und zerreissend l a c h e n —

d a s, d a s i s t d e i n e S e l i g k e i t,
eines Panthers und Adlers Seligkeit,
eines Dichters und Narren Seligkeit!...   [80]

Bei abgehellter Luft,
wenn schon des Monds Sichel
grün zwischen Pupurröthen
und neidisch hinschleicht,
— dem Tage feind,
mit jedem Schritte heimlich
an Rosen-Hängematten
hinsichelnd, bis sie sinken,
nachtabwärts blass hinabsinken:
so sank ich selber einstmals,   [90]

aus meinem Wahrheits-Wahnsinne,
aus meinen Tages-Sehnsüchten,
des Tages müde, krank vom Lichte,
— sank abwärts, abendwärts, schattenwärts,
von Einer Wahrheit
verbrannt und durstig
— gedenkst du noch, gedenkst du, heisses Herz,
wie da du durstetest? —
d a s s i c h v e r b a n n t s e i
v o n a l l e r W a h r h e i t !   [100]
N u r Narr! N u r Dichter!...

Only Fool! Only Poet![8]

In air where the light has dimmed,
when the dew's comfort
already wells down to the earth
unseen and unheard—
for tender is the footwear
of the comforter dew, as of all that gently comforts—:
do you remember then, remember, hot heart,
how you once thirsted
for heavenly tears and dripping dew,
thirsted, scorched and weary,   [10]
while on yellowed grass paths
the evening sunlight-glances
were running maliciously around you through black trees,
blinding, glowing glances of the sun, deriving pleasure from their vindictiveness?

"The suitor of *truth*? You?" So they mocked—
"No! Only a poet!
An animal, a cunning, preying, prowling animal
that must lie,
that must knowingly, willingly lie:
lusting for prey,   [20]
colorfully masked,
a mask for itself,
prey for itself,
this—the suitor of truth?
No! Only fool! Only poet!
Only speaking colorfully,

---

[8] Grundlehner, *The Poetry of Friedrich Nietzsche*, 189–91. Grundlehner translates the version in *Thus Spoke Zarathustra*, which although very similar is not identical. Most of my alterations in brackets are places where I follow the diction of the *Dionysos Dithyrambs*. Starting in line 30, the line numbering diverges from Grundlehner's because the *Zarathustra* version has an additional line after "between false heavens."

only [speaking] colorfully out of fools' masks,
climbing around on mendacious word-bridges
on mendacious rainbows,
between false heavens [/]   [30]
roaming, hovering about—
only fool! *only* poet!

This—the suitor of truth?
Not still, stiff, smooth, cold,
become an image,
a pillar of God,
not placed before temples,
a god's entrance guard:
no! An enemy to such memorials of virtue,
more at home in any wilderness than [in] temples,   [40]

full of cats' mischievousness,
leaping through every window
swish! Into every chance,
sniffing for every jungle,
sniffing longingly, like one addicted,
that in jungles,
among colorful beasts of prey,
you might run, sinfully healthy and colorful and beautiful
with lusting animal lips
blissfully scornful, blissfully hellish, blissfully bloodthirsty—
preying, prowling, *lying* you might run—   [50]

Or like the eagle that gazes long,
long with a fixed eye into abysses,
into *its own* abysses...
—O how they circle downward,
under and in,
and into deeper and deeper depths!—
Then,
suddenly,
with a straight flight,
with a brandished flight   [60]
they pounce on *lambs*,
abruptly down, ravenous,
greedy for lambs,
hating all lamb-souls,
grimly hating everything that looks
virtuous, lamb-eyed, curly-wooled,
[dumb], with lambs'[-milk] good [will] ...

Thus,
eaglelike, panther like,
are the poet's longings   [70]

are *your* longings under a thousand masks,
you fool! you poet!...
You who saw man
As *god* and *sheep* —,
to *tear to pieces* the god in man
as the sheep in man,
and to *laugh* while you tear —
this, this is your bliss[,]
a panther's and eagle's bliss [,]
a poet's and a fool's bliss!...

[80]

In air where the light has dimmed,
where the moon's sickle
creeps along, green
and envious between crimson-reds:
—an enemy to the day
with every step secretly
sickling down the rose-hammocks
until they sink,
sink down, pale, down into the night [:]
Thus I myself once sank,
from my craze for truth
from my daytime longings,
weary of the day, sick from the light,
[—] sank downward, down toward evening, toward shadows:
burned and parched
by one truth:
—do you still remember, do you remember, hot heart,
how you thirsted then?—
[that I should be banned
From all truth!]
Only fool! *Only* poet!...

[90]

[100]

Aporie Augustinus (Über die Zeit)[9]

Die brennende Hornhaut im Salzschaum
Im Tuffstein die Augenhöhlen, Alypius,
Das Meer das dein Wort schluckt—
Nichts was du kennst, ist die Zeit.

[4]

Die Wölbung des Himmels, den Schädel
Umfassend, die Hände in Hohlform
Über der kreisenden Töpferscheibe—
Nichts was du siehst, ist die Zeit.

[8]

[9] Durs Grünbein, "Aporia Augustinus (Über Die Zeit)," in *Nach Den Satiren* (Frankfurt: Suhrkamp Verlag, 1999), 33–6.

Die Stimmen längst Toter, im Herdloch
Das Rascheln der Knöchel, Alypius,
In den Schläfen dein Blut—
Nichts was du hörst, ist die Zeit.   [12]

Nichts was du fassen kannst, ist sie. Kein Brusthaar,
Das nach dem Baden gezupft wird, und keine Tafel,
Die in den Stadien die Runden anzeigt beim Wagenrennen.
Weder die Greisenstirn noch die rosa Fingerbeeren des Kindes.   [16]

Nichts was sich messen läßt, ist die Zeit. Weder der Staub
Im Tiegel der Goldwaage noch der gestiegene Kaufpreis für Fische.
Auch nicht der wandernde Schatten am Gnomon
Oder die Zahl der Regierungen in einem Leben, der Kriege.   [20]

Nichts was sich regt, ist die Zeit. (Vergiß den Skorpion...).
Doch auch kein Sternbild, nach dem sich die Seeleute richten.
Keine der Routen nach Troja, kein Heimweg von dort
Durch Familien und Länder ans bittere Ende—Erinnerung.   [24]

Keine der Krankheiten ist sie, nichts was zerstört.
Sie ist kein Gigant, der die Steine zermalmt in der Brandung,
Keiner der Erdrutsche, Wirbelstürme, keiner der Götter.
Noch das Gestöhn der Helden in den welken Ohren Homers.   [28]

Gestern habe ich angefangen mit zuzuhören, Alypius.
Aus jedem Satz sprang ein Wort, das mich älter zurückließ.
Irgend ein *Bald*, ein *Nicht mehr*, ein *Von altersher*.
Als wäre da immer nur Richtung im Sprechen, kein Stillstand.   [32]

Da war dieses Noch...
                    Dieses Schon...
                              Dieses Einst...
Und nichts davon ist die Zeit.
Was aber ist sie?   [35]

Die kleine Enttäuschung, wenn ein Kind sich davonstiehlt,
Weil es weitersieht als Dein zweifelndes Wort?
Ein Gedicht aus den Tagen des Plinius, in falschen Metren,
Das vom Verliebtsein handelt, und die zwei sind längst tot,
Und es kommt dennoch ein Lied an, ein Herzton, ein Schauder?   [40]

Ist sie das Wiedersehn, wenn der Pfirsich erkannt wird,
Weil es das Wissen vom Pfirsichkern gibt? Ist sie der Fluch,
Der auf allem, was schlachtet und Dämme baut, liegt?
Ist sie der stetige Herzschlag, der sich in Sicherheit wiegt:
Daß jemand lacht und weiß nichts vom Treppensturz morgen?
Daß wir uns selbst kaum kennen, den Blick zur Erde gerichtet,
Über uns Sirius, im Rücken Ödipus...ist sie das?   [47]

Ist sie die Maus, die im Kornspeicher raschelt, das Rieseln,
Wenn durch ein ganz kleines Loch die üppige Ernte,
Die Arbeit so vieler Wochen, verschwindet?
Ist sie ein Kind, ahnungslos, das mit Glimmstäbchen spielend
Bibliotheken in Brand setzt, und Tempel, und Gärten?
Ein Kind, das noch nie was gehört hat von Herostrat...   [53]

Ist sie die Panik, die zu erwachen scheint überall,
Seit der Große Pan tot ist, das Scheusal, der stinkende Tiergott.
Seit er die Landschaften räumte wie Städte nach einer Epidemie,
Grund daß sich jeder beeilt mit dem Sterben, die Paare,
Wie gehetzt kopulieren und alles beschleunigt geht und ins Leere? [58]

Fragen, Alypius, die ich mir selbst oft gestellt hab,
Betäubt von Veränderung, seekrank vom dauernden Wechsel.
Ach, und wenn ich der Mutter zusah beim Beten, befremdet. [61]

Drei Arten Gegenwart sind in dir aufgespart.
Die eine heißt *Gestern*, die andere *Heute* und *Morgen* die dritte.
Sie alle sind rege in dir, nur in dir, nirgendwo sonst. [64]

Und laß dich nicht täuschen von sterblichen Astrologen.
Daß Zeit nur Bewegung sei, sichtbar am Himmel.
Was messen sie, wenn sie die Phasen des Mondes vermessen? [67]

Oder Gedichte mit wechselndem Versfuß, zum Beispiel Horaz.
Zwischen *"Lydia, schläfst du?"* und *"...Erz überdauernd"*
Eilt sein Vers hin und her, die geschäftige Zunge—
Zwischen Schamhaar und Ewigkeit. [71]

Einmal kurz, einmal lang sind die Silben, und der sie spricht,
Dehnt die Zeit und wird selbst gedehnt, rafft sie und wird gerafft.
Oder der Mörder, totgeweiht längst bevor ihn die Strafe ereilt—
An jedem Grenzstein schätzt er den Weg ab zum Tatort.
Terminus wird ihm zum Quälgeist. Er läuft im Kreis.
Denn wie sonst soll er laufen, wenn Schuld immer vorn liegt? [77]

In jede Richtung reicht Raum, aber Zeit ist die Klammer,
Die nach vorn spannt die Stirnen, die Deichseln und jedes Lied,
Das in Strophen zerfällt wie ein Menschenleben in Anekdoten. [80]

Augenschein erst, bald schon Erinnern, genährt von Erwartung:
So hält uns hin, was sich Zeit nennt. Seltsam, Alypius,
Wenn niemand fragt, weiß ich genau, was es ist. Aber fragst du,
Fällt mir nur Unsinn ein. Zeit, eine Krankheit zum Tode.
Oder im leeren Amphitheater ein stummer Chor
Mit den Mundhöhlen schwarz vor Empörung und Schmerz. [86]

Sind hundert Jahre Gegenwart eine lange Zeit? [87]

Schläfrig bin ich, Alypius. Was hast du gesagt?
Zeit ist das Seil, das ein Esel frißt und herausscheißt, verknotet?
Und der Esel gehört einem Mann, der die Knoten löst
Und dem Tier von neuem das Seil hinhält, mangels Futter.
Und der Esel macht statt zu rülpsen den Laut,
Den nur Esel beherrschen, vollendet.

Zeit ist kein Rätsel, Alypius. Vergiß es. [94]

Aporia Augustine (On Time)[10]

The cornea burning with salt foam,
The eye sockets deep in the tuff, Alypius,
The word-drowning sea—
Time isn't something you know.   [4]

The vault of the sky that encloses
The skull, the hands cupped over
The spinning pottery wheel—
Time isn't something you see.   [8]

The long-deceased's voices, the rattling
Of bones in the fire pit, Alypius,
Your blood in the temples—
Time isn't something you hear.   [12]

Nor something you will ever grasp. No chest hair
You pluck after bathing, no billboard
Announcing the rounds of the chariot race in the stadium.
Neither the brow of the old man, nor the pink finger pulps of the child.   [16]

Time isn't something you measure. Neither the dust
In the pan of the gold scale, nor the risen prices of fish.
Not the gnomon's wandering shadow,
Or the number of governments, wars in a lifetime.   [20]

Time isn't something that stirs. (Forget the scorpion…).
And no constellation that seafarers use for direction.
None of the routes to Troy, no way home from its shores
Past countries and families to the bitter conclusion—remembrance.   [24]

None of the illnesses, either, nothing that kills.
It isn't a giant crushing the rocks in the surf,
None of the landslides or hurricanes, none of the gods.
Nor is it the groaning of heroes in Homer's faded ears.   [28]

Yesterday, I began listening to myself, Alypius.
Words leapt out from each sentence leaving me older.
Some *soon*…some *no more*…some *of old*.
As if there were only direction in speaking, no standstill.   [32]

There was the *still*…
            The *already*…
                    The *once*…
Time, though, is none of all that.
But what is it, then?   [35]

The slight disappointment when a child steals away
Because it sees more than your doubt-ridden words?

[10] Durs Grünbein, "Aporia Augustine (On Time)," in *Mortal Diamond. Poems*, trans. Michael Eskin (New York, NY: Upper West Side Philosophers, INC, 2013), 33–6.

A poem from Pliny's day, in uneven meters,
About being in love, and the two are long dead,
And still, a song does arrive, a heart sound, a shudder?   [40]

Is it the fleet recognition—when you know it's a peach
Because you know there's a pit? Is it the curse
That lies upon all that builds dams and that slaughters?
Is it the regular heartbeat that thinks itself safe:
Laughing, not knowing tomorrow you'll fall down the stairs?
Barely knowing yourself, eyes looking downward,
Sirius above, Oedipus at your back...is that it?   [47]

Is it the mouse in the granary rustling, the drizzle—
As when through the tiniest of holes the harvest, abundant,
The labor of so many weeks, disappears?
Is it a child, oblivious, playing with sparklers,
Setting libraries, temples, and gardens on fire?
A child that never knew Herostratus...   [53]

Is it the panic that seems to awaken all over
Since the death of great Pan, the savage, the stinking animal god.
Since he vacated landscapes like towns in the wake of a plague,
This being the reason why each of us hastens to die, why couples
Make love in a hurry and all's going faster and faster with no end in sight?   [58]

Questions, Alypius, I've often wondered about,
Numb with inconstancy, seasick with unceasing change.
Ah, when I'd watch my mother in prayer, bewildered.   [61]

Three kinds of presence are held in reserve within you.
One is called *yesterday*, another *today*, and *tomorrow* the third.
They all are alive within you, only in you, nowhere else.   [64]

And don't be deceived by mortal astrologer's talk.
That time is but movement observed in the sky.
What is it they measure when they measure the moon's different phases? [67]

Or poems with varying meters—Horace, for instance.
Between "*Lydia, are you sleeping?*" and "*more lasting than bronze*"
Scurries his verse, that sedulous tongue—
Between pubic hair and eternity.   [71]

Long, short, short, long are the syllables, and the one who recites them,
Drawing out time, being drawn out himself, contracting it, being contracted.
Or the murderer, already doomed long before his comeuppance—
Each milestone a gauge of the distance to the scene of the crime.
Dogged by his nemesis, divine Terminus, he is running in circles.
How else would he run with his guilt ever looming ahead.   [77]

Space branches out in every direction, but time is the bracket
That stretches the foreheads ahead, the drawbars, each song
Breaking up into strophes like the life of a man into so many scenes.   [80]

Appearance at first, remembering then, feeding on expectation:
Thus time, so-called, leads us on. Strange, Alypius,
When nobody asks, I think I know just what it is. If you ask, though,
Nonsense is all I come up with. Time, a sickness to death.

Or in the empty amphitheater a voiceless choir
With mouth cavities black with outrage and pain.   [86]

Is one hundred years of presence a long time?   [87]

I'm sleepy, Alypius. What did you say?

Time is the rope that a donkey eats and excretes, all knotted?
And the donkey belongs to a man who unties the knots
And offers the rope to the donkey again, wanting fodder.
And the donkey makes, instead of belching, the sound
Only donkeys know how to make sound perfect.

Time is no riddle, Alypius. Forget it.   [94]

Works Cited

Adelung, Johann Christoph. "Erzwingen." In *Grammatisch-kritisches Wörterbuch der Hochdeutschen Mundart mit beständiger Vergleichung der übrigen Mundarten, besonders aber der Oberdeutschen,* 1:Sp.1963–4. Vienna, 1811.

Adelung, Johann Christoph (ed.). "Das Verhältniß." In *Grammatisch-kritisches Wörterbuch der Hochdeutschen Mundart mit beständiger Vergleichung der übrigen Mundarten, besonders aber der Oberdeutschen,* 4. Col. 1057–60. Leipzig, 1793–1801.

Ahrend, Hinrich. *'Tanz zwischen sämtlichen Stühlen': Poetik und Dichtung im lyrischen und essayistischen Werk Durs Grünbeins.* Würzburg: Königshausen und Neumann, 2010.

Albertsen, Leif Ludwig. *Neuere deutsche Metrik.* Bern: Peter Lang, 1984.

Albrecht, Michael von. "Nach den Satiren. Durs Grünbein und die Antike." In *Mythen in nachmythischer Zeit. Die Antike in der deutschsprachigen Literatur der Gegenwart.* Edited by Bernd Seidensticker and Martin Vöhler, 101–16. Berlin: de Gruyter, 2002.

Amtstätter, Mark Emanuel. *Beseelte Töne. Die Sprache des Körpers und der Dichtung in Klopstocks Eislaufoden.* Studien und Texte zur Sozialgeschichte der Literatur 107. Berlin: De Gruyter, 2005.

Ansell-Pearson, Keith (ed.) "Friedrich Nietzsche: An Introduction to his Thought, Life, and Work." In *A Companion to Nietzsche,* 1–21. Oxford: Blackwell, 2006.

Apel, August. *Metrik,* 2nd ed., Vol. 1, 2 vols. Leipzig: Verlag der Weygand'schen Buchhandlung, 1834.

Apel, August. "Über Rhythmus und Metrum." *Allgemeine musikalische Zeitung* 10, no. 1, 2, 4, 18, 19, 20, 21, 41, 42, 44 (1807–1808): 1–10, 17–26, 33–40, 49–62, 273–84, 289–98, 305–12, 321–31, 641–49, 657–68, 689–98.

Arghavan, Mahmoud, Nicole Hirschfelder, Luvena Kopp, and Katharina Motyl. *Who Can Speak and Who Is Heard/Hurt?: Facing Problems of Race, Racism, and Ethnic Diversity in the Humanities in Germany.* Transcript Verlag, 2019.

Aristoxenus. *Aristoxenus Elementa Rhythmica: The Fragment of Book II and the Additional Evidence for Aristoxenean Rhythmic Theory.* Translated by Lionel Ignacius Cusack Pearson. Oxford: Clarendon Press, 1990.

Arndt, Erwin. *Deutsche Verslehre.* 13th ed. Berlin: Volk und Wissen Verlag, 1996.

Augustine. *Confessions.* Edited and translated by Carolyn J.B. Hammond. Vol. 2: Books 9–13. Loeb Classical Library 27. Cambridge: Harvard University Press, 2016.

Aurochs, Bernd. *Die Entstehung der Kunstreligion.* Göttingen: Vandenhoeck & Ruprecht, 2006.

Baldelli, Giulia. "Von Spechten und Lacerten: Nietzsches Auseinandersetzung mit der Epigrammtradition in 'Dichters Berufung.'" In *Nietzsche und die Lyrik. Ein Kompendium* Edited by Christian Benne and Claus Zittel, 173–90. Stuttgart: Metzler Verlag, 2017.

Baldick, Chris. "Knittelvers." In *The Oxford Dictionary of Literary Terms.* Oxford University Press, 2008.

Barsch, Achim. *Metrik, Literatur und Sprache. Generative Grammatik zwischen empirischer Literaturwissenschaft und generativer Phonologie.* Braunschweig: Friedrich Vieweg & Sohn Verlagsgesellschaft, 1991.

Baumgarten, Alexander. *Die Aesthetik Alexander Gottlieb Baumgartens unter besonderer Berücksichtigung der Meditationes philosophicae de nonnullis ad poema pertinentibus nebst einer Uebersetzung dieser Schrift.* Translated by Albert Riemann. Halle: Max Niemeyer Verlag, 1928.

Baumgarten, Alexander. *Meditationes philosophicae de nonnullis ad poema pertinentibus.* Translated by Karl Aschenbrenner and William B. Holther. Berkeley: University of California Press, 1954.

Bedetti, Gabriella, and Henri Meschonnic. "Interview: Henri Meschonnic." *Diacritics* 18, no. 3 (1988): 93–111. https://doi.org/10.2307/465257.

Benes, Tuska. *In Babel's Shadow: Language, Philology, and the Nation in Nineteenth-Century Germany.* Detroit, Mich: Wayne State University Press, 2008.

Benne, Christian. *Nietzsche und die historisch-kritische Philologie*. Monographien und Texte zur Nietzsche-Forschung. 49. Berlin: De Gruyter, 2005.

Benne, Christian. "*Incipit parodia*–noch einmal." In *Pathos, Parodie, Kryptomnesie. Das Gedächtnis der Literatur in Nietzsches* Also sprach Zarathustra. Edited by Gabriella Pelloni and Isolde Schiffermüller, 49–66. Heidelberg: Winter, 2015.

Benne, Christian. "The Philosophy of Prosopopoeia." *The Journal of Nietzsche Studies* 47.2. 2 (July 6, 2016): 275–86.

Benne, Christian, and Jutta Georg. "Einführung." In *Friedrich Nietzsche: Die fröhliche Wissenschaft*. Edited by Christian Benne and Jutta Georg, 1–6. Berlin: de Gruyter, 2015.

Benne, Christian, and Claus Zittel. "Einleitung." In *Nietzsche und die Lyrik. Ein Kompendium*. Edited by Christian Benne and Claus Zittel, 1–8. Berlin: de Gruyter, 2017.

Blackall, Eric A. *The Emergence of German as a Literary Language, 1700–1775*. Cambridge: Cambridge University Press, 1959.

Blasius, Leslie David. "Nietzsche, Riemann, and Wagner: When Music Lies." In *Music Theory and Natural Order from the Renaissance to the Early Twentieth Century*. Edited by Suzannah Clark and Alexander Rehding, 93–107. Cambridge: Cambridge University Press, 2001.

Böckh, August. *Über die Versmasse des Pindaros*. Berlin: Realschulbuchhandlung, 1809.

Bodmer, Johann Jakob (Transl.). *Homers Werke. Aus dem Griechischen übersetzt von dem Dichter der Noachide*. Zürich: Orell, Gessner, Füesslin und Compagnie, 1778.

Bodmer, Johann Jakob (presumed). "Aufgefangener Brief." In *Die Lehre von der Nachahmung der antiken Versmaße im Deutschen. In Quellenschriften des 18. und 19. Jahrhunderts. Mit kommentierter Bibliographie*. Edited by Hans-Heinrich Hellmuth and Joachim Schröder, 9–13. Munich: Wilhelm Fink Verlag, 1976.

Bonds, Mark Evan. "Aesthetic Amputations: Absolute Music and the Deleted Endings of Hanslick's Vom Musikalisch-Schönen," *19th-Century Music* 36, no. 1 (2012): 3–23, https://doi.org/10.1525/ncm.2012.36.1.003;

Bormann, Alexander von. "Im Dickicht des Nicht-Ich. Durs Grünbeins Anapäste." In *Signaturen der Gegenwartsliteratur. Festschrift für Walter Hinderer*. Edited by Dieter Borchmeyer, 171–84. Würzburg: Königshausen und Neumann, 1999.

Boyd, Brian. *Why Lyrics Last. Evolution, Cognition, and Shakespeare's Sonnets*. Cambridge: Harvard University Press, 2012.

Boyd, Brian, Joseph Carroll, and Jonathan Gottschall, eds. *Evolution, Literature, and Film: A Reader*. New York: Columbia University Press, 2010.

Brambach, Wilhelm. "Kritische Streifzüge. II. Metrik und Musik." *Rheinisches Museum für Philologie* Neue Folge 25 (1870): 232–52.

Brambach, Wilhelm. *Rhythmische und metrische Untersuchungen*. Leipzig: Teubner, 1871.

Breitinger, Johann Jacob. *Fortsetzung der Critischen Dichtkunst: Worinnen die poetische Mahlerey in Absicht auf den Ausdruck und die Farben abgehandelt wird, mit einer Vorrede von Johann Jacob Bodemer*. Facsimile print based on the 1740 edition. Stuttgart: Metzler, 1966.

Breuer, Dieter. *Deutsche Metrik und Versgeschichte*. 4th ed. Munich: Wilhelm Fink Verlag, 2008.

Brücke, Ernst. *Die physiologischen Grundlagen der neuhochdeutschen Verskunst*. Vienna: Carl Gerold's Sohn, 1871.

Buchenau, Stefanie. *The Founding of Aesthetics in the German Enlightenment: The Art of Invention and the Invention of Art*. Cambridge: Cambridge University Press, 2013.

Bunia, Remigius. *Metrik und Kulturpolitik. Opitz, Klopstock, Bürger*. Berlin: Rippenger und Kremers Verlag, 2014.

Bürger, Gottfried August. *Sämmtliche Werke*. Vol. II/IV vols. Göttingen: Verlag der Dieterichschen Buchhandlung, 1844.

Bürger, Gottfried August. "An einen Freund über seine teutsche Ilias." In *Die Lehre von der Nachahmung der antiken Versmaße im Deutschen. In Quellenschriften des 18. und 19. Jahrhunderts. Mit kommentierter Bibliographie*. Edited by Hans-Heinrich Hellmuth and Joachim Schröder, 158–71. Munich: Wilhelm Fink Verlag, 1976.

Burt, S. "What Is This Thing Called Lyric?," *Modern Philology* 113, no. 3 (February 2016): 422–40, https://doi.org/10.1086/684097.

Buschendorf, Bernhard. "Die Geburt der Lyrik aus dem Geiste der Parodie. Friedrich Nietzsches Gedicht 'An die Melancholie.'" In *Jedes Wort ist ein Vorurteil": Philologie und Philosophie in Nietzsches Denken*. Edited by Manfred Riedel. Colone: Böhlau, 1999.

Büttner, Urs. "Erkenntnisse des Schnees. Grünbeins cartesische Anthropologie und Ästhetik." In *Bildlichkeit im Werk Durs Grünbeins*. Edited by Christoph auf der Horst and Miriam Seidler, 163–84. Berlin: de Gruyter, 2015.

Byers, Thomas B. "The Closing of the American Line: Expansive Poetry and Ideology." *Contemporary Literature* 33, no. 2 (Summer 1992): 396–415.

Caduff, Renzo. "Sebastian Donat: Deskriptive Metrik. (Reihe Comparanda. Literaturwissenschaftliche Studien zu Antike und Moderne). Innsbruck/Wien/ Bozen: StudienVerlag, 2010, Band 15, 180 Seiten." *Arcadia* 47, no. 1 (July 2012). https://doi.org/10.1515/arcadia-2012-0014.

Caplin, William E. "Theories of Musical Rhythm in the Eighteenth and Nineteenth Centuries." In *The Cambridge History of Western Music Theory*. Edited by Thomas Christensen, 657–94. Cambridge: Cambridge University Press, 2002.

Collinge, N.E. "156. The Introduction of the Historical Principle into the Study of Languages: Grimm. XXIV. The Establishment of New Philologies in the 19th Century / Die Herausbildung neuer Philologien im 19. Jahrhundert/Le Développement des Nouvelley Philologies au XIXe Siècle." In *History of the Language Sciences - Geschichte der Sprachwissenschaften - Histoire des Sciences du Langage*. Edited by Sylvain Auroux, E.F.K. Koerner, Hans-Josef Niederehe, and Kees Versteegh, 2: 1210–23. Berlin/Boston: de Gruyter, 2008.

Collins, Christopher. *Paleopoetics. The Evolution of the Preliterate Imagination*. New York: Columbia University Press, 2013.

Cooper, Ian. "Direction, Disruption, Voice: Durs Grünbein's 'Historien' and 'Neue Historien.'" *Germanic Review* 84, no. 2 (2009): 99–121.

Corbineau-Hoffmann, Angelika. "Rhythmus." In *Historisches Wörterbuch der Philosophie. Gesamtwerk. R - Sc*. Edited by Joachim Ritter and Karlfried Grunder, 1026–33. Basel: Schwabe Verlag 1992.

Corn, Alfred. *The Poem's Heartbeat: A Manual of Prosody*. Port Townsend, WA: Copper Canyon Press, 1997.

Couturier-Heinrich, Clémence. "Gottfried Hermann, un philologue kantien." *Revue germanique international* 14 (2011): 73–90.

Couturier-Heinrich, Clémence. "Autorität und Konkurrenz. Zur Reaktion von Goethe und Schiller auf Vossens Hexameterlehre und –praxis." In *Voß' Übersetzungssprache. Voraussetzungen, Kontexte, Folgen*. Edited by Anne Baillot, Erica Fantino, and Josefine Kitzbichler, 71–92. Berlin: De Gruyter, 2015.

Cowper, William (Transl.). *The Iliad and Odyssey: Of Homer, Translated into English Blank Verse, by W. Cowper, of the Inner Temple, Esq.* Dublin, 1792.

Culler, Jonathan. *Theory of the Lyric*. Cambridge: Harvard University Press, 2015.

Culler, Jonathan. "Why Rhythm?," In *Critical Rhythm: The Poetics of a Literary Life Form*. Edited by Ben Glaser, Jonathan Culler, Lazar Fleishman, and Haun Saussy, 21–39. New York: Fordham University Press, 2019.

Curran, Jane Veronica. *Horace's "Epistles," Wieland and the Reader: A Three-Way Relationship*. Bithell Series of Dissertations. London: W.S. Maney and Son Ltd, 1999.

Dabrowska, Anna. "Die Dichtung von Durs Grünbein und die Musik." In *Authentizität und Polyphonie. Beiträge zur deutschen und polnischen Lyrik seit 1945. Für Gerhard R. Kaiser zum fünfundsechzigsten Geburtstag*. Edited by Jan Volker Röhnhart, 225–36. Heidelberg: Winter, 2006.

Dehrmann, Mark-Georg. "Klopstocks totaler Krieg - Zur Neuedition von Klopstocks Hermann-Dramen": literaturkritik.de," accessed July 5, 2022, https://literaturkritik.de/id/14395).

Deleuze, Gilles and Félix Guattari. *A Thousand Plateaus: Capitalism and Schizophrenia*. Translated by Brian Massumi. Minneapolis: University of Minnesota Press, 1987.

Denham Kristin and Anne Lobeck. *Linguistics for Everyone*. 2nd ed. Boston: Wadsworth, 2013.

Detering, Heinrich. "Stagnation und Höhenflug: 'Die Lieder des Prinzen Vogelfrei.'" In *Friedrich Nietzsche: Die fröhliche Wissenschaft*. Edited by Christian Benne and Jutta Georg, 151–74. Berlin: de Gruyter, 2015.

Diesen, Deborah. *The Pout-Pout Fish*. New York: Farrar, Straus and Giroux, 2008.

Donat, Sebastian. *Deskriptive Metrik.* Comparanda 15. Innsbruck: Studien Verlag, 2010.

Donington, Robert. "Ictus." In *Grove Music Online.* Accessed July 5, 2022. http://www. oxfordmusiconline.com.ezproxy.library.wisc.edu/view/10.1093/gmo/9781561592630.001.0001/ omo-9781561592630-e-0000013699.

Dürbeck, Gabriele. "'Wenn es stimmt, dass wir schwierige Tiere sind.' Anatomie und Anthropologie in Durs Grünbeins 'Mensch ohne Großhirn.'" *Zeitschrift für Germanistik* 19, no. 1 (2009): 133–45.

Ekman, Ulrik, and Hans Ulrich Gumbrecht. "The Speed of Beauty: Hans Ulrich Gumbrecht, Interviewed by Ulrik Ekman." *Postmodern Culture* 16, no. 3 (2006).

Eldridge, Hannah Vandegrift. "Towards a Philosophy of Rhythm: Nietzsche's Conflicting Rhythms." *Journal of Literary Theory* 12, no. 1 (2018): 151–70. https://doi.org/10.1515/jlt-2018-0009.

Emden, Christian J. *Nietzsche's Naturalism: Philosophy and the Life Sciences in the Nineteenth Century.* Cambridge: Cambridge University Press, 2014.

Erhart, Walter. "Literaturwissenschaft und Physik. Aus Anlass von Durs Grünbeins *Vom Schnee oder Descartes in Deutschland* (2003)." In *Literaturwissenschaft—interdisciplinär.* Edited by Lothar van Laak and Katja Malsch, 115–26. Heidelberg: Synchron, 2010.

Ertel, Anna. *Körper, Gehirne, Gene: Lyrik und Naturwissenschaft bei Ulrike Draesner und Durs Grünbein.* Berlin: de Gruyter, 2011.

Eskin, Michael. "Descartes of Metaphor. On Durs Grünbein's 'Vom Schnee.'" In *Schaltstelle. Neue deutsche Lyrik im Dialog.* Edited by Karen Leeder, 163–79. Amsterdam: Rodopi, 2007.

Eskin, Michael. "Denkbilder: Zu einem Motiv bei Durs Grünbein." In *Bildlichkeit im Werk Durs Grünbeins.* Edited by Christoph auf der Horst and Miriam Seidler, 141–62. Berlin: de Gruyter, 2015.

Esser, Jürgen. *Rhythm in Speech, Prose and Verse. A Linguistic Description.* Berlin: Logos Verlag, 2011.

European Commission. "Women Professors on the Increase in German Universities." *CORDIS EU research results.* Accessed July 5, 2022. https://cordis.europa.eu/article/id/28031-women-professors-on-the-increase-in-german-universities.

Ewell, Philip A. "Music Theory and the White Racial Frame." *Music Theory Online* 26, no. 2 (September 2020). https://doi.org/DOI:10.30535/mto.26.2.4.

Fabb, Nigel. *Linguistics and Literature: Language in the Verbal Arts of the World.* Oxford: Blackwell, 1997.

Fabb, Nigel, and Morris Halle. *Meter in Poetry: A New Theory.* 1 edition. Cambridge: Cambridge University Press, 2008.

Facts I Just Made Up, "Can you explain how crackers are made?". Accessed July 5, 2022. https://facts-i-just-made-up.tumblr.com/post/86186032503/i-spent-like-15-hours-on-this.

Fantino, Erica. "Johann Heinrich Voß als junger Dichter und Übersetzer antiker Lyrik. Zur Entfaltung seiner rigoristischen Methode." In *Voß' Übersetzungssprache. Voraussetzungen, Kontexte, Folgen.* Edited by Anne Baillot, Erica Fantino, and Josefine Kitzbichler, 1–32. Berlin: De Gruyter, 2015.

Farr, Arnold. "Wie *Weiß*sein sichtbar wird. Aufklärungsrassismus und die Struktur eines rassifizierten Bewusstseins." In *Mythen, Masken und Subjekte. Kritische Weißseinsforschung in Deutschland.* Edited by Maureen Maisha Eggers et al. Münster: Unrast Verlag, 2005.

Forrer, Thomas. "Rhythmische Parodie. Friedrich Nietzsches Gedicht 'Dichters Berufung.'" In *Der Witz der Philologie. Rhetorik-Poetik-Edition.* Edited by Felix Christen, Thomas Forrer, Martin Stingelin, and Hubert Thüring, 108–22. Frankfurt a.M.: Stroemfeld, 2014.

Forster, Michael. "Johann Gottfried von Herder." In *The Stanford Encyclopedia of Philosophy.* Edited by Edward N. Zalta. Metaphysics Research Lab, Stanford University, 2019. https://plato.stanford.edu/archives/sum2019/entries/herder/

Fortson, Benjamin. *Language and Rhythm in Plautus: Synchronic and Diachronic Studies.* Walter de Gruyter, 2008.

Frank, H.J. *Handbuch der deutschen Strophenformen.* Munich: Hanser Verlag, 1980.

Fuchs, Carl. *Präliminarien zu einer Kritik der Tonkunst.* Leipzig: E.M. Fritzsch, 1871.

Fuchs, Carl. *Die Zukunft des musikalischen Vortrages und sein Ursprung.* Danzig: A.W. Kafemann, 1884.

Fuchs, Stefan. "Gender Disparities in Higher Education and Academic Careers in Germany and the United States." AICGS Policy Papers, 1999.

Fuhrmann, Manfred. "'Von Wieland bis Voss: Wie verdeutscht man antike Autoren?'" *Jahrbuch des Freien Deutschen Hochstifts* (1987): 1–22.

Gane, Nicholas, and Geoffrey Winthrop-Young. "Friedrich Kittler: An Introduction." *Theory, Culture & Society* 23, no. 7–8 (2006): 5–16.

Gasparov, Mikhail L. *A History of European Versification*. Translated by G.S. Smith and Marina Tarlinskaja. Oxford: Clarendon Press, 1996.

Gerber, Natalie. "Stress-Based Metrics Revisited: A Comparative Exercise in Scansion Systems and Their Implications for Iambic Pentameter." *Thinking Verse* 3 (2013): 131–68.

Gibbon, Dafydd. "Intonation in German." In *Intonation Systems. A Survey of Twenty Languages*. Edited by Daniel Hirst and Albert di Cristo, 78–95. Cambridge: Cambridge University Press, 1998.

Gilman, Sander L. "Incipit Parodia: The Function of Parody in the Lyrical Poetry of Friedrich Nietzsche." *Nietzsche-Studien* 4 (1975): 52–74.

Gilman, Sander L. and Carole Blair in Friedrich Nietzsche. *Friedrich Nietzsche on Rhetoric and Language*. Edited by Sander L. Gilman, Carole Blair, and David J. Parent. New York: Oxford University Press, 1989.

Glaser, Ben. "Introduction." In *Critical Rhythm: The Poetics of a Literary Life Form*. Edited by Ben Glaser, Jonathan Culler, Lazar Fleishman, and Haun Saussy, 1–18. New York: Fordham University Press, 2019.

Goltschnigg, Dietmar. "Vorindustrieller Realismus und Literatur der Gründerzeit." In *Geschichte der deutschen Literatur*. Edited by Viktor Žmegač. Band II/1 1848-1918:1–108. Königstein: Athenäum 1980.

Görner, Rüdiger. "Nur Narr, Nur Dichter. Musikalität und Poetik." *Nietzsche-Studien* 41, no. 1 (2012): 43–57. https://doi.org/10.1515/niet.2012.41.1.43.

Gottsched, Johann Christoph. "Gutachten, von der heroischen Versart unsrer neuen biblischen Epopeen." In *Die Lehre von der Nachahmung der antiken Versmaße im Deutschen. In Quellenschriften des 18. und 19. Jahrhunderts. Mit kommentierter Bibliographie*. Edited by Hans-Heinrich Hellmuth and Joachim Schröder, 15–24. Munich: Wilhelm Fink Verlag, 1976.

Gottsched, Johann Christoph. *Versuch einer critischen Dichtkunst. Vierte, sehr vermehrte Auflage*. 4th ed. Darmstadt: Wissenschaftliche Buchgesellschaft, 1977.

Grey, Thomas. "Wagner." In *The Routledge Companion to Philosophy and Music*. Edited by Theodore Gracyk and Andrew Kania, 380–90. New York: Routledge, 2011.

Grimm, Erk. "Mediamania? Contemporary German Poetry in the Age of New Information Technologies: Thomas Kling and Durs Grünbein." *Studies in 20th Century Literature* 21, no. 1 (1997): 275–301.

Grimm, Jacob. *Deutsche Grammatik*. 2nd ed. Vol. 1. Gütersloh: Druck und Verlag von C. Bertelsmann, 1893.

Grimm, Jacob, and Wilhelm Grimm (eds). "Erzwingen." In *Deutsches Wörterbuch von Jacob und Wilhelm Grimm. 16 Bde. in 32 Teilbänden*, Sp.1104. Leipzig, 1854–1961.

Groddeck, Wolfram. *Friedrich Nietzsche. "Dionysos-Dithyramben."* Vol. 2. Die "Dionysos-Dithyramben" Bedeutung und Entstehung von Nietzsches letztem Werk. 2 vols. Berlin: de Gruyter, 1991.

Große, Wilhelm. "Descartes/Grünbein oder das Dreieck aus Philosophie, naturwissenschaftlichem Dehken und Literaturpoesie. Anmerkungen zu Durs Grünbeins *Vom Schnee oder Descartes in Deutschland*." *Literatur im Unterricht* 6, no. 5 (2005): 219–27.

Grünbein, Durs. "Drei Briefe." In *Galilei vermißt Dantes Hölle und bleibt an den Maßen hängen. Aufsätze 1989–1995*, 40–54. Frankfurt a.M.: Suhrkamp Verlag, 1996.

Grünbein, Durs. "Katze und Mond." In *Galilei vermißt Dantes Hölle und bleibt an den Maßen hängen. Aufsätze 1989–1995*, 55–60. Frankfurt a.M.: Suhrkamp Verlag, 1996.

Grünbein, Durs. "Mein babylonisches Hirn." In *Galilei vermißt Dantes Hölle und bleibt an den Maßen hängen. Aufsätze 1989–1995*, 18–33. Frankfurt a.M.: Suhrkamp Verlag, 1996.

Grünbein, Durs. "Biologischer Walzer/Biological Waltz." Translated by Andrew Shields. *Poetry Magazine*, November 1998. https://www.poetryfoundation.org/poetrymagazine

Grünbein, Durs. "Aporia Augustinus (Über Die Zeit)." In *Nach den Satiren*, 33–36. Frankfurt: Suhrkamp Verlag, 1999.

Grünbein, Durs. "Zwischen Antike und X." *Text + Kritik* 153 (2002): 68–71.

Grünbein, Durs. "Schlaflos in Rom. Versuch über den Satirendichter Juvenal." In *Antike Dispositionen. Aufsätze*, 328–68. Frankfurt a.M.: Suhrkamp Verlag, 2005.

Grünbein, Durs. *Gedichte. Bücher I-III.* Frankfurt am Main: Suhrkamp Verlag, 2006.

Grünbein, Durs. "Das Gedicht und sein Geheimnis." In *Gedicht und Geheimnis. Aufsätze 1990-2006*, 84–95. Frankfurt a.M.: Suhrkamp Verlag, 2007.

Grünbein, Durs. "Ein kleines blaues Mädchen." In *Gedicht und Geheimnis. Aufsätze 1990-2006*, 135–54. Frankfurt a.M.: Suhrkamp Verlag, 2007.

Grünbein, Durs. "Der Indianer des Geistes. Bagatellen über das Leben des Philosophen Pascale." *Zeitschrift für Ideengeschichte* 2, no. 1 (2008): 69–84. München: Verlag C. H. Beck, 2008.

Grünbein, Durs. "A Little Blue Girl." In *The Bars of Atlantis. Selected Essays.* Edited by Michael Eskin, translated by John Crutchfield, 209–27. New York: Farrar, Straus and Giroux, 2010.

Grünbein, Durs. "Accented Time." In *The Bars of Atlantis. Selected Essays.* Edited by Michael Eskin, translated by Andrew Shields, 116–31. New York: Farrar, Straus and Giroux, 2010.

Grünbein, Durs. *Descartes' Devil. Three Meditations.* Edited by Michael Eskin, translated by Anthea Bell. New York: Upper West Side Philosophers, INC, 2010.

Grünbein, Durs. "My Babylonish Brain." In *The Bars of Atlantis. Selected Essays.* Edited by Michael Eskin, translated by Michael Hofmann, 59–71. New York: Farrar, Straus and Giroux, 2010.

Grünbein, Durs. "The Poem and Its Secret." In *The Bars of Atlantis. Selected Essays.* Edited by Michael Eskin, translated by Andrew Shields, 59–71. New York: Farrar, Straus and Giroux, 2010.

Grünbein, Durs. "The Thinker's Voice." In *The Bars of Atlantis. Selected Essays.* Edited by Michael Eskin, translated by John Crutchfield, 228–45. New York: Farrar, Straus and Giroux, 2010.

Grünbein, Durs. "Vom Schnee." In *Zeitschrift für Germanistik* 21, Nr. 2 (2011): 256–58. Bern: Verlag Peter Lang, 2011.

Grünbein, Durs. "Aporia Augustine (On Time)." In Mortal Diamond. Poems. Translated by Michael Eskin, 33–36. New York, NY: Upper West Side Philosophers, INC, 2013.

Grünbein, Durs, and Hans-Jürgen Heinrichs. "Gespräch mit Durs Grünbein." *Sinn und Form* 1 (2008): 47–66.

Grünbein, Durs, and Heinz-Norbert Jocks. *Durs Grünbein im Gespräch mit Heinz-Norbert Jocks.* Köln: DuMont Buchverlag, 2001.

Grundlehner, Philip. *The Poetry of Friedrich Nietzsche.* New York: Oxford University Press, 1986.

Gumbrecht, Hans Ulrich. "Rhythm and Meaning." In *Materialities of Communication.* Edited by Hans Ulrich Gumbrecht and Ludwig K. Pfeiffer, translated by William Whobrey, 170–82. Stanford: Stanford University Press, 1994.

Gumbrecht, Hans Ulrich. *The Production of Presence. What Meaning Cannot Convey.* Stanford: Stanford University Press, 2003.

Gumbrecht, Hans Ulrich. "Media History as the Event of Truth: On the Singularity of Friedrich A. Kittler's Works." In *The Truth of the Technological World: Essays on the Genealogy of Presence*, by Friedrich A. Kittler, 307–29, translated by Erik Butler. Stanford: Stanford University Press, 2013.

Günther, Friederike Felicitas. *Rhythmus beim frühen Nietzsche.* Berlin: de Gruyter, 2008.

Guyer, Paul. "18th Century German Aesthetics." In *The Stanford Encyclopedia of Philosophy.* Edited by Edward N. Zalta. Stanford, January 16, 2007. https://plato.stanford.edu/archives/win2016/entries/aesthetics-18th-german/.

Guyer, Paul. *A History of Modern Aesthetics: The Eighteenth Century.* Cambridge University Press, 2014.

Hall, Robert W. "Schopenhauer's Philosophy of Music." In *A Companion to Schopenhauer.* Edited by Bart Vandenabeele, 165–77. Malden, MA: Wiley-Blackwell, 2012.

Hamilton, John T. *Soliciting Darkness: Pindar, Obscurity, and the Classical Tradition. Harvard Studies in Comparative Literature 47.* Cambridge, MA: Harvard University Press, 2004.

Hanslick, Eduard. *Vom Musikalisch-Schönen. Ein Beitrag zur Revision der Ästhetik der Tonkunst.* Edited by Dietmar Strauss. Mainz: Schott, 1990.

Hanson, Kristin, and Paul Kiparsky. "A Parametric Theory of Poetic Meter." *Language* 72, no. 2 (1996): 287–335.

Haugen, Kristine Louise. *Richard Bentley. Poetry and Enlightenment.* Cambridge, MA: Harvard University Press, 2011.

Hayes, Bruce. "The Prosodic Hierarchy in Meter." In *Rhythm and Meter*. Edited by Paul Kiparsky and Gilbert Youmans, 201–60. Academic Press, 1989. https://doi.org/10.1016/B978-0-12-409340-9.50013-9.

Hayes, Bruce. "Meter in Poetry. Nigel Fabb, Morris Halle, Cambridge University Press, Cambridge (2008)." *Lingua* 120, no. 10 (October 1, 2010): 2515–21. https://doi.org/10.1016/j.lingua.2010.04.001.

Hellmuth, Hans-Heinrich. *Metrische Erfindung und metrische Theorie bei Klopstock*. Munich: Wilhelm Fink Verlag, 1973.

Hempfer, Klaus. "Some Aspects of a Theory of Genre." In *Linguistics and Literary Studies / Linguistik und Literaturwissenschaft: Interfaces, Encounters, Transfers / Begegnungen, Interferenzen und Kooperationen*. Edited by Monika Fludernik and Daniel Jacob. Linguae & litterae 31. Berlin: de Gruyter, 2014.

Heng, Geraldine. "The Invention of Race in the European Middle Ages II: Locations of Medieval Race." *Literature Compass* 8, no. 5 (2011): https://doi.org/10.1111/j.1741-4113.2011.00795.x.

Hennig, Ursula. "Einleitung." In *Über althochdeutsche Prosodie und Verskunst (1823/24). Mit Beiträgen von Jacob Grimm*. Edited by Ursula Hennig, 1–56. Hermaea Germanistische Forschungen. Tübingen: Max Niemeyer Verlag, 1990.

Herder, Johann Gottfried. "Kritische Wälder oder Betrachtungen über die Wissenschaft und Kunst des Schönen. Viertes Wäldchen: Über Riedels Theorie der Schönen Künste (1769)." In *Werke*, Vol. 2. Edited by Wolfgang Pross. Munich: Carl Hanser Verlag, 1984.

Herder, Johann Gottfried. "Über die neuere deutsche Literatur. Fragmente. Zweite, völlig umgearbeitete Ausgabe." In *Werke*, Vol. 1. Edited by Wolfgang Pross, 63–210. Munich: Carl Hanser Verlag, 1984.

Herder, Johann Gottfried. "Versuch einer Geschichte der Lyrik." In *Werke*, Vol. 1. Edited by Wolfgang Pross, 7–61. Munich: Carl Hanser Verlag, 1984.

Hermann, Gottfried. *Handbuch der Metrik*. Leipzig: Gerhard Fleischer dem Jüngern, 1799.

Hillebrandt, Claudia, Sonja Klimek, Ralph Müller, William Waters, and Rüdiger Zymner. "Theories of Lyric." *Journal of Literary Theory* 11, no. 1 (2017): 1–11. https://doi.org/10.1515/jlt-2017-0001.

Hilliard, Kevin. *Philosophy, Letters, and the Fine Arts in Klopstock's Thought*. London: Institute of Germanic Studies, 1987.

Hilliard, Kevin. "Die»Baumgartensche Schule«und der Strukturwandel der Lyrik in der Gefühlskultur der Aufklärung." In *Gefühlskultur in der bürgerlichen Aufklärung*. Edited by Achim Aurnhammer, Dieter Martin, and Robert Seidel, 11–22. Frühe Neuzeit 98. Tübingen: Niemeyer, 2004.

Hilliard, Kevin, and Katrin Kohl. "Einleitung." In *Wort und Schrift: Das Werk Friedrich Gottlieb Klopstocks*. Edited by Kevin Hilliard and Katrin Kohl, 1–5. Hallesche Forschungen 27. Tübingen: Niemeyer, 2008.

Hoffmann, Torsten. *Körperpoetiken: Zur Funktion des Körpers in der Dichtungstheorie des 18. Jahrhunderts*. Munich: Wilhelm Fink Verlag, 2015.

Hollander, John. *Rhyme's Reason: A Guide to English Verse* 3rd ed. New Haven: Yale Nota Bene, 2001.

Holub, Robert C. *Nietzsche in the Nineteenth Century: Social Questions and Philosophical Interventions*. Philadelphia: University of Pennsylvania Press, 2018. https://doi.org/10.9783/9780812295146.

Holzmüller, Anne. *Lyrik als Klangkunst. Klanggestaltung in Goethes Nachtliedern und ihren Vertonungen von Reichardt bis Wolf*. Freiburg: Rombach Verlag, 2015.

Hoorn, Tanja van. "Keine Tiergeister im ‚Schnee.' Grünbeins Descartes-Ideen." *Zeitschrift für Germanistik* 21, no. 2 (2011): 284–95.

Horace. *Odes and Epodes*. Edited and translated by Niall Rudd. Vol. 33. Loeb Classical Library. Cambridge: Harvard University Press, 2004.

Horst, Christoph auf der. "Durs Grünbein, Descartes und die Neurologie: Kennt Grünbeins Psychopoetik einen *Embodied Cognition*-Ansatz?" In *Bildlichkeit im Werk Durs Grünbeins*. Edited by Christoph auf der Horst and Miriam Seidler, 185–215. Berlin: de Gruyter, 2015.

Irmer, Thomas. "Durs Grünbein." In *Deutschsprachige Lyriker des 20. Jahrhunderts*. Edited by Ursula Heukenkamp and Peter Geist, 711–21. Berlin: Erich Schmidt, 2007.

Jackson, Virginia. "Lyric." In *Princeton Encyclopedia of Poetry and Poetics*, 4th edn, Edited by Stephen Cushman, Clare Cavanagh, Jahan Ramazani, and Paul Rouzer, 826–34. Princeton: Princeton University Press, 2012.

Jackson, Virginia. "The Cadence of Consent: Francis Barton Gummere, Lyric Rhythm, and White Poetics." In *Critical Rhythm: The Poetics of a Literary Life Form*. Edited by Ben Glaser, Jonathan Culler, Lazar Fleishman, and Haun Saussy, 87–105. New York: Fordham University Press, 2019.

Jacobs, Arthur M. "Neurocognitive Poetics: Methods and Models for Investigating the Neuronal and Cognitive-Affective Bases of Literature Reception." *Frontiers in Human Neuroscience* 9 (April 16, 2015) https://doi.org/10.3389/fnhum.2015.00186.

Jakobson, Roman. "Closing Statement: Linguistics and Poetics." In *Style in Language*. Edited by T.A. Sebeok, 350–77. Cambridge: Cambridge University Press, 1960.

Jensen, Anthony K., and Helmut Heit. "Introduction." In *Nietzsche as a Scholar of Antiquity*. Edited by Anthony K. Jensen and Helmut Heit, xvii–xxii. London: Bloomsbury, 2014.

Joseph, John E. "Language-Body Continuity in the Linguistics-Semiology-Poetics-Traductology of Henri Meschonnic." *Comparative Critical Studies* 15, no. 3 (October 1, 2018): 311–29. https://doi.org/10.3366/ccs.2018.0298.

Joseph, John E. *Language, Mind and Body: A Conceptual History*. Cambridge University Press, 2018.

Joseph, John E. "Introduction." In *The Henri Meschonnic Reader: A Poetics of Society*. Edited by Marko Pajević, 1–14. Edinburgh: Edinburgh University Press, 2019.

Kaiser, Gerhard. "Wortwelten, Weltworte. Die ersten beiden 'Dionysos-Dithyramben' Nietzsches." In *Augenblicke deutscher Lyrik: Gedichte von Martin Luther bis Paul Celan*, 300–52. Frankfurt a.M.: Insel Verlag, 1987.

Kaufmann, Sebastian. "'Die letzte Entscheidung über den Text zwingt zum scrupulösesten ‚Hören' von Wort und Satz' – Textgenese und Druckgeschichte der *Fröhlichen Wissenschaft*." In *Friedrich Nietzsche: Die fröhliche Wissenschaft*. Edited by Christian Benne and Jutta Georg, 7–18. Berlin: de Gruyter, 2015.

Kaufmann, Sebastian. "Heiterkeit, Heroismus, Sentimentalität. Nietzsches *Idyllen aus Messina* und sein poetologisches Konzept der Idylle." In *Nietzsche als Dichter. Lyrik - Poetologie - Rezeption*. Edited by Katharina Grätz and Sebastian Kaufmann, 95–119. Berlin: de Gruyter, 2017.

Kaufmann, Sebastian. "'verbessert, verlängert, zum Theil verkürzt, dieser Sammlung einverleibt.' Nietzsches 'Rezyklierung' der 'Idyllen aus Messina' in den 'Liedern des Prinzen Vogelfrei.'" In *Nietzsche und die Lyrik. Ein Kompendium*. Edited by Christian Benne and Claus Zittel, 115–34. Stuttgart: Metzler Verlag, 2017.

Kellner, Ulrich. "'Zwischen Antike und X.' Zur Poetologie Grünbeins." In *Zwischen Globalisierung und Regionalisierung. Zur Darstellung von Zeitgeschichte in deutschsprachiger Gegenwartsliteratur.* Edited by Martin Hellström and Edgar Plate, 41–52. Munich: Iudicum, 2008.

Kittler, Friedrich A. "Homer and Writing." In *The Truth of the Technological World: Essays on the Genealogy of Presence*. Translated by Erik Butler, 259–66. Stanford: Stanford University Press, 2013.

Kittler, Friedrich A. "Lullaby of Birdland." In *The Truth of the Technological World: Essays on the Genealogy of Presence*. Translated by Erik Butler, 31–44. Stanford: Stanford University Press, 2013.

Kittler, Friedrich A. "In the Wake of the *Odyssey*." In *The Truth of the Technological World:Essays on the Genealogy of Presence*. Translated by Erik Butler, 275–89. Stanford: Stanford University Press, 2014.

Kittler, Friedrich A. "Nietzsche (1844–1900)." In *The Truth of the Technological World: Essays on the Genealogy of Presence*. Translated by Erik Butler, 17–30. Stanford: Stanford University Press, 2014.

Kittler, Friedrich A. "Poet, Mother, Child: On the Romantic Invention of Sexuality." In *The Truth of the Technological World: Essays on the Genealogy of Presence*. Translated by Erik Butler, 1–16. Stanford: Stanford University Press, 2014.

Kittler, Friedrich A. "The God of the Ears." In *The Truth of the Technological World: Essays on the Genealogy of Presence*. Translated by Erik Butler, 45–56. Stanford: Stanford University Press, 2014.

Kitzbichler, Josefine, Katja Lubitz, and Nina Mindt. *Theorie der Übersetzung antiker Literatur in Deutschland seit 1800*. Transformationen der Antike 9. Berlin: De Gruyter, 2009.

Klopstock, Friedrich Gottlieb. *Über die deutsche Rechtschreibung. Eine Beilage zum zweiten Theile der Campischen Erziehungsschriften*, 1778.

Klopstock, Friedrich Gottlieb. "Die Deutsche Gelehrtenrepublik. Ihre Einrichtung, ihre Gesetze, Geschichte des letzten Landtags." In *Friedrich Gottlieb Klopstock. Ausgewählte Werke*. Edited by Karl August Schleiden. Munich: Carl Hanser Verlag, 1962.

Klopstock, Friedrich Gottlieb. "Der doppelte Mitausdruck." In *Epigramme. Text und Apparat* Edited by Klaus von Hurlebusch, 1: 53. Berlin: de Gruyter, 1982.

Klopstock, Friedrich Gottlieb. *Der Messias*. Edited by Elisabeth Höpker-Herberg. Werke und Briefe. Vol. IV.1–6. Berlin: de Gruyter, 1984–2000.

Klopstock, Friedrich Gottlieb. "Vom deutschen Hexameter." In *Gedanken über die Natur der Poesie. Dichtungstheoretische Schriften*. Edited by Winfried Menninghaus, 60–157. Frankfurt a.M.: insel taschenbuch, 1989.

Klopstock, Friedrich Gottlieb. "Vom gleichen Verse. Aus einer Abhandlung vom Silbenmaße." In *Gedanken über die Natur der Poesie. Dichtungstheoretische Schriften*, edited by Winfried Menninghaus, 35–54. Frankfurt a.M.: insel taschenbuch, 1989.

Klopstock, Friedrich Gottlieb. "Von der Sprache der Poesie." In *Gedanken über die Natur der Poesie. Dichtungstheoretische Schriften*. Edited by Winfried Menninghaus, 22–34. Frankfurt a.M.: insel taschenbuch, 1989.

Klopstock, Friedrich Gottlieb. *Werke und Briefe: Abteilung Briefe IV: Briefe 1759–1766, Band 1: Text*. Edited by Helmut Riege. Briefe Vol. IV.1, XII vols. Berlin: De Gruyter, 2003.

Klopstock, Friedrich Gottlieb. "Braga." In *Oden*. Edited by Horst Gronemeyer and Klaus Hurlebusch, 1: 280–2. Berlin: de Gruyter, 2010.

Klopstock, Friedrich Gottlieb. "Der Bach." In *Oden*. Edited by Horst Gronemeyer and Klaus Hurlebusch, 1: 270–5. Berlin: de Gruyter, 2010.

Klopstock, Friedrich Gottlieb. "Der Eislauf." In *Oden*. Edited by Horst Gronemeyer and Klaus Hurlebusch, 1: 249–51. Berlin: de Gruyter, 2010.

Klopstock, Friedrich Gottlieb. "<Wen der Morgen in dem Mei ... > / Der Kamin." In *Oden*. Edited by Horst Gronemeyer and Klaus Hurlebusch, 1: 252–7. Berlin: de Gruyter, 2010.

Klopstock, Friedrich Gottlieb. "Eisode. / Die Kunst Tialfs." In *Oden*. Edited by Horst Gronemeyer and Klaus Hurlebusch, 1: 310–9. Berlin: de Gruyter, 2010.

Klopstock, Friedrich Gottlieb. "Sponda." In *Oden*. Edited by Horst Gronemeyer and Klaus Hurlebusch, 1: 243–5. Berlin: de Gruyter, 2010.

Knoblich, Aniela. *Antikenkonfigurationen in der deutschsprachigen Lyrik nach 1990*. Berlin: de Gruyter, 2014.

Koelb, Clayton, and Eric Downing. "Introduction." In *German Literature of the Nineteenth Century, 1832–1899*, 9: 1–19. Camden House History of German Literature. Rochester, NY: Camden House, 2005.

Kohl, Katrin. *Friedrich Gottlieb Klopstock*. Stuttgart: Metzler Verlag, 2000.

Komska, Yuliya, Michelle Moyd, and David Gramling. *Linguistic Disobedience: Restoring Power to Civic Language*. Springer, 2018.

König, Christoph. "'Ich bin dein Labyrinth...' Zur poetischen Klugheit in Nietzsches 'Dionysos Dithyramben.'" In *Nietzsche und die Lyrik. Ein Kompendium*. Edited by Christian Benne and Claus Zittel, 331–49. Stuttgart: Metzler Verlag, 2017.

Korte, Hermann. "Habemus poetam. Zum Konnex von Poesie und Wissen in Durs Grünbeins Gedichtsammlung 'Nach den Satiren." In *Text + Kritik* 153 (2002). Edited by Heinz-Ludwig Arnold, 19–33.

Korte, Hermann. "Zivilisationsepisteln. Poetik und Rhetorik in Grünbeins Gedichten." In *Die eigene und die fremde Kultur. Exotismus und Tradition bei Durs Grünbein und Raoul Schrott*. Edited by Dieter Burdorf, 79–95. Iserlohn: Institut für Kirche und Gesellschaft, 2004.

Krämer, Olav. "Ich und Welt. Durs Grünbeins Zyklus 'Niemands Land Stimmen' und sein Gedicht 'Nach den Satiren I." *Jahrbuch der deutschen Schillergesellschaft* 48 (2004): 348–74.

Krämer, Sybille. "The Cultural Techniques of Time Axis Manipulation: On Friedrich Kittler's Conception of Media." *Theory, Culture & Society* 23, no. 7–8 (December 2006): 93–109. https://doi.org/10.1177/0263276406069885.

Kuhlmann, Hauke, and Christian Meierhofer. "Descartes à la Grünbein. Philosophiegeschichtliche und erkenntnistheoretische Implikationen von *Vom Schnee oder Descartes in Deutschland.*" *Zeitschrift für Germanistik* 21, no. 2 (2011): 308–20.

Kutas, M., and S. A. Hillyard. "Reading Senseless Sentences: Brain Potentials Reflect Semantic Incongruity." *Science (New York, N.Y.)* 207, no. 4427 (January 11, 1980): 203–5. https://doi.org/10.1126/science.7350657.

Lachmann, Karl. *Über althochdeutsche Prosodie und Verskunst (1823/24). Mit Beiträgen von Jacob Grimm.* Edited by Ursula Hennig. Vol. 59. Hermaea Germanistische Forschungen. Tübingen: Max Niemeyer Verlag, 1990.

Lampart, Fabian. "Der junge Dichter als Sphinx. Durs Grünbein und die deutsche Lyrik nach 1989." In *Schreiben am Schnittpunkt. Poesie und Wissen bei Durs Grünbein.* Edited by Kai Bremer, Fabian Lampart, and Jörg Wesche, 19–36. Freiburg: Rombach Verlag, 2007.

Lamping, Dieter. "Eine Theorie des lyrischen Gedichts." *Recherches germaniques* 14 (2019): 31–7.

Landerer, Christoph, and Nick Zangwill. "Hanslick's Deleted Ending." *The British Journal of Aesthetics* 57, no. 1 (January 1, 2017): 85–95. https://doi.org/10.1093/aesthj/ayw056.

Latacz, Joachim. "On Nietzsche's Philological Beginnings." In *Nietzsche as a Scholar of Antiquity.* Edited by Anthony K. Jensen and Helmut Heit, 3–26. London: Bloomsbury, 2014.

Leeder, Karen. "The Poetry of Science and the Science of Poetry: German Poetry in the Laboratory of the Twentieth Century." *German Life and Letters* 60, no. 3 (2007): 412–29.

Lessing, Gotthold Ephraim. "Rezension zu Johann Jacob Bodmers Noah." In *Die Lehre von der Nachahmung der antiken Versmaße im Deutschen. In Quellenschriften des 18. und 19. Jahrhunderts. Mit kommentierter Bibliographie.* Edited by Hans-Heinrich Hellmuth and Joachim Schröder, 14. Munich: Wilhelm Fink Verlag, 1976.

Leyland, Maureen L. "An Introduction to Some of the Ideas of Humberto Maturana." *Journal of Family Therapy* 10, no. 4 (January 1988): 357–74. https://doi.org/10.1046/j.1988.00323.x.

Liberman, Gauthier. "Hermann et la colométrie pindarique de Boeckh. Révolution et contre-révolution en métrique." In *Gottfried Hermann (1772–1848).* Edited by Kurt Sier and Eva Wöckener-Gade, 197–219. Tübingen: Narr Francke Attempo Verlag, 2010.

López, Héctor Julio Pérez. "Die doppelte Wahrheit von Nietzsches Tätigkeit 1870–1872. Zur Beziehung griechischer Rhythmik und moderner Musikästhetik im Umkreis der 'Geburt der Tragödie.'" *Nietzscheforschung* 2, no. 1 (December 1, 1995): 219–36. https://doi.org/10.1524/nifo.1995.2.jg.219.

Lösener, Hans. *Der Rhythmus in der Rede: Linguistische und literaturwissenschaftliche Aspekte des Sprachrhythmus.* Tübingen: Niemeyer, 1999.

Lubkoll, Christine. "Rhythmus und Metrum." In *Literaturwissenschaft. Einführung in ein Sprachspiel.* Edited by Heinrich Bosse and Ursula Renner, 103–22. Freiburg: Rombach, 1999.

Luck, Steven J. *Introduction to the Event-Related Potential Technique.* MIT Press: Cambridge, 2014.

MacPherson, James (Transl.). *The Iliad of Homer.* Translated by James Macpherson, Esq; in Two Volumes. London: 1773.

Malinowski, Bernadette, and Gert-Ludwig Ingold. "'…im andern dupliziert.' Zur Rezeption cartesischer Erkenntnistheorie und Naturwissenschaft in Durs Grünbeins *Vom Schnee oder Descartes in Deutschland.*" In *Schreiben am Schnittpunkt. Poesie und Wissen bei Durs Grünbein.* Edited by Kai Bremer, Fabian Lampart, and Jörg Wesche, 271–306. Freiburg: Rombach Verlag, 2007.

Martus, Steffen, and Claudia Benthien. "Schnee von gestern—Schnee von heute: Die 'Wiederkehr der Frühen Neuzeit' bei Durs Grünbein." *Zeitschrift für Germanistik* 21, no. 2 (2011): 241–55.

Mecheril, Paul. "Der doppelte Mangel, der das Schwarze Subjekt hervorbringt." In *Mythen, Masken und Subjekte. Kritische Weißseinsforschung in Deutschland.* Edited by Maureen Maisha Eggers et al. Münster: Unrast Verlag, 2005.

Meier, Georg Friedrich. "Vom Werthe der Reime." In *Horatzische Oden*, by Samuel Gotthold Lange, 2–21. Edited by Georg Friedrich Meier. Halle: Carl Herrmann Hemmerde, 1747.

Meier, Georg Friedrich. *Beurtheilung des Heldengedichts, der Meßias.* Halle: Carl Herrmann Hemmerde, 1749.

Menninghaus, Winfried. "Klopstocks Poetik der schnellen 'Bewegung.'" In *Gedanken über die Natur der Poesie. Dichtungstheoretische Schriften*, by Friedrich Gottlieb Klopstock, 259–361. Edited by Winfried Menninghaus. Frankfurt a.M.: insel taschenbuch, 1989

Menninghaus, Winfried. *Hälfte des Lebens. Versuch über Hölderlins Poetik*. Frankfurt: Suhrkamp Verlag, 2005.

Menninghaus, Winfried. *Kunst als Beförderung des Lebens. Perspektiven transzendentaler und evolutionärer Ästhetik*. Munich: Carl von Siemens Stiftung, 2008.

Menninghaus, Winfried. *Wozu Kunst? Ästhetik nach Darwin*. Berlin: Suhrkamp Verlag, 2011.

Menninghaus, Winfried, Isabel C. Bohrn, Christine A. Knoop, Sonja A. Kotz, Wolff Schlotz, and Arthur M. Jacobs. "Rhetorical Features Facilitate Prosodic Processing While Handicapping Ease of Semantic Comprehension." *Cognition* 143 (October 1, 2015): 48–60. https://doi.org/10.1016/j.cognition.2015.05.026.

Merritt, Adrienne. "A Question of Inclusion: Intercultural Competence, Systemic Racism, and the North American German Classroom." In *Diversity and Decolonization in German Studies*. Edited by Regine Criser and Ervin Malakaj, 177–96. London: Palgrave MacMillan, 2020.

Mersch, Dieter. "Wozu Medienphilosophie? Eine programmatische Einleitung." *Internationales Jahrbuch für Medienphilosophie* 1, no. 1 (January, 2015). https://doi.org/10.1515/jbmp-2015-0103.

Mersch, Dieter. "*Meta/Dia*: Two Different Approaches to the Medial." *Cultural Studies* 30, no. 4 (July 3, 2016): 650–79. https://doi.org/10.1080/09502386.2016.1180751.

Meschonnic, Henri. "Metrics: Pure Metrics or Discourse Metrics." In *The Henri Meschonnic Reader: A Poetics of Society*. Edited by Marko Pajević, translated by John E. Joseph.115–54. Edinburgh: Edinburgh University Press, 2019.

Meschonnic, Henri. "Realism, Nominalism: The Theory of Language Is a Theory of Society." In *The Henri Meschonnic Reader: A Poetics of Society*. Edited and translated by Marko Pajević, 312–20. Edinburgh: Edinburgh University Press, 2019.

Meschonnic, Henri. "Rhyme and Life." In *The Henri Meschonnic Reader: A Poetics of Society*. Edited by Marko Pajević, translated by Andrew Eastman, 179–97. Edinburgh: Edinburgh University Press, 2019.

Meschonnic, Henri. "Rhythm: What Is at Stake in a Theory of Rhythm." In *The Henri Meschonnic Reader: A Poetics of Society*. Edited by Marko Pajević, translated by Chantal Wright and David Nowell Smith, 66–114. Edinburgh: Edinburgh University Press, 2019.

Meschonnic, Henri. *The Henri Meschonnic Reader: A Poetics of Society*. Edited by Marko Pajević. Edinburgh: Edinburgh University Press, 2019.

Meves, Uwe. "160. Die Entstehung und frühe Entwicklung der Germanischen Philologie. XXV. The Establishment of New Philologies in the 19th Century/Die Herausbildung neuer Philologien im 19. Jahrhundert/Le développement des nouvelley philologies au XIXe siècle." In *History of the Language Sciences - Geschichte der Sprachwissenschaften - Histoire des Sciences du Langage*. Edited by Sylvain Auroux, E.F.K. Koerner, Hans-Josef Niederehe, and Kees Versteegh, 2: 1286–94. Berlin/Boston: de Gruyter, 2008.

Miall, David S., and Ellen Dissanayake. "The Poetics of Babytalk." *Human Nature* 14, no. 4 (December 1, 2003): 337–64. https://doi.org/10.1007/s12110-003-1010-4.

Mills, Charles W. *Blackness Visible: Essays on Philosophy and Race*. Ithaca, NY: Cornell University Press, 1998.

Milton, John. *Paradise Lost*. London, 1795.

Mönig, Klaus. "Sie hätte singen sollen, diese 'neue Seele'—und nicht reden!' Nietzsches späte Lyrik." In *Nietzsche als Philosoph der Moderne*. Edited by Barbara Neymeyr and Andreas Urs Sommer, 193–221. Heidelberg: Winter, 2012.

Mukařovský, Jan. "Standard Language and Poetic Language." In *Linguistic and Literary Studies in Eastern Europe*. Edited by Josef Vachek and Libuše Dušková, 12: 165. Amsterdam: John Benjamins Publishing Company, 1983. https://doi.org/10.1075/llsee.12.11muk.

Müller, Alexander. *Das Gedicht als Engramm. Memoria und Imaginatio in der Poetik Durs Grünbeins*. Oldenburg: Igel Verlag Wissenschaft, 2004.

Müller, Armin Thomas. "Nietzsches Gimmelwalder Melancholie-Gedichte aus dem Sommer 1871." In *Nietzsche als Dichter. Lyrik - Poetologie - Rezeption*. Edited by Katharina Grätz and Sebastian Kaufmann, 47–77. Berlin: de Gruyter, 2017.

Naumann, Barbara. "Gewalt der Sprache. Nietzsches Descartes-Kritik, Grünbeins Descartes." In *Die Literatur der Literaturtheorie*. Edited by Boris Previšić, 133–44. Bern: Peter Lang, 2010.

Neill, Alex. "Schopenhauer." In *The Routledge Companion to Philosophy and Music*. Edited by Theodore Gracyk and Andrew Kania, 339–49. New York: Routledge, 2011.

Nelson, Ingrid. "Poetics of the Rule: Form, Biopolitics, Lyric." *New Literary History* 50, no. 1 (2019): 65–89. https://doi.org/10.1353/nlh.2019.0004.

Nicolai, Friedrich. "Rezension zu F.W. Zachariae, Das Verlohrne Paradies." In *Die Lehre von der Nachahmung der antiken Versmaße im Deutschen. In Quellenschriften des 18. und 19. Jahrhunderts. Mit kommentierter Bibliographie*. Edited by Hans-Heinrich Hellmuth and Joachim Schröder, 61–9. Munich: Wilhelm Fink Verlag, 1976.

Nicolai, Friedrich. "Zu einer Young-Übersetzung eines Ungenannten." In *Die Lehre von der Nachahmung der antiken Versmaße im Deutschen. In Quellenschriften des 18. und 19. Jahrhunderts. Mit kommentierter Bibliographie*. Edited by Hans-Heinrich Hellmuth and Joachim Schröder, 70–9. Munich: Wilhelm Fink Verlag, 1976.

Nietzsche, Friedrich. "Nietzsche: On the Theory of Quantitative Rhythm." *Arion: A Journal of Humanities and the Classics* 6, no. 2 (1967). Translated by James W. Halporn.

Nietzsche, Friedrich. "Encyclopaedie der klass. Philologie." In *Nietzsche Werke. Kritische Gesamtausgabe*. Edited by Fritz Bornmann, II.3 Vorlesungsaufzeichnungen (SS1870-SS1871): 339–437. Berlin: de Gruyter, 1993.

Nietzsche, Friedrich. *Digitale Kritische Gesamtausgabe Werke und Briefe (eKGWB), index*. Edited by Paolo D'Iorio. Paris: Nietzsche Source, 2009. Accessed July 5, 2022, http://www.nietzschesource.org/#eKGWB.

Norton, Robert E. *Herder's Aesthetics and the European Enlightenment*. Ithaca, NY: Cornell University Press, 1991.

Nowell Smith, David. "The Poetry-Verse Distinction Reconsidered." *Thinking Verse* 1 (2011): 137–60.

Nowell Smith, David. "Editor's Introduction: Scansion." *Thinking Verse* 3 (2013): 1–14.

Nowell Smith, David. "Training the Ear, or: On Learning to Hear the *Alexandrin*." *Thinking Verse* 3 (2014), 137–38.

Nowell Smith, David. "Verse Scored Free: Scansion, Recording, Notation." *Revue Française d'études Américaines* 153, no. 4 (2017), 45.

Nowell Smith, David. "Rhythm-Sense-Subject, or: The Dynamic Un/Enfolding of Sense." *Comparative Critical Studies* 15, no. 3 (October 1, 2018): 349–67. https://doi.org/10.3366/ccs.2018.0300.

Nowell Smith, David. "What Is Called Rhythm." In *Critical Rhythm: The Poetics of a Literary Life Form*. Edited by Ben Glaser, Jonathan Culler, Lazar Fleishman, and Haun Saussy, 1–17. New York: Fordham University Press, 2019.

Obermeier, Christian, Sonja A. Kotz, Sarah Jessen, Tim Raettig, Martin von Koppenfels, and Winfried Menninghaus. "Aesthetic Appreciation of Poetry Correlates with Ease of Processing in Event-Related Potentials." *Cognitive, Affective, & Behavioral Neuroscience* 16, no. 2 (2016): 362–73. https://doi.org/10.3758/s13415-015-0396-x.

Obermeier, Christian, Winfried Menninghaus, Martin von Koppenfels, Tim Raettig, Maren Schmidt-Kassow, Sascha Otterbein, and Sonja A. E. Kotz. "Aesthetic and Emotional Effects of Meter and Rhyme in Poetry." *Frontiers in Psychology* 4 (2013). https://doi.org/10.3389/fpsyg.2013.00010.

Opitz, Martin. *Buch von der deutschen Poeterey. Jn welchem alle jhre eigenschafft vnd zuegehör gründtlich erzehlet/ vnd mit exempeln außgeführet wird*. Breslau, 1624.

Pabst, Stephan. *Post-Ost-Moderne. Poetik nach der DDR*. Göttingen: Wallstein Verlag, 2016.

Pajević, Marko. "A Poetics of Society: Thinking Language with Henri Meschonnic." *Comparative Critical Studies* 15, no. 3 (October 1, 2018): 291–310. https://doi.org/10.3366/ccs.2018.0297.

Pajević, Marko. "Meschonnic's Theory of Rhythm, his Key Concepts and their Relation." In *The Henri Meschonnic Reader: A Poetics of Society*. Edited by Marko Pajević, 15–31. Edinburgh: Edinburgh University Press, 2019.

Pajević, Marko, Pier-Pascale Boulanger, Andrew Eastman, John E. Joseph, David Nowell Smith, and Chantal Wright (eds.). *The Henri Meschonnic Reader A Poetics of Society*. Edinburgh: Edinburgh University Press, 2019.

Pajević, Marko, and David Nowell Smith. "Introduction: Thinking Language with Henri Meschonnic." *Comparative Critical Studies* 15, no. 3 (October 1, 2018): 279–87. https://doi.org/10.3366/ccs.2018.0396.

Peters, John Durham. "Introduction: Friedrich Kittler's Light Shows." In Friedrich A. Kittler, *Optical Media: Berlin Lectures 1999*. Translated by Anthony Enns, 1–17. Cambridge: Polity Press, 2010.

Peters, John Durham. "Assessing Kittler's *Musik und Mathematik*." In *Kittler Now: Current Perspectives in Kittler Studies*. Edited by Stephen Sale and Laura Salisbury, 22–43. Cambridge: Polity Press, 2015.

Pfau, Thomas. "Between Sentimentality and Phantasmagoria: German Lyric Poetry, 1830-1890." In *German Literature of the Nineteenth Century, 1832–1899*. Edited by Clayton Koelb and Eric Downing, 9: 207–50. Camden House History of German Literature. Rochester, NY: Camden House, 2005.

Pfeiffer, K. Ludwig. "The Materiality of Communication." In *Materialities of Communication*. Edited by Hans Ulrich Gumbrecht and Ludwig K. Pfeiffer, translated by William Whobrey, 1–12. Stanford: Stanford University Press, 1994.

Pinker, Steven. "Toward a Consilient Study of Literature." *Philosophy and Literature* 31 (2007): 162–78.

Pliny the Younger. *The Letters of Caius Plinius Caecilius Secundus: The Tr. of Melmoth, Revised and Corrected with Notes and a Mem. by F.C.T. Bosanquet*. Bell, 1878.

Poiss, Thomas. "Zur Idee der Philologie. Der Streit zwischen Gottfried Hermann und August Boeckh." In *Gottfried Hermann (1772–1848)*. Edited by Kurt Sier and Eva Wöckener-Gade, 143–63. Tübingen: Narr Francke Attempo Verlag, 2010.

Polak, Rainer, Nori Jacoby, Timo Fischinger, Daniel Goldberg, Andre Holzapfel, and Justin London. "Rhythmic Prototypes Across Cultures: A Comparative Study of Tapping Synchronization." *Music Perception: An Interdisciplinary Journal* 36, no. 1 (September 1, 2018): 1–23. https://doi.org/10.1525/mp.2018.36.1.1.

Porter, James I. *Nietzsche and the Philology of the Future*. Stanford: Stanford University Press, 2000.

Porter, James I. "Nietzsche, Rhetoric, Philology." In *Philology and Its Histories*. Edited by Sean Gurd, 164–91. Columbus: Ohio State University Press, 2010.

Pourciau, Sarah M. *The Writing of Spirit. Soul, System, and the Roots of Language Science*. New York: Fordham University Press, 2017.

Praamstra, Peter, and Dick F. Stegeman. "Phonological Effects on the Auditory N400 Event-Related Brain Potential." *Cognitive Brain Research* 1, no. 2 (April 1, 1993): 73–86. https://doi.org/10.1016/0926-6410(93)90013-U.

Preston, William A. "Nietzsche on Blacks." In *Existence in Black: An Anthology of Black Existential Philosophy*. Edited by Lewis R. Gordon, 165–72. New York: Routledge, 1997.

Prins, Yopie. "Metrical Translation: Nineteenth-Century Homers and the Hexameter Mania." In *Nation, Language, and the Ethics of Translation*. Edited by Sandra Bermann and Michael Wood, 229–56. Princeton: Princeton University Press, 2005. https://doi.org/10.1515/9781400826681.229.

Prins, Yopie. "Sapphic Stanzas: How Can We Read the Rhythm?" In *Critical Rhythm: The Poetics of a Literary Life Form*. Edited by Ben Glaser, Jonathan Culler, Lazar Fleishman, and Haun Saussy, 247–73. New York: Fordham University Press, 2019. https://doi.org/10.2307/j.ctv8jp01t.14.

Ramazani, Jahan. *A Transnational Poetics*. Chicago: University of Chicago Press, 2015.

Ramazani, Jahan. "Lyric Poetry: Intergeneric, Transnational, Translingual?" *Journal of Literary Theory* 11, no. 1 (2017): 97–107. https://doi.org/10.1515/jlt-2017-0011.

Ramazani, Jahan. *Poetry in a Global Age*. University of Chicago Press, 2020.

Ramler, Carl Wilhlem. "Ist der römische Hexameter der deutschen Sprache möglich?" In *Die Lehre von der Nachahmung der antiken Versmaße im Deutschen. In Quellenschriften des 18. und 19. Jahrhunderts. Mit kommentierter Bibliographie*. Edited by Hans-Heinrich Hellmuth and Joachim Schröder, 35–45. Munich: Wilhelm Fink Verlag, 1976.

Reber, Rolf, Norbert Schwarz, and Piotr Winkielman. "Processing Fluency and Aesthetic Pleasure: Is Beauty in the Perceiver's Processing Experience?" *Personality and Social Psychology Review: An*

Official Journal of the Society for Personality and Social Psychology, Inc 8, no. 4 (2004): 364–82. https://doi.org/10.1207/s15327957pspr0804_3.

Rehding, Alexander. *Hugo Riemann and the Birth of Modern Musical Thought*. Cambridge: Cambridge University Press, 2003.

Riemann, Hugo. *Musikalische Dynamik und Agogik. Lehrbuch der musikalischen Phrasirung auf Grund einer Revision der Lehre von der musikalischen Metrik und Rhythmik*. Hamburg: D. Rahter, 1884.

Riemann, Hugo. "Ueber musikalischen Phrasirung." In *Die Zukunft des musikalischen Vortrages und sein Ursprung*. Edited by Carl Fuchs. Danzig: A.W. Kafemann, 1884.

Riemann, Hugo, and Carl Fuchs. *Katechismus der Phrasierung. Praktische Anleitung zum Phrasieren*. Leipzig: Max Hesse's Verlag, 1886.

Rinsum, Annemarie van, and Wolfgang van Rinsum. "III.3.5 Politische Lyrik des Vormärz." In *Deutsche Literaturgeschichte*, Band 6: Frührealismus 1815–1848: 168–78. Munich: dtv, 1992.

Rinsum, Annemarie van, and Wolfgang van Rinsum. "IV.4.1 Biedermeier als kulturhistorischer Begriff." In *Deutsche Literaturgeschichte*, Band 6: Frührealismus 1815–1848: 181–4. Munich: dtv, 1992.

Rinsum, Annemarie van, and Wolfgang van Rinsum. "IV.4.2 Die Lyriker." In *Deutsche Literaturgeschichte*, Band 6: Frührealismus 1815–1848: 185–213. Munich: dtv, 1992.

Ritschl, Friedrich. "Zur Metrik." *Rheinisches Museum für Philologie* Neue Folge, 1 (1842): 277–302.

Ronzheimer, Elisa. "'Sceptische Beweglichkeit.' Metren in Goethes *Faust II*." In *Poetologien des Rhythmus um 1800. Metrum und Versform bei Klopstock, Hölderlin, Novalis, Tieck und Goethe*. Berlin/Boston: de Gruyter, 2020.

Ronzheimer, Elisa. "'Wie wenn am Feiertage…' Hölderlins Projekt eines individuellen Metrums." In *Poetologien des Rhythmus um 1800. Metrum und Versform bei Klopstock, Hölderlin, Novalis, Tieck und Goethe*. Berlin/Boston: de Gruyter, 2020.

Rossbach, August. *Metrik der griechischen Dramatiker und Lyriker nebst den begleitenden musischen Künsten*. Vol. 1. 2 vols. Leipzig: Teubner, 1854.

Rossbach, August. "Westphal, Rudolf." In *Allgemeine Deutsche Biographie, Band 42*, 1897 https://www.deutsche-biographie.de/pnd117327026.html#adbcontent.

Rothermich, Kathrin, Maren Schmidt-Kassow, and Sonja A. Kotz. "Rhythm's Gonna Get You: Regular Meter Facilitates Semantic Sentence Processing." *Neuropsychologia* 50, no. 2 (January 2012): 232–44. https://doi.org/10.1016/j.neuropsychologia.2011.10.025.

Rowell, Lewis. "Time in the Romantic Philosophies of Music." *Indiana Theory Review* 25 (2004): 139–75.

Rugg, Michael D. "Event-Related Potentials and the Phonological Processing of Words and Non-Words." *Neuropsychologia* 22, no. 4 (January 1, 1984): 435–43. https://doi.org/10.1016/0028-3932(84)90038-1.

Rugg, Michael D., and Sarah E. Barrett. "Event-Related Potentials and the Interaction between Orthographic and Phonological Information in a Rhyme-Judgment Task." *Brain and Language* 32, no. 2 (1987): 336–61. https://doi.org/10.1016/0093-934X(87)90132-5.

Ryan, Judith. "'Spurlose Frühe.' Durs Grünbeins *Vom Schnee* und das Problem der Wende." In *Weiterschreiben. Zur DDR-Literatur nach dem Ende der DDR*. Edited by Holger Helbig and Katrin Felsner, 163–81. Berlin: Akademie Verlag, 2007.

Sabban, Adela Sophia. "Zitternd und zuckend ein Preislied. Nietzsches Gedicht 'An die Melancholie.'" In *Nietzsche und die Lyrik. Ein Kompendium*. Edited by Christian Benne and Claus Zittel, 59–77. Stuttgart: Metzler Verlag, 2017.

Saussy, Haun. *The Ethnography of Rhythm: Orality and Its Technologies*. New York: Fordham University Press, 2016.https://doi.org/10.1515/9780823270491.

Saussy, Haun. "Contagious Rhythm: Verse as a Technique of the Body." In *Critical Rhythm The Poetics of a Literary Life Form*. Edited by Ben Glaser, Jonathan Culler, Lazar Fleishman, and Haun Saussy, 106–27. New York: Fordham University Press, 2019. https://doi.org/10.2307/j.ctv8jp01t.8.

Savarese, Ralph James. "What Some Autistics Can Teach Us about Poetry." In *The Oxford Handbook of Cognitive Literary Studies*. Edited by Lisa Zunshine, 393–417. Oxford: Oxford University Press, 2015.

Savarese, Ralph James, and Lisa Zunshine. "The Critic as Neurocosmopolite; Or, What Cognitive Approaches to Literature Can Learn from Disability Studies: Lisa Zunshine in Conversation with

Ralph James Savarese." *Narrative* 22, no. 1 (January 2014): 17–44. https://doi.org/10.1353/nar.2014.0000.

Schäfer, Armin. "Wieland liest die Briefe des Horaz." In *Wieland/Übersetzen: Sprachen, Gattungen, Räume.* Edited by Bettine Menke and Wolfgang Struck, 83–103. Berlin: de Gruyter, 2010.

Schiller, Friedrich. "Das Distichon." In *Sämtliche Werke. 3rd Edition,* Volume 1. Munich: Hanser, 1962.

Schlitz, Michael. "Form and Medium: A Mathematical Reconstruction." *Image & Narrative* III, no. 2 (6) (2003): online.

Schneider, Joh. Nikolaus. *Ins Ohr geschrieben. Lyrik als akustische Kunst zwischen 1750 und 1800.* Wallstein Verlag, 2004.

Schramm, Michael. "Hermann und Kant. Philologie als (Kantische) Wissenschaft." In *Gottfried Hermann (1772–1848).* Edited by Kurt Sier and Eva Wöckener-Gade, 83–121. Tübingen: Narr Francke Attempo Verlag, 2010.

Schuster, Marc-Oliver, and Christoph Landerer. "›Die Musik kann niemals Mittel werden‹:Nietzsches Ästhetik und ihre Wurzeln bei Hanslick." *Österreichische Musikzeitschrift* 55, no. 6 (2000): 17–24.

Seidel, Wilhelm. "Rhythmus." In *Ästhetische Grundbegriffe,* Volume 5. Edited by Karl Barck, Martin Fontius, Dieter Schlenstedt, Burkhart Steinwachs, and Friederich Wolfzettel, 291–314. Stuttgart: Metzler, 2003.

Shapiro, Lisa. "Elisabeth, Princess of Bohemia." In *The Stanford Encyclopedia of Philosophy.* Edited by Edward N. Zalta, Winter 2014. Metaphysics Research Lab, Stanford University, 2014. https://plato.stanford.edu/archives/win2014/entries/elisabeth-bohemia/.

Shklovsky, Victor. "Victor Shklovsky: 'Art as Technique.'" In *Twentieth-Century Literary Theory: A Reader.* Edited by K. M. Newton. London: Macmillan Education UK, 1997. https://doi.org/10.1007/978-1-349-25934-2_1.

Siegert, Bernhard. "Cultural Techniques: Or the End of the Intellectual Postwar Era in German Media Theory." *Theory, Culture & Society* 30, no. 6 (November 2013): 48–65. https://doi.org/10.1177/0263276413488963.

Skowron, Michael. "Dionysische Perspektiven. Eine philosophische Interpretation der Dionysos-Dithyramben." *Nietzsche-Studien* 36, no. 1 (2008): 296–315. https://doi.org/10.1515/9783110192827.1.309.

Sousa, Tiago. "Was Hanslick a Closet Schopenhauerian?" *The British Journal of Aesthetics* 57, no. 2 (April 1, 2017): 211–29. https://doi.org/10.1093/aesthj/ayx008.

Spoerhase, Carlos. "Über die Grenzen der Geschichtslyrik: Historischer Anachronismus und ästhetische Anachronie in Durs Grünbeins Werk, am Beispiel seiner Arbeiten über Descartes." *Zeitschrift für Germanistik* 21, no. 2 (2011): 263–83.

Starr, G. Gabrielle. *Feeling Beauty. The Neuroscience of Aesthetic Experience.* Cambridge, MA: MIT Press, 2013.

Stöckmann, Ernst. "Von der sinnlichen Erkenntnis zur Psychologie der Emotionen.Anthropologische und ästhetische Progression der Aisthesis in der vorkantischen Ästhetiktheorie." In *Physis und Norm. Neue Perspektiven der Anthropologie im 18. Jahrhundert.* Edited by Manfred Beetz, Jörn Garber, and Heinz Thoma, 69–106. Göttingen: Wallstein Verlag, 2007.

Storost, Jürgen. "158. Die 'neuen Philologien,' ihre Institutionen und Periodica: Eine Übersicht. XXV./The Establishment of New Philologies in the 19th Century Die Herausbildung neuer Philologien im 19. Jahrhundert/Le développement des nouvelley philologies au XIXe siècle." In *History of the Language Sciences - Geschichte der Sprachwissenschaften - Histoire des Sciences du Langage.* Edited by Sylvain Auroux, E.F.K. Koerner, Hans-Josef Niederehe, and Kees Versteegh, 2: 1240–72. Berlin/Boston: De Gruyter, 2008.

Strabone, Jeff. *Poetry and British Nationalisms in the Bardic Eighteenth Century: Imagined Antiquities.* Basingstoke, U.K.: Palgrave Macmillan, 2018.

Strathausen, Carsten. "A Rebel Against Hermeneutics: On the Presence of Hans Ulrich Gumbrecht." *Theory & Event* 9, no. 1 (March 27, 2006). https://doi.org/10.1353/tae.2006.0021.

Sulzer, Johann Georg. "Dichtkunst. Poesie." In *Allgemeine Theorie der Schönen Künste,* 1: 250–8. Leipzig, 1771.

Sulzer, Johann Georg. "Empfindung (Schöne Künste)." In *Allgemeine Theorie der Schönen Künste,* 1: 311–16. Leipzig, 1771.

Sulzer, Johann Georg. "Gedicht." In *Allgemeine Theorie der Schönen Künste*, 1: 433–38 Leipzig, 1771.

Sulzer, Johann Georg (ed.). "Hexameter." In *Allgemeine Theorie der Schönen Künste*, 1: 536–7. Leipzig, 1771.

Sulzer, Johann Georg. "Metrum; Metrisch (Schöne Künste)." In *Allgemeine Theorie der Schönen Künste*, 2: 764–5. Leipzig, 1774.

Sulzer, Johann Georg. "Prosodie." In *Allgemeine Theorie der Schönen Künste*, 2: 928–9 Leipzig, 1774.

Sulzer, Johann Georg. "Rhythmus; Rhythmisch (Redende Kunst, Musik, Tanz)." In *Allgemeine Theorie der Schönen Künste*, 2: 975–85. Leipzig, 1774.

Sulzer, Johann Georg. "Sylbenmaaß." In *Allgemeine Theorie der Schönen Künste*, 2: 1119–21. Leipzig, 1774.

Tarlinskaja, Marina. "What Is 'Metricality'? English Iambic Pentameter." In *Formal Approaches to Poetry: Recent Developments in Metrics*. Edited by B. Elan Dresher and Nila Friedberg, 53–74. Berlin: De Gruyter, 2006.

Treadwell, James. "The Urge to Communicate: The Prose Writings as Theory and Practice." In *Cambridge Companion to Wagner*. Edited by Thomas S. Grey, 177–91. Cambridge Companions to Music. Cambridge: Cambridge University Press, 2011.

Tsur, Reuven. *Toward a Theory of Cognitive Poetics, Second, Expanded and Updated Edition.* 2nd ed. Brighton: Sussex Academic Press, 2008.

Tsur, Reuven. *Poetic Rhythm: Structure and Performance: An Empirical Study in Cognitive Poetics.* Brighton: Sussex Academic Press, 2012.

Turner, Frederick, and Ernst Pöppel. "The Neural Lyre: Poetic Meter, the Brain, and Time." *Poetry* 142, no. 5 (1983): 277–309.

Twain, Mark. "A Literary Nightmare." *The Atlantic Monthly* (February 1876): 167–9.

Vogl, Joseph. "Becoming-Media: Galileo's Telescope." *Grey Room* 29 (October 2007): 14–25. https://doi.org/10.1162/grey.2007.1.29.14.

Voß, Johann Heinrich. *Homers Werke (Ilias und Odyssee). Übersetzt von Johann Heinrich Voß; mit 25 Radirungen nach Zeichnungen von Bonaventura Genelli.* Stuttgart: J.G. Cotta, 1876.

Voß, Johann Heinrich. "Aus der Vorrede zur *Georgica* Übersetzung." In *Die Lehre von der Nachahmung der antiken Versmaße im Deutschen. In Quellenschriften des 18. und 19. Jahrhunderts. Mit kommentierter Bibliographie.* Edited by Hans-Heinrich Hellmuth and Joachim Schröder, 242–9. Munich: Wilhelm Fink Verlag, 1976.

Wagenknecht, Christian. *Deutsche Metrik. Eine historische Einführung.* 5th ed. Munich: C.H. Beck, 2007.

Wagner, Richard. "Über das Dirigieren." In *Beethoven/Über das Dirigieren.*, 69–140 Darmstadt: Wissenschaftliche Buchgemeinschaft, 1953.

Wagner, Richard. "Oper und Drama." In *Richard Wagner: Dichtungen und Schriften.* Edited by Dieter Borchmeyer, 7: 9–370. Frankfurt a.M.: Insel Verlag, 1983.

Wellbery, David E. *Lessing's Laocoon. Semiotics and Aesthetics in the Age of Reason* (Cambridge: Cambridge University Press, 1984).

Wellbery, David E. "Foreword." In Friedrich A. Kittler, *Discourse Networks 1800/1900.* Translated by Michael Metteer, vii–xxxiii. Stanford: Stanford University Press, 1990.

Wellbery, David E. "Interpretation vs. Lesen. Posthermeneutsiche Konzepte der Texterörterung." In *Wie international ist die Literaturwissenschaft? Methoden- und Theoriediskussion in den Literaturwissenschaften: kulturelle Besonderheiten und interkultureller Austausch am Beispiel des Interpretationsproblems, 1950–1990.* Edited by Lutz Danneberg, 123–38. Stuttgart: Metzler Verlag, 1996.

Westphal, Rudolf. "Zur vergleichenden Metrik der indogermanischen Völker." *Zeitschrift für vergleichende Sprachforschung auf dem Gebiete des Deutschen, Griechischen und Lateinischen* 9, no. 6 (1860): 437–58.

Westphal, Rudolf. *Die Fragmente und die Lehrsätze der griechischen Rhythmiker.* Leipzig: Teubner, 1861.

Westphal, Rudolf. *Allgemeine griechische Metrik.* Leipzig: Teubner, 1865.

Westphal, Rudolf. *Theorie der Neuhochdeutschen Metrik.* Jena: Carl Doebereiner, 1870.

Westphal, Rudolf. *Elemente des musikalischen Rhythmus mit besonderer Rücksicht auf unsere Opern-Musik.* Jena: Hermann Constenoble, 1872.

Westphal, Rudolf. *Allgemeine Theorie der musikalischen Rhythmik seit J.S. Bach.* Leipzig: Breitkopf und Härtel, 1880.

Westphal, Rudolf. *Geschichte der alten und mittelalterlichen Musik.* Breslau: Verlag von F.E.C. Leuckart, 1865.

Winthrop-Young, Geoffrey. "The Kittler Effect." In *New German Critique* 44, no. 3 (132) (November 1, 2017): 205–24, https://doi.org/10.1215/0094033X-4162322.

Youmans, Gilbert. "Generative Tests for Generative Meter." *Language* 59, no. 1 (1983): 67–92. https://doi.org/10.2307/414061.

Zelle, Carsten. "Klopstocks Diät – das Erhabene und die Anthropologie um 1750." In *Wort und Schrift: Das Werk Friedrich Gottlieb Klopstocks.* Edited by Kevin Hilliard and Katrin Kohl, 101–27. Hallesche Forschungen 27. Tübingen: Niemeyer, 2008.

Zöller, Günter. "Schopenhauer." In *Music in German Philosophy: An Introduction.* Edited by Stefan Lorenz Sorgener and Oliver Fürbeth, translated by Susan H. Gillespie, 121–40. Chicago: University of Chicago Press, 2010.

Index